Improving LCSH
for Use in Online Catalogs

Improving LCSH
for Use in Online Catalogs

Exercises for Self-Help
with a
Selection of Background Readings

Pauline A. Cochrane

1986

LIBRARIES UNLIMITED, INC. • Littleton, Colorado

Copyright © 1986 Pauline A. Cochrane
All Rights Reserved
Printed in the United States of America

No part of this publication may be reproduced, stored in a retrieval system, or transmitted, in any form or by any means, electronic, mechanical, photocopying, recording, or otherwise, without the prior written permission of the publisher.

LIBRARIES UNLIMITED, INC.
P.O. Box 263
Littleton, Colorado 80160-0263

Library of Congress Cataloging-in-Publication Data

Cochrane, Pauline Atherton, 1929-
    Improving LCSH for use in online catalogs.

    Includes bibliographies and index.
    1. Library of Congress. Subject Cataloging Division. Library of Congress subject headings. 2. Subject headings. 3. Subject cataloging. 4. Catalogs, On-line. 5. On-line bibliographic searching. I. Title.
II. Title: Improving Library of Congress subject headings for use in on-line catalogs.
Z695.C646   1986   025.4'9   85-23655
ISBN 0-87287-484-2 (pbk.)

Libraries Unlimited books are bound with Type II nonwoven material that meets and exceeds National Association of State Textbook Administrators' Type II nonwoven material specifications Class A through E.

To Sandy, for his work on the outside
and for his book, *Prejudices and
Antipathies* which inspired us all

and

To Gene, for his work on the inside
which inspired me to persevere

Our aim as librarians is not merely to accumulate books. It is to help the reader to the books he wants—or ought to want. In a large library the only tool which accomplishes this result is the catalog, and of this the subject catalog is the part most difficult to make, most useful when well made.

—William Warner Bishop
1906

Contents

PREFACE xiii

SECTION 1

    INTRODUCTION 3

1   **LCSH: What It Is and Is Not, and What It May Become within the Online Catalog** 13
        LCSH: What It Is and Is Not 13
        What LCSH May Become in the Online Catalog 24
        Exercises 25
        Notes 26
        Selected Readings 26
        Appendix to Chapter 1 26

2   **FORM OF LCSH HEADINGS IN LIBRARY CATALOGS: Suggestions for Improvement and for More Scope Notes** 31
        Form of Headings 31
        Exercises 34
        Scope Notes 36
        Exercises 40
        Notes 43
        Selected Readings 43

3   **LCSH CROSS-REFERENCE STRUCTURE: Suggested Improvements** 45
        Background 47
        See References 49
        Exercises 50
        See Also References 51
        Exercises 52
        Notes 53
        Selected Readings 53

4   **LCSH SUBDIVISIONS: Suggested Improvements** 54
        Period Subdivisions 57
        Place Subdivisions 57
        Form and Topical Subdivisions 57

4 LCSH SUBDIVISIONS *(continued)*

Pattern Headings..59
Online Display of Subdivisions....................................59
Permutation/Rotation of Subject Heading String....................62
Exercises...67
Notes...67
Selected Readings...68

5 LCSH, LCC, AND DDC: Suggested Relationships..................69

Background..72
Links between Subject Headings and Classification Numbers.........73
Preparation for Links between Subject Headings and Class Numbers..74
Linkages to Improve Online Searching..............................76
Moves toward Shelf Browsing Online................................77
Exercises...80
Notes...81
Selected Readings...81

6 LCSH AND SUBJECT ACCESS ONLINE: Improvements through Enhancements and User Assistance..........................82

Improvements through Enhancements.................................83
User Assistance...91
Exercises...93
Notes...94
Selected Readings...95

SECTION 2

INTRODUCTION..99

**"LIBRARY OF CONGRESS SUBJECT HEADINGS—
Review and Forecast"**..103
Richard S. Angell

**AUSTRALIAN BIBLIOGRAPHIC NETWORK
SUBJECT CATALOGUING MANUAL. PART B.2**.........................119

"PROPOSAL FOR REFORMS TO IMPROVE SUBJECT SEARCHING".........121
Sanford Berman

**"LIBRARY OF CONGRESS SUBJECT HEADINGS AS AN ONLINE
RETRIEVAL TOOL: Structural Considerations"**...................123
Lois Mai Chan

"THE PERIOD SUBDIVISION IN SUBJECT HEADINGS"................134
Lois Mai Chan

SUBJECT CATALOGUES: Headings and Structure..................140
Eric James Coates

"CLASSIFICATION AS AN ONLINE SUBJECT ACCESS TOOL: Challenge and Opportunity"..148
   Pauline Cochrane

"LCSH-EVP NOTEBOOK OF PROCEDURES" and "USING LCSH AS A SUBJECT ACCESS TOOL IN ONLINE PUBLIC ACCESS CATALOGS"..........151
   Pauline Cochrane

THE GRAMMAR OF SUBJECT HEADINGS: A Formulation of Rules for Subject Headings Based on a Syntactical and Morphological Analysis of the Library of Congress List..159
   Jay E. Daily

"SCOPE NOTES IN LIBRARY OF CONGRESS SUBJECT HEADINGS"..........165
   Alan M. Greenberg

SUBJECT HEADINGS: A Practical Guide..................................175
   David Judson Haykin

"ONLINE CLASSIFICATION NUMBER ACCESS: Some Practical Considerations"..181
   Janet Swan Hill

ANALYSIS OF VOCABULARY CONTROL IN LIBRARY OF CONGRESS CLASSIFICATION AND SUBJECT HEADINGS..................................192
   John Phillip Immroth

"INTEGRATING SUBJECT PATHFINDERS INTO ONLINE CATALOGS".......209
   William E. Jarvis

SUBJECT CATALOGING MANUAL: Subject Headings......................213
   Library of Congress, Subject Cataloging Division

"SUBJECT CATALOGERS – EQUAL TO THE FUTURE?".....................226
   Manuel D. Lopez

"ENRICHING THE LIBRARY CATALOG RECORD FOR SUBJECT ACCESS"..231
   Carol A. Mandel

"HELPING LC IMPROVE LCSH ONLY CONSTRUCTIVE APPROACH".........241
   Carol A. Mandel

SUBJECT SEARCHING IN LIBRARY CATALOGS............................243
   Karen Markey

AN EXPLORATORY STUDY OF THREE SUBJECT ACCESS SYSTEMS IN MEDICINE: LCSH, MeSH, PRECIS......................................257
   H. Mary Micco

"AUTHORITY CONTROL IN THE RETROSPECTIVE
CONVERSION PROCESS"..269
   Dan Miller

"NATURAL VERSUS INVERTED WORD ORDER IN SUBJECT
HEADINGS"..276
   Jessica L. Milstead

"EXPANDED SUBJECT ACCESS TO LIBRARY COLLECTIONS
USING COMPUTER-ASSISTED INDEXING TECHNIQUES"....................281
   William H. Mischo

"STUDY OF THE SEE-ALSO REFERENCE STRUCTURE IN
RELATION TO THE SUBJECT OF INTERNATIONAL LAW"...................287
   Vaclav Mostecky

PAIS SUBJECT HEADINGS..292

SUBJECT HEADINGS: The History and Theory of the Alphabetical
Subject Approach to Books..298
   Julia Pettee

"AN APPROACH TO THEORY AND METHOD IN GENERAL
SUBJECT HEADINGS"...303
   Marie Prevost

"CATS: An Example of Concealed Classification in Subject Headings"..............309
   Phyllis Allen Richmond

"INTELLIGENT INDEXING AND RETRIEVAL"..............................318
   R. A. Wall

"LANGUAGE OF THE LIBRARY OF CONGRESS SUBJECT
HEADINGS PERTAINING TO SOCIETY"..................................326
   Jan Wepsiec

INDEX..333

Preface

In many respects the idea for this book came to me when I was in library school more than thirty years ago, and recurred to me every time I taught cataloging. Students, as a general rule, find it easy to criticize existing practices and engage in exercises which will improve the work of their predecessors, but they often lose the zeal for engaging in such projects once they join the league of professionals. In an attempt to facilitate a continuing effort to improve professional tools such as LCSH I offer this book of discussion, exercises, and readings as a stimulus for all librarians and catalog designers who have an interest in their users' welfare. Our efforts to make improvements can be greatly facilitated by the computer systems we now use to produce and access catalog information, but how many improvements we make will be limited by our ability to generate creative ideas and see that they are implemented.

Some of the ideas expressed here are mine, but many of them come from former students (Jarvis, Markey) and colleagues. I am especially happy to bring together the work of Angell, Coates, Daily, Immroth, and Richmond, for these five stimulated me greatly early in my career. I am also glad to bring their work together under one cover with such authors as Pettee and Prevost, Mischo, Wall, and Micco so that younger professionals can see how these earlier works blend in with the new. My only regret is that I could not include many more selections.

The title of this book should have included the phrase "and other related subject authority files," but for the sake of brevity it was omitted. The intention throughout the book is *not* to improve LCSH at the Library of Congress, but to improve this tool's use in developing a subject authority file in an individual library or in a network of libraries. My aim is to reach the audience of interested persons, be they library school students, reference librarians or catalogers, computer programmers or administrators, any and all who are concerned about the lack of proper subject access services in our libraries today. If that readership is stimulated by the content of this book, we may see some definite improvement in our online catalogs before 1990.

Besides the two to whom this book is dedicated, I would like to thank Monika Kirtland who helped me find more recent references to LCSH improvements than those cited in our bibliography, Karen Markey and Lois Mai Chan who kept me supplied with their latest thinking on the subject, and the staff at the Library of Congress who were always ready to discuss the idea of improving LCSH, and who opened their files and meetings to me while I was in the Automated Systems Office at LC from 1982 to 1985. The editorial staff at Libraries Unlimited and the indexer, Robert Burger, helped make my job as author and compiler less arduous and almost painless, for which I am very grateful.

Section 1

Introduction

> If the *Subject Catalog* is continued in its present form, it will attain its highest usefulness only if the subject-heading system upon which it is based is constantly criticized and improved. The subject headings must be carefully selected, continually revised to keep them abreast of current usage and responsive to contemporary needs in all fields, clearly defined through adequate explanatory notes, and logically organized by sufficient but not overly elaborated *see* and *see also* references. The LC subject-heading list has been notably improved in recent years, but it still has many shortcomings. Changes in card catalogs are expensive, and, naturally, the tendency is toward conservatism. It is unfortunate that the *Subject Catalog*, itself not tied to past practice, must, because of the manner of its production, perpetuate the errors and misjudgments of the past and reproduce the obsolescent headings and the inadequate or overly minute subdivisions of its parent card catalog.
>
> —Mary Hardy
> "The Library of Congress *Subject Catalog*: An Evaluation,"
> *Library Quarterly*, 1952

Obviously the library world missed the opportunity to improve subject access which Hardy mentioned in the early 1950s. Another opportunity was missed in the late 1970s when the Library of Congress made preparations to close its card catalog, but made no plans for a major revision of the subject heading system. Now, in the 1980s we think we have another opportunity because the long-awaited, up-to-date, machine-readable file of the Library of Congress *Subject Authorities*, a version of *Library of Congress Subject Headings* (*LCSH*), will soon be available while many libraries are transforming their card catalogs to online public access catalogs.[1]

The availability of *LCSH* in this form and on a continuing basis, beginning sometime in 1986, will make it possible for many libraries with online catalogs to contemplate projects to improve their subject access services. The availability of *LCSH* in this form will also mean that those libraries with automated technical services will be able to obtain some of the data they need to develop their own computer-based subject authority files.

The unavailability of this file has hampered many attempts to improve subject access in library catalogs. From many corners we have heard that there are weaknesses and problems with subject access. It would appear that we cannot begin too soon to make corrections and improvements.[2]

There will still be much that individual libraries or networks will have to do for themselves to develop their own online subject authority file. The availability of "MARC Distribution Service-Subject Authorities" from the Library of Congress will not be the panacea some make it out to be. (See Appendix to Introduction.) This file from the Library of Congress can be used as a reference tool but it does not represent a subject authority file which is geared to an individual library's catalog for its collections. This file is not, strictly speaking, a "subject authority file," but it will have great utility as a start toward such a file. (See chapter 1.)

During the two-day ALA institute on *LCSH*, which was held at seven different U.S. locations from 1982 to 1984, Library of Congress staff alerted audiences to the practices and procedures of the Subject Cataloging Division that were not documented in the *LCSH* file, and they also pointed up inaccuracies and anomalies in the "red book," as the *LCSH* is called. The introduction to each printed version of *LCSH* documents what headings are not to be found in the list, even though such headings are used for subject cataloging. Commonly used subdivisions are listed in the introduction, but the alphabetical list of subject headings does not show their use with every heading. Some guidance is given on "pattern" or "model" headings, but the list of headings does not indicate which specific headings follow these models.

For the most part libraries have neglected the maintenance of subject headings in their catalogs and have long ago given up keeping their own subject authority files. As a result, subject access in many library catalogs does not include the required cross-references and explanatory notes which the introductory quotation by Hardy discusses.

Over the eighty or more years that *LCSH* has existed as a subject heading list, it has undergone several changes in philosophy and procedure at the hands of different librarians.[3] This is evident when one compares the editions of *LCSH* in print, but an "audit trail" of changes cannot be made because of the lack of a history note with each *LCSH* record. In figure 1.7 of chapter 1 there is an example of such an audit trail or history note, which could help repair the inconsistency and inaccuracies in the subject headings on catalog records.

The subject headings the Library of Congress has assigned to books cataloged for the Library of Congress collection may not create a proper subject catalog for other libraries. Many libraries have reported modifications and additions they have deemed necessary to help their library users.[4] Their individual subject authority records document these variations from *LCSH*, as well as keep a record of LC practice. For example, if a library selects only some of the cross-references from *LCSH* or chooses not to use all the subdivisions suggested by the Library of Congress, then the library's subject authority file should reflect those differences. Most library users who refer to *LCSH* in print as they are searching a catalog would find it an inaccurate representation of what that library had in the way of subject access. Caution must be the watchword if the red book is the only source of assistance for subject searching.

Information cards or scope notes are often added to the catalog because they were suggested either by *LCSH* or by the cataloger or reference staff. Over time these explanatory notes, definitions, and explanations of practice can help a library's users.

All of this kind of subject catalog maintenance work has been lamentably neglected in many libraries over the years as the number of professional staff in catalog departments was reduced. The problem was acerbated when libraries began the practice of acquired cataloging via OCLC or other utilities and these records were accepted with few changes; little catalog maintenance was done to add cross-references and scope notes. There should be a revitalization of this work now that catalog maintenance can be done with the aid of computers. The objective of this book, with suggestions for self-help to improve subject authority files based on *LCSH*, is to make a contribution to that renascence.

The Library of Congress published its *Subject Cataloging Manual: Subject Headings* in 1984 but now, as the day when *LCSH* will be available as a machine-readable file, it is obvious that LC practice alone will not provide all the guidance needed for the development of new subject authority files in the online environment. Lucia Rather and Mary K. Pietris have said as much: "Both the search strategy design and the loading of LC authorities are a responsibility of individual libraries and utilities."[5] Australia may have taken the lead in this regard by producing its own version of the LC *Cataloging Manual for Subject Headings*. It will serve as the source for decisions about subject cataloging on records in the Australian Bibliographic Network.[6]

In this book I have proposed a few areas where improvements in a subject authority record (i.e., a record like *LCSH*), made on an individual library basis, will help create better subject authority records and more useful subject access information in the online catalog. These improvements are called "self-help exercises" and not "projects" because they are not complete plans, but they point the way to full-scale improvements. It will be up to each individual library to decide what kind of effort to expend to bring about needed improvements in the subject catalog. The reader embarking on a program of improved subject access will choose from this book those exercises which are the most useful for his or her library. These self-help exercises should not upset any plans for network development or exchange of files, any more than the individual library's name authority file would affect cooperative ventures.

There is no suggestion here that the subject headings in the LC MARC catalog records should be changed. The focus here is on elements of the subject authority (i.e., *LCSH* records) which will affect subject access features of an interactive online catalog. Chapters 2-5 in section 1 of this book discuss ways to improve several elements of a subject authority record if the system of headings being used is based on *LCSH*. Particular attention is paid to scope notes, cross-references, subdivisions, and the relationship of subject headings to the classification scheme used.

For too long the library field has talked about *LCSH* as an entity instead of talking about it as a set of records with data elements, describing some but not all of the subject headings and related information found in library catalogs. There are differing descriptions of what an LC subject heading is and what an *LCSH* record is. The latter forms a part of a subject authority file. The former should be seen as a series of subject strings, resembling some, but not all, of the *LCSH* file.

It is time we began to look at subject authority records as online displays for searchers and to conceive ways to present these records (or elements from them) for online browsing. The first and last chapters of section 1 will review what *LCSH*, or any subject authority file like it, is and is not, and what a subject authority file may become within the online catalog.

To supplement the suggested exercises, readings have been selected which document the origin of many of these exercises. Some of these readings are classics: Prevost, Haykin, Angell, Chan, Richmond, Immroth, Daily, etc. As we enter a new era of catalog design, it is only proper that we reread these authors and glean from them something that can help us today and tomorrow.

The idea for this book originated in 1981 when Monika Kirtland and I produced *Critical Views of LCSH: A Bibliographic Essay* (ED 208 900) for the ERIC Clearinghouse on Information Resources. This publication pulled together all the references to the literature which critically evaluated the weaknesses in *Library of Congress Subject Headings* (*LCSH*) and attempted to make suggestions for improvements. The references cited covered a span of more than thirty-five years. In a table within that document, some twenty weaknesses with suggested improvements were itemized. That table is reproduced here.

Table 1.1. Selective Catalog of Twenty *LCSH* Weaknesses or Defects with Suggested Improvements, 1898-1979

	LCSH Weaknesses or Defects	Suggested Improvements	Critic and/or Suggestor/Date
1)	No code for application	Attempt at "code" of practice	Cutter-1898; Haykin-1951; L.C.-1975; Chan-1978
2)	No rules for grammatical forms	15 rules	Daily-1957
3)	Inconsistent form of headings	Noun rule	Prevost-1946; Reich-1949
4)	No structure specified	Leave as mixed system	L.C. Staff-1890s
5)	Restructuring needed	?	Angell-1971
6)	"1940 standards of definition" not maintained	?	Frarey-1954
7)	Need for more scope notes	Provide more scope notes	Kanwischer-1975
8)	Need connective references for compound subjects	Make more references	Coates-1960; Kanwischer-1975
9)	Lack of references from geographic subdivisions to subject headings & variant forms	Create references *from* geographic subdivisions	Hardy-1952
10)	Subject-place ordering is confusing	Use direct subdivision for all topical headings	Wellisch-1978
11)	Loose, inconsistent syndetic structure	a) Chain-indexing of LC class and Thesaurus as one vocabulary system b) Adopt classification principles for s.a. references	a) Immroth-1970 b) Richmond-1959; Mosteckey-1956
12)	Lack of currency	Discontinue subject added entries and replace with machine produced subject catalogs	McClure-1976
13)	Prejudicial headings	Counter-lists	Berman-1971; Dickinson-1974; Ferrington-1976; Marshall-1977
14)	Lack of specificity	Add more specific and direct terms	Enyingi-1975; Atherton-1978; Clack-1978
15)	Wide conceptual gulf and inadequate designation of concepts	Careful study of words and their function	Christ-1972
16)	Need for fuller subdivisions	Provide more subdivisions	Hardy-1952
17)	Period subdivisions need revision for uniform human and computer filing	Six different forms for period subdivisions	Chan-1972

Table 1.1. *(continued)*

	LCSH Weaknesses or Defects		Suggested Improvements		Critic and/or Suggestor/Date
18)	Sparseness of headings assigned to items	a)	Add headings to tracing	a)	Dornfest-1975; McClure-1976
		b)	Add subject description (contents, book index terms) for computer searching	b)	Atherton-1973, 1978
		c)	Duplication at specific and general levels	c)	L.C. Staff according to Wilson-1979
19)	No reconciliation between LCSH and LC class		Use LCSH and LC class captions and index together		Daily-1957; Immroth-1970; Williams, Manheimer and Daily-1972
20)	Need for machine-readable form and style of LCSH		?		Harris-1970

Source: ED 208 900.

On the basis of this table, the chapters in section 1 were organized around several suggestions which occurred often in the literature:

1. Need to improve form of heading and add more scope notes

2. Need to improve cross-reference structure

3. Need to improve subdivision access

4. Need to improve syndetic structure by use of classification

    This 1981 bibliography has been useful for the student new to the subject, but I felt a collection of the text of some of the selections in the bibliography might be more helpful to the busy librarian who is facing a problem on which the readings have some bearing. Such a collection can help reduce the time spent in document retrieval and increase the time available for information retrieval. The selections chosen for this book came for the most part from the original 1981 bibliography, but I have attempted to update that bibliography and select some papers written after 1979. All the selections are in section 2 of this book, in alphabetical order by author; they are cited in the chapters where their remarks are most pertinent background reading. I regret that severe limitations of space required that I be very selective.
    I ask the reader to remember that this book is neither a textbook on subject cataloging nor a subject cataloging manual. Wynar, Chan, and the Library of Congress have provided those tools.[7] Neither is it a history of subject cataloging nor a treatise on the theory of subject analysis. Pettee, Ranganathan, Foskett, Haykin, Chan, Miksa, Coates, and Immroth, among others, have made the most valuable contributions in this area.[8] This book is for the subject cataloger, the student, the online catalog designer, and others whose interests go beyond the information in existing textbooks and histories.

Notes

[1] Robert P. Holley and Robert E. Killheffer, "Is There an Answer to the Subject Access Crisis?" *Cataloging & Classification Quarterly* 1 (1982): 125-33. See also appendix to this introduction (p. 9).

[2] *Using Online Catalogs: A Nationwide Survey* (New York: Neal-Schuman, 1983); Karen Markey, *Subject Searching in Library Catalogs: Before and after the Introduction of Online Catalogs* (Dublin, Ohio: OCLC, 1984).

[3] Francis Miksa, *The Subject in the Dictionary Catalog from Cutter to the Present* (Chicago: American Library Association, 1983).

[4] Sanford Berman, ed., *Subject Cataloging: Critiques and Innovations* (New York: Haworth, 1984).

[5] Lucia Rather and Mary K. Pietris, "Comments from the Library of Congress," *American Libraries* 15 (May 1984): 337.

[6] Elaine N. Hall, "W(h)ither LCSH?" *Cataloguing Australia* 10 (June 1984): 3-11.

[7] Lois Mai Chan, *Cataloging and Classification: An Introduction* (New York: McGraw-Hill, 1981); Bohdan S. Wynar, *Introduction to Cataloging and Classification*, 7th ed. by Arlene G. Taylor (Littleton, Colo.: Libraries Unlimited, 1986); Library of Congress, Subject Cataloging Division, *Subject Cataloging Manual: Subject Headings*, preliminary ed. (Washington, D.C.: Library of Congress, 1984).

[8] Julia Pettee, *Subject Headings: The History and Theory of the Alphabetical Subject Approach to Books* (New York: H. W. Wilson Co., 1947); S. R. Ranganathan, *Theory of Library Catalogue* Madras Library Association Publication Series, no. 7 (London: Edward Goldston, 1938); A. C. Foskett, *The Subject Approach to Information*, 4th ed. (London: Clive Bingley, 1982); David Judson Haykin, *Subject Headings: A Practical Guide* (Washington, D.C.: U.S. Government Printing Office, 1951); Lois Mai Chan, *Library of Congress Subject Headings: Principles and Application*, 2d ed. (Littleton, Colo.: Libraries Unlimited, 1986); Francis Miksa, *The Subject in the Dictionary Catalog from Cutter to the Present* (Chicago: American Library Association, 1983); Eric James Coates, *Subject Catalogues: Headings and Structure* (London: Library Association, 1960); John Phillip Immroth, *Analysis of Vocabulary Control in Library of Congress Classification and Subject Headings* (Littleton, Colo.: Libraries Unlimited, 1971).

Introduction 9

Appendix to Introduction

THE LIBRARY OF CONGRESS
WASHINGTON, D.C. 20541

PROCESSING SERVICES
CATALOGING DISTRIBUTION SERVICE

ANNOUNCEMENT

MARC Distribution Service—Subject Authorities

The Cataloging Distribution Service is currently developing a subscription service to MARC Distribution Service—Subject Authorities. The following general information on the nature and scope of this service is provided to assist subscribers in their initial planning.

DISTRIBUTION SERVICE OVERVIEW

MDS—Subject Authorities will follow the same overall distribution pattern as MDS—Name Authorities. Although both name/series and subject authorities are accommodated in the same USMARC authorities format, the two groups of authorities will be distributed separately.

MARC Distribution Service—Subject Authorities tapes will be shipped weekly on 9-track tapes at 1600 cpi. The cumulated master file will be available at either 1600 or 6250 cpi. A test tape will be available with a small file of representative records in the USMARC authorities format. *Authorities: A MARC Format*, and Update No. 1 will be included with the test tape and subscription service. The exact availability dates and costs of these products have not yet been established. This information will be published as soon as it is available.

A cumulated master file of approximately 137,000 subject authority records in the USMARC authorities format will be distributed initially. The base file will contain all machine-readable subject authority records available at the time the distribution service goes into production. The regular weekly distribution service will consist of current authority work completed by the Subject Cataloging Division. New, changed, and deleted records will be distributed as full records according to the usual pattern for other CDS distribution services.

The LC control numbers of records in the new cumulative master file will be different from those previously distributed. Unlike previous versions of the master file, a control number will now be permanently assigned to each record and will conform to the standard LC control number practice. These control numbers will each carry the prefix "sh∅". Records in the new cumulated file will not use any superseded numbers from previously distributed cumulations in the ∅∅1 or ∅1∅ field.

COVERAGE OF THE RECORDS

Under current policy, authority records are created only for those heading and heading-subdivision combinations which are to be printed in *Library of Congress Subject Headings*. Records are *not* created for every unique heading-subdivision combination assigned to a bibliographic record.

Categories which currently are not printed and for which no MARC subject authority records are created are:

(1) names of persons, unless used as a pattern or example, or unless a subdivision must be printed;

(2) names of corporate bodies and jurisdictions, unless used as a pattern or example, or unless a subdivision must be printed;

(3) headings incorporating free-floating subdivisions, unless needed for use as a reference to another heading, or followed by a nonfree-floating subdivision;

(4) phrase headings created by incorporating free-floating terms (e.g., ... Region, ... Valley, ... in art, ... in literature).

For categories 1 and 2 above, name authority records are created and distributed in MDS—Name Authorities. Authority records will be created for some categories of headings not printed in the past (e.g., systematic names in botany and zoology) when they are needed for new cataloging. Many headings were made incorrect by the adoption of AACR 2 (e.g., geographic names). Most of these incorrect headings have been removed from the file. Authority records for replacement headings in correct form are created only when the headings are needed for new cataloging.

The file does not contain:

(1) records for subdivisions. The USMARC authorities format does not allow encoding of records for subdivisions. No LC policy has been developed for any possible future implementation of subdivision records.

(2) records for non-LC authority systems (e.g., MESH, NAL, NLC);

(3) records for LC juvenile headings. The Library of Congress will not maintain authority records for these headings as part of its internal automated authority system. Printed lists of these headings will be available. The headings will continue to be used in bibliographic records in the Annotated Card program.

It may be useful to note:

(1) Deleted subject authority records (Record Status "d") will contain field 682, "Deleted Heading Information", when additional information is deemed necessary to explain the reason for the cancellation. Record Status values of "s" and "x" will not be implemented.

(2) Coding in the 4xx and 5xx control $w byte 0 for "related" and "broader" terms for authority records in the master file will be done based on the reference structure at the time of LC's internal file conversion. However, the coding of some "broader" and "related" term references may require reconsideration on a case by case basis. "Narrower" term references will not be carried in LC subject authority records.

(3) Dewey Decimal Classification numbers are not yet included in the authority records.

(4) Source data information is not present in existing authority records. However, newly created records will carry source data.

Questions and comments regarding the sale and distribution of MARC Distribution Service—Subject Authorities should be directed to:

> Customer Services Section
> Cataloging Distribution Service
> Library of Congress
> Washington, D.C. 20541
> (202) 287-6171

Questions about subject cataloging policy should be directed to:

> Chief, Subject Cataloging Division
> Library of Congress
> Washington, D.C. 20540

June 1985

1

LCSH:
What It Is and Is Not, and What It May Become within the Online Catalog

> ... the extent to which we can make good use of LC and LCSH depends on our awareness of the problems involved in the maintenance of such large-scaled tools. Uncritical acceptance of Library of Congress cards, complete with call numbers and subject headings, will lighten the work of the cataloguer, but we should be aware of the possible pitfalls for the reference librarian.
>
> —A. C. Foskett
> *The Subject Approach to Information*,
> 1982

LCSH: What It Is and Is Not

In 1951 Haykin defined a "subject heading" as "a word or a group of words indicating a subject under which all material dealing with the same theme is entered in a catalog or a bibliography, or is arranged in a file."[1] Following Library of Congress practice, the form of a subject heading can be a heading proper, sometimes called a "main heading," made up of a noun or phrase, or it may be an "amplified heading," with a parenthetical qualifier or with a subdivision, of which there are four kinds: topic, place, time, and form. (See Angell in section 2.)

The *Library of Congress Subject Headings*, sometimes called *LCSH* or the big red book, contains the headings established and applied by the Library, "with some exceptions noted" in the introduction. The operative word in the previous sentence is "established." This means that *LCSH* as a publication is a record of all the headings which have been approved for establishment by an editorial committee at the Library of Congress.

Some headings applied by catalogers at the Library of Congress do not need to go through the editorial process because they follow time-honored rules for construction and application, and therefore need no additional approval. (These rules are recorded in the Subject Cataloging Division's *Manual for Subject Headings*, published in 1984.) Many of the headings which catalogers apply were established in part as main headings, to which it is permissible to apply "free-floating subdivisions" as long as certain rules in the divisional manual are followed.

For the above reasons, and others recorded in the introduction to *LCSH, LCSH* is not a subject authority list or file because, by definition, it does not record every heading in the catalogs at the Library of Congress. Nor does it record all the references which may be made to relate headings in those catalogs to each other. Nor does *LCSH* include all the scope notes defining headings or subdivisions. Nor does it include the citation of appropriate sources for choice of form of headings. Haykin's definition of a subject authority file includes all of these functions.

Because the above statements seem incredible, a few illustrations are included here to prove that *LCSH*, in its present form, is not complete enough to be called a subject authority file for the Library of Congress or any other library which acquires its cataloging records from that source.

Figure 1.1 shows the entry in *LCSH* for **Quality of life** and a partial list of the subject headings beginning with **Quality of life** which have been applied to books cataloged at the Library of Congress. A quick scan of this abridged list of subject headings from catalog records (with a count of the number of times each heading has been used) illustrates how the *(Indirect)* rule allows the cataloger to subdivide by place, and the rule for free-floating subdivisions allows the cataloger to subdivide by form. None of these constructed headings had to go through the editorial "establishment" process for approval and therefore they do not appear in the printed *LCSH*.

As of 1984, the master file of subjects at the Library of Congress (the machine-readable file from which *LCSH* is printed) contained about 125,000 different subject heading records like the *LCSH* record illustrated in figure 1.1. It has been estimated that in 1984 the MARC bibliographic file contained more than a million different subject headings in the 6*xx* fields. One hundred twenty-three of these headings are in figure 1.1, but only one can be matched to the *LCSH* record in figure 1.1, namely the heading **Quality of life**.

Some of the subject headings in MARC bibliographic records are known to contain spelling errors,[2] unauthorized subdivisions, and possibly unauthorized or out-of-date headings. (Four pages in the appendix to this chapter come from the material distributed at the ALA institute on *LCSH* in 1982. They document some of the announcements the Library of Congress has made about discrepancies between cataloging records and the contents of recent editions of *LCSH*.)

The number of erroneous subject headings on catalog cards has been estimated to be in the thousands, affecting hundreds of thousands of bibliographic records. For example, in figure 1.1 **Quality of life – Germany (West)** and **Quality of life – Germany, West** both appear. Only one form is currently correct. Several records must be changed if the file is to contain only currently correct subject headings. Some changes, if one-to-one, can be made automatically by the computer if programs for such "global changes" are written. Another approach would be to make either form of heading allowable when the cataloging records are checked against the subject authority file, even though one is preferred.

Another reason that the headings on bibliographic records will not match *LCSH* records is the practice of following a pattern of subdivisions and references governed by a model or pattern heading. For example, for any *LCSH* heading which would be grouped in the category of headings called "Languages and groups of languages," the pattern of subdivisions and references to be applied are found by consulting only one heading in that group, namely the *LCSH* heading **English language** followed by all of the *LCSH* records for that heading and its subdivisions. (These records take up fifteen columns of print in *LCSH*!) Figure 1.2 shows the *LCSH* record for **Quechua language**, which has no *LCSH* records for that heading plus "pattern" subdivisions. The browse list of subject headings on catalog records shows the frequency of use of that main heading alone, and that heading with subdivisions. Some twenty-two different subdivisions have been used with this heading, all approved because they appear under the model heading, **English language**, or because they follow the free-floating rules. For example, **Quechua language** and the subdivision **Dialects** form the first portion of several different subject headings in the list, followed by a place subdivision. This practice is controlled by the *LCSH* record for **English language – Dialects (Indirect)**. This is the model which tells the cataloger how to construct a

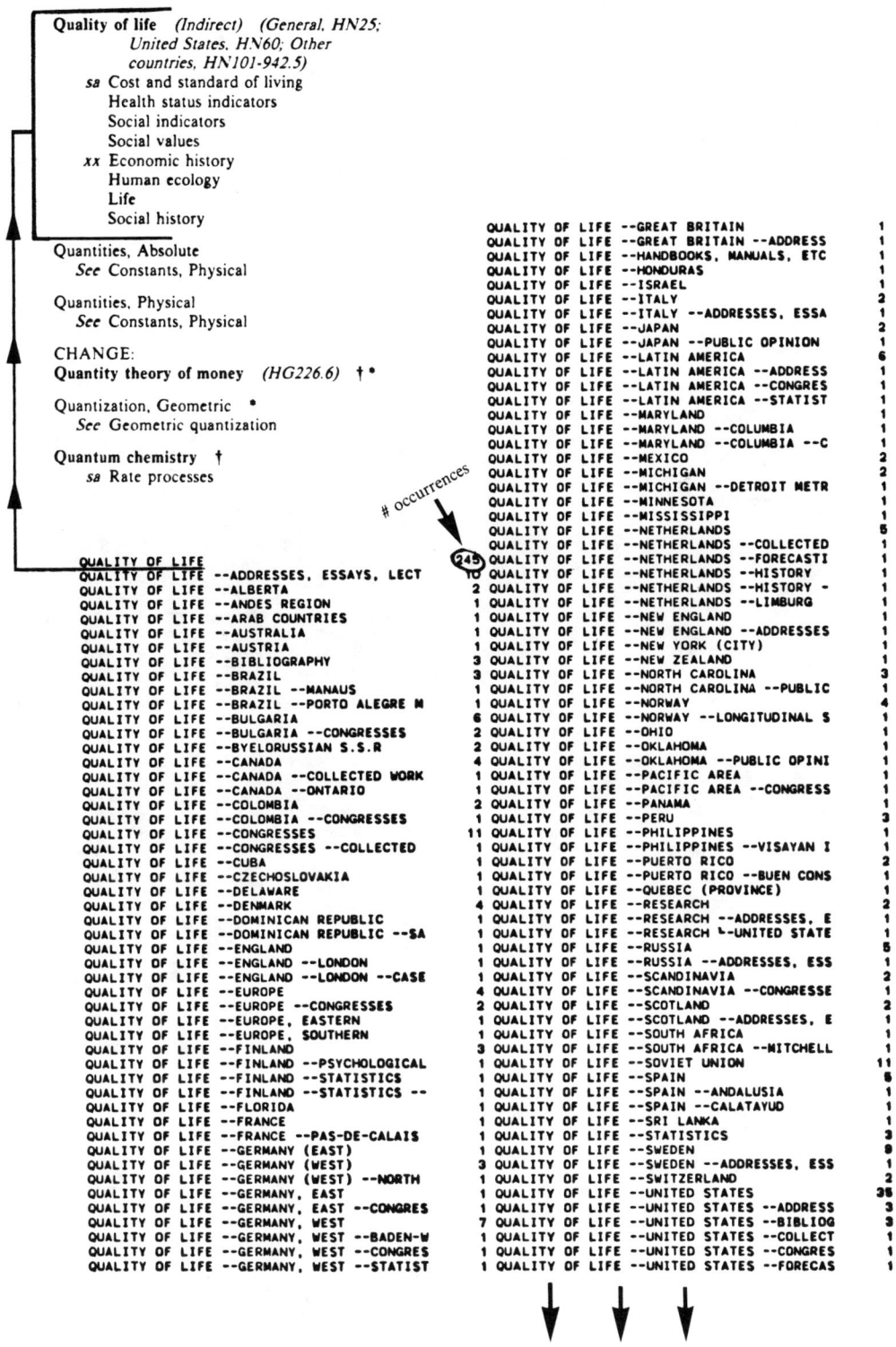

Fig. 1.1. Comparison of entries in *Supplement to LC Subject Headings (January-December 1980): Quarterly Cumulative Supplement to the 9th Edition* and subject headings found in cataloging records online at the Library of Congress (LCCC).

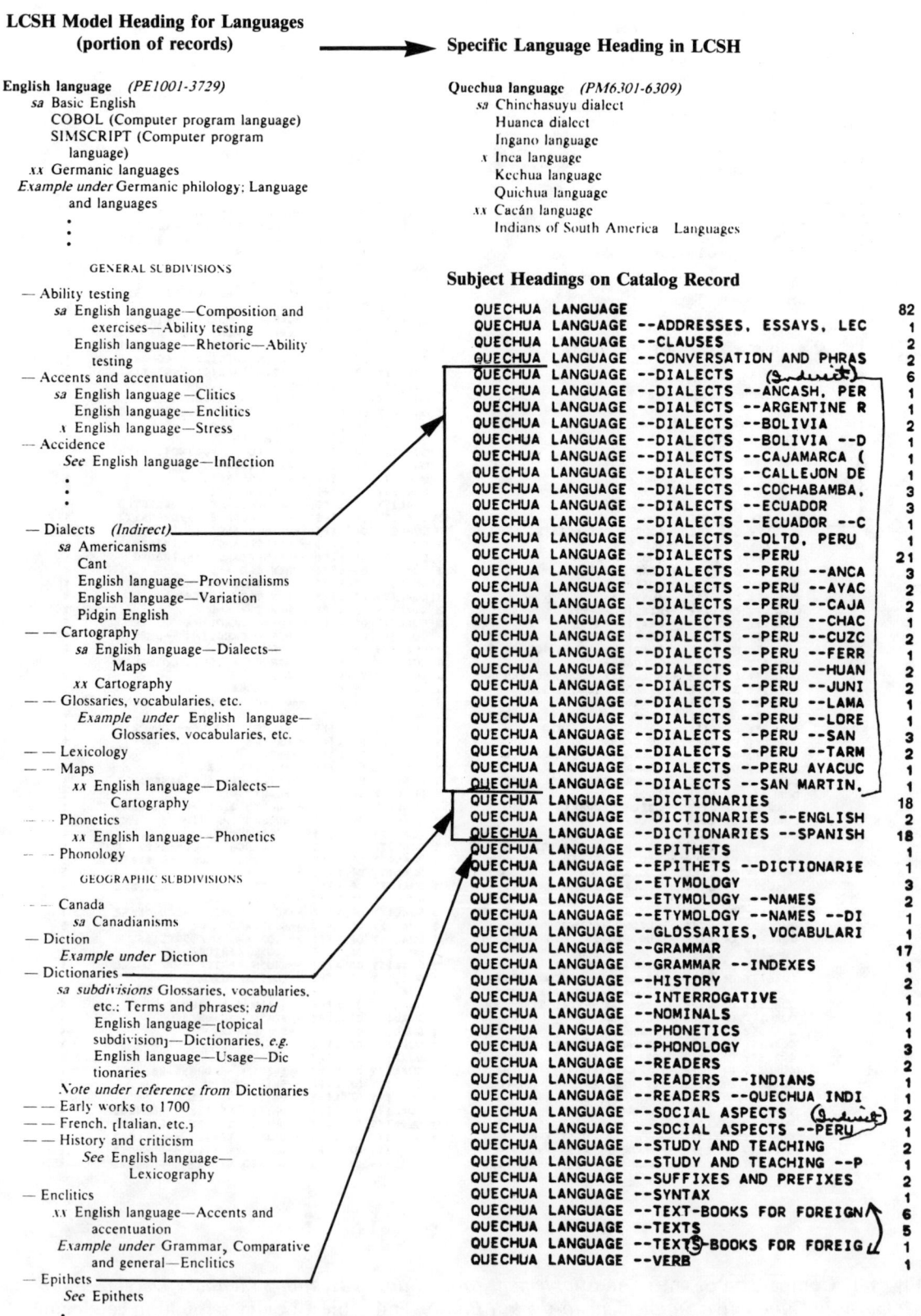

Fig. 1.2. LCSH model heading (with pattern subdivisions) and actual use in a catalog.

heading for any language when a subject heading is needed for a dialect of the language spoken in a particular place. As figure 1.2 makes clear, a few such headings were not constructed following that pattern, e.g., the heading for Olto, Peru dialects of Quechua.

The *LCSH* record for **Quechua language** has no pointer to the model heading **English language**. Catalogers are supposed to know to follow the model, or to look in the pattern file if they are working at the Library of Congress.

If a cataloger wanted to make some *see also* references from **Quechua language—Dialects**, the model heading would be consulted and the references listed would be checked out for their applicability. For example, if the subdivision **Provincialisms** or **Variation** had already been used with **Quechua language**, then the cataloger could rightfully relate these headings in the way indicated under the model, and subject access in that catalog would have been improved somewhat.

According to Haykin and other experts on vocabulary control, every library—including the Library of Congress—should maintain some record of every heading used and every reference made to relate these headings and to record *see* references made to headings used. The current debate concerns how to do this efficiently with the help of computers. The questions being asked are:

1. Can some computer-based mechanism for quality control be designed which will check every heading used in cataloging and make all the necessary references automatically?

2. For such control will there need to be a subject authority record for each main heading and for each main heading combined with one or more subdivisions?

3. Is there some way to control subdivisions separate from their use to make up different subject headings?

4. Is there some way to verify cross-references which is not linked to individual subject heading records?

Until recently, a subject authority record as Haykin described it was seen to be the only way to do vocabulary control in libraries. Now this approach is gradually being replaced by more modern methods. (See Miller in section 2.)

Traditional subject authority records do not exist in many libraries. When *LCSH* is available in machine-readable form, many libraries will again have the opportunity to begin to have control over their subject headings if they will use the computer for checks on their headings and references, and then go beyond that to create more modern vocabulary control mechanisms for staff and user benefit.

Over time, *LCSH* in its various editions has undertaken to record use of subdivisions, scope notes, and references. Figure 1.3, taken from a 1981 publication by Cochrane and Kirtland, records the changes in one *LCSH* record over eight editions of the printed *LCSH*. If a library used one heading and was maintaining its own subject authority file, the library would have to check every LC change to see if it were valid for its list of headings; the library would not want to make references to headings which it had not used simply because LC had made the reference. This is the kind of work which the computer will be able to do: check the validity of headings; if valid, then make references; if no longer valid, then report need to change or alter bibliographic records and references.

Subject Heading: SEXUAL ETHICS	Features in LCSH: Qualifier	Direct/ Indirect	LC Classification	Scope Notes	s.a.	x	xx
1st edition			HQ 31		Chastity, Free love, Prostitution, Sex and religion		
2nd edition			Same		Same as above		
3rd edition			Same		Same, plus: Birth Control, Hygiene, Sexual		
4th edition			Same		Same, plus: Sex crimes	Ethics Sexual purity Social purity	Birth Control, Conception-Prevention, Ethics, Hygiene, Sexual Marriage, Prostitution, Social ethics
5th edition			Same		Same as above		Same, but purged: Birth control
6th edition			Same		Same, plus: Promiscuity		Same
7th edition			Same		Same, plus: Dating		Same
8th edition			Same		Same, *but* Dating qualified—Dating (Social custom)	Same, plus: Sexual Behavior	Same
1974-75 suppl.			Same		Same as above	Same	Same
1974-76 suppl.			Same		Same as above	Same	Same
1977 suppl.			Same		Same, plus: Contraception, Premarital sex, Sterilization (Birth Control)—Moral and religious aspects	Same	Same, but purged: Conception—Prevention

Source: ED 208 900.

Fig. 1.3. Record of changes in cross-reference structure in *LCSH* (edition 1 to 8).

In the USMARC Authorities, the Library of Congress format allows for some, but not all, of the information which could be recorded in a subject authority record of the kind described by Haykin. If that format is followed, the missing information includes fields for *see also* references, citation of source for heading, citation of work which occasioned new heading, and some information which modern thesauri have in their records.

Figure 1.4 is a mockup of a computer display of a MARC subjects record, and the corresponding *LCSH* record. Notice that the *sa (see also)* references are not included in this record. As envisioned, these references would only be recorded in the reciprocal records as traced references. Most thesaurus makers have chosen to record such references in both records, labeling one relationship as *broader* and the other as *narrower* if the relationship is hierarchical; if not hierarchical, then the label for the relationship is *related*. Traditional library labels for these relationships are *sa, x* and *xx*. In the USMARC Authorities format, the tags, or labels, for the *x* and *xx* tracings are field 450, and 550. There is no field tag for the *sa* reference and there is no provision to create a record for the *see* reference. Some libraries who have modified their subject authority records to include the *sa* reference have labeled the field 350. When they create a record for the *see* reference, that entry is in field 250. This is the case in the RLIN (Research Libraries Information Network) GAF (General Authority File), but not in their RLIN LCR (Library of Congress Resource) file (see fig. 1.5).

Note that the computer processes the *LCSH* information differently for the two files. The first record in GAF is an exact duplicate of the *LCSH* record except for the changed labels. In addition, three new records are created to show that the relationship is reciprocal, and field tags note the type of relationship. A record for the referred heading must already exist or the reference is considered invalid.

In the case of the LCR file, two records are created for the *LCSH* information, one to record the *x* and *xx* relationships and the other to trace the *sa* reference. The reciprocal of the *x* and *xx* (namely *see*, and *see also*) references are not recorded in the LCR file.

An individual library or network, when creating its own subject authority file, will be able to choose how it will process the MARC subjects file from the Library of Congress. Besides creating records like the LCR and GAF examples from RLIN shown above, another kind of record or display can be generated. Figure 1.6 shows a subject authority record designed for display in an online catalog. It gives all the information which was contained in an *LCSH* record, but it includes new, more understandable labels for parts of the record. These parts are rearranged to bring forward the most essential information for the online catalog searcher. Each subject heading on the record is referenced on a tagged line. For example, the user may call up a T11 heading's authority record or use that heading for searching without having to key in anything more than a command and that tag.

Mock-up of Computer Display

```
 1  PAGE s Radiobiology; file subjects   1 of 1 records
 2  09/30/83          [SUBJ]          [FIND]           PAGE 1 OF 1
 3  0*UPD* RECORD HAS BEEN ADDED TO WEEKLY LIST QUEUE
 4
 5  THIS RECORD IS FOR USE BY LC STAFF. IT IS NOT A BIBLIOGRAPHIC
 6  RECORD.
 7
 8  001   sh 75-410147
 9  150   RADIOBIOLOGY
10  450   [used for] Radiation biology
11  550   [broader term] Biological physics
12  550   [broader term] Biology
13  550   [broader term] Nuclear physics
14  550   [broader term] Radioactivity
15  360   subdivision Physiological effect under radiation subjects,
16        e.g. Light--Physiological effect; Radiation--Physiological
17        effect; X-rays--Physiological effect
18  053   QH652
```

LCSH Record (9th ed.)

Radiobiology *(QH652)*
    sa Insect radiosterilization
       Radioactive tracers
       Radioecology
       Radiogenetics
       Radioisotopes in biology
       Radioisotopes in parasitology
       Radioisotopes in the body
       Space radiobiology
       subdivision Physiological effect *under*
          radiation subjects, e.g. Light—
          Physiological effect; Radiation—
          Physiological effect; X-rays—
          Physiological effect

    x Radiation biology
   xx Biological physics
       Biology
       Nuclear physics
       Radioactivity

Fig. 1.4. Computer display on LOCIS/MUMS of "full" subject authority record (i.e., *LCSH*) and actual "full" record in *LCSH*, 9th ed.

In *LCSH*:

Art, Abstract

x Abstract art
xx **Art, Modern — 20th century**
sa **Abstract expressionism**

GAF File in RLIN:		*LCR File in RLIN:*	
150	**Art, Abstract**	150	**Art, Abstract**
350	**Abstract expressionism**		
450	Abstract art	450	Abstract art
550	**Art, Modern — 20th century**	550	**Art, Modern — 20th century**
150	**Abstract art**		
250	**Art, Abstract**		
150	**Art, Modern — 20th century**		
350	**Art, Abstract**		
150	**Abstract expressionism**	150	**Abstract expressionism**
550	**Art, Abstract**	550	**Art, Abstract**

Fig. 1.5.

Online Catalog Display

```
RADIOBIOLOGY

    Narrower terms:
T01    INSECT RADIOSTERILIZATION
T02    RADIOACTIVE TRACERS
T03    RADIOECOLOGY
T04    RADIOGENETICS
T05    RADIOISOTOPES IN BIOLOGY
T06    RADIOISOTOPES IN PARASITOLOGY
T07    RADIOISOTOPES IN THE BODY
T08    SPACE RADIOBIOLOGY
       see also subdivision Physiological effect under
       radiation subjects, e.g. LIGHT--PHYSIOLOGICAL EFFECT;
       RADIATION--PHYSIOLOGICAL EFFECT; X-RAYS--PHYSIOLOGICAL
       EFFECT.  For a list of radiation subjects,  type B GREF

    Broader terms:
T09    BIOLOGICAL PHYSICS
T10    BIOLOGY
T11    NUCLEAR PHYSICS
T12    RADIOACTIVITY
 Page 1 of 2.  Ready for New Command or Page #(For Next Pg, XMIT):
```

```
RADIOBIOLOGY (continued)

    Used for: Radiation biology
    For a list of subdivisions used with this subject heading
    consult the Browse list.  Type B (term)--

    For more items on this subject consult the Browse list
    for call numbers.  Type B CALL QH652

PAGE 2 OF 2..READY FOR NEW COMMAND:
```

Radiobiology *(QH652)*
  sa Insect radiosterilization
      Radioactive tracers
      Radioecology
      Radiogenetics
      Radioisotopes in biology
      Radioisotopes in parasitology
      Radioisotopes in the body
      Space radiobiology
      subdivision Physiological effect *under*
         radiation subjects, e.g. Light—
         Physiological effect; Radiation—
         Physiological effect; X-rays—
         Physiological effect
  x Radiation biology
  xx Biological physics
       Biology
       Nuclear physics
       Radioactivity
  — Research
       xx Biological research

**Two Printed LCSH Records
for Same Subject**

Fig. 1.6. Online catalog display of subject authority record designed for users (mock-up) compared with *LCSH*.

Other decisions that an individual library or network will have to make when it creates a computer-based subject authority file will be how to record any special practices or catalogers' notes, what to do with the class marks (for the Library of Congress classification in *LCSH* and for Dewey Decimal classification numbers in *Sears* or other public library lists), and how to handle standard subdivisions, pattern headings and other rules. The incorporation of this information may lengthen the record, but it may also aid novice catalogers and searchers. (See figs. 1.4 and 1.6.)

Some libraries may want to include the content of auxiliary files in their subject authority files. At the present time, the Library of Congress maintains separate card files for qualifiers, pattern headings, subdivisions, biological names, chemical names, geographic headings with references and tracings, and many more pieces of special information. LC has no plans at present to incorporate this information in its subjects master file, but as TOSCA (Total Online Support for Cataloging Activities) is planned for the Subject Cataloging Division, LC may think again about those auxiliary card files. The information which only exists in the official catalog or LC shelflist may prove to be valuable for the subjects master file, too.

LCSH, having been planned for use in manual catalogs and printed listings, did not develop along the lines of a thesaurus which is usually associated with a machine-readable bibliographic file indexed using descriptors. The fine distinctions between descriptors and subject headings escape most people, but the differences between *LCSH*, taken as a whole, and the ERIC thesaurus, for example, are easily discernible. For one, *LCSH* is an alphabetic list of some of the subject headings used by LC, while a thesaurus lists all the descriptors used by an information service, first alphabetically, then hierarchically, and lastly in a rotated descriptor display (with each keyword in every descriptor accessed). A thesaurus unambiguously labels all the relationships between headings, while *LCSH* alludes to some relationships by means of the general *see also* reference. (See Angell in section 2 and chapter 3 for a discussion of cross-references.)

Additional thesaurus features, missing in *LCSH*, include:

1. A tally of the frequency of use of each term

2. The date on which a term was added to the vocabulary, with notes to indicate which descriptors (if any) were previously used for the concept

3. Publication indicators if the term can be used for different purposes, e.g., in a computer file or printed index

4. Codes to indicate a category or group arrangement of the term, which may form microthesauri or be useful to display terms in a tree structure

Figure 1.7 exhibits what a full subject authority record might contain. Notice that this is an example from *MeSH*, a modern thesaurus, but it still has the title *Medical Subject Headings*.

The very nature of subject headings in *LCSH* may preclude their being treated as descriptors, easily combinable in a postcoordinate fashion during searching in an online catalog. Many people, however, have suggested this as a first approximation toward the conversion of *LCSH* for the online catalog. (See chapter 6.) Special considerations involve the form of *LCSH* headings for compound and complex subjects and the treatment of subdivisions and relationships between terms. The following chapters will treat these aspects in more detail.

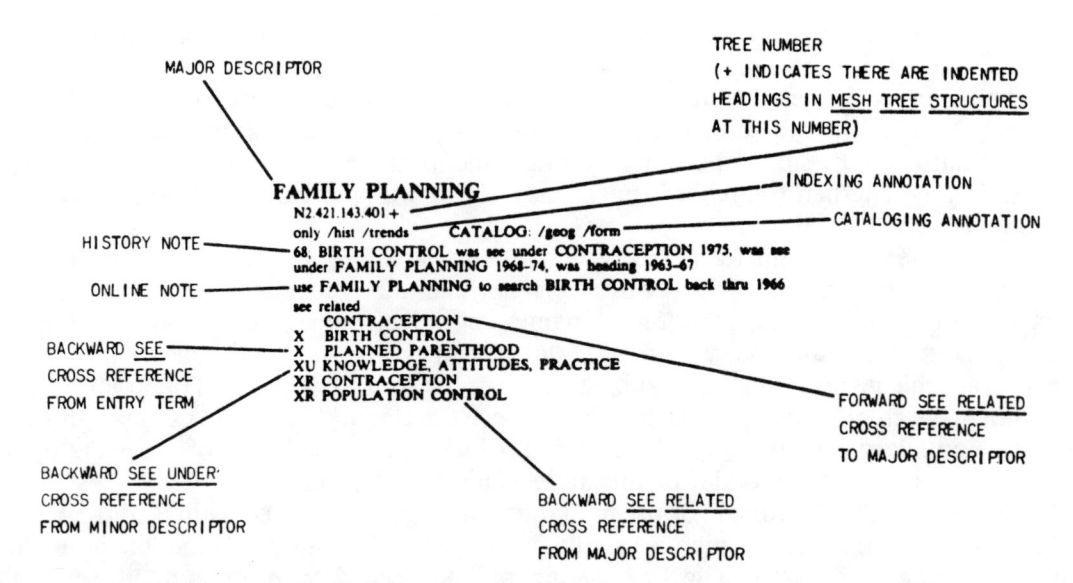

```
                                              TREE NUMBER
                                              (+ INDICATES THERE ARE INDENTED
             MAJOR DESCRIPTOR                 HEADINGS IN MESH TREE STRUCTURES
                                              AT THIS NUMBER)

                    FAMILY PLANNING                    INDEXING ANNOTATION
                    N2.421.143.401+
                    only /hist /trends   CATALOG: /geog /form     CATALOGING ANNOTATION
  HISTORY NOTE      68, BIRTH CONTROL was see under CONTRACEPTION 1975, was see
                    under FAMILY PLANNING 1968-74, was heading 1963-67
  ONLINE NOTE       use FAMILY PLANNING to search BIRTH CONTROL back thru 1966
                    see related
                       CONTRACEPTION
                    X  BIRTH CONTROL
  BACKWARD SEE      X  PLANNED PARENTHOOD
  CROSS REFERENCE   XU KNOWLEDGE, ATTITUDES, PRACTICE
  FROM ENTRY TERM   XR CONTRACEPTION
                    XR POPULATION CONTROL              FORWARD SEE RELATED
                                                       CROSS REFERENCE
                                                       TO MAJOR DESCRIPTOR
  BACKWARD SEE UNDER
  CROSS REFERENCE          BACKWARD SEE RELATED
  FROM MINOR DESCRIPTOR    CROSS REFERENCE
                           FROM MAJOR DESCRIPTOR
```

Source: *Medical Subject Headings Annotated Alphabetic List*, 1983. Reprinted in *Journal of the American Society for Information Science* 35 (January 1984): 42.

Fig. 1.7. A full subject authority record.

What LCSH May Become in the Online Catalog

> I believe that when all of LCSH is widely available in machine readable form and when the card catalog is replaced by the machine catalog, there should be a major effort to revise the terminology of LCSH and to provide more (and more reader-responsive) links between subject headings.
>
> LCSH, which seeks to embrace the universe ... is at present (in the words of S. R. Ranganathan) flabby and listlessly drifting. The machine may well bring improvements and be the agent by which the investment which LCSH represents can be recouped for the benefit of future library users.
>
> —Michael Gorman
> "Toward Bibliographic Control—Fate, Time, Occasion, Chance, and Change: Or How the Machine May Yet Save LCSH,"
> *American Libraries*

Many people are recommending that *LCSH* become more like a thesaurus when it is used as the control vocabulary in the online catalog.[3] No one is suggesting the reindexing of the millions of cataloging records now in catalogs in countries throughout the world. Instead there are suggestions to transform those headings in catalog records into segments so that access to all parts of a subdivided heading is possible, and to treat subdivisions more as headings in their own right with separate records in the *LCSH* file. (See chapter 4.)

Also, suggestions have been made to use other parts of the bibliographic records for subject access and link indexes to those access points with headings in *LCSH*. (See chapter 6.)

As an entity, *LCSH* can be revised, restructured, annotated, categorized, rotated, and recoded without making any significant changes in the bibliographic file. The links between the contents of the two files will determine how the changes in *LCSH* affect the other file. The selection included in this book by Dan Miller shows how authority control can be done at the present time. Other possibilities can also be explored.

Robert H. Burger has discussed the two ways of relating the authority file and the bibliographic file: (1) as unlinked, separate entities where the authority file is consulted as a dictionary to determine the correct form for retrieval in the bibliographical file, and (2) where the two files are linked so that the proper form is exhibited as a search begins.[4]

The challenge for designers of online catalogs and online subject authority files will be to decide how these files will be linked and displayed. A useful compendium on this subject is the 1979 Institute proceedings entitled *Authority Control: The Key to Tomorrow's Catalog* edited by Mary W. Ghikas (Phoenix, Ariz.: Oryx, 1982).

Exercises

1. Expand the number of fields allowed in the record format for subject authorities. (Consult fig. 1.7.) Try to provide for:

    a) All relationships between headings and label these relationships unambiguously

    b) Separate notes for catalogers and for the public

    c) Codes to groups headings in microlists

    d) A field for frequency of use data

2. Devise online displays which are browsing lists of the subject headings used in bibliographic records and *LCSH* records. Also devise displays of full subject authority records which would be self-explanatory to the novice catalog user and another display for the staff and the more experienced user of the library's catalog. Consider which data elements from the subject authority record are needed for each user, what the arrangement of these elements will be, and what explanatory information will be added as display constants.

3. Review what information pertinent to vocabulary control efforts is contained in auxiliary files in your library. Decide what should be added to the machine-readable subject authority file. Estimate the cost in both time and effort for that augmentation. Try to determine if that cost could be shared with other libraries interested in a similar project.

4. Determine how to handle record keeping for changes you will make or have made to the subject headings provided on catalog records acquired from the Library of Congress. Create a data element on your subject authority record for "LC version." Then devise computer programs to make one-to-one changes in the future whenever that subject heading appears on new catalog records, replacing the LC version with your version. If you ever want to search for the LC version, program for automatic switching from one form to the other.

Notes

[1] David Judson Haykin, *Subject Headings: A Practical Guide* (Washington, D.C.: U.S. Government Printing Office, 1951), 103.

[2] Edward T. O'Neill and Rao Aluri, *Subject Heading Patterns in OCLC Monographic Records* (Washington, D.C.: ERIC, 1979) ED 183 167.

[3] Pauline A. Cochrane, "Modern Subject Access in the Online Age," *American Libraries* (March 1984): 145-50.

[4] Robert H. Burger, "Artificial Intelligence and Authority Control," *Library Resources & Technical Services* 28 (October-December 1984): 340.

Selected Readings

(See section 2 for texts, which are renumbered in this edition.)

Angell, Richard S. "Library of Congress Subject Headings—Review and Forecast." In *Subject Retrieval in the Seventies*, edited by H. Wellisch and T. D. Wilson, 143-62. Westport, Conn.: Greenwood Publishing and University of Maryland, School of Library and Information Services, 1972.

Haykin, David Judson. *Subject Headings: A Practical Guide*. Washington, D.C.: U.S. Government Printing Office, 1951. pp. 92-94.

Miller, Dan. "Authority Control in the Retrospective Conversion Process." *Information Technology and Libraries* (September 1984): 286-92. (*See also* Authority Control Services brochures from various suppliers such as Blackwell North America, UTLAS, RLIN, and OCLC.)

Appendix to Chapter 1

Material distributed at ALA Institute on *LCSH* in 1982:

1. Comparison of *LCSH 8* (1973) and *LCSH 9* (1978)

2. *AACR2* Changes (1981 Supplement to *LCSH*)

3. Examples of Headings That Have Changed

4. Split Files and Their Impact on Subject Headings Corrections at LC

Comparison of LCSH 8 (1973) and LCSH 9 (1978)

<u>LCSH 8 (1973) column:</u>

Albite
   xx Feldspar
Ålborg Værft Strike, 1971-1972
Albright's hereditary osteodystrophy
   See Pseudo-pseudohypoparathyroidism
Albuera, Battle of, 1811 (DC233.A5)
   xx Peninsular War, 1807-1814
✓ Albumin (QP551)
   sa Serum albumin
   x Toxalbumins
Albumin metabolism
   xx Metabolism
✓ Albuminuria (RC905; Diseases of children, RJ476.A3; Diseases of pregnancy, RG575)
   sa Bright's disease
      Urine—Analysis and pathology
   xx Bright's disease
      Kidneys—Diseases
      Proteinuria
✓ Albumose (QP551)
✓ Albumosuria (RC905)
Albums
Albums, Autograph
   See Autograph albums
Albums, Postage-stamp
   See Postage-stamps—Albums
Alcaldes
   See Mayors
Alcaloids
   See Alkaloids

✓ = in LCSH 1 (1910-1914)

0,1,2,3 = number of hits in MARC data base at LC in Jan. 1981

Reasons for increase between editions:

1. Natural growth of new headings
2. Printing of former non-prints (1976+)

<u>LCSH 9 (1978) middle column:</u>

1 Albion, Mount, Colo.
   x Albion Peak, Colo.
     Kiowa Peak, Colo.
     Mount Albion, Colo.
     Sheep Mountain, Colo.
   xx Mountains—Colorado
Albion Peak, Colo.
   See Albion, Mount, Colo.
0 Albite (Indirect)
   xx Plagioclase
1 Albitite (Indirect)
   xx Rocks, Igneous
Albizo family
   See Albizzi family
1 Albizzi family
   x Albizo family
     Albizzo family
0 Albizzia falcata (Botany, QK495.L52; Forestry, SD397.A385)
Albizzia lebbeck
   See Lebbek tree
Albizzo family
   See Albizzi family
0 Ålborg Værft Strike, 1971-1972
2 Albright family
   x Albrite family
     Allbright family
     Allbrite family
     Allright family
Albright's hereditary osteodystrophy
   See Pseudo-pseudohypoparathyroidism
Albrite family
   See Albright family
0 Albuera, Battle of, 1811 (DC233.A5)
   xx Peninsular War, 1807-1814
0 Albula (QL638.A335)
   xx Albulidae
0 Albulidae
   sa Albula
     Pterothrissus
2 Albumen paper (TR285)
   xx Paper
     Photography—Printing papers
2 Albumin (QP551)
   sa Serum albumin
     Toxalbumins
2 Albumin metabolism
   xx Metabolism
0 Albuminuria (RC905; Diseases of children, RJ476.A3; Diseases of pregnancy, RG575)
   sa Bright's disease
   xx Bright's disease
     Kidneys—Diseases
     Proteinuria
     Urine—Analysis
0 Albumose (QP551)
0 Albumosuria (RC905)
0 Albums
   sa Photographs—Albums
Albums, Autograph
   See Autograph albums
Albums, Postage-stamp
   See Postage-stamps—Albums

<u>LCSH 9 (1978) right column:</u>

0 Alburnus (QL638.C94)
   xx Cyprinidae
1 Alburquerque, Dukes of (DP60.A)
   xx Spain—Nobility
Alburt family
   See Albert family
1 Albuterol (RM666.A33)
   x Butylaminomethylhydroxyxylenediol
   xx Amino alcohols
     Bronchodilator agents
     Phenethylamines
     Sympathomimetic agents
Alcaldes
   See Mayors
Alcaloids
   See Alkaloids
3 Alcatraz Island, Calif.

1981 Supplement to LCSH

AACR2 Changes

Because of the implementation of AACR2 at the beginning of 1981, many headings currently in *LCSH*, both subject headings and name headings, are in obsolete form. Numerous instances of such headings being converted to AACR2 form may be noted in the present quarterly. Because decisions involving these corrections are not exactly the same as those used in normal cancellation and substitution operations, explanation is provided here.

All headings in *LCSH* influenced by AACR2 must be carefully reevaluated before being assigned to AACR2 cataloging. Subject headings of the following types are normally affected: geographic names, including geographic features; buildings and structures; events; and other named entities which have a geographic aspect. Special rules for formulating such subject headings in AACR2 form have been set forth in *Cataloging service bulletin*, nos. 11 and 12. All name headings established by descriptive catalogers but printed in *LCSH* are subject to review and possible update. Many jurisdictional names in *LCSH*, including the names of all cities, require conversion. Because all subject and name headings listed in *LCSH* will be reviewed on a continuing basis as new works are cataloged, it will be some time before all headings in obsolete form will have been removed from *LCSH*. Meanwhile, any heading requiring conversion should be regarded as unusable in its obsolete form.

The following decisions were made regarding the processing of individual headings:

(1) All subject or name headings in *LCSH* which are not AACR2-compatible will be cancelled.

(2) These cancelled headings will be reinstated at the time of cancellation only if they are required for new cataloging; or if a non-free-floating subdivision has been established for use under the heading; or if the heading is needed as a reference or is used in an example note. For example, *Memphis—Parks—Overton Park* was originally provided under *Memphis*. When *Memphis* was cancelled in this quarter, the park heading was not reinstated because it was not needed for any of the above reasons.

(3) The standard note normally used to explain cancellations in *LCSH* is not being provided in connection with AACR2-generated cancellations, even when the heading is reinstated in AACR2 form and there is no *see* reference from the cancelled heading to the reinstated heading. It was felt that AACR2 changes have been so well publicized that it would be redundant to include further explanation in *LCSH*.

(4) If a heading is being reinstated in AACR2 form after the cancellation of its obsolete form, free-floating subdivisions previously listed under the heading will be omitted, except when such subdivisions are required as references. This includes such subdivisions as *—Fire, [date]; —Riot, [date]; —Siege, [date]* used under cities. For example, *Lyons* is being cancelled and reinstated as *Lyon (France)*. Three subdivisions of this type formerly listed under *Lyons* were not relisted because they are free-floating. Similarly, two of the three subdivisions formerly under *Memphis* were not reinstated because they are free-floating; the third, the subdivision for Overton Park, was not necessary for reasons explained above. Since no non-free-floating subdivisions remained under the city, the city name itself was not reinstated.

(5) When geographic names are cancelled, especially names of cities, all associated headings for individually named entities are cancelled at the same time without reinstatement unless such a heading is needed for new cataloging. This decision refers to the following types of headings cancelled in connection with a city cancellation:

—Names of buildings, monuments, institutions, etc., designated by subheadings under the name of a city (for example, *see* the cancellations involving *Chicago*, e.g., *Chicago. Chicago Tribune Tower*).

—"In headings" involving the city, e.g., *[city] in moving-pictures.*

—Inverted event headings involving the city, such as names of battles, e.g., *[city, larger jurisdiction], Battle of, [date].* As an exception, battle names will be left unaltered in *LCSH* if the city in the original heading was not qualified by a larger jurisdiction. For this reason the heading *Memphis, Battle of, 1862* was left intact when the city *Memphis* was cancelled.

—All inverted legal headings which formerly were subject headings, but which now are name headings governed by AACR2. For example, the following two headings were associated with the city *Lyons: Lyons, Council of, 2d, 1274; Lyons, Treaty of, 1601.* When *Lyons* was cancelled, these were cancelled at the same time and not reinstated.

—*See* references associated with the city, if made to individual entities. Both the references and the headings referred to are cancelled along with the city heading. For example, numerous *see* references formulated as subheadings of Tokyo were made to city sections of Tokyo. Not only the references but also the city sections themselves were cancelled and not reinstated.

(6) A heading converted from former nonprint status to a heading listed in *LCSH*, even if altered because of AACR2, is treated as a new heading and receives no special notation. For example, *Death Valley* was an LC heading that had been authorized for many years, but had never been listed in *LCSH*. It appears now in this quarterly in the form of *Death Valley (Calif. and Nev.).* Similarly, *Beale Street (Memphis, Tenn.)* appears as a new heading, but had actually existed as an unprinted heading in the form *Memphis—Streets—Beale Street.*

Examples of Headings That Have Changed

1. Heading replaced by see reference

   LC card says "Miniature computers"

   LCSH fiche: Miniature computers, see Minicomputers

2. Heading disappears, no see reference, but can deduce what happened

   LC card says "Nurses and nursing"

   LCSH fiche: does not have this, but has "Nurses"; "Nursing"

3. Heading disappears completely

   A. LC card says: "Christian education as a profession"

   LCSH fiche: nothing

   Action:
   Check in past supplements for the cancellation and the 699
   Check in past supplements in the major changes lists
   Check in CSB 15 for the list of changes in patterns

   B. LC card says: "Defective and delinquent classes"

   LCSH fiche: nothing

   Action: note that cataloging dates are 50 years old, and recatalog, reanalyzing the books and assigning available headings

In any case in which a heading on an old card does not appear in LCSH, if you have searching access to the MARC data base, check to see if LC has updated the cataloging by searching under the card number.

Split Files and Their Impact on Subject Headings Corrections at LC

In 1975 the Library adopted the "split files" method to handle major subject heading changes. This technique avoided changing cards in the Library's catalog and allowed many needed changes to take place. The adoption of this new method was coupled with the anticipation that subject heading changes could be made to the records in the MARC data base with a simple instruction to change a heading from one set of words to another. Since the Library did not implement such a method of changing MARC records, many subject headings that were changed several years ago have not yet been changed in the MARC data base.

The list below represents some of the subject headings still remaining in the MARC files:

Former heading	Current heading
Africa, South	South Africa
Aeroplanes	Airplanes
Buddha and Buddhism	Buddhism; Gautama Buddha
Ceylon	Sri Lanka
Cities and towns—Planning	City planning
Czechoslovak Republic	Czechoslovakia
Dahomey	Benin
East (Far East)	East Asia
Gipsies	Gypsies
Hygiene, Public	Public health
Insurance, Social	Social security
Languages—Psychology	Psycholinguistics
Negroes	Afro-Americans; Blacks
Phonorecords	Sound recordings
Rime	Rhyme
Textile industry and fabrics	Textile industry; Textile fabrics

These headings will be changed only by special project. Continued existence in the MARC data base of these and similar headings should not be reported to the Subject Cataloging Division. AACR1 jurisdictional names also need not be reported to the Library of Congress for change, since these will be handled as a group in an update process known as the "bibliographic flip."

A full explanation of split files appeared in *Cataloging Service Bulletin*, no. 119, Fall 1976.

2

Form of LCSH Headings in Library Catalogs:
Suggestions for Improvement and for More Scope Notes

Form of Headings

The subject headings printed in boldface in *LCSH* are the purview of the Library of Congress. In the Subject Cataloging Division at the Library of Congress, these headings are added to or revised as needed when new books are cataloged by subject. Over the years critics have commented on the many inconsistencies in the form devised for these headings by the Library of Congress. (See Berman, Coates, Daily, Milstead, Prevost, and Wepsiec in section 2.)

Some of the inconsistencies noted by these critics include inverting some multiple-word phrased headings while not inverting others and using subdivisions for some topics while forming a phrased heading for similar topics. William Warner Bishop, in a library meeting as long ago as 1906, had this to say about the problem: "... as a matter of *form of heading*, the practice of inversion is to be regarded as fully as pernicious in the subject catalog as in the author catalog.... The worse thing about inversion is the utter lack of certainty as to which of several forms may be used.... My own opinion is for the regular use of the phrase in current use in the form in which it habitually occurs in titles, save in the numerous cases in which a caption with proper subhead better expresses the idea."[1] (For more reading on the stylistic forms of these headings, see Angell and Chan in section 2.)

In this chapter we will concentrate on a few forms of *LCSH* headings which will cause problems when the headings are manipulated for display in the online environment. The suggestions made by people before the advent of online catalogs may still be useful both for card or online catalogs.

What we will not be reviewing are the various suggestions made to change the terminology in *LCSH*. Comments by Berman to change **Aeronautics—Accidents** to **Airplane Accidents** or **Clothing, Cold Weather** to **Winter Clothing**[2] or by Kanwischer to delete such headings as **Creative Activities and Seatwork**, **Wild Men**, and **Yellow Peril**,[3] to mention only a few, will be beyond our limited purpose because we cannot overrule the Library of Congress choice of heading. About the most we will do is suggest that if some other terminology is preferred, at least a cross-reference (*see*) from that terminology to *LCSH* should be made. Many library groups, notably the British and Australian, have described how they will, whenever possible, stay with the *LCSH* terminology, but how they will be sure to provide access from their preferred form so that their users will always find a link to the used form. Bonnici of the British Library has suggested a "table of equivalences" between *LCSH* and standard British terms: for example, **Inventory control—Stock control; Job analysis—Work study**, etc.[4] John McKinley, in *Cataloguing Australia*, reported on the ABN Standards Committee Subject Heading Review Panel's guidelines for the use of non-*LCSH* headings.[5] These guidelines permit only minor deviation from *LCSH*. How these headings are handled with cross-references is discussed in chapter 3.

In this chapter we will try to draw attention to some of the suggestions which have stressed "natural order" and the use of subdivisions instead of phrases, either inverted or uninverted, because these suggestions appear to lead to greater ease of use and display. Several authors have tried to provide an underlying theory for the choice and form of heading: Wepsiec, Milstead, Steinweg, and Wellisch in recent years, and Prevost and Daily in the 1940s and 1950s.

The Prevost rule is, All headings begin with the noun indicating the direct subject, followed by subheads for several aspects. (See selection in section 2.) There would be no composite headings and no use of the conjunction *and*. Subject would take precedence over place, but where subject subheads under place are desired, reverse entry could be made.

Daily reviewed Prevost's suggestions and came up with fifteen rules, several of which focused on punctuation, glosses (i.e., parenthetical qualifiers), the need for a classified approach to subject heading formation, and the use of the subdivision to handle geographic area, historical period, and form of work. (See selection in section 2.) Wepsiec reiterated the preference for "natural language" and the need to employ subdivisions rather than inverted headings or compound phrases. (See selection in section 2.)

It would appear from the various suggestions made by these authors that the advent of the online catalog gives librarians an opportunity to seriously consider changes which could bring about more consistency in form of headings *displayed* to catalog users. I emphasize "displayed" because the actual record of subject heading chosen for a book need not change. The display would be governed by the computer-based subject authority record linked to those catalog records. The headings used by a particular library would be indicated in its subject authority record file as well as the form the display of subject headings will take in its online catalog.

For any library, a review of the form of headings most in use could help to clarify what should be done before the online catalog displays of headings are generated. Remember, the headings can stay as they are on the catalog records while displays from these records are governed by an authority record which shows the preferred form. For example see figure 2.1.

Heading on Catalog Record	Preferred Heading for Online Catalog
Decentralization in government	**Decentralization** **Government**
Decentralization in management	**Decentralization** **Management**
Decision-making in political science	**Decision-making** **Political science**
Decision-making in school management	**Decision-making** **School management**
Decision-making, Group	**Decision-making** **Group decision-making**

Fig. 2.1.

All of the above decisions for changes in display put into effect the suggestions to prefer uninverted order, no compound headings, and direct access to nouns. Similar decisions could be made for other phrase headings so that browse lists in online catalogs will look more uniform and will open up access to concepts hidden in a phrased heading. In card catalogs or printed lists the display could still be in the fixed citation order recorded on the original catalog record. These changes in display are part of the one-to-one changes which could be done automatically by computer when subject headings in catalog records are "controlled" by subject authority records.

Many people have suggested an automated rotation of all words in subject headings to the filing position. We are suggesting something a little more labor intensive, but more carefully produced. The exercises for this chapter test the value of the Daily and Prevost suggestions.

A special class of headings with form problems are those which contain dates in the main heading and/or historical period subdivisions. Daily and Prevost have also commented on the various inconsistencies. Coates described these inconsistencies because they cause problems in specificity. (See selection in section 2.) Earlier Haykin[6] and then Chan[7] described the practice, as does procedure H1075 in the Library of Congress' *Subject Cataloging Manual*, revised 15 December 1983. To try to limit a query by specifying a "time dimension" in the online catalog is almost impossible now because of the practices described or discussed by these authors. They highlight the problems to be faced, but they do not offer many constructive suggestions other than to treat all historical periods as numerals in a subdivision instead of by some adjectival phrase such as "Modern" or "Ancient." They do suggest regularizing ad hoc divisions of time because the same country's chronological subdivisions of history, politics, and government, etc., are not always identical. A review of this problem in a library's catalog, where this aspect of a subject is important, could help answer the question: In the online catalog, how can we limit a subject search on the basis of date or chronological period?

When two concepts are involved in one subject heading (combined by a conjunction, prepositional phrase or topical subdivision), subject searching can be difficult and the syndetic structure for such headings can become confused. Coates, Prevost, Wepsiec, Daily, and many others have suggested the abandonment of such headings. Prevost's suggestion of double entry indexing in order to split the heading could be accommodated automatically without changing the indexing. (See selection in section 2.) An algorithm could be written where conjunction words (such as *and*) would point to candidates for splitting in online displays of the headings. This same identification could help find candidates for cross-reference structure revision, new scope notes, etc. Some interesting exercises result from a review of these suggestions.

Chan,[8] Prevost (see section 2), and others have discussed place name main headings and geographic subdivisions. The form of the geographic name is governed by AACR2 and will not be discussed here, but a suggested change in access to this information in online displays follows the same reasoning as that mentioned above and follows the suggestions of Prevost and others.

In the Chan selection in section 2 of this book, the form of heading which includes a qualifier is reviewed because it has some special considerations in online displays. H350, H351, and H357 in the *Subject Cataloging Manual* govern the construction of such headings. Daily has described the utility of glosses, a related issue. As parenthetical expressions, the qualifiers could easily be handled by the computer via specific instructions. One exercise in the following list suggests a review of such headings to determine what to do with them online.

Exercises

1. To improve on the consistency of form of some headings and to test the applicability of the Prevost rules or Daily's fifteen rules, this exercise consists of a review of almost one hundred headings in the general area of sports and recreation. If this is not a subject of great interest in your library, then perhaps a group of headings from a subject like science or education could be chosen. Look at all, or at least some, of these headings; and try to reconstruct them on the basis of the Prevost or Daily rules. (See selections in section 2.) Then try to answer the question: What would be a better form of heading, the present *LCSH* heading or the form suggested by either Prevost or Daily?

    Remember to examine entry word for multiple-word headings, subdivision punctuation, and time and place subdivisions, and to consider how these headings would look in an online browse list. (We will come back to this list to check syndetic structure, but feel free to look at *see* references to see if the Library of Congress has a reference from the form suggested by Daily or Prevost.) For those headings which are obviously compound, perhaps cataloging practice should be checked to see if double entry was attempted by a cataloger.

LCSH Headings for Review

LCSH form	Prevost or Daily form
Hunting customs	
Recreation leadership	
Games, Greek and Roman	
Olympic games (Ancient)	
Olympic games—History	
Youth recreation	
Family recreation	
Outdoor recreation	
Recreation areas	
Camping—Outfits, supplies, etc.	
Camp sites, facilities, etc.	
Packhorse camping	
Physical education and training	
Snow and ice climbing	
Rock climbing	
Desert survival	
Wilderness survival	
Physical education for children	
Physical education for handicapped children	
Exercise—Juvenile literature	
Reducing exercises	
Beauty, Personal	
Weight lifters	
Weight lifting	
Bodybuilding for women	
Sports and state	
Professional sports	
Segregation in sports	
Athletes, American	
Athletes' wives	

Form of LCSH Headings in Library Catalogs

LCSH form	Prevost or Daily form
Coaches (Athletics)	
Sports stories	
Sports for children	
Mentally handicapped — Recreation	
Sports for the physically handicapped	
Radio broadcasting of sports	
Public relations — Sports	
Boats and boating	
Canoes and canoeing	
White-water canoeing	
Hockey — Biography	
Hockey players — Canada — Biography	
Hockey coaching	
Stanley Cup (Hockey)	
Field hockey	
Roller-skate hockey	
Roller-skating	
Skating — Competitions	
Automobile racing	
Automobile racing drivers	
Sports car events	
Soap box derbies	
Automobile rallies	
Weight throwing	
Knife throwing	
Hand-to-hand fighting, Oriental	
Hand games	
Indoor games	
Bridge whist	
Contract bridge	
Duplicate contract bridge	
Video games	
Crossword puzzles, Biblical	
Dancing — Germany — History	
Folk dancing — Europe	
Folk dancing, Scottish	
Folk dancing — Greece	
Modern dance	
Religious dance, Modern	
Belly dance	
Tap dancing	
Dancing — Children's dances	
Amateur circus	
Amusement parks	
Animals, Training of	
Trout fishing	
Brown trout fishing	
Atlantic salmon fishing	
Ice fishing	
Bluefishing	
Waterfowl shooting	
Duck shooting	
Turkey hunting	

LCSH form	Prevost or Daily form
Hunting with bow and arrow	
Fox-hunting	
Red deer hunting	

2. Scan pages of *LCSH* for headings with time expressions. Review ways these should appear in online displays.

3. Scan your catalog or *LCSH* for geographic names and subdivisions. Review ways these could be displayed.

4. Scan *LCSH* to find headings with qualifying phrases. Are the words in these qualifiers useful for access? If yes, determine whether a cross-reference would suffice or if the authority record for the heading should specifically indicate access under that term in online displays.

Scope Notes

> The one essential for securing continuity and correctness in subject work is definition of the subject heading combined with sharp directions as to its use in the library's practice.
> — William Warner Bishop
> "Subject Headings in Dictionary Catalogs,"
> *Library Journal*,
> 1906

Haykin considered scope notes an important element in helping the readers orient themselves in catalogs. (See selection in section 2.) The *Subject Cataloging Manual* contains five pages on the construction of scope notes because they will "help to limit the scope of a heading, thereby making it possible for catalogers to maintain consistency in assigning the heading." (See Library of Congress H400 in section 2.) Considering their usefulness, it may come as a surprise to some that scope notes do not exist for every heading in *LCSH*. Less than one-third of the headings in *LCSH* have scope notes. There is some debate as to whether they are needed for each and every heading, but there is general agreement that more would be useful.

Greenberg examines the scope notes in *LCSH* in some detail because Chan, in her book on *LCSH*, omitted any discussion of them. (See Greenberg in section 2.) Pettee considers definitions essential in determining the correct heading to use when terms are closely related. (See selection in section 2.)

The discussion of notes is part of this chapter on form of subject headings because notes in the authority record for the heading often relate to the form chosen, the relationship to other headings, or a statement of the meaning of the term. In the USMARC Authorities format, as presently designed, the field for scope notes may also contain cataloger's notes, definitions, and information about reference department files or other information and guidance to catalog users. An individual library may want to differentiate these notes, dividing them into separate fields for ease of manipulation and choice for various displays in their online catalog or cataloging subsystem.

This is an area where an individual library could improve its subject authority file by adding more notes, or by tailoring the existing notes for catalog users and staff. Online, these notes will enhance any subject authority record displayed and may be useful for free text searching. Take the following example:

Current events

>Here are entered works on the study and teaching of current events. Accounts, discussions, etc. of the events themselves, issued serially or covering a stated year, are entered under the headings History — Periodicals; History — Yearbooks.

If someone were searching for material on a given recent year and used the term "current events," this scope note would be a tremendous help.

Another example of a chain of notes, taken from the catalog of the State Library of New South Wales in Sydney, Australia, alerts the user to information not to be found in the book collection of the library:

(1) TOILETS
   See WATER-CLOSETS (the preferred LCSH form until 1980)

(2) WATER CLOSETS
   See also PUBLIC CONVENIENCES
   For other information on this subject apply at the Inquiry Desk for the RESEARCH DEPARTMENT'S LIST OF REFERENCES on Dual Flush Toilets
   Date of Research: 1981

(3) PUBLIC CONVENIENCES
   See the subhead *Public conveniences* under the names of cities and towns
   For other references on this subject see the RESEARCH DEPARTMENT'S CATALOGUE under the heading
   PARKS AND PICNIC AREAS - PARKING AND TOILET FACILITIES

A further example shows how the *LCSH* record contains scope notes in two places:

Civil law systems

>Here are entered works on the legal systems derived from Roman law. Material on the laws of one or several states or nations regulating all the private relations of citizens to each other are entered under the heading Civil law.
>
>*sa subdivision* Roman influence
> *under names of legal systems* or
>   *under the law of a particular jurisdiction, e.g.,*
>   Common law — Roman influence;
>   Law — Brazil — Roman influence

This record contains a scope note and a general *see also* reference note. A library may choose to include these notes together in their online subject authority file, or they may choose to handle them as the present USMARC Authorities format does, i.e., as a "refer from" note, not in this record, but in the one referred to, namely **Common law — Roman influence**, etc.

A more generous provision of notes might be very useful when searching online because often there is no exact match between search words and words in the headings used for cataloging. As scope notes often contain definitions, statements of the limited use of the heading for cataloging purposes, or an explanation of the heading's use in special cases, they are rich in subject content. Often the scope note will refer to closely related or overlapping headings and contain referrals which do not exist as part of the cross-reference structure for that heading. For example, look at this record:

Currency exchanges (Domestic) *(Indirect)*

Here are entered works on enterprises engaged in the business of cashing checks, drafts, money orders, etc., for a fee.

xx Checks
Negotiable instruments

Obviously someone would be helped by this scope note if they had searched using the words "cashing checks"—helped that is, if the online catalog system, finding no matches in the heading field, automatically matched the search words with words in the scope note field.

Some libraries may want to review the notes with the headings they use most often and check the content of each note with other parts of record for that heading (e.g., *see* and *see also* references, general *see* and general *see also* notes, qualifiers, or glosses, etc.). Depending upon how the displays are designed for online catalogs, this information may have to be revised. Scope notes designed to be read on a printed page may lose their value in an online display. For example, a single scope note in print can show how all related headings (e.g., all headings with same first word followed by inverted ethnic or linguistic modifiers) are to be scoped. Online, this scope note might never be seen by catalog users if they enter a term farther down in the list. It may be useful for individual libraries to add such scope notes to each and every heading to which they pertain.

There is a group of notes which need special attention. They are the scope notes for commonly used subdivisions. These will not exist in the 1986 edition of the machine-readable file of *LCSH*. These subdivision notes were first printed in the introduction to *LCSH* (8th edition) and then as a separate publication in 1981, entitled *Library of Congress Subject Headings: A Guide to Subdivision Practice.* An ALA committee has suggested to the Library of Congress that records for these subdivisions and their scope notes be added to the machine-readable version of *LCSH* because they would be so helpful to catalogers and catalog users alike. These notes are revised from time to time (during weekly editorial meetings at the Library of Congress). For example, at the editorial meeting held on 9 March 1982, when a cataloger suggested a new heading, **AGED—SUICIDAL BEHAVIOR**, it was decided that "The subdivision **—SUICIDAL BEHAVIOR** may now be used as a free-floating subdivision under names of ethnic groups and classes of persons for works about suicide or attempted suicide among those groups." This decision made the proposal for a new heading unnecessary because the construction of such a heading was now governed by the procedure for free-floating subdivisions and this subdivision was added to the list of common subdivisions. Catalogers at the Library of Congress then manually updated their list of common subdivisions. With a computer record of this list, every catalog could benefit from this note.

The following examples of such records illustrate how valuable their content is:

CARE AND TREATMENT *(Direct)*

> Use under classes of physically or mentally handicapped persons for nonmedical care received, e.g., *Mentally ill*—Care and treatment; *Epileptics*—Care and treatment. For the medical care and treatment of diseased persons, i.e., the therapy for particular diseases, assign the name of the disease without subdivision.

> *sa* Almshouses
> Health and hygiene
> Medical care
> Rehabilitation
> *x* Treatment and care

MEDICAL CARE *(Direct)*

> Use under classes of persons, particular occupational groups, or ethnic groups for professional medical care received, e.g., *Aged*—Medical care; *Merchant seamen*—Medical care; *Negroes*—Medical care.

> *sa* Care and hygiene
> Dental care
> Diseases and hygiene
> Hospitals
> Rehabilitation
> *x* Health care

The cross-references which form a part of these records refer to other subdivisions, but not to main headings in *LCSH*. As these are valuable notes and they do cover the many distinctions made between topical and form subdivisions, it is indeed a good suggestion to add such records to a subject authority file as long as some distinctions can be made between topical headings and topical subdivision records.

Other thesaurus makers have solved this problem. (See *Legislative Index Vocabulary*, a Congressional Research Service thesaurus, or the National Library of Medicine's *Medical Subject Headings*, or the 1984 publication entitled *PAIS Subject Headings*.) *PAIS Subject Headings*, for example, which is an offshoot of *LCSH*, has printed subheading entries on blue paper and included a note to show when the subheading is also a main heading. Here is an example:

Economic conditions

> Main heading which may also be used as a subheading under geographic headings and under headings for specific population groups, e.g., Great Britain—Economic conditions; Blacks—Economic conditions.

In the record for the main heading, **Economic conditions**, a note appears which indicates that this may also be used as a subheading. (See *PAIS Subject Headings* in section 2.)

Exercises

The exercises which follow are plans for projects which would bring about improvements in scope notes found in a library's subject authority file. As an added benefit, a library might send its new scope notes to the Library of Congress. They might be well received if they were constructed following the procedures laid down in H400 of the *Subject Cataloging Manual*.

1. Review the various scope notes with the following headings.

State governments *(Indirect) (United States. JK2408-9595)*
    Here are entered works on state governments in general and in the United States.
    Works dealing with state governments in other countries organized on a federal basis are entered under State governments—[local subdivision], *e.g.* State governments—Canada, State governments—Mexico.
    Works dealing with administrative divisions of a centralized state are entered under the heading Local government.
    Works on the government of an individual state are entered under the subdivision Politics and government under the name of the state. *e.g.* New York (State)—Politics and government.
  sa Constitutions, State
      Exclusive and concurrent legislative powers
      Federal government
      Governors—United States
      Interstate agreements
      Interstate controversies
      Interstate relations
      Legislative power
      Lieutenant-governors
      Statehood (American politics)
      Taxation, State
  xx Federal government
      Legislative power
      Political science
      Statehood (American politics)
  — Officials and employees
    x State officials and employees
    xx Public officers
    Example under reference from Officials and employees
  — — Health and hygiene
    x State governments—Officials and employees—Medical care
    xx Hygiene
  — — Medical care

Local color in literature *(PN56.L)*
  sa Poetry of places
    France in literature; Italy in literature; *and similar headings*
  x Literature—Local color
  xx Manners and customs
    National characteristics

Local elections *(Indirect)*
    Works on the electoral systems of individual cities or other local government units are entered under the headings Election law, or Elections, subdivided by the name of the respective city or other local government unit.
  sa Elections, Nonpartisan
  x County elections
    Elections, County
    Elections, Local
    Elections, Municipal
    Municipal elections
  xx Election law
    Elections
    Local government
    Municipal corporations
    Municipal government

Metronome *(ML1080)*
  x Chronometer (Music)
    Metrometer
  xx Tempo (Music)

Metropolitan areas *(Indirect)*
    For individual metropolitan areas *see* name of the central city, unless separate provision is made for the metropolitan area, *e.g.* Washington metropolitan area.
  sa Annexation (Municipal government)
    Metropolitan finance
    Metropolitan government
    Municipal powers and services beyond corporate limits
    Open spaces
    Suburbs
    Urban renewal
  x Conurbations
    Urban areas
  xx Cities and towns—Growth

Local geography *(G75)*
   x Geography, Local
     Home geography
   xx Geography
Local government *(Indirect) (JS)*
   Here are entered works which deal with local government of districts, counties, townships, etc. Works dealing with government of municipalities only are entered under Municipal government; those dealing with government of counties only are entered under County government.
   sa Administrative and political divisions
     Annexation (County government)
     Annexation (Municipal government)
     Block wardens (Local government)

Local government and the press *(Indirect)*
   xx Government and the press
     Journalism
     Press
Local government bonds
   See Municipal bonds
Local history
   Here are entered works on the writing and compiling of local histories. Collective histories of several local units are entered under names of countries, states, etc. with subdivision History, Local. Individual local histories are entered under the name of the place, with or without subdivision History.
   x History, Local
   xx Historiography

Current events
   Here are entered works on the study and teaching of current events. Accounts, discussions, etc. of the events themselves, issued serially or covering a stated year, are entered under the headings History—Periodicals; History—Yearbooks.
   xx History, Modern—Study and teaching

Governmental investigations *(Indirect)*
   Here are entered works on investigations initiated by the legislative, executive, or judicial branches of the government and usually conducted by ad hoc or permanent bodies for the purpose of investigating some particular problem of public interest.
   sa Criminal investigation
     Executive privilege (Government information)
     Legislative hearings
     Police
     names of specific investigative bodies
   x Commissions of inquiry
     Executive investigations
     Government investigations
     Investigations, Governmental
     Judicial investigations
     Legislative investigations
   xx Investigations
     Justice, Administration of
     Legislation
     Legislative bodies—Committees
     Legislative oversight
     Public administration
  — United States
     x Congressional investigations

Governors
   Works on governors of the United States are entered under the heading Governors—United States. Works on governors in other countries are entered under the name of the country with subdivision Governors, *e.g.* Russia—Governors.
   Works on governors of any state or province, including collective biography, are entered under the name of the state or province with subdivision Governors, *e.g.* Louisiana—Governors.
  — Wives
     Works on the wives of governors of all jurisdictions except the United States are entered under the name of the jurisdiction with subdivision Governors—Wives, *e.g.* New York (State)—Governors—Wives.
     Works discussing collectively the wives of the governors of the United States are entered under Governors—United States—Wives.

Civil law systems
    Here are entered works on the legal systems derived from Roman law. Material on the laws of one or several states or nations regulating all the private relations of citizens to each other are entered under the heading Civil law.
  sa subdivision Roman influence *under names of legal systems or under the law of a particular jurisdiction. e.g.* Common law—Roman influence; Law—Brazil—Roman influence
  xx Roman law
      Roman law—Influence

Currency act of March 14, 1900 *(Speeches in Congress, HG534)*
  xx Bimetallism
      Silver question
Currency areas
  See Monetary unions
Currency changers (Coins)
  See Coin changing machines
Currency convertibility
  x Convertibility of currency
  xx Commercial policy
      Currency question
      Foreign exchange
      Gold standard
      Industrial management and inflation
      Money
Currency devaluation
  See Currency question
Currency exchanges (Domestic) *(Indirect)*
    Here are entered works on enterprises engaged in the business of cashing checks, drafts, money orders, etc. for a fee.
  xx Checks
      Negotiable instruments

Loans, Personal *(Indirect) (HG2052-2069)*
    Here are entered works on loans to individuals for personal rather than business uses, for consumption rather than production purposes.
  sa Banks and banking, Cooperative
      Building and loan associations
      Finance charges
      Industrial loan associations
      Pawnbroking
  x Consumer loans
      Loan sharking
      Loans, Consumer
      Loans, Small
      Personal loans
      Small loans
  xx Consumer credit
      Loans
  Note under Consumer credit

Corporations, Nonprofit *(Indirect)*
    Here are entered works on the law of incorporated associations established for other than business purposes. Works on corporations established to administer endowment funds are entered under the heading Charitable uses, trusts, and foundations.
  sa By-laws
      Unincorporated societies
  x Associations (Law)
      Corporations, Membership
      Membership corporations
      Nonprofit corporations
  xx Corporation law
      Juristic persons
      Unincorporated societies
  — Registration and transfer *(Indirect)*
  — Taxation *(Indirect)*
    sa Church property—Taxation
        Cooperative societies—Taxation
        Taxation, Exemption from
        Universities and colleges—Taxation
    x Charities—Taxation
    xx Taxation, Exemption from
  — Tort liability
    See Tort liability of charitable organizations
    Tort liability of corporations

Would all parts of these scope notes be useful for catalog searchers? How might these scope notes be revised for display in online catalogs?

2. Provide dictionary definitions as scope notes for the following headings:

    New thought
    Sandwich construction
    Open and closed shelves

Would these scope notes help with synonym searching if they were provided free text searching? Consider other headings that could use such scope notes. (Consult Pettee selection for background.)

3. Scan an area of your catalog where you know there has been some difficulty in user's understanding of cataloging practice, for example, headings beginning with the words "Local," "State," "Municipal," or "Metropolitan." Devise scope notes which would include more explanation about the use of each heading. Consult *LCSH* to see if it has added similar scope notes.

4. Determine if the scope notes found in other thesauri might be useful additions to your subject authority file. Choose ten or more of the most used headings in your catalog. Check to see if there are scope notes for these headings in the vocabularies for other online databases, for example, PAIS or ERIC. Would these enrich your subject authority file?

Notes

[1] William Warner Bishop, "Subject Headings in Dictionary Catalogs," *Library Journal* 31 (June 1906): supplement, 118.

[2] Sanford Berman, "Where Have All the Moonies Gone?" *The Reference Librarian* 9 (Fall/Winter 1983): 133-43.

[3] Dorothy Kanwischer, "Subject Headings Trauma," *Wilson Library Bulletin* (May 1975): 651-54.

[4] Norbert Bonnici, "PRECIS and *LCSH* in the British Library: Problems of Consistency and Equivalence," *Catalogue and Index* 56 (Spring 1980): 9-11.

[5] John McKinley, "Australia, *LCSH* and FLASH," *Library Resources & Technical Services* 26 (April/June 1982): 100-109.

[6] David J. Haykin, *Subject Headings: A Practical Guide* (Washington, D.C.: U.S. Government Printing Office, 1951), 33-35.

[7] Lois Mai Chan, *Library of Congress Subject Headings: Principles and Applications* (Littleton, Colo.: Libraries Unlimited, 1978), 70-74.

[8] Chan, 66-69, 120-24.

Selected Readings

(See section 2 for texts, which are renumbered in this edition.)

Berman, Sanford. "Proposal for Reforms to Improve Subject Searching." *American Libraries* (April 1984): 254.

Chan, Lois Mai. "Library of Congress Subject Headings as an Online Retrieval Tool: Structural Considerations." Paper presented at the Symposium on Subject Analysis, 29-30 March 1985, Durham, N.C., sponsored by the School of Library and Information Science, North Carolina Central University.

Coates, Eric James. *Subject Catalogues: Headings and Structure.* London: Library Association, 1960. 69-79.

Daily, Jay E. *The Grammar of Subject Headings: A Formulation of Rules.* Doctoral diss., School of Library Service, Columbia University, 1957. pp. 152-61.

Greenberg, Alan M. "Scope Notes in *Library of Congress Subject Headings.*" *Cataloging & Classification Quarterly* 1 (1982): 95-104.

Library of Congress, Subject Cataloging Division. *Subject Cataloging Manual: Subject Headings.* Washington, D.C., 1984. H400.

Mandel, Carol. "Helping LC Improve LCSH Only Constructive Approach." *American Libraries* (May 1984): 336.

Milstead, Jessica L. "Natural versus Inverted Word Order in Subject Headings." *Library Resources & Technical Services* 24 (Spring 1980), 174-78.

Pettee, Julia. *Subject Headings: The History and Theory of the Alphabetical Subject Approach to Books.* New York: H. W. Wilson Co., 1947. pp. 73-80.

Prevost, Marie. "An Approach to Theory and Method in General Subject Heading." *Library Quarterly* 16 (1946): 144-47, 149-51.

Wepsiec, Jan. "Language of the Library of Congress Subject Headings Pertaining to Society." *Library Resources & Technical Services* 25 (April/June 1981): 196-203.

3 LCSH Cross-Reference Structure:
Suggested Improvements

Cross-references are the very heart and soul of the dictionary catalog. Without cross-references, the dictionary catalog is about as impossible for readers to use as the bookstack would be if we failed to provide readers with an index to the classification. Every library has a public index to its classification in the form of the subject entries in its catalog. Every library should provide an equally good cross-reference network.

A cataloger who thinks that all we need to do is buy printed subject cards from either the Library of Congress or from the so-called professional cataloging services and file them in the card catalog without providing the cross-reference network is not a professional librarian but a clerk.

A cataloger who is not permitted to make cross-references because they are too expensive is not a professional librarian nor necessarily a clerk, but rather the victim of a chief clerk.

And the so-called cataloger who is ignorant of the cross-reference network and thinks that filing printed cards is all there is to cataloging, and who publishes articles advertising his ignorance in professional library journals and in the journals of the other professions which librarians are honored to serve, is not a librarian but a jerk.

—Harry Dewey
Conference on Reclassification,
1968

...Let's pour out the stuff without this time-consuming predilection for cross-references, *see froms, see alsos,* and even finally *see me*.... This obsession of the cataloger with providing the poor ignorant public with *see also's* to everything related is an elaborate conceit.... We cannot possibly make all the connections, just as we

> cannot know everything, and we should do one thing at a time. We should and will index as much material as possible, using recognizable terms, terms which can usually be found in the material itself, and leave the connections for posterity.
> —Jerrold Orne
> "Subject Analysis—A Rising Star,"
> *Special Libraries*,
> 1948

Apparently not everyone agrees that someone searching in a library catalog for something on a subject appropriate to the library's collection should be able to find items of interest under a subject heading which matches the search words or that there should be an adequate way to lead the searcher to the subject headings under which those items have been cataloged.

Cross-references for loosely related subjects are open to much more criticism because, as William Warner Bishop said in 1906, "these loose [i.e., related] *see also* references are the refuge of careless catalogers.... I believe we should not suffer greatly were they excluded entirely from the subject catalog."[1] Nevertheless, many have suggested that *LCSH* should find a more adequate way to direct the searcher to more specific or more general headings.

Numerous studies of catalog use and of *LCSH*'s syndetic structure (i.e., the connection of entries by cross-references) have found that these leads, relationships, and directions to elsewhere in *LCSH* are often missing or confusing. As important as the work of syndetics is, according to Dewey and others, too little effort has been spent on cross-references in library catalogs. Few libraries make the cross-references suggested in *LCSH*, and many have faulted the Library of Congress for not making enough. Statistics show that 73 percent of the headings have no leads, i.e., *see* references leading to the subject heading, and 44 percent have no *see also* references which would relate the headings to other headings in the list. It is estimated that there are now about 25 percent of the headings with *related* references, meaning that there are *see also* references going in both directions between headings. (See fig. 3.1.)

	Type of reference
Ice-boats (GV843) 　sa　**Iceboating** 　xx　**Boats and boating** 　　　**Iceboating** 　　　**Sailing**	Related Traced *see also* (Broader) 　Related-traced 　Traced *see also* (Broader?)
Ibsen family 　x　Ibson family	Traced *see*
Ibson family 　*See* **Ibsen family**	*See*

Fig. 3.1. Types of cross-references in *LCSH*.

This chapter will focus on the suggestions offered by many people for improving the syndetic structure of *LCSH*. Some have suggested more of everything so that no heading would exist without some relationship to other headings. In other words, there would be no "orphans." Some suggestions dealt only with the need for an improved lead-in vocabulary, i.e., more *see* references. Many have suggested that the relationships could be less loose and inconsistent (see fig. 3.1) and more logical if some code for hierarchical (*broader-narrower*) relationships were followed and other rules were followed for *related* references. Some have suggested that each type of cross-reference—*see, see also* (*broader-narrower*), and *see also* (*related*)—and their traced references should have new designators. Some background on developments in this area at the Library of Congress and in the library profession may help to explain why these suggestions have finally been heeded and may account for major changes in *LCSH* syndetic structure by 1990.

Background

During July of 1974, staff at the Library of Congress were considering changing the term relationship designators for subject headings. John C. Rather, then Chief, Technical Processes Research Office, presented the case to Edward J. Blume, then Chief of the Subject Cataloging Division that "the designators (BT-broader term, NT-narrower term, and RT-related term) would lend themselves to more compact display, would provide information that would make possible graphic computer display of the tree structure of a subject heading and headings linked with it, and would facilitate efforts to achieve compatibility between the LC subject heading list and other indexing vocabularies."[2] Rather recommended at that time that there be the means of conveying this information in the MARC format for subject heading authority records. C. Sumner Spalding, then Assistant Director for Cataloging, was strongly in favor of these proposals because they would bring about a more intelligible tool for readers.

Spalding recommended an information card in the LC catalogs which would display a "map of where the reader is in the topical system."[3] For each Heading in the Catalog, the card would look like the one in figure 3.2.

```
(heading in caps)                              INFORMATION CARD

    For more specific topics see
    _____
    _____


    For related topics see
    _____
    _____


    For more general topics see
    _____
```

Fig. 3.2.

As we know when we look at the ninth edition of *LCSH*, this project never began back in 1974, but the same proposal kept coming up because standards for thesaurus construction, both national and international, indicated such designators for relationships were useful.

In 1983, the Council on Library Resources convened a meeting on subject access to which were invited several experts, researchers, and practitioners. Two recommendations from that meeting focused on the cross-reference structure of *LCSH*:

Edit the LCSH see-also structure so that true hierarchical relationships are made explicit and both broader terms and narrower terms can be distinguished and retrieved.

Evaluate the LC subject headings themselves to determine if they can be rearranged and displayed hierarchically and whether such a change would be useful to users of online catalogs and catalogers. If such a display is not feasible, major improvements can and should be made in the syndetic structure of LCSH.[4]

The ALA Subject Analysis Committee was also busy, looking to make recommendations for similar improvements. By January 1985 there was a report of the SAC (Subject Analysis Committee of RTSD/ALA) Format of *LCSH* Subcommittee. In a survey of 1,200 libraries and library schools, the committee had heard from 294 respondents about their perferences for a replacement of the designations *x, xx* and *sa* by BT, NT, RT (spelled out as broader term, narrower term, and related term). More than 60 percent of the respondents thought this replacement should be made, even though they were warned that "it would be a long and labor-intensive project for LC because they would want to do it accurately."[5]

By 1985, the Subject Cataloging Division of the Library of Congress revised its rules for *see also* references (see H370 in the *Subject Cataloging Manual* in section 2). This revision paves the way for the labor-intensive work of reviewing the *see also* reference structure and the revision of the designators. A new way of constructing the syndetic structure which relates one heading to another has been spelled out. As new headings are added to *LCSH*, their relationship to other terms already in the list will be reviewed and the *see also* references changed according to the new rules. Projects for the revision of existing references may get underway in time for the tenth or eleventh edition of *LCSH*.

Unfortunately, the USMARC Authorities format does not now explicitly allow for a separate field for the NT relationship in a subject authority record. As shown in chapter 1, this specific relationship can be derived from the other records in the file and added if the library wishes to follow RLIN/GAF example. (See chapter 1 for some examples of how this can be done.) This would then bring *LCSH* in line with the standards for thesaurus construction, and would facilitate hierarchical displays similar to those found in the ERIC thesaurus.

The USMARC Authorities format was initially designed to accommodate the name authority records which are maintained by the Descriptive Cataloging Division at the Library of Congress. The rules for references for names are in the *Anglo-American Cataloguing Rules—AACR2* (chapter 26). *See* references are discussed in great detail because there need to be references to the different names a person or corporate body can use (pseudonym, real name, secular name, earlier name, later name, etc.), different forms of name (different completeness of initials or full name, different language, different spelling), and different entry elements (for compound name entered direct or inverted, etc.).

There is scant notice of the need for *see also* references because these references are needed only if a person or corporate body's works are entered under two different headings. Tracing these references is most important for a descriptive cataloger. But a subject cataloger is more bi-directional, looking to and from headings before deciding on the conceptual match between the subject of a book and a subject heading in *LCSH*. These differences between subject and descriptive catalogers accounts for the differences needed in their respective authority records.

The *Subject Cataloging Manual*, the closest thing to a counterpart *AACR2* for subject catalogers, has elaborate rules for both *see* and *see also* references. The references made between subject headings, unlike names, are not based on the need to link differences. They are based on the need to provide logical and conceptual relationships, and to direct the searcher into the vocabulary used to identify subjects.

Many authors have analyzed the structural relationships between subject headings. The selections by Coates, Angell, Immroth, Richmond, Wall, Micco, and Mostecky in section 2 represent some, but by no means all, of the writings on this subject. Space permits only a small sampling of them. Those included offer the reader the clearest methodology for analysis and improvement of the syndetic structure. The rest of this chapter will cover suggestions for improving *see* references, and secondly, suggestions for improving *see also* references.

See References

See references are a special part of the syndetic structure of *LCSH*. They form the entry vocabulary which allows a catalog searcher to access the correct subject heading for a concept even if the search terms entered do not match headings used in *LCSH*. See figure 3.3 for example.

Women's Lib *See* **Feminism**	Latrines *See* **Toilets**
Ice age *See* **Glacial epoch**	Marshall Day *See* **John Marshall Day**
John-dory *See* **Dory (Fish)**	Animals—Abnormalities *See* **Abnormalities (Animals)**

Fig. 3.3.

The reasons for *see* references are many. H373 in the *Subject Cataloging Manual* (reproduced in section 2) is the main policy governing the construction of these references in *LCSH*. Beside this policy, there are more than forty other policies which contain some elaboration of this main policy. The manual and the files at the Library of Congress can help the cataloger at the Library of Congress, but others may do this work on an ad hoc basis. This problem of providing lead-in vocabulary became so pronounced that the Council on Library Resources sponsored a project in 1982 to facilitate a process whereby other libraries might help improve *LCSH* as far as entry vocabulary was concerned. The "Notebook of Procedures" from that project is in section 2 of this book. (See Cochrane, *LCSH Entry Vocabulary Project*.) It can help those wanting to improve the *see* references in their own library catalog or those who may want to make suggestions direct to the Library of Congress for improvements to *LCSH*.

In the Entry Vocabulary Project sponsored by the Council on Library Resources, four types of lead-in vocabulary were discovered which would help improve access for the catalog searcher:

1. For *word-order changes* caused by inversion of multi-term headings, subdivision or phrase headings, parenthetical qualifiers, etc.

2. For *alternative forms* such as popular or technical terms, foreign or English language terms, old or new terms, alternative coined phrases, synonymous subdivisions

3. For *grammatical variants* such as spelling, singular or plural forms, adjectival or noun forms

4. For *related term scattering* with need for point of access to more general terms (sometimes called "upward" *see* references, e.g., Ethnic—aged *See* Minority-aged), quasi-antonyms, cluster terms, etc.

The exercises which follow serve to isolate various ways in which the lead-in vocabulary in a subject authority file can be improved.

Exercises

N.B.: Refer to H373 in *The Subject Cataloging Manual* and the *LCSH Entry Vocabulary Project* "Notebook of Procedures."

1. Scan *LCSH* or subject headings in a library catalog, looking for multi-term headings. Check what *x* references (i.e., traced *see* references) have been made or suggested. Make additional ones if you think they would be warranted by following H373.

2. Scan subject headings which are heavily subdivided topically or geographically to see if all useful *see* references have been made. For example, if **Evolution** is subdivided by the subdivision **Religious aspects**, you would want to make the following *see* reference:

    Evolution and religion
    see
    Evolution—Religious aspects

    If you found the subject heading **Palestinian Arabs** in your catalog and you knew you had the heading **Arabs** subdivided by place, then you would want to be sure to have the following cross-reference:

    Arabs—Palestine
    see
    Palestinian Arabs

3. Many subject headings begin with an adjective. Some of these are descriptive, but still "hide" the concept unless a cross-reference is made from the noun in the heading. (Remember Prevost's noun rule from chapter 2.) Check *LCSH* or your library catalog under such adjectives as "Used," "New" or gerunds such as "Selling." Have all the necessary *see* references been made? Return to the list of headings in chapter 1, exercise 1, and see how many have *see* references which you consider adequate as lead-in vocabulary.

4. Scan the pages of *LCSH* looking for headings which have no traced *see* references. Can you think of a *see* reference that should be made because it is called for by H373 or the *LCSH Entry Vocabulary Project* "Notebook"? Remember that some of the headings in *LCSH* have not been touched since they were first approved. A newer term might be useful as a cross-reference, especially if the effort to change the heading to the newer term is not possible. For example, this cross-reference is very helpful:

    Road safety
    see
    Traffic safety

See Also References

> Retrieving information involves finding the path, in a network of interconnected paths, that leads from a query to relevant answers. The choice of appropriate entry points and turns—in other words, the search strategy—is crucial to the success of the search. To help searchers find the right path, cross-reference structures provide systems of directional signs.
> —Manfred Kochen and Renata Tagliacozzo
> "A Study of Cross-referencing,"
> *Journal of Documentation*,
> 1968

Some, like Bishop and Orne (quoted earlier in this chapter), have viewed a *see also* reference as an unstructured indicator that the cataloger has placed some books on a related subject elsewhere in the catalog. More view these references as Kochen and Tagliacozzo do, namely that they provide the logical framework for guiding the searcher to *more specific* topical headings or to *more general* headings. But besides those "on target" headings which merit cross-reference, there are other headings that would be of interest and are listed. It is this latter group, called "loosely related" headings, which have met with the most criticism.

Angell, Richmond, Coates, Wepsiec, Mostecky, Daily, Immroth, and many others have written to explain how *see also* relationships in an alphabetic list could be seen to provide a classified, or logical, structure for the subjects covered by the subject vocabulary. For them, the *see also* references to *narrower* or *broader* terms are essential. The 1985 revision of H370 in the *Subject Cataloging Manual* now clearly distinguishes the two types of *see also* references, one hierarchical, the other merely related. Until the designators change from *sa* and *xx*, it will not be easy to tell which are hierarchical and which related, but we know from examples earlier in this book that the machine-readable version of *LCSH* can be manipulated to make the subject authority records more accurately represent those relationships. It is up to the library staff, either at the Library of Congress or other libraries, to review the existing references to make sure they are accurately marked as hierarchical or related.

The *Art and Architecture Thesaurus*, part of the Getty Art History Information Program, is attempting to restructure *LCSH* headings in its area so that hierarchical structures, similar to *MeSH* tree structures, can be displayed.[6] In the process many *LCSH* headings have been changed, and many headings not in *LCSH* have been added. These activities are beyond the scope of this book. Nevertheless, the work is worthy of note, and the prototype issue of the thesaurus indicates how far one could go to modernize *LCSH*.

The selections by Richmond, Mostecky, and Micco point the way to study hierarchical relationships in different subject fields (cats, international law, and medicine, respectively). In all cases, established treatises in their respective fields are the established source for determining form of headings and relationships. Even if the reader of this book is not interested in the subjects these authors used for their analysis, a great deal can be learned from examining their methodology and their results. A great deal has changed in *LCSH* because their work was reviewed at the Library of Congress.

R. A. Wall (see a portion of his paper in section 2) has tried to analyze related terms (which are not hierarchical) into groups of "overlapping" terms (from variant hierarchies), "coordinate" terms (at same level with same Broader Terms), and "associated" terms (without hierarchical relationships). He argues that if this analysis were charted in a thesaurus like *LCSH*, then the computer could track relationships automatically and new terms could fit in quite easily without redrawing the relationships. His examples are easy to follow and may entice the computer-aided catalog designer to develop such displays. At the beginning this will require some human analysis, similar to that now being required by H370, referred to above.

Because computers can now graph relationships, the work of people like Micco and Wall needs to be viewed by online catalog designers to determine if there are ways to graphically display *LCSH* hierarchical relationships, once they are established. Perhaps the syndetic structure is now too complicated for simple displays, but eventually, after review and revision, we may be able to guide our online catalog users through the maze of references via "maps" rather than alphabetic lists.

The exercises are modeled on the work of these authors, and serve to indicate how much work may be involved in the revision of the present *see also* reference structure in *LCSH*.

Exercises

1. Choose a subject of interest, starting with the broadest subject heading which could cover it in *LCSH*. On a large sheet of paper, chart the "downward' or "more specific" subject headings in the list of *see also* references. (Consult the Lopez selection in section 2 of this book for some ideas if you want to compare your library with LC or other libraries.)

    Eliminate all headings which are listed as both *xx* and *sa* references because according to *LCSH*, they are merely related.

    Narrower headings that appear on several levels express "round and round" relationships and should be eliminated. When you are happy with your chart, change all the subject authority records affected by your revision.

2. Review the latest edition of *LCSH* and compare it with the suggestions made by either Richmond or Mostecky. If the change they suggested was not made and you agree that it should have been made, revise your subject authority records accordingly.

3. Scan *LCSH* or the library catalog for subject headings which express a multiple concept. Trace the hierarchical relationships as suggested above in (1). If there are two different hierarchies that must be accommodated, decide how to make the task easier. Will such headings need to be split? If the subject is an important one for your users, then perhaps a break with *LCSH* is warranted—as long as accurate records of your deviations are kept.

4. After reading the Coates selection, and chapter 5, review the necessity of hierarchical references if the relationships between classification and subject headings is made more evident to online catalog users. Do you agree with the opinion expressed in the Cochrane selection on the *Entry Vocabulary Project* or with the following statement of Francis Miksa:

    > the cross-reference structure of contemporary dictionary subject catalogs, in which one confronts the question of how subjects should be related, also suffers the same sort of erratic appearance. It reflects and perpetuates the highly variable approach to classificatory order begun by Hanson eighty years ago. Thus, the cross-references and the use of collocation by heading structure, with which cross-references in a sense compete, are of dubious systematic value.[7]

Notes

[1] William Warner Bishop, "Subject Headings in Dictionary Catalogs," *Library Journal* 31 (June 1906): 119.

[2] John C. Rather, in private communication to Pauline A. Cochrane.

[3] C. Sumner Spalding, in private communication to Pauline A. Cochrane.

[4] "Subject Access" in *Proceedings of the Council on Library Resources* at Dublin, Ohio, in June 1982 (Washington, D.C.).

[5] American Library Association. RTSD. Subject Analysis Committee, "Format of *LCSH*: Report of Survey" (January 1985, mimeographed).

[6] Toni Peterson, "The AAT: A Model for the Restructuring of *LCSH*," *The Journal of Academic Librarianship* 9 (September 1983): 207-10.

[7] Francis Miksa, *The Subject in the Dictionary Catalog from Cutter to the Present* (Chicago: American Library Association, 1983), 403.

Selected Readings

(See section 2 for texts, which are renumbered in this edition.)

Cochrane, Pauline A. *LCSH Entry Vocabulary Project*. Final Report to the Council on Library Resources and to the Library of Congress, March 1983, "LCSH-EVP" Notebook of Procedures and appendix entitled "Using LCSH as a Subject Access Tool in Online Public Access Catalogs." ED 234 780.

Library of Congress, Subject Cataloging Division. *Subject Cataloging Manual: Subject Headings*. Washington, D.C., 1984. H373 and in supplement, H370 (draft).

Lopez, Manuel D. "Subject Catalogers—Equal to the Future?" *Library Resources & Technical Services* 9 (Summer 1965): 371-75.

Micco, H. Mary. *An Exploratory Study of Three Subject Access Systems in Medicine: LCSH, MeSH, PRECIS*, Ph.D. diss., University of Pittsburgh, 1980. 45-51, 58-60, 82-92, 147, 148, 153.

Mostecky, Vaclav. "Study of the *See-also* Reference Structure in Relation to the Subject of International Law." *American Documentation* 7 (1956): 309-13.

Richmond, Phyllis A. "Cats: An Example of Concealed Classification in Subject Headings." *Library Resources & Technical Services* 3 (Spring 1959): 102-12.

Wall, R. A. "Intelligent Indexing and Retrieval." *Information Processing and Management* 16 (1980): 80-86.

4 LCSH Subdivisions:
Suggested Improvements

We can't eliminate subheadings from our alphabetical subject catalog. At least, if we can, no one has arisen to show us how.
—William Warner Bishop
Library Journal,
1906

It will be seen that the only formal distinctions between subdivisions and main headings are typographical.... This leads to the conclusion that the choice of the form of heading is dependent on the skill and experience of the cataloguer in evaluating the composition of the list as he finds it and the necessity of fitting in a new heading.
—Jay E. Daily
The Grammar of Subject Headings,
1957

The various LC subject heading strings of today were not devised for online operations. They are in fact artifacts of another era, the card catalog era, when "main entry" catalogs were the best that we could do. Any further access was normally prohibited by excessive costs. Even by 1910 two principal types of strings had been put into use: (1) a string in which the name of a place was the entry element.... (2) a string in which the entry element was a topic.... In each case all other possible elements in various combinations were arbitrarily lined up behind the entry element regardless of whether the string made much sense or led to a successful search ... today we are no longer bound by the rule of single entry; catalogers do attempt to provide several access points when designating topics of a work. But the conventions governing the creation of the strings are inflexible, arbitrary and often downright illogical.... I have actually had librarians recently say to me that they could not possibly construct one of our strings themselves and get the place right: it all appears to be mumbo jumbo.... They are right, I feel.
—Eugene Frosio
Principal Subject Cataloger, Library of Congress,
1983

> When I first began looking at PAIS indexing with more than cursory interest, I felt that the linking of heading, subheading, and sometimes sub-subheading, was cumbersome for database searchers. In particular, I felt that having to search a linked heading and subheading set in an order that was really determined by the needs of the print publication, was cumbersome. Now, I understand that DIALOG has developed a new linking symbol that will search the linked headings in any permutation.
> — Barbara M. Preschel
> Executive Director, PAIS,
> 1984

> In online retrieval, subdivisions not only provide subarrangement of large files and make the headings more specific, they also provide additional access points ... certain functions originally allocated to subdivisions can be performed more effectively in online systems by limiting according to information in the MARC fixed fields. This is true for form subdivisions that show document types, period subdivisions indicating dates of publication, language subdivisions indicating language of the text, and to a limited extent, indirect geographic subdivisions. Serious consideration should be given to maximizing the use of fixed-field information.
> — Lois Chan
> *Library of Congress Subject Headings,*
> 1986

The sentiments expressed in the statements quoted above show a progression of thinking about subdivisions or subheadings in *LCSH* and related subject authority files. The need to use subdivisions (or some other device) for identifying: (1) the *location* of the situation or activity described, (2) the *time frame* involved, (3) the *form* in which the work appears, or (4) the *audience* addressed is not denied. What seems to be questioned is the way this will be done now that we have the opportunity of accessing information in our catalog records that is much different from past opportunities in the card catalog or printed book-form catalog.

Jay Elwood Daily, in his 1957 doctoral dissertation (see excerpt in section 2) analyzed main headings and subdivisions in *LCSH*. He concluded that main headings had certain definite characteristics. They:

1. are printed in bold-face type,

2. rarely include a dash,

3. may be followed by a list of cross-references,

4. may be followed by scope notes,

5. may have an indication of direct or indirect subdivision,

6. are expressed as one-word terms, proper names, events, gloss terms, two-word and three-word terms, inverted terms, and terms which include a function word like "in," "of," and "with," or the function word "and,"

7. may be followed by suggested Library of Congress classification, and

8. may be followed by subdivisions.

Subdivisions, on the other hand:

1. are not printed in bold-face type, and

2. begin with a dash.

Daily's list of characteristics for subdivisions continues with five more points. They do not, however, differentiate subdivisions from main headings because these five points are identical to his last five characteristics for main headings.

Daily concluded from this analysis that the only formal distinctions between subdivisions and main headings are typographical. Subdivisions are printed from a different font of type, which is not bold-face like that from which main headings are printed. "The dash, the sign of a subdivision, is really a method of abbreviating the main heading.... There is no other distinction, not even to the form of heading.... The use of subject subdivision is a further resource for the grouping of headings when the inversion of a word is infeasible."[1] He concluded, basing his statement only on the form of subject headings, that some simplification of the list would be practical.

In an attempt at simplification, Daily formulated several rules affecting subdivisions:

Rule 9
"Indicate with a dash (—) subdivisions by geographic area, by historical period, and by form of work ..."[2]

Rule 11
"When certain headings tend to be used frequently together or when a heading is reasonably a subdivision of another heading, so far as a certain work is concerned, use the colon": to indicate this relationship and list with the term, other than the entry word in the classified guide. For instance, "Employment" and "Discrimination" in such phrases as "Discrimination in employment" may be listed in the catalogue as **Employment : Discrimination** and listed in the classified guide under **Discrimination**. Do not carry this grouping beyond two headings. For a third relationship make two headings."[3]

Rule 12
"In making subdivisions show the extent of time as exactly as possible, in numerals, not by some word like "modern," "ancient," and so forth. Make a *see* reference from such terms to the heading used. If subdivision by time is not a general feature of the list, such a heading as **Reconstruction, U.S.** may be preferred to **U.S. : History — 1865-1877**."[4]

Not all authors who have written about ways to improve *LCSH* subdivisions agree with Daily's rules, and no one to our knowledge has followed his rule for the use of the colon when two concepts are represented, although Wepsiec might approve of this. (Any of the suggestions he has made, by the way, could be incorporated into a library's subject authority file, as long as the *LCSH* form were preserved in some field and computer programs written to switch incoming subject headings from bibliographic records to the new form. Cross-references could be made from the LC form, of course, so that automatic switching for any searcher could be done.)

Period Subdivisions

Chan discovered six different ways of forming period (i.e., temporal) subdivisions (subfield *y* in the subject heading field on MARC records), and she suggested improvement by allowing only one formulation:

>Main heading—(subject subdivision if any)—dates (name of period or event, if desired)

She saw little reason for objecting to this revision, except "a tenacious adherence to tradition or habits." (See Chan's "The Period Subdivision in Subject Headings" in section 2.) This suggestion is not too different from Daily's. (See Daily, Rule 12, above.)

Place Subdivisions

Others have written about a more logical formulation of topical headings subdivided by place so that the practice of sometimes *indirect*, other times *direct* (i.e., sometimes country, then city; other times city first) could be made more consistent. Now that *AACR2* requires a qualifier to identify cities and other places by country, it may be moot to discuss this again, but the way the qualifier is handled in the online catalog still needs to be considered. Not providing access to qualifiers will deny any collocation of subject headings by country if they have been subdivided more specifically. The place subdivision is a matter of some concern because so many headings are affected by our choice of treatment. Remember neither *LCSH* nor other subject authority records are affected because most of these headings are not in *LCSH*. What is affected by the acceptance of these improvements is how headings from bibliographic records will be permuted and displayed in online catalogs and how our subject authority records would keep track of these manipulations.

Statistics about subject headings in the master file at the Library of Congress illustrate how many headings could be affected by changes in the treatment of place subdivisions. In 1983, I was able to analyze more than 1,220,000 bibliographic records. Over 360,000 records had subject headings subdivided by place; another 220,000 were subdivided by place and further subdivided by form or topic; and more than 100,000 were subdivided by multiple subdivisions for place (i.e., subfield tagged *z, zz,* etc.).

If place is a pertinent access point, then online catalogs can open up the subject heading string quite easily by permutation of the parts, treating them all as equals for access but holding the original string as the "correct" form in card catalogs. All this would require is a specification in a computer program to handle *z* subfields in a certain way.

Form and Topical Subdivisions

The third subfield or subdivision type in a subject heading is the *x* subfield, which is an ambiguous tag because it is an identical code for both form and topical subdivisions. At least half of the above-mentioned MARC file of over 1,200,000 records with subject headings, when analyzed in 1983, were found to contain an *x* subfield. Almost 100,000 had *xx, xxx, xxxx,* or *xxxxx* combinations. Another 220,000 had a *zx, zxx, zxxx, zxxxx,* or *zxxxxx* combination. Many people have recommended removing the ambiguous coding and recoding form subdivisions in a *k* subfield, or removing them entirely from the subject heading string and placing them in a separate field of the MARC record—the way the GAC field (Geographic Area Code) was created.

This would take a great deal of work, but once in place in a subject authority file, there would be great benefits for catalog users and catalog designers. Displays of subject heading strings could be shorter if form subdivisions were removed and "limit commands" used when necessary to select items on the basis of form.

Many suggestions for improvements in *LCSH* subdivisions start with the list of free-floating subdivisions. This list contains the most frequently used *x* subdivisions for form and/or topic. To date these subdivisions have not been listed separately in subject authority files like *LCSH* because these subdivisions by definition can be used to formulate subject headings without approval, and therefore need appear only if they are part of a subject heading string which is in *LCSH* to record some note or some cross-reference. As they have such a profound effect on subject access in our catalogs, they were described by the Library of Congress in a separate publication, which reprinted the list from the eighth edition of *LCSH*'s introduction. The entries for these subdivisions have useful scope notes and cross-references which do not appear in *LCSH* proper. As explanations of practice, they are also useful to catalogers away from the Library of Congress who must formulate subject headings for books on their own. PAIS, an indexing service whose vocabulary is based on *LCSH*, has published a list of both its main headings and subheadings, with notes on their usage. (See PAIS in section 2.) Figures 4.1 and 4.2 show how useful these notes can be for catalogers and catalog searchers alike:

Directories -- Telephone

    Use under names of regions, countries, cities, etc., or under names of corporate bodies.

   x Telephone directories

(This cross-reference does not appear in *LCSH* proper.)

Fig. 4.1.

Environmental aspects

    Use under types of industries, processes, machines, constructions, or chemicals for environmental problems associated with their operation, creation or use, e.g.,
Atomic power-plants -- Environmental aspects;
Automobiles -- Environmental aspects;
Pesticides -- Environmental aspects.

   sa Dust control
        Fume control

(These *sa* cross-references are to subdivisions, not to main headings.)

Fig. 4.2.

If there were records for such subdivisions in authority files, they could be used to control parts of subject headings in MARC bibliographic records so that misspellings would not occur. (In the MARC file there are at least twenty-two versions of the subdivision **Addresses, essays, lectures**!)

There is a provision for authority records in the USMARC Authorities format which are not main heading records—namely "260 records." This would accommodate records for these free-floating subdivisions and their scope notes, but the way in which the internal cross-references would be handled has not been covered. Figure 4.3 is an example of such a 260 record in *LCSH*, but the cross-references are traced on other *LCSH* records as "examples under."

> Entrance requirements
>
> *See subdivision* Entrance requirements under types of schools and names of individual schools, e.g. High schools -- Entrance requirements
> Harvard University -- Entrance requirements

Fig. 4.3.

Pattern Headings

Subdivisions governed by pattern headings (such as "Soccer" for the category of headings under **Sports**; "Corn" for the category of headings, **Plants and crops**, etc.) are governed by the LC *Subject Cataloging Manual*, Policy H1146 and a host of related policies. We have mentioned earlier that there is no notation linking all the individual headings in a category to the pattern heading in *LCSH* proper, nor could such an annotation be easily accommodated in the USMARC Authorities format. Nevertheless, these changes would be one way to improve *LCSH* and related subject authority files. The lack of explicit guidance for the use of these subdivisions causes problems for the cataloger trying to maintain cross-references between headings with these subdivisions; it also causes problems for catalog users who do not know that certain subdivisions are part of a pattern which they might be able to use for comprehensive searching of several headings in a category. Automatic comparisons could be made between bibliographic records and subject authority records if notes for these subdivisions were included in machine-readable subject authority records. An ingenious way of handling these subdivisions as a class of records might make it unnecessary to have separate subject authority records for each and every main subject heading and pattern subdivision. The selection by Miller in section 2 gives some ideas of how this could be handled. The fast-developing automated authority control systems described by Taylor, Maxwell, and Frost will also bear watching.[5]

Online Display of Subdivisions

Over and above the need to clarify the subfield tags for subdivisions in the USMARC Authorities format and to make provision for recording free-floating subdivisions in subject authority files, there are suggestions for improving the display of subdivisions online. Figures 4.4, 4.5, 4.6 represent some current online displays of subject headings.

```
BRWS TERM FILE:LCCC; BEGIN WITH:SPAIN--CIVILIZATION--POETRY--
B01+SPAIN--CIVILIZATION--POETRY//(INDX=1)
B02 SPAIN--CIVILIZATION--STUDY AND TEACHING//(INDX=1)
B03 SPAIN--CIVILIZATION--STUDY AND TEACHING -//(INDX=1)
B04 SPAIN--CIVILIZATION--TO 711//(INDX=1)
B05 SPAIN--CIVILIZATION--1516-1700//(INDX=9)
B06 SPAIN--CIVILIZATION--1516-1700--CONGRESS//(INDX=1)
B07 SPAIN--CIVILIZATION--18TH CENTURY//(INDX=4)
B08 SPAIN--CIVILIZATION--18TH CENTURY--CONGR//(INDX=1)
B09 SPAIN--CIVILIZATION--19TH CENTURY//(INDX=4)
B10 SPAIN--CIVILIZATION--19TH CENTURY--ADDRE//(INDX=1)
B11 SPAIN--CIVILIZATION--19TH CENTURY--BIBLI//(INDX=1)
B12 SPAIN--CIVILIZATION--19TH CENTURY--EXHIB//(INDX=1)
B13 SPAIN--CIVILIZATION--20TH CENTURY//(INDX=5)
B14 SPAIN--CIVILIZATION--20TH CENTURY--ADDRE//(INDX=2)
B15 SPAIN--CIVILIZATION--20TH CENTURY--BIBLI//(INDX=1)
B16 SPAIN--CIVILIZATION--20TH CENTURY--COLLE//(INDX=1)
B17 SPAIN--CIVILIZATION--711-1492//(INDX=8)
B18 SPAIN--CIVILIZATION--711-1492--ADDRESSES//(INDX=1)
B19 SPAIN--CIVILIZATION--711-1492--JUVENILE//(INDX=1)
B20 SPAIN--CIVILIZATION--711-1516//(INDX=7)
READY FOR NEW COMMAND (FOR NEXT PAGE, XMIT ONLY):
```

Fig. 4.4. Browse list on SCORPIO at the Library of Congress for SPAIN—.

```
BRWS TERM FILE:LCCC; BEGIN WITH:JESUS CHRIST--BIOGRAPHY--MEDITATIONS--
B01+JESUS CHRIST--BIOGRAPHY--MEDITATIONS//(INDX=7)
B02 JESUS CHRIST--BIOGRAPHY--MISCELLANEA//(INDX=2)
B03 JESUS CHRIST--BIOGRAPHY--PASSION WEEK//(INDX=11)
B04 JESUS CHRIST--BIOGRAPHY--SERMONS//(INDX=3)
B05 JESUS CHRIST--BIOGRAPHY--SOURCES//(INDX=16)
B06 JESUS CHRIST--BIOGRAPHY--SOURCES--BIBLIC//(INDX=1)
B07 JESUS CHRIST--BIOGRAPHY--SOURCES, BIBLICA//(INDX=32)
B08 JESUS CHRIST--BIOGRAPHY--SOURCES, JEWISH//(INDX=2)
B09 JESUS CHRIST--BIOGRAPHY--STUDY//(INDX=10)
B10 JESUS CHRIST--BRETHREN//(INDX=2)
B11 JESUS CHRIST--BURIAL//(INDX=3)
B12 JESUS CHRIST--BURIAL--ART//(INDX=2)
B13 JESUS CHRIST--CARTOONS, SATIRE, ETC//(INDX=2)
B14 JESUS CHRIST--CHARACTER//(INDX=6)
B15 JESUS CHRIST--CHARACTER--JUVENILE LITERAT//(INDX=1)
B16 JESUS CHRIST--CHILDHOOD//(INDX=13)
B17 JESUS CHRIST--CHILDHOOD--JUVENILE LITERAT//(INDX=6)
B18 JESUS CHRIST--CHILDHOOD--MEDITATIONS//(INDX=2)
B19 JESUS CHRIST--CHILDHOOD--STUDY AND TEACHI//(INDX=1)
B20 JESUS CHRIST--CHRONOLOGY//(INDX=7)
READY FOR NEW COMMAND (FOR NEXT PAGE, XMIT ONLY):
```

Fig. 4.5. Browse list on SCORPIO at Library of Congress for JESUS CHRIST—.

LCSH Subdivisions

```
                                              AUTHORITY DISPLAY
     COLLECTION ID.ALL
        1. Papua New Guinea
        2.     —Antiquities
        3.          —Bibliography.
        4.     —Biography.
        5.     —Colonial influence.
        6. Papua-New Guinea—Commerce.
        7. Papua New Guinea—Constitutional law.
        8.     —Description and travel.
        9.          —Views.
       10.     —Economic conditions.
 b 10
```

```
                                              AUTHORITY DISPLAY
     COLLECTION ID.ALL
        1. Papua New Guinea—Economic conditions.
        2.     —Economic policy.
        3.     —History
 +      4.          —Anniversaries, etc.
        5.          —Fiction.
        6.          —Sources.
        7.     —Industries.
        8.          —Congresses.
 +      9.     —Languages
       10.          —Bibliography.
 b 10
```

```
                                              AUTHORITY DISPLAY
     COLLECTION ID.ALL
        1. Papua New Guinea—Languages—Bibliography.
        2.          —Maps.
        3.          —Syntax.
        4.     —Politics and government.
        5.     —Population.
        6.     —Race relations—History.
        7.     —Relations (general) with Australia—Addresses, essays,
               lectures.
        8.     —Relations (general) with Japan.
        9.     —Social conditions.
       10.     —Social life and customs.
 b 10
```

```
                                              AUTHORITY DISPLAY
     COLLECTION ID.ALL
        1. Papua New Guinea—Social life and customs.
        2.          —Addresses, essays, lectures.
        3. Papua-New Guinea (Ter.)—Description and travel.
        4. Papua-New Guinea (Ter.)—Economic Conditions—Maps.
        5. Papua-New Guinea (Ter.)—Pictorial works.
        6.     —Politics and government.
        7.          —Congresses.
        8.     —Social life and customs.
```

Fig. 4.6. Four screens of an online authority browse display at
Ohio State University Library.

The display screen of most online catalogs allows twenty-two to thirty lines of text at most. Some of this must be used for system messages, prompts and user responses. For frequently used headings like **Jesus Christ, Spain** and **Papua New Guinea,** many screens must be viewed before all the subdivisions with those headings can be displayed. At the Library of Congress, for the MARC file alone, the user would have to view more than fourteen screens for **Jesus Christ** (over 250 lines!) and well over fifty screens for **Spain**. Because many of these headings include more characters than a line on the screen will accommodate, they appear as truncated headings, so the form, place, and time subdivisions are abbreviated or not displayed when the searcher is browsing such a list. (See figures 4.4 and 4.5.)

In the authority displays at Ohio State University, they have tried to handle the length of the subject heading string, when many subdivisions are included, by not repeating the main heading and by second and third indentions. (See figure 4.6.) These illustrations point up two problems with the display of headings and their subdivisions, but they do not exhibit any innovative way of using the subfield tags ($x, y, z,$ separately or in combination) to guide users in need of a better search strategy. (See chapter 6 for more on this subject.)

If these long lists of a main heading with its subdivisions are considered a problem, then perhaps some special handling of these headings is in order in online catalogs. For example, it has already been suggested that all the subdivisions by form could be counted as retrieved with the main heading alone, but the system would provide a prompt to the user: "You may limit the output by form of material by typing x." The same could be done, perhaps, for time (y subfield) and location (z subfield), but, as mentioned above, each and every one of these subfields needs special attention to ready them for this kind of display and manipulation if consistent and logical user prompts are to be devised.

Permutation/Rotation of Subject Heading String

Regardless of the changes one may make in the form and coding of subdivisions, some have pointed to the need to permute the subject heading string as it now appears. This is recognized to be only a very rough start toward improving subject access. Mischo (see selection in section 2) and others have developed computer algorithms for these permutations.

There have been discussions at the Library of Congress about how the subject cataloging could be done differently in order to accommodate permutation of the subject heading string. Since the logic behind the string's construction is lost on most catalog users and some catalogers, a worksheet was devised to guide the cataloger who would analyze a work and assign subject headings in parts or "elements." These parts would then be available for computer manipulation to construct headings for catalog cards and for computer-based catalogs, with varying display options. Figures 4.7, 4.8, 4.9, and table 4.1 show the possible coding for subject which could replace the existing coding, a proposed MARC worksheet, some examples of such coding, and a discussion of the advantages of such proposed changes. This suggestion has not been implemented at the Library of Congress, but it is noteworthy and may stimulate another library to consider analyzing its subject headings in this way, recoding the parts of the headings in its subject authority files, and creating a new way of displaying subject headings in its online catalogs. Although this may seem revolutionary, remember that it still is within Library of Congress rules for construction of subject headings. It just makes the formulated headings more flexible and accessible for manipulation.

LCSH Subdivisions

600-630 = No change

HEADING STRING ASSIGNED

Tag
1.*   Place name entry
        a = place name (as established)
        d = topical subdivision (restricted list)
        e = chronological subdivision (as established)

SUBJECT ELEMENTS ASSIGNED SEPARATELY

2.   Topic of work
        a = basic topic (as established)
        f = topical subdivision

3.   Location of subject designated in Tag 2*
        a = place name (as established)

4.   Chronological aspects
        a = *History* [i.e. the heading itself]
        g = single date subdivision under the heading *History*
        h = century or date span subdivision under the heading *History*

5.   Special activity headings referring to the basic topic such as *Research*
        a = activity
        i = place name (as established) designating location of the activity

6.   Form of work
        a = statement of form
        j = addition form subdivision

7.   Intended audience
        a = category of persons

---

*SPECIAL IDENTIFICATION CODES

Tag 8.   Identification of place name types
        a = place name of Tag 3 is a city
        b = place name of Tag 3 is an entity within a single country (including names of cities)
        c = place name of Tag 3 is a country

Fig. 4.7. Possible coding for subjects.

Named entities:
Tag 1: Place name entry:

Subject elements assigned separately:
   Subject set 1: *Tag 2:* *Topic of work:*
 	
      Tag 3: Location of subject designated in Tag 2:
         1.
         2.
         3.
      Tag 4: Chronological aspects:
 	
      Tag 5: Special activity headings:
 	
      Tag 6: Form of work:
 	
      Tag 7: Audience:
 	
   Subject set 2: *Tag 2:* *Topic of work:*
 	
     * Tag 3: Location of subject designated in Tag 2:
         1.
         2.
         3.
     * Tag 4: Chronological aspects:
 	
     * Tag 5: Special activity headings:
 	
     * Tag 6: Form of work:
 	
     * Tag 7: Audience:
 	
   Subject set 3: *Tag 2:* *Topic of work:*
 	
     * Tag 3: Location of subject designated in Tag 2:
         1.
         2.
         3.
     * Tag 4: Chronological aspects:
 	
     * Tag 5: Special activity headings:
 	
     * Tag 6: Form of work:
 	
     * Tag 7: Audience:
 	
――――――――
*Need not repeat if identical to Subject set 1.

Fig. 4.8. Possible MARC worksheet for bibliographic records Subject Headings.

LCSH Subdivisions

		Codes
1.	White-water canoeing—Southern States—Referees—Directories.	
	Assign:	
	White-water canoeing—Referees	2af
	Southern States	3a
	Directories	6a
	Possible display: 1. 2af3a6a.	
	1. White-water canoeing—Referees—Southern States—Directories.	
2.	Technology—France—History—18th century—Pictorial works—Juvenile literature.	
	Assign:	
	Technology	2a
	France	3a
	History—18th century	4ah
	Pictorial works	6a
	Juvenile literature	7a
	Possible display: 1. 2a3a4ah6a7a.	
	1. [same heading as above]	
3.	Great Britain—History—Norman period, 1066-1154—Sources—Bibliography.	
	Assign:	
	Great Britain—History—Norman period, 1066-1154	1ade
	Sources—Bibliography	6aj
	Possible display: 1. 1ade6aj.	
	1. [same heading as above]	
4.	Art, Modern—20th century—France—Study and teaching—United States.	
	Assign:	
	Art, Modern	2a
	France	3a
	History—20th century	4ah
	Study and teaching—United States	5ai
	Possible display: 1. 2a3a4ah5ai.	
	1. Art, Modern—France—History—20th century—Study and teaching—United States.	
5.	Railroads—France—Paris—Trains—Dynamics—Congresses.	
	Assign:	
	Railroads—Trains—Dynamics	2aff
	Paris (France)	3a
	Congresses	6a
	Possible display: 1. 2aff3a6a.	
	1. Railroads—Trains—Dynamics—Paris (France)—Congresses.	
6.	Paris (France)—Police—Job stress—Statistics.	
	Assign:	
	Police—Job stress	2af
	Paris (France)	3a
	Statistics	6a
	Possible display: 1. 2af3a6a.	
	1. Police—Job stress—Paris (France)—Statistics.	

Fig. 4.9. Examples of coding subject headings in bibliographic records.
(Each given heading is formulated according to existing rules.)

Table 4.1. Advantages of a coding scheme for subjects.

1. *Less complexity.* Rules for the formulation of the present strings are so complicated that they are not readily understood by catalogers or the public. The principal feature of the proposed system is to reduce this anachronistic string to its constituent parts—thus, one less hurdle to all concerned in negotiating the system. Catalogers would no longer need to take the time to line up the elements of the string in just the correct manner to correspond to the situation in hand. The machine generated string would have internal arrangements that would be entirely predictable.

2. *Greater consistency.* The practice would result in more uniform and consistent indexing. The public would now be able to predict where the various elements in the string should invariably appear.

3. *LC products.* The proposal provides for the constituent parts of strings to be stored in the bibliographic data base, not full strings. In storage these elements would be instantly ready and available to the computer for further manipulation, the exact treatment depending upon the requirements of the special LC product in which they are to appear. For online searching at LC displays could be achieved using machine generated strings. For particular bibliographies or LC printed catalog cards the various elements could be combined in various ways to meet the requirements of the particular product, e.g. NUC, HLAS, etc.

4. *Separation of elements.* Advantages accrue from having each element of the analysis not impinging on the other. For example:

   If a hierarchical relationship were to be established between topical subjects, the fixed strings with other elements would not be in the way. If a geothesaurus were to be constructed to facilitate subject searching on this aspect, it could be constructed as an independent tool, an adjunct to LCSH for topics. This could be coordinated with the GAC more efficiently. If there were to be an effort to develop a format dictionary, the separate list maintained by the SCD for this element could be more easily updated and revised, because it would not be necessary to change cataloging records but indexes in the computer.

5. *Ease of corrections.* The capability of making corrections on bibliographic records would be greatly enhanced, since a change of a heading or subdivision would mean only correction of individual elements, not entire strings. Incidental information such as dates, form, audience, etc. could be corrected by indexes in the computer, not by the changing of individual records.

6. *Greater productivity.* The practice proposed here would result in a more efficient use of personnel in the cataloging assembly line. The cataloger would require less time in completing and proofreading the cataloging worksheet of a work since each element would be written only once. MARC editors would have less inputting of information. Chance of typos would be reduced. Today each of the various strings are repeated in full under each topic assigned. For example:

   1. [topic 1]—[place]—History—18th century—Addresses, essays, lectures.
   2. [topic 2]—[place]—History—18th century—Addresses, essays, lectures.
   3. [topic 3]—[place]—History—18th century—Addresses, essays, lectures.

7. *Storage of information.* The subject information stored in the data base would occupy less space since each element would be listed only once.

8. *Validation would be easier.* The proposal would make possible a situation whereby the validation problem for individual headings could be readily solved. If the system did not provide for the existence of full strings, there would no longer be the problem of validating full strings. It would be sufficient to validate only the information stored in the record, which would be in the form of separate elements.

9. *Geographic considerations.* The proposal is able to maintain the several different kinds of place names currently in the system: place names as true subjects, place names simply as the location or environment of a topic in question, and place names where the special investigation of the topic (such as *Research*) is undertaken.

Exercises

1. Examine the list of free-floating subdivisions and incorporate into your subject authority file a record for those which are most frequently used in your library. Determine if you can accommodate all the information in existing MARC fields or if you will have to create new fields (e.g., for the cross-references valid only between subdivisions). Determine how you will use such records to validate subject headings in your bibliographic file.

2. Consult the table of pattern headings in *LCSH*. For any category of headings which is popular in your library, e.g., **Sports**, review all the subject headings in that category to determine if the pattern of subdivisions and cross-references has been followed. Revise your subject authority records to show these subdivisions and references or devise a new type of authority record for the subdivisions, possibly following the format devised in exercise 1. This latter solution would also require some way of linking that subdivision record to the headings of that category. (Consult the *MeSH* list for some suggested codings and categories.)

3. After reading the Chan selection, "The Period Subdivision in Subject Headings," consider the impact of her suggestion by reviewing headings with dates in your catalog. How many headings would change and how could the change, if made, help users of your online catalog limit their searches by date?

4. Review the selection from PAIS. Would the explanation of main headings and subheadings suffice for your library? Try producing a list of subheadings with annotations and links to the main heading records that is similar to the list in PAIS.

5. Refer again to the list (p. 34) in chapter 2, and find their equivalent in your catalog. Would a different arrangement other than alphabetical be useful for these headings and their subdivisions? Would it be an improvement to permute some subdivisions (e.g., for location) with these headings? Review Daily's rules for compound headings and subdivisions. Would his suggestion for punctuation (namely the colon) improve the display of headings?

Notes

[1] Jay E. Daily, *The Grammar of Subject Headings: A Formulation of Rules for Subject Headings Based on a Syntactical and Morphological Analysis of the Library of Congress List*, Doctoral diss., School of Library Service, Columbia University, 1957. pp. 112-13.

[2] Daily, 154.

[3] Daily, 155.

[4] Daily, 156.

[5] Arlene G. Taylor, Margaret F. Maxwell, and Carolyn O. Frost, "Network and Vendor Authority Systems," *Library Resources & Technical Services* (April/June 1985), 195-205.

Selected Readings

(See section 2 for texts, which are renumbered in this edition.)

As subdivisions are one of the most pervasive topics concerning *LCSH*, the reader is referred to all the selections included in section 2 of this book because they are useful reading for their comments and suggested improvements. However, the following selections are specific only to that topic:

Chan, Lois Mai. "The Period Subdivision in Subject Headings." *Library Resources & Technical Services* 16 (Fall 1972): 453-59.

PAIS Subject Headings. New York: Public Affairs Information Service, Inc., 1984.

5 LCSH, LCC, and DDC: Suggested Relationships

> Besides serving as an inventory record of the library's classified collections, the shelflist can be used, within limits, as a classified, or systematic, catalog.... The relative index of the classification and the indexes to its individual parts may be used as an index to the shelflist. To a certain extent the subject headings for the books in the classified collections may also be used for this purpose.... If the shelflist is available to the public and is not too far removed from the catalog, a reference from the subject heading to the corresponding class number in the shelflist will take the place of many entries, yet guide the reader to most of the material on the subject. It will, furthermore, give the reader an insight into the significance of the number. The reference must, however, be worded to show clearly that only part of the material is to be found in the shelflist and that the rest is entered under the same heading immediately following the reference. —David J. Haykin
> *Subject Headings: A Practical Guide*, 1951

We would expect to find a fairly close relationship between the classification scheme used for shelf arrangement and the alphabetical headings used in the catalogue, but in practice this does not seem to be the case. The two systems are treated quite separately, and indeed it is often argued that there need be no connection because they serve different purposes. Even the structure of *see also* references does not appear to be based on the LC scheme; Coates suggests that the scheme to which it bears most affinity is DC!

It can be argued that a list of subject headings should not be tied to any classification scheme, since the freedom to make cross-references in an alphabetical sequence would be hampered by too close an adherence to a classified structure. However, unless the

> task of making cross-references is approached systematically the resulting network is likely to be less helpful than it might be. This does not mean that subject headings should reflect one and only one systematic approach. —A. C. Foskett
> *The Subject Approach to Information*, 1982

> The problem with classification lies in the attempt to carry out its two conflicting purposes—subject retrieval and the arrangement of individual items—using only one instrument. The solution requires separating the two purposes and the methods used to achieve them. Intelligent use of computers is the key to the separation and the solution.... The user can browse the whole collection online using a classification number....
> Both DDC and LC should produce shortened versions suitable for shelf arrangement. They should confine their elaborations and changes to full versions which would produce numbers suitable for machine manipulation. In this way, practicalities of shelf arrangement could be reconciled with the potential of machine subject retrieval. —Michael Gorman
> "The Longer the Number, the Shorter the Spine; or Up and Down with Melvil and Elsie,"
> *American Libraries*, 1984

Haykin, Foskett, Gorman and many others have encouraged librarians to consider the relationships between an alphabetical subject heading list like LCSH and a classification scheme like LCC (the Library of Congress Classification) or DDC (the Dewey Decimal Classification). They have argued that if they were used together as subject retrieval tools, there would be an improvement over the present subject access apparatus in our library catalogs.

Several authors have pointed out that only one-third of *LCSH* headings have class numbers attached to them, and that this is a weakness because there is no sufficiently reliable link to a systematic arrangement like LCC. The reading selections by Daily, Immroth, and Hill point up deficiencies in linking the two, but they all recommend that more work be done so that the user will benefit from the two displays of subjects. As the USMARC Authorities format for subjects includes fields for both the LCC class number and DDC class number which is associated with a particular subject heading, the way appears clear to begin some of this work. With the computer assistance we now have, perhaps the era of the online catalog will see a use in tandem of either *LCSH* and LCC or *LCSH* and DDC. But first, we must properly prepare for such use. Hill (see section 2) warns of some of the pitfalls of using the classification number on bibliographic records without thinking.

At the time of writing this chapter, the results of a very interesting and relevant research project were just coming in. I refer to the OCLC-Forest Press project on using DDC in an online catalog. This work is directed by Karen Markey at OCLC.[1]

Some libraries have already developed subject guides based on their files of assigned subject headings and class numbers (see fig. 5.1), but these are only crude approximations of what we should be able to develop for online use. The existing guides are by-products of an automated authority control system. (See Miller in section 2.) The selections by Cochrane and Markey (see section 2) suggest some advances beyond that type of guide for online use.

> CHILDREN–CARE AND HYGIENE, 649.1(36); 136.7(7); 155.4(7); 618.92(4); 371.911(2); 613.7(2); J613.71; 301.4120951; 301.431; 362.71; 371.71; 610.73; 612.821; 613; 614; 614.88; 617.6; 617.7; 618; 618.9; 641.1; 646.36; 649.103; 649.109; 649.8; SEE ALSO: BABY SITTERS; CHILDREN–DISEASES; CHILDREN–NUTRITION; CHILDREN–PREPARATION FOR MEDICAL CARE; COMMUNITY HEALTH SERVICES FOR CHILDREN; HEALTH EDUCATION; INFANTS–CARE AND HYGIENE; PEDIATRIC NURSING; PHYSICAL EDUCATION FOR CHILDREN; SCHOOL HYGIENE; SPORTS FOR CHILDREN

Fig. 5.1. *Subject Guide to the Collection of the Public Library of Columbus [Ohio] and Franklin County, 1984.**

---

*"This SUBJECT GUIDE enables you to find books and other materials on a subject in which you are interested. The GUIDE consists of a listing of subject terms used to describe the library materials. Following the subject term is a classification number which indicates the shelf location of material on that subject. Some subject terms are followed by more than one classification number indicating that there is material in more than one place on that subject. The figure in parentheses after some classification numbers is the number of books at that shelf location on that subject. The SUBJECT GUIDE represents the holdings of the entire library system. No single branch will have all the material listed here."

Background

Over the years, the Library of Congress has mentioned several times that it considers *LCSH* to be an index to LCC:

> The numbers, combined with letters, which follow the subject headings are the classmarks and subdivisions showing where the material dealing with these subjects is classified in the Library of Congress; pending the eventual publication of a complete general index to the Classification schedules, the list may therefore serve to a limited extent as a substitute.[2]

Library of Congress class numbers in parentheses follow many of the headings, e.g.

Atomic mass. (Chemistry, QD466; Physics, QC173)
Dilemma. (BC185)
Dingal language. (PK2461-9)

These class numbers are added only when there is a close correspondence between a specific subject heading and the Library of Congress Classification. Although such subject headings serve in part as a general index to the classification schedules, the suggested numbers should not be used without referring to the individual indexes.[3]

Class numbers. Many of the headings are followed by Library of Congress class numbers which generally represent the most common aspect of a subject. If several aspects of a subject are covered by different class numbers, the latter are qualified by a term indicating the specific discipline to show the distinction, e.g.

Diesel motor (TJ795)
Norwegian language (PD2571-2699)
Shellfish (Cookery, TX753; Public health, RA602.S2;
   Shellfish as food, TX387; Zoology, QL401-445)

Class numbers are added only when there is a close correspondence between the subject heading and the provisions of the Library of Congress classification schedules. Since these, as well as the subject heading list, are subject to continuous revision, the class numbers in the list should not be used without verification in the latest editions of the schedules and their supplements.[4]

David J. Haykin, in *Subject Headings: A Practical Guide*, devoted a chapter to the subject of "Subject Catalog vs. Shelflist." (See section 2.) He had this to say about the relationship between *LCSH* and class numbers:

> At the Library of Congress the device of referring from subject heading to class number was used to a limited extent before the shelflist and the public catalog were placed so far apart that access to the shelflist on the part of the public became difficult. The device of referring to the shelflist does

emphasize the relationship between subject heading and class number and represents one way of reducing the large number of entries under some headings without eliminating the reader's approach to them altogether.[5]

It seems obvious that the people at the Library of Congress once had the objective of linking the two subject access schemes they used, but they had to forego achieving this objective as time passed and the workload increased.

Links between Subject Headings and Classification Numbers

Now the subject catalog and the shelflist are virtually next to each other because they represent two file arrangements of the bibliographic records in an online catalog. At the Library of Congress, there is access to the shelflist or classed arrangement via a "Browse CALL" command and access to the subject heading arrangement via a "Browse INDX" command. Many other libraries have incorporated similar commands into their online catalogs: Ohio State University, University of Toronto, BLAISE, and Syracuse University. Nevertheless, no library to date has gone beyond such arrangements and begun to amplify its subject authority records so that each and every record would serve as a link between subject headings and class numbers. Only one-third of the headings in *LCSH* have class numbers and these have never been checked against the actual practice recorded on catalog records. To see if every subject heading ever used could be linked to LCC or DDC class numbers would be a formidable task, but the raw data, albeit incomplete, exists in a publication entitled *Subject Authorities*, published by Bowker, which presents data from more than ten years of MARC bibliographic records.[6] The work shows what subject headings had been used and how they related to either Dewey or Library of Congress class numbers found on those MARC records.

Although there has been some effort made to put the classification schedules and their indexes into machine-readable form, no one has as yet designed the MARC format for such a record.[7] For example, the OCLC-Forest Press project mentioned earlier is using a format originally designed for computer typesetting. It was modified, not redesigned for the project.

Immroth and later Williams, Mannheimer, and Daily have been the most outspoken about the value of a "classified" *LCSH* to overcome the weaknesses in *LCSH*'s hierarchical references. Daily makes a very strong argument for such an improvement.[8] The new policy for *see also* references will, in time, correct some of the hierarchical deficiencies in *LCSH*, but there is a powerful argument for combining the advantages of the two systems as well as cancelling out their disadvantages. R. A. Wall summarized these advantages and disadvantages. (See figure 5.2.)

Hierarchical classifications	Thesauri
ADVANTAGES	
long hierarchies, hence high recall	specific terms, hence high precision;
"consensus" hierarchies selected	accurate poly-hierarchical linking capability (if overlapping terms properly dealt with);
notation maps search routes	each term encompasses its topic
DISADVANTAGES	
frequently inflexible hierarchies;	frequently, short hierarchies;
increasing separation of like topics;	no "posting on" to very broad terms;
accompanies increasingly specific division;	
sacrifice of hierarchical accuracy to notation constraints	noise from automatic posting on

Source: R. A. Wall, "Intelligent Indexing and Retrieval," *Information Processing and Management* 16 (1980), 79.

Fig. 5.2. The thesaurus compared with hierarchical classifications.

Preparation for Links between Subject Headings and Class Numbers

Once a library has its catalog records in a file in machine-readable form, several reports, or files, can be prepared. Procedures can be developed for adding data to the subject authority file, such as the most frequently used class numbers with any given subject heading. This information could be displayed to catalog users, or used by the computer to find more relevant records.

The kinds of reports one might want to receive from an online technical services system which would help in this area could include the following:

1) A list of every subject heading used in the online catalog, with a count of the number of times a given class number appears with that subject heading. For this report, a decision must be made to ignore or include the subdivisions with a given main heading before such a count is made. If this list were compared with the machine-readable *LCSH* (or the library's own subject authority file built from that file), then each heading in the library's catalog could be compared with *LCSH* and a code attached when the two are identical. At the time of comparison, the LCC class number, if part of the *LCSH* record, could be given in the report.

2) A list of all class numbers (not call numbers) that are used more than five or ten or fifty times (the exact number of occurrences is left to the individual library), with a report of the subject headings (possibly only main headings) used with that class number.

Such reports go beyond the mere listing of relationships which were shown in the *Classified LCSH* and in Bowker's *Subject Authorities*. These reports could help a library decide how to relate class numbers and subject headings during the retrieval process, something suggested by Cochrane and illustrated by Markey as improved displays for online catalogs. (See Cochrane, "Classification as an Online Subject Access Tool: Challenge and Opportunity" in section 2 and figures 5.3 and 5.4.)

User: SUB/ISLAM—ADDRESSES, ESSAYS, LECTURES

LINE	NUMBER OF CLASS AREAS	SUBJECT HEADING	CLASS AREAS & (NO. OF BOOKS)
11	4	Islam in literature	PL216, PR149, PQ283, PQ6066
12	12	Islam—Addresses, essays, lectures	BP20(5), 297(5), BP165(4), BP25(2), BP161(2), BP170(2), BM42, BP49.5, BP88, DS33, DS35.4, 910
13	4	Islam—Africa	BP64(4), BP62, 276, 297
14	1	Islam—Africa—Addresses, essays, lectures	DT4
15	1	Islam—Africa—Bibliography	Z7835
16	1	Islam—Africa—Congresses	DS38
17	1	Islam—Africa, North—History	209
18	1	Islam—Africa, Sub-Saharan—Bibliography	Z7835
19	1	Islam—Africa, West	BP64(2), BP172
20	2	Islam—Africa, West—Addresses, essays, lectures	BP64

PAGE 2 - For other pages, enter "PS" and page number
- For titles on a subject enter "LN/" and line number/ and class area, e.g., "LN/16/DS38"
- To start over, enter "SUB/" and subject heading

Source: Karen Markey, *Subject Searching in Library Catalogs*. OCLC, 1984, p. 94.

Fig. 5.3. Suggested online display of subject headings and class areas.

```
User:  SUB/ISLAM—ADDRESSES, ESSAYS, LECTURES

       SUGGESTED
LINE   CLASS AREAS   ITEMS   SUBJECT HEADING
 11    PL216          4      Islam in literature
 12    BP20          26      Islam—Addresses, essays, lectures
 13    BP64           7      Islam—Africa
 14    DT4            1      Islam—Africa—Addresses, essays, lectures
 15    Z7835          1      Islam—Africa—Bibliography
 16    DS38           1      Islam—Africa—Congresses
 17    209            1      Islam—Africa, North—History
 18    Z7835          1      Islam—Africa, Sub-Saharan—Bibliography
 19    BP64           3      Islam—Africa, West
 20    BP64           1      Islam—Africa, West—Addresses, essays, lectures

PAGE 2 - For other pages, enter "PS" and page number
       - For titles on a subject, enter "LN" and line number
       - To start over, enter "SUB/" and subject heading
```

Source: Karen Markey, *Subject Searching in Library Catalogs.* OCLC, 1984, p. 93.

Fig. 5.4. Alphabetical display of assigned subject headings with class numbers for OPAC bookshelf browsers.

From these reports an individual library could begin to review the version of *LCSH* it has received from the Library of Congress to see if it represents the correct linkages between *LCSH* and LCC for its library. It would then be possible to create an accurate outline to the subjects in the library's collections. Such an outline would also be useful in writing online tutorials to help users with too little output.

Linkages to Improve Online Searching

Immroth's work, although done over fifteen years ago, contains the methodology for comparing *LCSH* and LCC; he investigates the value and validity of their content for computer manipulation so that together the two subject access systems could help the online searcher. (See section 2 for portions of his work.) As we are beginning to encourage free text searching in online catalogs, perhaps the searcher should have more than catalog records to search freely. The classification schedules, accompanying indexes, and our subject authority files are rich with synonyms and alternatives for searching. From these we can begin to contemplate designing an expert system when the fifth generation of computers are used in libraries.

Nancy Olson at Mankato State University attacked another, but related, problem when she produced something the Library of Congress wanted but never seemed to have the time or wherewithal to do. She created machine-readable files of all the separate indexes to the Library of Congress Classification schedules, and combined them. From these files she had printed in several volumes a *Combined Index to LCC*.[9] This was distributed by the United States Historical Documents Institute as a fifteen-volume set, with five major subsets: author/number; biographical subject index; classified index to persons; geographical name index; and subject keyword index (including geographical names). Because she worked from the schedules and indexes in print as of 1973, her work has become somewhat dated. Nevertheless, it showed what could be done with some work-study students and a diligent editor.

In print, these combined indexes provide a useful reference for catalogers. As an online file, the final set of six volumes, could offer many possibilities for manipulation and study of links between *LCSH* and LCC. I feel sure Immroth would have loved to have had the set for his studies.

Here is an example of what you could have if you could combine the count of a class number's use in a catalog file with a description of that number taken from index entries of the classification:

LCC Class Number	Index Entries	Item Count
HD 9743	Arms and Ammunition Firearms Trade Munitions Industry	167

Moves toward Shelf Browsing Online

The work reported by Markey and others on how people use the online catalog as a shelf browsing tool strongly suggests that preparations should be made to improve the online links between subject keyword searching and class number or systematic browsing. The suggested exercises in this chapter and in chapter 6 will focus on this prospective new development.

Much needs to be done before these subject access schemes can be interconnected and properly represent the subject analysis in our bibliographic records. Only one-third of the headings in *LCSH* have class numbers as part of their record, and many of these are suspected of being out-of-date or incorrect. Every library catalog is hiding errors in classification, and changes have not always been made to bring call numbers up to date with revisions in the classification system used. The indexes to each schedule of LCC are not linked to *LCSH*, although there are some efforts being made now to do this, just as the *National Library of Medicine (NLM) Classification Schedule* is linked to *MeSH* (*Medical Subject Headings*).

Immroth and Daily are two authors who have contributed much to our understanding of why these schemes should be related. Unfortunately their early work did not change *LCSH* and LCC into a combined subject access scheme, and their rigorous rules for forming *LCSH* and for chain indexing LCC were never adopted. Nevertheless their suggestions may provide useful ideas for the design of some new online tools if the reader keeps in mind that their work was carried out long ago.

The *AAT* (*Art and Architecture Thesaurus*) project has taken the approach that this subject area in *LCSH* needs a complete overhaul, which it will perform and then present the results to the art library world and to the Library of Congress. Using *MeSH* as the model, *AAT* will categorize terms and develop tree structures. This is a standard approach to thesaurus building and one which is a mammoth undertaking for a list as large and as diverse as *LCSH*.

The *AAT* effort is still in a preliminary stage, but its criticism of *LCSH* (referred to in chapter 3) is worth reading again for its relevance to this issue as well.[10]

The research now underway by Markey, creating subject access online via DDC and subject headings from bibliographic records, is perhaps the most revolutionary use of all the data available to date. Here the subject information in the catalog records is combined with the machine-readable DDC file, which contains the classification schedule, captions, notes, and class numbers as well as the Relative Index entries for each class number. (Missing from the system is an *LCSH* file, or subject authority file, which would be complete with references, scope notes, etc.)

The online search commands this project used to access and match words in the subject headings on catalog records and the DDC schedules and Relative Index are reviewed in figure 5.5. There is only one different command in which SOC and DOC differ, namely, the "SS" command, which allows access to the Dewey information and permits browsing systematically rather than alphabetically. The *source* of what is searched by the various commands, however, is different, and the user prompts the project created are of interest. (These are preliminary because the OCLC-Forest Press Project was still underway when this chapter was sent to the publisher.)

A Brief Guide to SOC and DOC Searching

Both SOC and DOC are easy to search. The catalogs are menu-based systems and always provide a list of options at the end of every system response which tell you the possible next actions in the search. Both systems also provide an initial screen which details the available subject search options and the system response.

SOC SEARCHING

SOC (or catalog A) has the traditional subject searching capabilities of online catalogs, namely, subject heading, and subject and title keyword searches. SOC's subject searching options are described below with respect to their functional description, sources of terms for indexing, and subsequent user actions.

SOC Option Code	Functional Description	Source of Subject Terms for Indexing	Wisest Subsequent User Action(s)
SA	Search for subject and browse an alphabetical list of subjects near your subject	Assigned *subject headings* from the library's bibliographic records	Select a listed subject heading (SL option) to display retrieved items, or browse backward or forward (BB or BF option)
SD	Search directly for subject and retrieve number of items on your subject	Keyword, implicit Boolean AND search of *title, subject heading, series,* and *notes* words in bibliographic records	Display retrieved items (DI option)
SC	Search directly for call number and retrieve number of items with your call number	*Class numbers* in 082a subfield of the library's bibliographic records	Display retrieved items (DI option)

DOC SEARCHING

DOC (or catalog Z) has both the traditional subject searching capabilities of SOC and enhanced subject searching capabilities because the DDC Relative Index and DDC Schedules and notes have been integrated into DOC's subject searching capabilities. DOC's subject searching options are described below with respect to their functional description, sources of terms for indexing, and subsequent user actions.

DOC Option Code	Functional Description	Source of Subject Terms for Indexing	Wisest Subsequent User Action(s)
SA	Search for subject and browse an alphabetical list of subjects near your subject	*DDC Relative Index entries* matching class numbers in the library's bibliographic records	Select a listed Relative Index entry to display retrieved items (SL option), or browse forward or backward in the alphabetical list (BF or BB option), or select a listed Relative Index entry to obtain a subject outline from the classification Schedules (ST option)
SS	Search for subject and browse an outline of subjects related to your subject	Keyword, implicit Boolean AND search of *DDC Relative Index entries, DDC Schedules* and *notes*, and the *first subject heading* listed in the library's bibliographic records directing users to outlines of *DDC Schedule captions* in the classification area(s) where there are records bearing user-entered terms	Select a listed DDC Schedule caption to display retrieved items (SL option), or browse more specific DDC Schedule captions (BS option)
SD	Search directly for subject and retrieve number of items on your subject	Keyword, implicit Boolean AND search of *title, subject heading, series, note, DDC Relative Index entry*, and *DDC Schedule* and *note* words in bibliographic records	Display retrieved items (DI option)
SC	Search for call number and browse an outline of meanings of call numbers	*Class numbers* in 082a subfield of bibliographic records directing users to outlines of *DDC Schedule captions* in the classification area matching user-entered call number	Select a listed DDC Schedule caption to display retrieved items (SL option), or browse more specific DDC captions (BS option)

Source: Karen Markey, OCLC-Forest Press/CLR Project, 1985.

Fig. 5.5. Online search commands in *A Brief Guide to SOC and DOC Searching*.

Exercises

These exercises will concentrate on the linkages between *LCSH* or typical subject authority files and the classification scheme which may be used for shelf arrangement of the collection. It is assumed that these suggested "improvements" are being undertaken to improve subject access in an online catalog and not merely for the better maintenance of these files.

1. If your library is classed according to LCC, review the class numbers most heavily used in your library, observing which subject headings are used most often with that class number. You could also peruse *The Classified LCSH* or the Bowker *Subject Authorities*. Compare the number you find in *LCSH* with the one in your shelflist. Is there agreement? Do these class numbers serve as a good collecting point for that subject? Devise some way to use this information in your subject authority file. If these headings do not have any class number in *LCSH* or your subject authority file, devise a routine for adding this information to each record.

   If your library is classed according to DDC, follow the same process but start with the Bowker *Subject Authorities*; then add the Dewey class number to your subject authority file.

2. Following the methodology of Immroth, compare the systematic arrangement of a subject, using first the syndetic structure of *LCSH* and then the LCC or DDC schedule. Remember to start with the most general heading for a topic and follow the hierarchical structure. (You may want to review the discussion of *see also* references in chapter 3.) This exercise should help you find missing links in your subject authority file, and it may help you uncover ways to use the outline of that topic in the classification schedule. (Look again at Micco, Richmond, and Mostecky for related ideas.)

3. Choose a topic of special interest. Collect the records for this topic from your subject authority file (or from *LCSH*), and photocopy the pages from LCC or DDC. Compare how the aspects of place, time, and form are represented in the classification schedules. Is this almost as good as, or better than, the arrangement you get using subdivisions with subject headings? Would the outline of this topic in the classification schedule be a useful display in your catalog instead of a long list of subject headings with subdivisions?

4. Consider how you would create online displays of *ranges* of class numbers so that subject searching could be done more easily. Choose your own subject for this exercise or look at the heading, **Cities and towns—Planning** in your catalog or subject authority file and the Library of Congress classification schedule (HT 166-177). Would you agree that the outline of the subject in the classification is very compact and perhaps more visually appealing than the list of headings with sub-subdivisions under this topic (more appealing, that is, after it has been edited somewhat!)?

Notes

[1]Pauline A. Cochrane and Karen Markey, "Preparing for the Use of Classification in Online Cataloging Systems and in Online Catalogs," *Information Technology and Libraries* 4 (June 1985): 91-111.

[2]C. M., "Introduction," *Library of Congress Subject Headings*, 3d ed. (Washington, D.C.: Library of Congress, 1927), iv.

[3]Richard S. Angell and John W. Cronin, "Introduction," *Library of Congress Subject Headings*, 6th ed. (Washington, D.C.: Library of Congress, 1957), iv.

[4]Richard S. Angell and John W. Cronin, "Introduction," *Library of Congress Subject Headings*, 7th ed. (Washington, D.C.: Library of Congress, 1966), iv. (Reprinted verbatim in the ninth edition of *LCSH*, signed by Joseph H. Howard and Mark K. P. Pietris.)

[5]David Judson Haykin, *Subject Headings: A Practical Guide* (Washington, D.C.: U.S. Government Printing Office, 1951), 71.

[6]*Subject Authorities: A Guide to Subject Cataloging* (New York: Bowker, 1981).

[7]Pauline A. Cochrane and Karen Markey, "Preparing for the Use of Classification in Online Cataloging Systems and in Online Catalogs," *Information Technology and Libraries* 4 (June 1985): 91-111.

[8]Jay E. Daily, "From Alphabetic Puzzle to Classified Order," in *Classified Library of Congress Subject Headings*, ed. James G. Willliams, Martha L. Manheimer, and Jay E. Daily (New York: Marcel Dekker, 1972, 1982), Part A: viii, xvii.

[9]Nancy B. Olson, *The Combined Indexes to the Library of Congress Classification Schedules* (Washington, D.C.: United States Historical Documents Institute, 1974).

[10]Toni Petersen, "The AAT: A Model for the Restructuring of *LCSH*," *The Journal of Academic Librarianship* 9 (September 1983): 207-10.

Selected Readings

(See section 2 for texts, which are renumbered in this edition.)

Cochrane, Pauline. "Classification as an Online Subject Access Tool: Challenge and Opportunity." Paper presented at a Subject Access meeting sponsored by the Council on Library Resources, June 1982, Dublin, Ohio.

Haykin, David Judson. *Subject Headings: A Practical Guide*. Washington, D.C.: U.S. Government Printing Office, 1951. pp. 69-71.

Hill, Janet Swan. "Online Classification Number Access: Some Practical Considerations," *Journal of Academic Librarianship* 10 (March 1984): 17-22.

Immroth, John Phillip. *Analysis of Vocabulary Control in Library of Congress Classification and Subject Headings*. Littleton, Colo.: Libraries Unlimited, 1971. pp. 90-101, 107-8.

6 LCSH and Subject Access Online: Improvements through Enhancements and User Assistance

From one point of view, this chapter is unnecessary because we have been discussing improvements for subject access online all through this book. Nevertheless, there is some need for a final chapter where the focus is on the online catalog and its users first and subject access second, instead of the other way around. This slight reorientation brings home very quickly the need to make improvements in our catalogs as we change over to computer-based online systems. As Michael J. Simonds put it:

> Prominent among the findings of the Council on Library Resources study of the patron and the online catalog was that patrons wanted subject access. They use it far more than previously suspected, they are frustrated with its current limitations and likely to grow even more frustrated in the future as their sophistication grows as a result of experience with other online services.... Although it was much discussed at the conference [1983 ALA Conference in Los Angeles], I'm not sure that most people understood the key point. The main problem with subject access is not with the online catalogs themselves. The problem lies with the database they use. The logical conclusion is that the MARC database itself is an inadequate foundation for the online catalog.... I do not oppose the introduction of elements such as tables of contents into our databases, I believe in the usefulness of keyword searching of titles. These methods, however, must be recognized for what they are: desperate attempts to overcome the basic inadequacy of access-deficient LC MARC cataloging.... The only hope for adequate subject access is through fundamental changes in the national standard.[1]

Simonds is echoing many people before him who have commented on the need to upgrade the MARC record because users need more subject access than is possible at present, but that is not the only change that needs to be contemplated. We have chosen to call all these suggestions "enhancements"—to catalog records, and to other associated files, and even to the computer system itself which provides the means for the user to take advantage of a library's catalog online.

The improvements discussed in this chapter will expand on those mentioned in chapters 1-5. Elsewhere I have described these improvements as "the capabilities of online catalogs":

- a) Access to subjects and their relationships
- b) Access to records for works on these subjects
- c) Browsing of subject or term lists
- d) Browsing of retrieved records
- e) Assistance in focusing search words to match subjects in file
- f) Displaying of subject records
- g) Displaying/printing of catalog records for works[2]

To have the capabilities listed above (e.g., access, browsing, assistance, and displaying), the online catalog must be seen as a kind of catalog different from any the library has designed previously. The idea of built-in assistance is a relatively new phenomenon, going beyond mere information cards and display of subject authority files. A great deal needs to be done to provide these capabilities in an imaginative way.

In this last chapter we will cover enhancements and user assistance, and relate them to improvements in *LCSH* and other subject authority files. As before, pertinent readings and exercises, designed to stimulate individual libraries to contemplate implementing some of these improvements, are included.

Improvements through Enhancements

In a six-part continuing education series in *American Libraries* in 1984, I asked several experts to make suggestions to the Library of Congress for improved subject access. Their comments were tabulated. (See Table 6.1.) The Library of Congress remarked on the experts' suggestions (reproduced here with Table 6.1). I have organized the collected suggestions about enhancements in a similar manner:

1. Enhancements to catalog records
2. Enhancements to subject authority records
3. Enhancements to subject terminology used in searching
4. Enhancements to retrieval features

Table 6.1. Suggestions to the Library of Congress for improved subject access and LC's comments.

Topic	Respondent(s)	Suggestion
CATALOG RECORDS	Petersen, Mischo, Wiberley, Mandel, Berman, Buckland	Enhance with aid of subject specialists; create more access points per record
MARC format for catalog records	Mandel, Mischo, Beckman	Add a field for uncontrolled subject descriptors*
SUBJECT AUTHORITY RECORDS	Petersen	Define elements of subject authority record separately from its subdivisions
SUBJECT TERMINOLOGY	Mischo, Petersen, Berman	Improve adequacy and specificity; correct inconsistency of form
Cross reference structure	Mischo	Change unsystematic network of references; form hierarchies*
Replacing LCSH with natural language	Beckman	Structure terminology using artificial intelligence (AI) techniques
RETRIEVAL FEATURES		
Sophisticated keyword searching	Mischo, Bates, Buckland, Beckman	Adopt for online catalog
Full text searching problems	Bates, Wiberley, Mandel	Remedy by automatic display of related term or hierarchy
Library catalogs or database for subject access?	Harper	Library catalogs only for inventory control
Integration of MARC and non-MARC records in files	Beckman	Put artificial intelligence in program for retrieval system to get dynamic results
POLITICAL ISSUES*		
Transform LCSH and LC classification into National Subject Authority Service	Mandel	Follow lead of NACO (Name Authority Cooperative project)
Form new entity—U.S. National Library	Wellisch	Such a library would serve the nation as a bibliographic center

*specific comment from Library of Congress on this point (see below)

Source: *American Libraries* (May 1984): 338.

Comments from the Library of Congress

We at the Library of Congress are pleased that Pauline Cochrane has made the reactions to Marcia Bates's statement of 1977 available to us.

We agree with Bates's reevaluation that the ability to search in online systems by individual words in titles, notes, and subject headings provides good access that overcomes some shortcomings of LC subject headings. When this searching capability is available in an online system that also includes LC subject authority records and cross references, the result can be a good system for finding works in a database.

Both the search strategy design and the loading of LC authorities are a responsibility of individual libraries and utilities. The Library of Congress is attempting to provide better service by designing an improved machine-readable subject authority system that will be updated in a manner similar to the updating of name authority records. However, implementation is not expected to begin for another two years.

Those such as Mandel and Mischo, who wish to augment LC bibliographic data with uncontrolled vocabulary, may use the 653 field in the MARC format for bibliographic records for such terms. This field is used by several bibliographic utilities. Lack of staff prevents the Library of Congress from adding such terms to its own records.

We hope to embark on a project to improve our *see also* reference structure by making the references more hierarchical and reducing the number of "orphaned" headings that have no references. This would address some of the concerns mentioned by Mischo and Mandel. However, even the best system of cross references in LCSH would not help libraries that are unable to place this information in their online catalogs. **We are aware that few libraries can afford to maintain *see also* references in their card catalogs, and we hope that this will not also be true in online catalogs.**

Some suggestions from the 10 respondents about what to do with LCSH appear to contradict each other. While Berman would have more headings assigned to individual works and to types of works that now receive no subject headings, Wiberley notes the problems of information overload and the need to aid users who find too much information. It may well be that the depth of analysis, and therefore the number of subject headings assigned to an individual work, inevitably depend on the size of the collection into which the work will be placed: many access points are needed for small libraries, whereas large libraries need few access points. This viewpoint assumes that the large library is more likely to have whole books devoted to subjects that may only be chapters of more general works in small libraries.

Harper points out an aspect of LC subject headings often forgotten: the purpose of subject headings is to serve as a finding device to locate items on a subject in a collection. Access to the detailed contents of books should be provided by indexes and indexing services, not by subject headings on bibliographic records.

One longstanding impediment to changing LC subject **headings continues to be the large number of catalog records bearing old subject headings in catalogs at LC and in other libraries. The economic implications of change must be considered as improvements to LCSH are contemplated.**

The suggestion from Mandel that LC **begin cooperative efforts to improve LCSH has been partially implemented with** the inauguration of the Entry Vocabulary Project (EVP), in which several libraries contribute *see* references to LCSH. We plan to expand participation in this program and to enable other libraries to propose new subject headings in ways similar to efforts underway in the Name Authority Cooperative program. Now that Judith J. Henderson has been named as the Coordinator for Cooperative Subject Cataloging Projects, we are able to explore these options.

MARY K. D. PIETRIS
Chief, Subject Cataloging Division
LUCIA J. RATHER
Director for Cataloging
Processing Services
Library of Congress

Source: Pauline Cochrane, "Modern Subject Access," *American Libraries* (May 1984): 337-38.

Enhancements to Catalog Records

Figure 6.1 shows a MARC record which is subject-rich because it contains fixed fields for bibliographic level, language, and date of publication, and it contains fields marked as = 3 (call number), = 6 (title), = 9 (notes or abstract), = 11 through = 13 (subject headings). Not every MARC record is so subject-rich and many people have lamented the fact that there are so few subject headings assigned (the average is under two) and so few records with content notes or abstracts (the estimate is less than 1 percent of MARC files have a "500" field).

Carol Mandel, at the 1984 American Library Association meeting, presented a paper entitled "Enriching the Library Catalog Record for Subject Access." (See text in section 2.) In it is a matrix describing the various alternatives for enhancement of the MARC records per se, or for adding databases which would be available with MARC records on existing utilities like RLIN or OCLC, or for additions to utility databases or online catalogs.

```
Screen 1 of 2
NO HOLDINGS IN OCC -   FOR HOLDINGS ENTER dh DEPRESS       DISPLAY RECD SEND
OCLC:   9888339        Rec stat:   n    Entrd:   830908    Used:    830908
Type:   a   Bib lvl:   m   Govt pub:        Lang:   eng    Source:  d   Illus:   a
Repr:       Enc lvl:   K   Conf pub:  0     Ctry:   miu    Dat tp:  r   M/F/B:  10
Indx:   0   Mod rec:       Festschr:  0     Cont:
Desc:       Int lvl:       Dates: 1967,1915

= 1  010
= 2  040         CNO c CNO
= 3  090         HN64 b .C43
= 4  049         OCCL
= 5  100   10    Carver, Thomas Nixon, d 1865-1961. w 1n
= 6  245   10    Essays in social justice, c by Thomas Nixon Carver ...
= 7  260    0    Cambridge, b Harvard university press, c 1915.
= 8  300         vii, 429 p. b diagrs. c 22 cm.
```

```
Screen 2 of 2
=  9  505  0   What is justice?--The ultimate basis of social conflict.--The
principle of self-centered appreciation commonly called self-interest.--The
forms of human conflict.--Economic competition.--How ought wealth to be
distributed?--How much is a man worth?--Interest.--Socialism and the present
unrest.--Constructive democracy.--The single tax.--The question of
inheritance.--The question of monopoly.--The cure for poverty.--The
responsibility of the rich for the condition of the poor.--Social service.--How
ought the burdens of taxation to be distributed?
= 10  533        Photocopy. b Ann Arbor, Mich., c University Microfilms, d 1967.
= 11  650   0    Social problems.
= 12  650   0    Sociology.
= 13  650   0    Economics.
```

Source: Karen Markey. *Subject Searching in Library Catalogs.* OCLC, 1984, p. 39.

Fig. 6.1. MARC record with subject-rich fields (= 3, 6, 9, 11-13).

Her suggestions cover the following enhancements:

a) Deeper indexing by LC for select set of monographs, e.g. collections of essays, festschriften, etc.

b) Acceptance of indexing of books by abstracting and indexing services as an addition to the subject headings on MARC records

c) Use of a book's index tapes as an enhancement to the MARC record for that book

d) Use SAP (Subject Access Project) procedures for excerpting from table of contents and indexes of books for select set of monographs

e) Use publishers' analytic abstracts and include in MARC records at LC

f) Apply SUPERINDEX techniques

The SAP method considered by Mandel was developed by the Subject Access Project at Syracuse University in the late 1970s. It has been described in a report (ED 156 131) and in a 1982 *Database* article.[3] The resulting augmented MARC record looks like the record included here as figure 6.2. Notice that this record has an LCH (Library of Congress Heading) which includes the subdivision "Addresses, essays, lectures." Catalog records for books like this collection are the ones Mandel says need special attention because they are so inadequately subject indexed using traditional LC subject cataloging.

```
RSN - 00683235
SNO - 2145
CCN - PN2189 B66
ME  - Brockett, Oscar Gross, 1923-
TI  - Perspectives on contemporary theatre
IM  - Baton Rouge, Louisiana State University Press, 1971
COL - 158p.
PY  - 1971
LCH - Theater - History - 20th century - Addresses, essays, lectures
LCH - Drama - 20th century   Addresses, essays, lectures
IT  - ARISTOPHANES (P. 108-12)
IT  - *ART : CHARACTERISTICS OF MODERN (P. 68-72) :PURPOSES OF (P.
      114-29)
IT  - ARTAUD ANTONIN : THEORETICAL VIEWS OF (P. 92-99) ; VIEWS OF
      CONTRASTED WITH / WAGNERS AND BRECHTS (P. 92-99 PASSIM)
IT  - *AUDIENCE : AND COMMUNICATIVE DEVICES (P. 80-103 PASSIM) ;
      PSYCHOLOGICALLY RELATED TO PERFORMER (P. 4-9)
IT  - BRECHT BERTOLT THEORETICAL VIEWS OF (P. 88-92)
IT  - COMMITMENT IN RECENT DRAMA (P. 121-29)
IT  - *COMMUNICATION DEVICES FOR (P. 80-108 PASSIM)
IT  - DETACHMENT TYPES OF IN DRAMA (P. 114-21)
IT  - DISCONTINUITY IN MODERN ART (P. 68-73)
IT  - *DRAMATIC STRUCTURE ; CAUSE TO EFFECT ARRANGEMENT IN (P. 58-64) ;
      CHANGES IN (P. 52-79 PASSIM) ; DISCONTINUITY IN (P. 68-73) ; IN
      DIDACTIC DRAMA (P. 64-68 74-78) ; DISPARATE ELEMENTS JUXTAPOSED
      IN (P. 68-73) ; RELATED TO PLAYWRIGHTS VIEW OF REALITY (P. 59-79
      PASSIM) ; THEMATIC ARRANGEMENT IN (P. 55-59 64-78)
IT  - *EMPATHY (P. 84-99 PASSIM); EPIC THEATRE (P. 88-92)
IT  - *FEELING ROLE OF IN THEATRE (P. 80-103 PASSIM)
IT  - FILM INCREASE IN POPULARITY OF (P. 11-15)
IT  - *INNOVATION (P. 135-51 PASSIM)
IT  - *INTELLIGENCE ROLE OF IN THEATRE (P. 80-103 PASSIM)
IT  - *RELEVANCE (P. 121-29 PASSIM 138-51 PASSIM)
IT  - REPERTORY (P. 139-44)
IT  - *THEATRE : AS REFLECTION OF CONTEMPORARY VALUES (P. 27-51 PASSIM)
      ; AS WEAPON (9P. 88-92 121-29) ; ATTEMPTS TO REDEFINE (P. 130-51
      PASSIM) ; CHANGES IN POPULARITY OF (P. 9-18) ; COMMITTED TO
      CAUSES (P. 104-29 PASSIM) ; EFFECT OF FILM ON (P. 11-15) ;
      PURPOSE OF (P. 81-85 104-29 PASSIM) ; SPECTATOR PERFORMER
      RELATIONSHIP IN (P. 4-9); *THOUGHT IN DRAMA (P. 55-59 64-78)
IT  - *UNITY : AND CAUSE TO EFFECT ARRANGEMENT (P. 58-64) ; AND
      THEMATIC ARRANGEMENT (P. 55-59 64-78) ; AS REFLECTION OF
      PLAYWRIGHTS VIEW OF REALITY (P. 59-79 PASSIM) ; CHANGING
      CONCEPTIONS OF (P. 52-59) ; OF DISPARAT (P. 68-73) SOURCES OF (P.
      54-59); *VALUES CONFLICTS IN (P. 25-51 PASSIM)
IT  - WAGNER RICHARD THEORETICAL VIEWS OF (P. 84-88)
```

Source: Pauline A. Cochrane, private data file.

Fig. 6.2. SAP augmented catalog record.

The IT lines in figure 6.2 are excerpts from the back-of-the-book subject index, hence they are in alphabetical order. With the current retrieval systems now being used in online catalogs, every word in every line of this record would be accessible if free text searching was available. No attempt was made by SAP to control vocabulary as we do when *LCSH* is used. Pagination was added to show what part of the book (and how many pages) contained information about a topic represented in an IT line—something like analytics in subject cataloging. The trouble with such uncontrolled vocabulary is that the searcher who was looking for something on "Brecht" would locate one record and read pages 88-92, but he might miss pages 92-99, which are located under "Artaud Antonin ... views of contrasted with/Wagners and Brechts." (See fig. 6.2.) We concluded from our SAP project that enhancements to retrieval systems would be necessary to correct for spelling variation, syntax, and minor inaccuracies.

SUPERINDEX is a commercial firm in Boca Raton, Florida which has put entire indexes into machine-readable form and creates databases which can be searched on commercial retrieval systems like BRS (Bibliographic Retrieval Services).

Maybe one of these suggestions in Mandel's matrix may become the new national standard Simonds spoke of. If none of these suggestions are adopted, we can still hope that some library networks will follow the lead of the Australian Bibliographic Network and provide a procedure for "analytical entries" to be added by individual libraries. (See their policy in section 2.)

Enhancements to Subject Authority Records

Displaying subject authority records in the online catalog is a foregone conclusion, but when we focus on users who may never have viewed *LCSH* in print, then we know much needs to be done to make that data understandable. To the naive or inexperienced user too much data is not a good thing. Figure 6.3 shows an early (1984) attempt at the Library of Congress to augment and redesign displays of subject authority records. Notice that two screens are needed for one fairly short subject heading record containing notes and references. For good reason the screen also includes "prompts": an infrequent user will need to be told what to do next after reading the record display. As you can see, the user who has found this heading and might use it in a search will be viewing 1,412 items unless he or she decides on narrower terms or some subdivision of the heading. Assistance with search strategy is inextricably linked to some of the data in the subject authority record. We will need to decide what various search strategies are possible and how information can be transmitted in order to help the user reach a search goal.

Figure 6.3 shows how much data can be conveyed, but it is not offered as a model to follow. This display has undergone many changes in the year since it was first offered as an improvement over the existing authority record display. The kind of information which can be added to authority records (such as frequency of use, automatic links to related records, etc.) will have to be creatively and selectively displayed.

```
                        LCSH SUBJECT HEADING

   T01  PHOTOGRAPHY, ARTISTIC                      item 1 of 6 in set 2
                                                          page 1 of 2
            1412 items currently indexed under this heading.

   SCOPE: For works on photography as a fine art, including aesthetic theory.

   NARROWER TERMS
     T02  Glamour photography
     T03  Photography, Abstract
     T04  Photography, Close-up
     T05  Photography, Humorous
     T06  Photography, Table-top
     T07  Photography of clouds
     T08  Photography of men
     T09  Photography of the nude
     T10  Photography of water
     T11  Photography of women
     T12  Photography of wood
     T13  Reflections
     T14  Ripples

   FOR NEXT PAGE, PRESS ENTER...
```

```
                        LCSH SUBJECT HEADING

   T01 PHOTOGRAPHY, ARTISTIC                       item 1 of 6 in set 2
                                                          page 2 of 2
   BROADER TERMS
     T15  Art
   RELATED TERMS
     T16  Photography--Landscapes
   USED FOR
     T17  Artistic photography
     T18  Photography--Aesthetics
     T19  Photography, Pictorial
     T20  Pictorial photography
   GROUPS OF RELATED WORKS
     T21  TR650-682
     T22  TR183 (Aesthetics)

   END OF RECORD. SELECT T01 FOR A LISTING OF BIBLIOGRAPHIC RECORDS INDEXED
   UNDER THIS TERM. RETRIEVE T01 FOR A LISTING OF SUBDIVISIONS OF THIS HEADING
   AND ADDITIONAL HEADINGS WHICH FOLLOW IN ALPHABETICAL ORDER. THERE ARE NO
   GEOGRAPHIC SUBDIVISIONS. RETRIEVE LINE NUMBER, e.g., T07, FOR FULL
   DESCRIPTION OF THAT TERM.
```

Source: Developed by Retrieval Advisory Group Authorities Committee at the Library of Congress (5/10/84)

Fig. 6.3. *LCSH* full record display on SCORPIO.

Enhancements to Subject Terminology Other Than Subject Headings

Index lists generated by the computer from catalog record fields other than subject headings can be useful in searching. An enhancement to the usual kind of list would be a keyword title index linked to subject authority records (almost like synonym control features in thesauri) and structured networks of concepts (something we discussed in chapter 5). Many people have suggested such an improvement, but Sara D. Knapp is one of the few who has actually developed such a tool.[4] She calls it TERM, and it is on the retrieval service BRS. It helps searchers:

1. Find descriptors (i.e., subject headings) via corresponding natural language words or phrases

2. Find corresponding descriptors in additional databases, and

3. Find free-text words or phrases if the user has either a descriptor or free-text phrase

She has organized this file around three thousand social and behavioral science concepts (called "titles") and lists descriptors from five controlled vocabularies or thesauri along with a paragraph of free-text terms gleaned from dictionaries, newspapers, reference books, and other sources. Using the computer, every word in the record for each "title" provides access to the record which shows all the related terms. This is better than *Roget's Thesaurus* online because it provides links to vocabularies which were used in indexing several databases. Some may gasp at the size such a file would be for the free-text terms associated with every subject heading in *LCSH* or other library subject authority files, but, as R. A. Wall has said, "With an online facility, the complexity and/or size of a thesaurus (or a TERM file) should be factors of no concern to the user, subject of course to the technical constraints of the facility. There would be no need to print out the structure in full, though selected parts might be useful."[5]

Mischo's selections in this book (see section 2) and his other work[6] show some ways of using the data in these indexes, as do the examples we have from the commercial vendors of retrieval services (DIALOG, BRS, etc.) who have been providing such access for many years. The mass of information retrieved if only one keyword is searched requires some retrieval system features which can handle postcoordinate searching (Boolean operators) and truncation, which I will discuss in the next section.

Enhancements in Retrieval System Features

> "The problem with that damn computer is that it will only give you exactly what you ask for," said Arnold Compton of Arlington, a graying, retired school teacher reading up on medieval weaponry....
>
> "Browsing through a tray of catalogue cards, you often have your mind tickled by a title or author that has nothing at all to do with what you're looking for. That can get you thinking about your subject in a whole new way.
>
> "You can't do that in a computer, or at least I haven't figured out how. Without that quality of thought, book titles are just so much data."
>
> — *Washington Post*, 1984

Browse displays, done in a creative way, might help the catalog user quoted above, but there also are many other features of modern retrieval systems which would help, too, if he gave the system a chance. Charles Hildreth, to mention only one of several people who is monitoring and criticizing the development of online catalogs, has written extensively on the system features which will improve the interface between the user and the system. He has devised an "OPAC Interface Adequacy Assessment Guide" in which he itemizes essential features such as "self service usability," "suggestive prompts," and easy user command and control of the system.[7] Some of the retrieval features suggested, which bear directly on subject access problems, included the following:

1. Situation-specific help available at the point of need

2. Current search request and its status displayed throughout the search

3. Ability to guide the user with the formulation or refinement of a search

4. Authority control for automatic access to variant forms, with *see* references to direct user to established headings, and related terms online during search.

Hildreth commented that the movement from the second to the third generation of online catalogs was marked by authority-based/guided access instead of mere keyword access and index browsing; it was also marked by interactive definition of search groups and individualized, tailored displays instead of multiple display formats and only two dialogue modes. The interactive search refinements which the user must now activate rather awkwardly (such as Boolean searching and limiting by date, publication form, etc.) would be replaced in the third generation online catalog by ordinary language search expressions, automatic point-of-need search strategy/formulation guidance, and automatic integration of alternate search approaches. This will all be a tall order for retrieval system designers, but it will no doubt come about, along with augmented, enriched bibliographic records and linked databases, of which we spoke earlier.

Various system features for subject access in the online catalog have been reviewed by Gary S. Lawrence in a recent article.[8] Many of these have been discussed here, if only briefly. I agree with his conclusion that the challenge is formidable, but that online catalogs have an enormous potential as subject access tools.

User Assistance

There is a great need to be creative about presenting all the data to be found on the subject authority record and to provide suggestive prompts which will help the user proceed with a search. The difficulty with this concept of "user assistance" is that we still cannot model user behavior so we cannot decide what information and which prompts will be needed during the search process. We will need several models (for technical processing staff, for patrons, for reference staff, etc.) and we must allow for the flexibility of each model. Karen Markey (see section 2) itemizes five models related to subject searching and itemizes required features to help the search.

Linda Arret, in a 1985 *American Libraries* article, warned that we may be making online catalogs too easy to use by designing menu systems which discourage memorization and provide no incentive for progression to searching more sophisticated than that provided by search options displayed on the bottom of the screen. She went on to remind us all that "users have told us they want this sophistication in order to control and modify retrieval results."[9]

There must be a happy medium. If user assistance is not a menu system, then perhaps it takes the form of a menu-driven system with all available options displayed. If there is no automatic substitution of an authorized term for a natural language phrase, then there should at least be assistance with synonyms and related terms, but not done without the searcher knowing why this has happened. If users are willing to learn, and there is a lot of evidence that they are, then the system design must provide a learning environment. If users expect a dialog with a computer, which is more than they expected from a card catalog, then the interaction between user and machine must be more of a conversation than a command and control session. Interestingly enough, some people realized this as far back as the beginning of the century:

> The catalog must be so constructed that he [the student] can discover easily and quickly what he wants to know. This seems a simple requisite. Yet practice shows that it is one of the most difficult ends to secure. No amount of ingenuity can make a subject catalog which shall be absolutely without flaw in the matter of uniformity; no one can always consult it without effort.... But his road must be made straight and the *rough places* made plain for him. Ease of consultation, then, may be laid down as a fundamental basis for work.[10]

Online aids for vocabulary and search strategy, online training about system features, and improved displays of indexes, subject authority records, and catalog records will all be improvements over existing online catalogs. But there is still more that we can do in the area of user assistance. Norman Stevens, in a short but provocative article, put his finger on the additional problem we can help solve with some kind of user assistance online:

> In seeking to overcome the apparent flaws of subject access we must not lose sight of this major flaw either in the design of those catalogs or in our efforts to persuade patrons to use the catalog for subject information. We need to continue to caution them about its major limitations ... the catalog can provide only very partial and incomplete information about the availability of information on a particular subject in that library's collections.... We need to begin to identify ways in which the vastly superior subject access to information found in indexing and abstracting services and similar tools can be effectively integrated with the online catalog.[11]

Stevens goes on to extoll the virtues of the reference librarian, as rightly he should, but it was good to find some suggestions which were less labor intensive. Such suggestions must be implemented if we are to overcome the limitations he mentioned. Others have suggested linking the online catalog database with the databases of pertinent abstracting and indexing services. The Ohio State University Library online catalog does just that, in a rudimentary way, with the ERIC database. Eventually someone may do this with the H. W. Wilson indexes, too. But until then, the suggestion of Willilam Jarvis is worth noting. (See section 2.) Jarvis suggests that "Pathfinders," designed by individual reference librarians to guide users to the many sources of information on a given topic, may have their place online if they can be designed and displayed creatively. The availability of printers attached to online catalogs makes this suggestion especially appealing because someone could walk away from the online catalog with a pathfinder and start searching reference books, periodical indexes, microfilm files, and the book shelf without needing staff assistance.

Maybe we will even think of a way to automatically call the library staff to the online catalog when the user is completely unsuccessful and needs human help. This might come as a pleasant surprise to the user who would be too bashful to ask for help. If it is considered welcome help, then we know we have vastly improved both subject access and user assistance. User studies in the future should help us assess what the impact of our improvements have been. The data from current user studies have certainly lead us to think that improvements were necessary.[12]

Exercises

1. After reading the suggestions for augmenting catalog records (Mischo, Mandel, Markey), choose a subject area of great interest to your library clientele and experiment with the various ways of augmenting the records for ten to twenty titles. Which way offers the best results with the least amount of effort?

2. Devise suggestive prompts and tutorial messages which could be used after someone has viewed a subject authority record or a browsing list of subject headings and title words in your online catalog. Try several "paper" designs on a group of users (both staff and public) until you come up with one that is satisfactory to almost everyone.

3. If your online catalog provides browsing capabilities for text from titles and subject headings, devise displays which are both informative and discriminating so that the user can be lead from one to the other, and also get assistance with related terms. (The selection by Markey will be useful reading.)

4. Online catalog use studies have concluded that users are having the following difficulties:

    a. Many retrieve nothing

    b. Many retrieve too much

    c. Many view only some of the retrieval results

    d. Many use heavily posted common words in a free text search and then abort their search with no display of records

    Devise a diagnostic message with some user assistance for each of these difficulties. Again try your "paper" display screens on some users (both staff and public) until you come up with one that most agree would be helpful.

5. If your library staff has developed any pathfinders or other short "subject information sheets," devise some way of displaying them online, and decide how they would be made available to the online user. Test these display screens with several users until you come up with one that almost everyone finds useful. (The Jarvis selection is background reading here.)

Notes

[1] Michael J. Simonds, "Database Limitations & Online Catalogs," *Library Journal* (15 February 1984): 329-30.

[2] Pauline Cochrane, "Subject Access—Free Text and Controlled—The Case of Papua New Guinea," *Online Public Access to Library Files: Conference Proceedings* (Oxford: Elsevier International Bulletins, 1985): 83-95.

[3] Barbara Settel and Pauline Cochrane, "Augmenting Subject Descriptions for Books in Online Catalogs," *Database* (December 1982): 15-23.

[4] Sara D. Knapp, "Creating BRS/TERM, a Vocabulary Database for Searchers," *Database* (December 1984): 70-75.

[5] R. A. Wall, "Intelligent Indexing and Retrieval: A Man-machine Partnership," *Information Processing and Management* 16 (1980): 88.

[6] William H. Mischo, "Library of Congress Subject Headings: A Review of the Problems and Prospects for Improved Subject Access," *Cataloging & Classification Quarterly* (1982): 117-21.

[7] Charles Hildreth, "The User Interface in Online Catalogues: The Telling Difference," *Online Public Access to Library Files: Conference Proceedings* (Oxford: Elsevier International Bulletins, 1985): 111-32.

[8] Gary S. Lawrence, "System Features for Subject Access in the Online Catalog," *Library Resources & Technical Services* 29 (January/March 1985): 16-33.

[9] Linda Arret, "Can Online Catalogs Be Too Easy?" *American Libraries* (February 1985): 120.

[10] William Warner Bishop, "Subject Headings in Dictionary Catalogs," *Library Journal* 31 (June 1906): 123.

[11] Norman Stevens, "The Flaw of Subject Access in the Library Catalog: An Opinion," *The Reference Librarian* 9 (Fall/Winter 1983): 110-11.

[12] Pauline A. Cochrane and Karen Markey, "Catalog Use Studies—Since the Introduction of Online Interactive Catalogs: Impact on Design for Subject Access," *Library and Information Science Research* 5 (1983): 337-63.

Selected Readings

(See section 2 for texts, which are renumbered in this edition.)

Australian Bibliographic Network. *Subject Cataloguing Manual.* Part B.2 "Analytical Entries." Canberra, 1985.

Jarvis, William E. "Integrating Subject Pathfinders into Online Catalogs," *Database* (February 1985): 65-67.

Mandel, Carol A. "Enriching the Library Catalog Record for Subject Access," *Library Resources & Technical Services* 29 (January/March 1985): 5-15.

Markey, Karen. *Subject Searching in Library Catalogs Before and After the Introduction of Online Catalogs.* Dublin, Ohio: OCLC, 1984. pp. 108-17.

Mischo, William H. "Expanded Subject Access to Library Collections Using Computer-assisted Indexing Techniques." *Proceedings of the ASIS Annual Meeting, 1983* 20 (1983): 155-57.

Section 2

Introduction

This section contains either full or partial reprints of several papers which contain useful suggestions for improving *LCSH*. When this book was first conceived, I planned to include selections with each chapter, but as the selections were reread, it became obvious that many of the authors did not limit themselves to only one suggestion for the improvement of *LCSH* and their papers did not fall into neat piles matching the focus of each chapter. For this reason it has seemed more sensible to gather all the selections together and refer to them, in whole or in part, when needed to give background to the improvements being suggested in each chapter.

Over the years many authors have written on this subject. Not all could be included in this book. For a comprehensive bibliography on the subject, the reader is referred to the 1981 ERIC Information Analysis Product, IR-53, ED 208 900. In abbreviated form, this report was also published in *Cataloging and Classification Quarterly* 1 (1982): 71-94.

For ease of use, the selections reprinted here are arranged in alphabetic order by author.

Angell, Richard S. "Library of Congress Subject Headings – Review and Forecast." In *Subject Retrieval in the Seventies*, edited by H. Wellisch and T. D. Wilson, 143-62. Westport, Conn.: Greenwood Publishing and University of Maryland, School of Library and Information Services, 1972.

Australian Bibliographic Network. *Subject Cataloguing Manual.* Part B.2., "Analytical Entries." Canberra, 1985.

Berman, Sanford. "Proposal for Reforms to Improve Subject Searching." *American Libraries* (April 1984): 254.

Chan, Lois Mai. "Library of Congress Subject Headings as an Online Retrieval Tool: Structural Considerations." Paper presented at the Symposium on Subject Analysis, 29-30 March 1985, Durham, N.C., sponsored by the School of Library and Information Science, North Carolina Central University.

Chan, Lois Mai. "The Period Subdivision in Subject Headings." *Library Resources & Technical Services* 16 (Fall 1972): 453-59.

Coates, Eric James. *Subject Catalogues: Headings and Structure.* London: Library Association, 1960. pp. 69-79.

Cochrane, Pauline. "Classification as an Online Subject Access Tool: Challenge and Opportunity." Paper presented at a Subject Access meeting sponsored by the Council on Library Resources, June 1982, in Dublin, Ohio.

Cochrane, Pauline. *LCSH Entry Vocabulary Project.* Final Report to the Council on Library Resources and to the Library of Congress, March 1983, "LCSH-EVP Notebook of Procedures" and appendix entitled "Using LCSH as a Subject Access Tool in Online Public Access Catalogs." ED 234 780.

Daily, Jay E. *The Grammar of Subject Headings: A Formulation of Rules for Subject Headings Based on a Syntactical and Morphological Analysis of the Library of Congress List*, Doctoral diss., School of Library Service, Columbia University, 1957. pp. 1-3, 74, 152-61. (University Microfilms No. 59-03116)

Greenberg, Alan M. "Scope Notes in *Library of Congress Subject Headings.*" *Cataloging & Classification Quarterly* 1 (1982): 95-104.

Haykin, David Judson. *Subject Headings: A Practical Guide.* Washington, D.C.: U.S. Government Printing Office, 1951. pp. 18-19, 69-71, 92-94.

Hill, Janet Swan. "Online Classification Number Access: Some Practical Considerations." *Journal of Academic Librarianship* 10 (March 1984): 17-22.

Immroth, John Phillip. *Analysis of Vocabulary Control in Library of Congress Classification and Subject Headings.* Littleton, Colo.: Libraries Unlimited, 1971. pp. 83-88, 90-101, 107-8.

Jarvis, William E. "Integrating Subject Pathfinders into Online Catalogs." *Database* (February 1985): 65-67.

Library of Congress, Subject Cataloging Division. *Subject Cataloging Manual: Subject Headings.* Washington, D.C., 1984. H373, H400, and in supplement, H370.

Lopez, Manuel D. "Subject Catalogers—Equal to the Future?" *Library Resources & Technical Services* 9 (Summer 1965): 371-75.

Mandel, Carol A. "Enriching the Library Catalog Record for Subject Access." *Library Resources & Technical Services* 29 (January/March 1985): 5-15.

Mandel, Carol A. "Helping LC Improve *LCSH* Only Constructive Approach." *American Libraries* (May 1984): 336.

Markey, Karen. *Subject Searching in Library Catalogs Before and After the Introduction of Online Catalogs.* Dublin, Ohio: OCLC, 1984. pp. 108-17.

Micco, H. Mary. *An Exploratory Study of Three Subject Access Systems in Medicine: LCSH, MeSH, PRECIS*, Ph.D. diss., University of Pittsburgh, 1980. Abstract, 45-51, 58-60, 82-92, 147-53.

Miller, Dan. "Authority Control in the Retrospective Conversion Process." *Information Technology and Libraries* (September 1984): 286-92.

Milstead, Jessica L. "Natural versus Inverted Word Order in Subject Headings." *Library Resources & Technical Services* 24 (Spring 1980): 174-78.

Mischo, William H. "Expanded Subject Access to Library Collection Using Computer-assisted Indexing Techniques." *Information Interaction: Proceedings of the 45th ASIS Annual Meeting, 1982* 19 (1982): 155-57.

Mostecky, Vaclav. "Study of the *See-also* Reference Structure in Relation to the Subject of International Law." *American Documentation* 7 (1956): 309-13.

PAIS Subject Headings. New York: Public Affairs Information Service, Inc., 1984. "User's Guide to PAIS Subject Headings" and sample pages.

Pettee, Julia. *Subject Headings: The History and Theory of the Alphabetical Subject Approach to Books*. New York: H. W. Wilson Co., 1947. pp. 73-80.

Prevost, Marie. "An Approach to Theory and Method in General Subject Headings." *Library Quarterly* 16 (1946): 144-47, 149-51.

Richmond, Phyllis A. "Cats: An Example of Concealed Classification in Subject Headings." *Library Resources & Technical Services* 3 (Spring 1959): 102-12.

Wall, R. A. "Intelligent Indexing and Retrieval: A Man-machine Partnership." *Information Processing and Management* 16 (1980): 80-86.

Wepsiec, Jan. "Language of the Library of Congress Subject Headings Pertaining to Society." *Library Resources & Technical Services* 25 (April/June 1981): 196-203.

"Library of Congress Subject Headings — Review and Forecast"

Richard S. Angell

A description of the Library of Congress list of subject headings is followed by an indication of the bibliographical records and services in which it is employed. Recommendations for review and improvement of the list are offered within the framework of certain general assumptions and enumerated under six commonly identified problems of the alphabetical subject catalog: Terminology, Specificity, Form and structure of headings, Reference provisions, Complexity and size, and Maintenance. A technique for adopting revised headings within the constraints of the present card catalogs is illustrated and suggestions offered for fuller publication of the total LC subject heading system in future editions.

Note

In the preparation of this paper the author has had the benefit of the advice and assistance of Library of Congress colleagues. The views expressed, however, are his own. Some have the status of recommendations for the review, analysis, and future development of the Library's Subject Heading List. *The paper has been cleared in the Library for presentation in this symposium, but no decision has been made on the extent, if any, to which the recommendations will be put into effect.*

Introduction

The principal means of subject access to the collections of libraries in the United States is the subject-entry component of the dictionary catalog. For the most part, the subject headings used in these catalogs derive from statements of "objects" and "means" formulated by Charles Ammi Cutter in his *Rules for a Dictionary Catalog.*[1]

Reprinted, by permission, from H. Wellisch and T. D. Wilson, eds. *Subject Retrieval in the Seventies* (Westport, Conn.: Greenwood Publishing and University of Maryland, School of Library and Information Services, 1972), 143-62.

The final formulation of Cutter's objectives and rules was taking place at the same time that the Library of Congress was expanding and reorganizing the collections at the turn of the century. His work had a considerable influence on the founders of the Library of Congress catalog. While the early officers were in accord with Cutter and the majority of United States libraries in rejecting the classified or alphabetico-classed catalog in favor of the dictionary catalog, they were unwilling to contemplate the dispersion of headings that could follow from full adherence to Cutter's rule of specific entry, at least in its application to compound headings. They preferred to combine elements of a dictionary and a classified arrangement. The fact that the Library's subject headings began as a mixed system opened the door to inconsistent decisions as the catalog grew.

Another historical circumstance affecting the development of the list is the pattern of organization of subject heading work in the first decades of the century. It was not until 1941 with the establishment of the Subject Cataloging Division that classification and the assignment of subject headings were combined under one technical and administrative direction. Formerly the Catalog Division was responsible for descriptive cataloging and the assignment of subject headings, and the Classification Division for the development and application of the LC schedules. This disposition of responsibilities resulted in some subject heading work being done by non-specialists and led to a rather generalized approach in the assignment and development of subject headings, of which evidences are still found on entries and in the list.

Description of *LCSH*

A thorough exposition of the Library's subject heading principles and practice would manifestly carry us beyond the proper limits of this paper. For those not already acquainted with the list the most useful exposition is contained in *Subject Headings, a Practical Guide*[2] by David J. Haykin, first chief of the Subject Cataloging Division under the reorganization referred to above. The introduction to the latest edition is also relevant[3]. For purposes of completeness in this document, however, and as a point of reference for later discussion, some basic facts about the list should be set forth.

The Library's list of subject headings (hereafter sometimes referred to as LCSH) is a member of the class of controlled pre-coordinate indexing vocabularies. Headings proper have the grammatical form of noun or phrase, the principal types of the latter being adjective-noun, phrases containing a preposition, and phrases containing a conjunction. Phrases may be in normal order of words, or inverted.

Headings are amplified as required by 1) the parenthetical qualifier, used principally to name the domain of a single noun for the purpose of resolving homographs; and 2) the subdivision, of which there are four kinds: topic, place, time, and form. References are provided between related headings and from terms not used as headings.

The complete vocabulary of headings and references exists only in the subject portion of the Library's Official Catalog. The published list, as set forth in the Introduction to the 7th edition[3], omits a number of categories of headings. Besides names of persons, families, and corporate bodies, some of the principal omitted categories are: chemical compounds; natural features; structures; metropolitan areas and their features; places and regions, except when needed to show subdivisions; and systematic names of families, genera, and species in botany and zoology.

An entry in the published list is either a heading or a *see* reference to a heading from an expression not used. Under each heading are shown the references from it to other headings and a record, or "tracing," of references made to the heading from other entries. The entry for a heading may also contain one or more of the following features: an indication that it is to be subdivided by place, and in what manner ("direct" or "indirect"); a class number from the LC classification (for some 8 to 10 percent of the headings); and a scope note, specifying the field of application of the heading or any special sense in which it is used. The entry includes a list of subdivisions used with the heading.

The 7th edition of the list and its supplements have been computer-produced from magnetic tape. A consolidated tape of the 7th edition and the first supplement (July 1964-December 1965) is available.

The following auxiliary records are maintained in order to promote uniformity in formulation and usage and to make possible revisions of headings and subdivisions:

1. A file of subdivisions (except form subdivisions) indicating all main headings under which each subdivision has been used.

2. A list of the terms used as qualifiers with a list of the headings after which they appear.

3. A list of the adjectives in adjective-noun phrases which have been entered in the list as inversions, e.g., Art, Primitive.

4. A list of conjunctions and prepositions subarranged by the phrase headings in which they appear, e.g.,
   Kings *and* rulers
   Music *and* war.

5. A record of the scientific headings not included in the published list.

6. A list of geographic names used as main headings or subdivisions.

Uses of *LCSH*

The subject headings have been applied to the Library's collection of more than 4.6 million titles, which is without limit as to subject field and language. The entries form the subject part of two card catalogs in the Library: the Main Catalog, primarily for use by the general public and the reference staff; and the Official Catalog, primarily for the staff of the Processing Department. These catalogs contain, respectively, approximately 15 and 17 million entries, of which an estimated 6 million in each catalog are topical subject entries. In the present fiscal year some 285,000 subject entries will be filed in each catalog for 228,000 currently cataloged titles. Since April of 1968 the Official Catalog has been a divided catalog; that is, it is separated into two sections, name-title and topical subject. Many special divisional catalogs are also maintained, among them those for music and maps. In the *Library of Congress Catalog Books - Subjects*, published since 1950, LC printed cards are displayed under the subject headings assigned to each entry.

In addition to the Library's internal use of the list in its catalogs, other libraries and agencies use it in whole or in part in their subject catalogs and services.

As many have pointed out, and some have deplored, the Library of Congress printed card service carries LC subject headings into the libraries of some 25,000 card subscribers in the United States and 1,200 in other countries. It can be assumed that a certain number of these libraries use the subject headings in their catalogs—often, no doubt, with modification.

A notable example of the subject bibliographies based on LCSH is the *Subject Guide to Books in Print* published annually by the R. R. Bowker Company in New York. The 1970 volume lists 225,000 books under 41,500 headings and includes 49,000 references. LC headings appear in such current lists as the weekly record of current U.S. book publication in *Publisher's Weekly*.

The indexing services of the H. W. Wilson Company use LCSH in one or two cases, and for most others the *Sears' List of Subject Headings*[4] which is very largely derived from LC's. The Sears' list is used for entries in the company's card distribution service.

The presence of LC subject headings on MARC tapes carries them into the new domain of machine-readable bibliographical records. Coverage of English language monographs in the 1969 and later card series is now complete and as of April 30, 1971, the total number of entries included was 130,000. Forty-six libraries and commercial processing services are now subscribers to the MARC tape distribution service. Regional and state networks are among those using the tapes. The Library exchanges its MARC tapes with those of the *British National Bibliography's (BNB)* MARC service. For titles cataloged by *BNB* before receipt of an LC entry, *BNB* assigns LC subject headings to entries appearing on its tapes.

Need for Review

This factual description of LCSH, besides furnishing an inventory of the parts of the system, is intended to convey the size and extent of the bibliographical enterprises of which it is a part. The enormous size of the Library's catalogs, the magnitude of the current cataloging effort as evidenced in the rate of growth of the catalogs, the wide-spread use of the subject heading list, are all impressive, perhaps, in quantitative terms. Unfortunately, in the course of the seven decades in which the Library's catalogs and subject heading list have been growing, certain inconsistencies and anomalies have developed. It would be difficult to imagine a contrary condition, unless perhaps the Library had disposed at every point in time the resources adequate for the necessary continuous revision to reflect changes in usage, semantic shift, abandonment of earlier orthography, and other vagaries of the language. These inconsistencies and anomalies have not escaped the attention of critics, some of whom object to the scheme itself. It would be well, therefore, to take a general look at the status of our subject headings.

In order to lay the basis for a comprehensive review of the Library's subject heading list, I have prepared and submitted to Library officers an outline entitled, "Library of Congress Subject Headings—Problems and Prospects," with the subtitle, "An agenda for analysis and consideration of current criticisms and acknowledged defects." The principal parts of this outline are the following: Uses and purposes of the list, Criteria for judging the list, Criticisms of the list (a synopsis of observations from the literature, experience of LC officers, etc.), Consideration of the criticisms in relation to our criteria, Decision on future course for the list. The last two sections of the outline contain sets of alternatives. The criticisms are to be sorted into valid and invalid; the valid into remediable and irremediable. The decision on future course is divided between Abandon and Maintain. If the former, abandon in favor of ... (the alternatives are to be supplied); if to maintain, there would follow a program for remedial actions.

General Considerations

If the suggestions implicit in the foregoing are adopted, a review of LCSH would proceed without preconceptions as to its future. While open-mindedness can be advocated in technical matters, certain general considerations should be borne in mind for their relevance to the ultimate decisions. They do not all point in the same direction.

In considering the future of the list, it seems a reasonable assumption that, as the Library moves toward a machine-readable bibliographic store, we will continue to maintain for an indefinitely long time card catalogs for the use of public and staff, and that this will be true for an even longer period for many of the libraries and other agencies using our bibliographic services. Accordingly, a set of considerations arises from the need to take account of the effect on existing catalogs and services of any changes we might make. For example, if we should decide to use coordinate indexing for certain categories of material we would still have to continue present techniques for the benefit of card subscribers who will still be using conventional displays of subject information.

We also need to be mindful of the objective of compatibility and convertibility with other indexing vocabularies, in particular with the subject authority lists of the National Library of Medicine and the National Agricultural Library.

We should also have in mind the developments toward a switching or intermediary language that would make possible the exchange of bibliographic information between agencies through a single medium.[5]

There is one approach to the review and analysis of LCSH that would seriously impede progress, in my opinion. This would be the assumption that the subject component of the Library's card catalogs is to remain open-ended for the indefinite future. If we accepted this constraint, it would be manifestly impossible to adopt a different system of subject cataloging. Nor, in my opinion, could we make the present system (and therefore the catalogs) materially better unless we can study LCSH as if we were revising it for a new subject catalog. I am persuaded that the Library's list of subject headings can become and remain an up-to-date and responsive instrument for subject access to the collections only if it is developed and maintained under conditions which permit the adoption of changes without the necessity of complete revision of earlier cataloging. Such conditions would be largely provided either by setting a cut-off date for the addition of subject entries to the present card catalogs and starting a new subject catalog at periodic intervals, of a span to be agreed on, or by developing techniques for the introduction of subject heading changes and additions without revision of existing entries. Both alternatives are under study in the Library.

Topics for Review

The analytic review of LCSH proposed in the foregoing observations might well choose as technical topics the problems enumerated by Frarey in his review of the state of the art of subject headings and the subject catalog. They are: Terminology, Specific entry, Form and structure, Reference apparatus, Complexity and size, and Maintenance.[6] The remarks which follow under these topics contain both exposition and recommendations, expressed or implied.

Terminology

Common usage as the basis for the selection of indexing terms is advocated in American practice. In the absence of evidence to the contrary, it seems a reasonable hypothesis that this basis offers the best chance of maximum correspondence between the prescriptions of indexers and searchers.

A corollary of this principle in the practice of the Library of Congress is that new headings have to be "established." We require evidence that the term or phrase for a new topic has some acceptance in the authoritative current journals and monographs in its field. This enables us to avoid coined terms that do not gain general acceptance, jargon, and other transitory expressions. This policy has its problems and its critics, some of whom have not understood it fully. Although I consider the policy sound, it should be reconsidered in the course of any such general examination as that suggested.

In the present list itself, an obvious element in a thorough revision would be the change from obsolete to current forms. Some of these cases are matters of orthography, e.g., Aeroplanes has become Airplanes; some are dictated by changes in usage, e.g., European War, 1914-1918, to World War, 1914-1918.

Specificity

As a topic in the theory and practice of the alphabetic subject catalog, specificity has proved a difficult attribute to define. For Cutter specific entry meant above all "*not* class entry." We shall see that his antipathy to the latter affected his prescriptions on the formulation of headings.

Some time ago Lilley called attention to the relative nature of the concept[7], and Frarey finds evidence that "the relativity of the principle of specific entry is the major source of difficulty in either its application or its comprehension."[8]

Dunkin observes that "In the discussion of subject headings, 'specific' is often used as if it meant 'narrow' (in contrast with 'broad' or 'general') subjects."[9] He correctly points out that "A specific entry is sometimes for a broad subject, sometimes for a narrow subject."[10] This view is implicit in Haykin's prescription under specificity, "The heading should be as specific as the topic it is intended to cover."[11] He allows, however, that, rather than use a heading broader than the topic, "the cataloger should use two specific headings which will approximately cover it."[12]

For a representative British view of this question we can adduce the following observation by Jack Mills: "Normal British indexing practice ... is to use for the index description of a document a class which is a summarization of the overall theme of the document. It does not attempt to embrace explicitly the detailed contents of the document... The summarization is, however, 'specific'... The practice might be called 'single entry specific'." Mills' example is a document on the bacterial diseases of grain crops in storage. The summarization would convey "just this and not something less specific."[13] Mills goes on to characterize American practice as tending "to reject the aim of specific description in a single index heading."[14] He notes some advantages and disadvantages of each method. (The fact that these remarks are made in a paper on classification does not lessen the force of their application to subject headings).

These observations suggest perhaps that we could more usefully deal with the problem of specificity if we substituted for "specific" the notion of "expressive." In this sense specificity is not an attribute of a subject access vocabulary as such (i.e., of its terms) but is rather a function of the total resources of the indexing system, and of the way in which it is used.

In order to achieve expressiveness, American library practice, as exemplified in the list and practices of the Library of Congress, relies in considerable part on the resources of the English language. It uses natural language as naturally as possible. This accounts for the presence in the list of a variety of standard phrase forms, in which relationships between terms are made clear by the syntax of the language. In this respect the principle of common usage, which governs the choice of single terms, is also invoked.

Qualification

Use of the parenthetical qualifier, principally for the resolution of homographs, has been mentioned. LCSH has been criticized for using marks of punctuation, including this one, for more than one purpose.[15] Since it is not a characteristic of English usage that each punctuation sign be used in only one way, it does not seem a reasonable demand to make of an indexing vocabulary. It is proper to expect, however, that in any particular set or complex of headings the parenthesis, for example, be used with a consistent meaning. From this point of view our use of parentheses in headings for cook books, e.g., Cookery (Beef), Cookery (Garnishes), and many others; and for musical compositions, e.g., Concertos (Violin), Sonatas (Flute and piano), etc., is proper in both cases but inconsistent in the first. The use of all marks of punctuation should be scrutinized from this point of view.

Subdivision

It is evident, however, that the limits of expressiveness and precision in index characterizations of document content can not be achieved only by the assignment of single words, by phrases in common use, and by others constructed on the models of common usage. And so, in Haykin's words, "Subdivision ... is resorted to when no invariable, commonly used and accepted phrase is available with which to express the intended limitation of a subject."[16] However, following Cutter in rejection of the alphabetico-classed heading, he urges, "Subdivision should as far as possible be limited to the form in which the subject matter is presented and the place and time to which it is limited."[17]

Topic. The attempt to exclude subdivision by topic or aspect in Library of Congress practice was never wholly successful. In the absence of a phrase sanctioned by usage, the topical subdivision is allowed by Haykin; for example, SOCIAL PHYCHOLOGY—RESEARCH. He also allows that the topical subdivision may be used in certain cases for uniformity of treatment under a subject, e.g., HEART—DISEASES.[18]

Forms like the following are now used:

>   AUTOMOBILES—MOTORS—BEARINGS
>   —...
>   —VALVES

Place. Subdivision by place is used only with headings for which it is indicated in the authority file and the list. Two styles are used: Direct and Indirect. The meaning and application of these signals is explained in the introduction to the 7th edition of the list.[3] The difference can be generally illustrated by these examples:

>   *Direct:*   BANKS AND BANKING—CLEVELAND
>
>   *Indirect:*   MUSIC—SWITZERLAND—ZURICH

At one time a criterion for designating a new heading for place subdivision was the likelihood that large files would accumulate under the heading. This is no longer the case; the sole criterion is suitability of this qualification to the literature of the subject. It may be of interest to note here that the geographic code developed as part of the MARC format has a built-in hierarchy, with the result that all subject headings in our machine-readable records to which this code has been assigned are in effect divided "Indirect."

Period. Time divisions under the history of a country express the periods into which its history is commonly divided. Sometimes a period is denoted by a name, sometimes by a century or other span of dates. The list should be reviewed to express all historical period subdivisions by dates or centuries, followed as appropriate by the period's name. One could say that we have operated on the assumption, for example, that filers in the Library of Congress catalogs could convert U.S.—HISTORY—CIVIL WAR into U.S.—HISTORY—1860-65. This assumption is no longer tenable. The same observations apply to time divisions under headings for literature, art, and other headings, chiefly in the humanities.

Form. Review of the Library's form subdivisions is well under way. A working group of the U.S. National Libraries Task Force on Automation and other Cooperative Activities, consisting of representatives of the Library of Congress, the National Agricultural Library, and the National Library of Medicine, has reviewed a composite list of form subdivisions used with the subject headings of each library. The group will soon be able to recommend adoption of a single list for use by all three libraries. Each subheading will have a scope note stating the appropriate field of application and examples of typical usage. In this review, almost all of the subheadings in the Library of Congress list consisting of terms in series, e.g., "Cartoons, satire, etc.," "Quotations, maxims, etc." would be eliminated by the adoption of the standard list.

Language of text. Although not part of our present practice, I believe that provision for this designation as a part of subject subdivision should be made. Again, the MARC format provides this search capability by including a fixed field for the language or languages of the text.

Complex Subjects

Expression of complex subjects often requires the assignment of more than one heading. We can identify, and should distinguish, two kinds of cases: 1) the multi-topic work and 2) the multi-element work. The assignment of two or more headings for the former is common practice in all systems, to the best of my knowledge. It has to be distinguished, of course, from analytical subject indexing of a work's contents. The difference, to be sure, is not easy to define or to maintain in operational terms.

The expression "multi-element work" is intended to characterize the kind of document, common in technical fields, which is on a narrow topic—"specific" in that sense—and that can only be fully expressed by the representation of all of its elements. This kind of document is not new, but in the post-war period its number, both absolutely and in proportion to the total range of library materials, has greatly increased.

A pre-coordinate system like LCSH has often dealt with this kind of document by the assignment of a heading to each of its elements, for example:

Title: The phenology and growth habits of pines in Hawaii. 1966, 25 pages

Headings: 1. Pine—Hawaii
2. Phenology
3. Trees—Growth

The objection to this kind of treatment is not that the entry under any one of the headings is inaccurate, but that the unmodified heading for Phenology, for example, should be reserved for general works. The consequence is that entries under Phenology have to be "sorted through" to find documents with the limitations of this one. Moreover, we can assume that in most searches the practice entails the unnecessary examination of this entry and its rejection as unlikely to have any material of substance on Phenology in general.

According to the "single-entry specific" practice, the heading for this example would presumably be

PINE—GROWTH—HAWAII

The systematic introduction of this kind of heading would have several consequences. The incidence of the alphabetico-classed form of heading would be increased. The "distributed relative" problem, for which we often use the illustrative *see* or *see also* reference (e.g., "STORAGE *See* ... subdivision Storage under names of stored products, e.g. ... FARM PRODUCTS—STORAGE") would require systematic attention. Most of the solutions have been developed for and used in indexes to classified catalogs and bibliographies. Among them are:

cross reference for each element after the first, chain index to a classification schedule, and rotation or selective permutation of the elements of the index string.

Form and Structure of Headings

In a pre-coordinate indexing system the form of the heading is affected by two factors: 1) the means of making the heading expressive; 2) the choice of lead term. In the foregoing observations on specificity we have dealt with some of the problems and alternatives of the first. The second, choice of lead term, can be dealt with under the heading of form.

Cutter's attempt to avoid inversion as much as possible (his rule on this point is avowedly equivocal) can not be considered an aspect of specificity regarded as expressiveness. If inversion is possible in the grammar of the language, it is surely as expressive as the direct form, e.g., Pheasant, Ring-necked instead of Ring-necked pheasant. Cutter avoided inversion because he regarded it as logically a classed entry. To be sure, it is so in the sense that it groups entries for works on aspects or subtopics of a subject with those for works on the subject as a whole. But surely the inverted adjective-noun phrase is a far cry from the lengthy taxonomic string which he was chiefly aiming to extirpate from library catalogs in the United States.

If establishment of criteria for inversion of phrase headings is a problem in the alphabetical subject catalog, it must be because experience or intuition or both have told us that a single rule is not acceptable, either for direct form always or inverted form always.

A rule that all such headings should be inverted runs at once into unacceptable results. Cutter offers a representative list, beginning with ALIMENTARY CANAL, of headings whose inversions would put them where no one would expect to find them.[19] On the other hand, a fisherman no doubt has a plausible case against a set of headings such as BASS, BLACK BASS, SMALL-MOUTH BASS even if we assume *see also* references from BASS to the last two and *see* references to them from the inversions. The case for using inversion in an example like this lies in the assumption that the searcher would prefer this collocation of entries to the dispersion of the direct forms.

The treatment of this problem by several authorities is reviewed by Dunkin.[20] As he implicitly concludes, attempts to solve the inversion problem by adoption of the "noun rule" result in constructions which sacrifice intelligibility to form and order. A possible test for avoiding unacceptable inversions might be to ask the question: If the second term were used without the first, would the result be accurate, even if imprecise? If the answer is No, the inversion is unacceptable. This gives us ALIMENTARY CANAL without difficulty, and also many phrases beginning with a proper adjective, e.g., BROWNIAN MOVEMENT. Using this question as a test would furnish a ready means of determining whether or not the modifying adjective or noun has removed the generic character of the substantive. If it has, we do not want to invert. If it has not, we may still prefer inversion. In LC practice at least, inversion of most phrases beginning with a linguistic, ethnic, or geographical adjective, or one denoting an historical period is well established, e.g., ART, FRENCH; ARCHITECTURE, MEDIEVAL. But there are exceptions and firmer criteria are needed.

Reference Provisions

In common with many other controlled indexing vocabularies, the LCSH reference structure consists of *see* references from terms not used to headings that are used, and *see also* references from a heading to one of lower rank, and between headings related other than hierarchically. This pattern is diagrammed in Figure 1 and explained in the following statement.

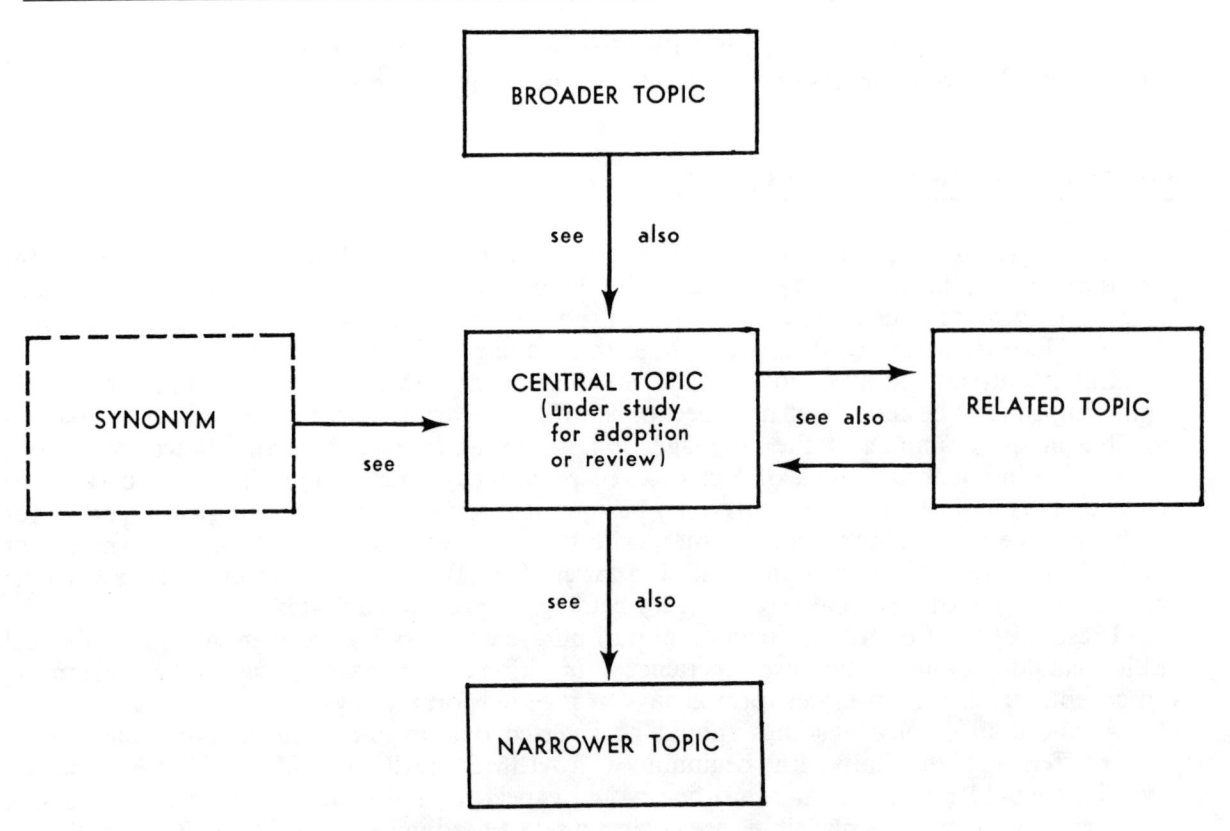

Fig. 1. Pattern of cross-reference provisions in the
Library of Congress subject heading list.

Figure 1 is designed to furnish a graphic display of the basic reference structure of the Library of Congress subject heading list and to suggest the systematic set of considerations associated with the adoption of a new heading or the review of an existing one. The following exposition summarizes current practice; that is, it describes the basis for development and revision of the vocabulary, not the published list of headings. For the purpose of this display, the expression "Central Topic" has been used to identify the term under consideration. Its relationships to other entries in the list are shown in the other boxes:

Broader topic. If the central topic is on a lower level in a hierarchy or is a part of a larger subject, a *see also* reference is made from the broader topic. This is the "downward *see also*" reference and is made from the next higher level only. ("Hierarchy" is used in a general sense, to include not only relations of genus—species but also class—member, topic—subtopic, activity—example, etc.)

Narrower topic. If the central topic is itself a broader topic to another, the downward *see also* reference is made, but only to a topic at the next lower level.

Related topic. If the central topic is related to another topic but the relationship is coordinate rather than hierarchical, a *see also* reference is made both from and to the central topic.

Synonym. For the purposes of the diagram, this single term is used to comprehend also the *see* reference from antonyms and alternative forms. The dotted box lines are intended to emphasize the fact that these entries in the list are not subject headings.

While only a single box is shown for each relationship, the full diagram for a central term may show more than one relationship of any one kind. Conversely, all of the relationships would not appear in every diagram.

Attention is called to the statement that this diagram represents the systematic set of considerations associated with the adoption of a new heading or the review of an existing one. The diagram is intended to demonstrate the following points: the list does indeed have a classificatory base, though not one directly related to a classification schedule; the *see also* hierarchical references are made in downward direction only and from one level to the next lower level only; related headings have reciprocal references; and *see* references are made in a lateral direction only and not to headings at a higher hierarchical level.

This systematic approach to the integration of new headings into the list has been followed for a considerable number of years. We are aware that it is not possible to derive from the published subject heading list that this represents our practice because 1) the list has not been completely revised and so contains survivals of other practices; 2) our judgments on the nature of relations may not accord with those of others; 3) errors may escape detection in editorial review.

In the reconstruction of LCSH it would be desirable to change the abbreviations for references and tracings to those in common use in thesauri, in the interest of making the list more intelligible to users and of fostering compatibility with other indexing vocabularies. This can be accomplished by means of a simple conversion table, as indicated in Figure 2. There are reasons to prefer "heading" for LCSH instead of "term" because the meaning of hierarchical and collateral references in subject headings lists and thesauri are not precisely the same. This is a consequence of the different kinds of material to which the two kinds of lists are typically applied, i.e., the monograph and the technical report. But this variation in the designations is perhaps not worth maintaining.

	LCSH		**Thesauri**	
	Reference	Tracing	Reference	Reciprocal
From unused terms to valid terms	see	x	USE	UF
Between valid terms				
General to specific	sa	xx	NT	BT
Specific to general	1		BT	NT
Collateral	sa^2	xx^2	RT	RT

---

1. Not made as such, but the xx tracing of the general-to-specific maintains the connection.
2. When this reference is made and traced in both directions.

BT   Broader term
NT   Narrower term
RT   Related term
sa   see also
UF   Use for

Fig. 2. Conversion table for typical subject heading
and thesaurus reference designations.

In my opinion all valid *see* references can be reduced to the relation of synonym, antonym, or alternative form. I would review the list to conform to this prescription. Any surviving *see* references to more general terms should be converted to headings and placed in the NT relation to the general term.

The kinds of hierarchies appropriate to the BT/NT relation should be made explicit. They should be expressed at each level by a downward *see also* (NT) reference to the term at the next lower level only. References not meeting this specification should be removed.

The BT designation supplies in acceptable form the "upward *see also*" advocated by many writers. Expressed as "*see also*" this reference is incorrect, in my opinion, except in Margaret Mann's formulation of a general reference information card, her example being:

GLACIERS

Chapters on this subject will often be found in the books entered in this catalog under the heading Geology.[21]

The collateral "see also" reference (RT). It seems likely that anyone who has undertaken a comparison of the provisions for related terms in subject heading lists and thesauri would agree that this is an element of indexing vocabulary construction that deserves careful study. The observations in general thesaurus guidelines and in prefaces to thesauri themselves contain for the most part only the most general kind of prescription for their use. *Thesaurofacet*[22] is an exception: 9 categories of related terms are suggested and illustrated.

Since the related term reference is avowedly suggestive and without precision, it might be considered unnecessary to subject it to rigorous analysis. In my opinion, however, this is not the proper view. Coates has observed that, in the absence of definition of what collateral subjects are, "the collateral relationship may be invoked to justify indiscriminate reference linkages."[23] His suggestion that it be considered "restricted to terms which lie within the same facet of a given generic subject"[24] has been adopted, perhaps independently, in the *Information Retrieval Thesaurus of Education Terms*[25] in which most RT references consist of the number of a subfacet in the thesaurus' faceted array where the subfacet terms are listed.

In its examination of this feature of LCSH the Library now has a valuable resource in a computer program which converts our term relation designations to the set commonly used in thesauri as shown in the conversion table of Figure 2. It has been used to print out certain blocks of headings in LCSH to facilitate comparison with those in the same section of the alphabet in the National Agricultural Library's vocabulary.[26] A printout of the complete tape would greatly facilitate review of the entire reference structure of LCSH. In particular, many NT tracings would be recognized as "one-way collateral *see also's*" and removed or made reciprocal as the case required.

Complexity and Size. Maintenance

The dimensions of Frarey's last two problems as they affect the Library of Congress subject heading list have perhaps been suggested in the earlier account of the size of the catalogs and their rate of growth. The problems can be illustrated by reference to the earlier suggestion that one of the conditions that would make it possible to keep the subject heading list up to date would be the development of techniques for introducing changes without the necessity of complete revision of earlier cataloging. In a study of this problem the Technical Processes Research Office and the Subject Cataloging Division have identified seven principal problems in maintaining currency and accuracy of subject entries in the LC catalogs.

1. Headings originally incorrect

2. Headings which have become incorrect through
    a. change of spelling
    b. change of usage

3. Headings which have become imprecise

4. Headings which have been used imprecisely

5. Invalid two-topic headings: "A and B"

6. Deficiencies resulting from faulty references

7. Problems of long files

Exposition of the details of this study would be inappropriate in this paper, but an illustrative case and an indication of the general nature of the proposed solutions may be of interest.

The problem chosen for illustration is "Deficiencies resulting from faulty references." An example can be found under EROSION on page 441 of the 7th edition of the subject heading list.[3] While there are *see also* references to such headings as BEACH EROSION, DUST STORMS, and RUN-OFF among others, SOIL EROSION is a *see* reference to EROSION. This anomaly was corrected in August of 1968, but until then the consequence of the reference provisions was that entries for SOIL EROSION had to be found in the file of general works under EROSION. Moreover, this incorrect reference resulted in an indirect connection between SOIL EROSION and SOIL CONSERVATION.

The following statement suggests the general nature of the solutions proposed by the study, namely, information cards filed with the affected entries and a prescription for the changes to be made in references:

Information Cards

SOIL EROSION
Here are entered works on soil erosion cataloged after September 1, 1968. Works on this topic cataloged before this date will be found among those entered under Erosion.

EROSION
Use of this heading for works on soil erosion was discontinued on August 31, 1968. Works on soil erosion cataloged after this date are entered under Soil erosion.

References

Cancel   Erosion
        sa   Soil conservation
           Soils
    Soil erosion see Erosion

Add   Erosion
        sa   Soil erosion
    Soil conservation
        sa   Soil erosion
    Soil erosion
        sa   Soil conservation

The study recognized that the examples of this possible technique could not provide a demonstration of its effect on the texture of the catalog, but accepted it as self-evident that a vastly more complex reference structure would be adverse to ready catalog consultation by users. The importance of communicating any such changes to card subscribers so that they could adopt or reject our solution was also recognized. Let me make it clear that these procedures have only been offered for consideration and have not been put into effect for any heading. The SOIL EROSION case has been taken care of in our catalogs by changing the affected entries and references. It is therefore a hypothetical example of how it might have been dealt with.

Publication of Future Editions of *LCSH*

In conclusion I should like to make some comments and suggestions on the content of future editions of the published list. They arise from a belief in the importance of making the list and its appurtenant records available as fully as possible to the users of the Library's bibliographical services and all others having an interest in the list. As the topics of recorded discourse multiply and as collections consequently grow in size and diversity, it becomes more and more important that the first step in the effort to find relevant materials by subject should be to examine the vocabulary of the indexing language. It follows that in more and more searches it will be economical to make them in two stages: first in the vocabulary and then in the catalog or display of subject entries.

The following outline suggests the sections into which future editions of LCSH might be organized:

Section 1   *Description, Conventions, Rules*
      2   *Alphabetical list of headings, including see and see-also references*
      3   *Subdivisions*
            Form (generally applicable)
            Topic, each with headings under which it is used
            Period, as used under names of places
      4   *Keyword list of headings and subdivisions*
      5   *Musical compositions*

A few observations on some of the sections may be appropriate.

Section 2 would include subject category designations for each heading in order to make possible the development of automatic techniques for extracting lists in special fields. Use of the main classes and principal subclasses of our schedules is assumed. A heading would have as many category designations as required to place it in each of the special lists of headings in which its membership would be appropriate.

Except for personal and corporate names, names of natural features, and categories of similar character, the headings excluded from the 7th edition and its supplements would be included in future editions. This is important in order that the references associated with the presently excluded headings be available. This is also a necessary basis for the establishment of conversion algorisms with other vocabularies.

The three lists of subdivisions in *Section 3* would include the standard list of forms now being developed, the subdivision control file, and a list of period subdivisions under names of places formerly published separately.

The keyword list proposed for *Section 4* would be a rotated list of headings and subdivisions, in order to provide comprehensive access to terms whenever they occur. Subdivisions would be identified by an arbitrary sign and this would constitute a reference to the list of topical subdivisions in the preceding section. If kept up to date with supplementary files between editions, this list might serve as a substitute for the *see* references now made in the card catalog between alternative forms, since all terms in phrase headings, for example, would be displayed.

The suggestion that headings for musical compositions constitute a separate section derives from the special nature of the materials and the consequent special character of the headings. The headings for music history, criticism, and pedagogy would be contained in the general list of *Section 2*. These headings could be extracted for separate publication, to be used with the composition headings in special music libraries.

Conclusion

The study of the Library's subject heading list suggested in the foregoing review could result in a different system in the course of time. The most reasonable path of progress, however, is considered to be the improvement of the list in its present terms, as suggested under the several topics for review. This course provides the obvious advantages of orderly evolution. It also recognizes the fact that, during the course of its seven decades of growth, the list and the catalogs in which it is embodied have been of substantial service in the library community.

Notes

[1] Cutter, C. A. *Rules for a Dictionary Catalog.* 4th ed. Washington, Government Printing Office, 1904. (First edition, 1876, has title: *Rules for a Printed Dictionary Catalogue.*)

[2] Haykin, D. J. *Subject Headings; a Practical Guide.* Washington, U.S. Government Printing Office, 1951.

[3] Library of Congress. *Subject Headings Used in the Dictionary Catalogs of the Library of Congress.* 7th ed. Ed. by M. V. Quattlebaum. Washington, 1966.

[4] *Sears' List of Subject Headings.* 9th ed. Ed. by B. M. Westby. New York, The H. W. Wilson Company, 1965.

[5] Coates, E. J. "Library Science and Documentation Literature: a New Development in International Co-operation." *Library Association Record*, v. 70, no. 7, 1968, p. 178-179.
―――. "Switching Languages for Indexing." *Journal of Documentation*, v. 26, no. 2, 1970, p. 102-110.

[6] Frarey, C. J. "Subject Headings." *In: The State of the Library Art.* Ed. by R. R. Shaw. New Brunswick, Rutgers—The State University, 1960, v. 1, pt. 2.

[7] Lilley, O. L. "How Specific is Specific?" *Journal of Cataloging and Classification*, v. 11, no. 1, 1955, p. 3-8.

[8] Frarey, C. J. *Op. cit.* p. 59.

[9] Dunkin, P. S. *Cataloging U.S.A.* Chicago, American Library Association, 1969, p. 68.

[10]*Ibid.*

[11]Haykin, D. J. *Op. cit.* p. 9.

[12]*Ibid.*

[13]Mills, J. "Some Current Problems of Classification for Information Retrieval." *Classification Society Bulletin*, v. 1, no. 4, 1968, p. 24.

[14]*Ibid.*

[15]Daily, J. E. "Many Changes, no Alteration." *Library Journal*, v. 92, no. 1967, p. 3962.

[16]Haykin, D. J. *Op. cit.* p. 27.

[17]Haykin, D. J. *Loc. cit.*

[18]Haykin, D. J. *Op. cit.* p. 36.

[19]Cutter, C. A. *Op. cit.* p. 73.

[20]Dunkin, P. S. *Op. cit.* Chapter 5, p. 65-95 *passim*.

[21]Mann, M. *Introduction to Cataloging and the Classification of Books.* 2d ed. Chicago, American Library Association, 1943, p. 151.

[22]*Thesaurofacet*, a thesaurus and faceted classification for engineering and related subjects. Compiled by J. Aitchison, et al. Whetstone, Leicester, The English Electric Co. Ltd., 1969, p. xviii.

[23]Coates, E. J. *Subject Catalogues, Headings and Structure.* London, The Library Association, 1960, p. 73-74.

[24]*Ibid.* p. 74.

[25]Barhydt, G. C., et al. *Information Retrieval Thesaurus of Education Terms.* Cleveland, Case Western Reserve University Press, 1968.

[26]National Agricultural Library. *Agricultural/Biological Vocabulary.* 1st ed. Washington, United States Department of Agriculture, 1967, 2 vols. and 1st supplement, 1968.

Australian Bibliographic Network *Subject Cataloguing Manual.* Part B.2.

B.2 ANALYTICAL ENTRIES

Participants wishing to assign headings additional to those which would be assigned by conforming to the general guidelines in section B.1, theoretically have three options open to them:

1. assignment of such additional headings in shareable subject heading fields;

2. assignment of such additional headings as institution-specific subject heading fields;

3. assignment of such additional headings on their local system, and not on ABN. It is hoped that participants will consider options 1 and 2 before restricting enhancements to their in-house systems.

B.2.1 *Option 1.*

The assignment of headings additional to those assigned according to the general guidelines in shareable subject heading fields are permissible provided:

i) that they are additional - that is, that subject headings assigned according to the general guidelines in section B.1 are also assigned;

ii) that such additional headings are valid Library of Congress Subject Headings, or ABN-approved headings;

iii) that they do not contravene guideline B.1.1 on specificity.

Reprinted, by permission, from Australian Bibliographic Network, *Subject Cataloguing Manual* (Canberra, 1985), Part B.2, "Analytical Entries."

Generally such additional headings will be analytical - analysing either fully or in part the contents of the item. The subject analysis may be at the level of the titles of the volumes of a multi-volume work, or e.g. the sections, chapters or articles of a work.

For example:

i) a book on physical geography may have additional headings assigned for each of the specific sections, namely climate, soils, and landforms.

ii) a book of photographs of cities of the world may have an additional heading assigned for a chapter on Melbourne, the one Australian city covered, purely because it is of particular interest to Australians.

iii) a book on tropical agriculture may have an additional heading assigned for the chapter on Indonesia, because of the particular institution's research/teaching interest in that country.

Participants adding such analytical headings should bear in mind that these headings are being added to the shareable data fields, and exercise some restraint. For example, all participants may appreciate additional access for significant/substantial sections of a work. But neither ABN, nor LCSH, may be suitable for in-depth analysis involving dozens of additional headings.

B.2.2. *Option 2*

Because subject headings assigned according to this option are not shareable, several participants wanting perhaps the same additional headings would not only have to add them individually, but also would not be aware of which headings had been assigned by any other participant. The addition of many headings by different participants to a particular bibliographic record according to this option will reasonably readily result in the record reaching the upper limit of its permissible character length.

It is therefore recommended that the addition of subject headings according to this option generally be restricted to non-valid Library of Congress Subject Headings - that is headings tagged with second indicator equal to P.

Note that such participant subject headings include not only those where either the entry element and/or subdivision are not valid LCSH, but also those where all elements may be LCSH terms, but are not valid in the particular combination. For example, French language--Texts which must be tagged SUT-P, because Texts is a valid subdivision only under the names of rare or exotic languages.

"Proposal for Reforms to Improve Subject Searching"

Sanford Berman

Frankly, it would be irresponsible to advocate the destruction of LCSH, even though proposed substitutes might be "theoretically" purer and intellectually more appealing, because 1) most new systems—like PRECIS—would not mesh into existing files; 2) split files are anathema to maximum catalog use; 3) substitute schemes would still be no more effective than the people who apply them; and 4) all types of American libraries have an incalculable investment in an existing scheme like LCSH.

The sane, conservative, and economic approach must necessarily be to make what we already have work better, and to introduce reforms at such a deliberate pace that understaffed and underfunded institutions can reasonably manage them.

The following basic reforms in both vocabulary and LC subject-heading-assignment policy would substantially improve subject searching in either conventional or online environments:

- Modernization of various awkward, archaic, or unfamiliar LCSH headings.

- Prompt recognition of new topics.

- Validation of still unestablished "old" topics.

- Introduction of appropriate *see* references, which could quickly switch a search on track.

- Greater number of subject tracings for a given work.

- Expansion of the assignment policy to include headings for literary genres and for thematic topics applied to individual novels, plays, and other literature.

- Gradual conversion of all inverted forms to natural order headings to achieve consistency and eliminate uncertainty.

Reprinted by permission of the American Library Association, "Proposal for Reforms to Improve Subject Searching" by Sanford Berman from *American Libraries*, April 1984, p. 254; copyright © 1984 by ALA.

Two final observations:

- The above "reforms" probably require a dramatic change in structure and/or management at the Library of Congress. They may also require more money and staff, something the entire library community should support.

- Some responsibility remains with the local or regional library or utility that performs maintenance and authority control to see that useful notes and cross-references actually appear in the catalog database and that notes and *see also* references are displayed for searchers.

"Library of Congress Subject Headings as an Online Retrieval Tool:
Structural Considerations"

Lois Mai Chan

Introduction

The Library of Congress Subject Headings (*LCSH*) system, originally designed for the manual, card catalog, is forging forward in the online environment. Since *Anglo-American Cataloguing Rules* (*AACR2*), *LCSH* has become the most discussed topic in the literature concerning bibliographic control. There have been many recent studies of subject access in the online environment.[1] Numerous articles have been written about the shortcomings and insufficiencies of the *LCSH* system in this regard, and many suggestions have been made for its improvement.[2] Most of these concern aspects of the vocabulary: its currency, its entry vocabulary (by far the most frequently mentioned), and the enrichment or enhancement of subject headings assigned to individual documents. This paper proposes to examine some of the structural aspects of *LCSH* in the context of online information and retrieval, to explore how various features of online retrieval may affect the performance of Library of Congress subject headings.

The Library of Congress (LC) MARC bibliographic database is available for retrieval in online catalogs in libraries, in a number of large commercial information retrieval systems, such as Lockheed's DIALOG and SDC's ORBIT, and through bibliographic utilities such as RLIN and WLN. Through the 6xx fields in those records we have opportunities for studying *LCSH* as a subject authority or thesaurus in the online environment. Such studies are particularly propitious as we look forward to having the Subject Authority File as an online thesaurus.

The features of online information retrieval to be discussed in this paper are: (1) keyword or component word search (including truncation), (2) Boolean operations (including word proximity or word adjacency), (3) limiting, (4) the synonym operator (including stemming), and (5) online thesaurus display. These features, which have been developed over the last two decades, are present to a greater or lesser degree in commercial retrieval systems such as DIALOG or ORBIT, in bibliographic utilities such as RLIN and WLN, and in online library catalogs. No current

---

Reprinted, by permission of the author, from a paper presented at the Symposium on Subject Analysis, 29-30 March 1985, Durham, N.C., sponsored by the School of Library and Information Science, North Carolina Central University.

system can boast all of them, but we can expect to see more and more of these features in more and more systems as time goes on. It is important, therefore, to take a theoretical look at the question: given a particular feature, what may be expected or considered in terms of the structure of *LCSH*.

Online Retrieval Features

By way of introduction, I will discuss briefly each of the online information retrieval features to be considered in this paper.

Keyword or Component Word Search

One of the major differences between manual and online information retrieval systems is the ability of the latter to provide multiple access points to a multi-word heading through keyword or component word search. A manual system is predicated on a linear approach; each subject entry, regardless of the number of words it contains, has one access point—the initial word, or entry element—only. In an online system, on the other hand, there may be as many access points as there are words in the entry: a heading such as **Beverage processing machinery industry** or **Automobiles—Motors—Carburetors—Maintenance and repair** can be accessed only through the entry word BEVERAGE or AUTOMOBILES in a manual catalog, while in an online system it can be accessed through any of the four or five words that make up the heading. This is true of headings with subdivisions and/or qualifiers as well as for phrase headings. In some systems, the additional access points may be limited to subfields, i.e., the initial words in subdivisions, only.

To enhance the keyword search capability, many systems also allow truncation which enables the retrieval of terms stemming from the same root and those with variant spellings. The most common truncation is single or multiple character terminal truncation. Some systems also provide middle or initial character truncation.

Boolean Operations

The capability of Boolean operations is probably the most distinctive feature of online information retrieval. The most common Boolean operators are AND, OR, and NOT. The ability to combine and exclude sets or terms in a search can only be laboriously achieved in a manual system but can be easily manipulated in an online system. Most of the commercial online systems and an increasing number of online catalogs provide this feature. It is this feature that makes the post-coordinate approach in information retrieval feasible and effective.

Basic keyword searching operates on individual words. A more sophisticated searching capability, called word proximity or word adjacency, operates on combinations of words defined by proximity and/or order. This capability greatly enhances the precision of keyword searching.

Limiting

Another online feature is the ability to limit a set of retrieved citations by certain criteria. The most common limiting features are year of publication, document type, and language. Some of the systems also allow limiting by geographic area.

Synonym Operation

The synonym operator, a less common feature, acts as a hidden *see* reference system. Internally, synonymous or equivalent terms are linked so that users may use any of them and achieve the same results as if they had put in the valid term. This feature requires that the bibliographic records are linked to the thesaurus.

Online Thesaurus Display

Online display of the thesaurus helps users select appropriate search terms. Online display of *LCSH* is not yet commonly available, and the methods and formats of displaying *LCSH* even in the more sophisticated systems leave much to be desired—particularly with respect to subdivisions and cross references. Nonetheless, online thesaurus display as applied to other indexing systems such as ERIC and MeSH gives an indication of what is possible and feasible in the online environment. The potential is very great. Online systems can display a thesaurus in various forms—alphabetical, classified, keyword—and by hierarchical clusters. Some though not all of these online thesaurus display systems include the number of items retrieved from the bibliographic file for each term used in indexing.

Library of Congress Subject Headings

For effective online information retrieval, there are a number of contributing factors, among which is the ability to retrieve relevant records, to broaden the recall if it is too small, and to narrow it if it is too large. In this section, we will examine how specific features of online retrieval systems and structural features of *LCSH* may be used together to achieve the best results in subject searching. In some cases, the two complement each other; in other cases, the two approaches overlap or duplicate each other's functions.

The structural aspects we will look at are the principles of uniform and unique headings, forms of main headings, subdivisions, and cross references.

Principles of Uniform and Unique Headings

Two of the fundamental principles of *LCSH* are that headings be uniform and unique: that each subject be represented by only one heading and that no heading stand for more than one subject. Although there has been some relaxation of the uniform heading principle over the years (for example, the duplicate entries made for bilateral foreign relations), the principle holds generally. Because of the linear access of manual catalogs, the principle greatly limits the accessibility of subjects represented by multi-term headings; it is for this reason that *LCSH* has not compared favorably with multiple-entry systems such as PRECIS in terms of access. However, with the multi-word access through keyword or component word searching available in online systems, the constraint of the single-entry approach is to a large extent eliminated. In the online environment, the principle of uniform headings retains its advantages of collocating materials on the same subject and minimizing the number of subject entries without the disadvantage of limiting access points.

The principle of unique headings, a corollary of the principle of uniform headings, requires that each heading represent only one subject. It was designed to ensure precision in retrieval by minimizing the adverse effects of homographs. For example, consider a botanist searching for information on the plant rape. He or she will find the unique heading **Rape (Plant)** much more effective as a search term than the single word **Rape**. The ability to achieve precision is even more important in online retrieval systems than in manual ones because of the different mechanism for browsing the records online. Using unique headings is an effective way to eliminate irrelevant records.

Forms of Main Headings

The various grammatical forms used in main headings in *LCSH* function in somewhat different ways in the online and manual environments. This is particularly true for phrase headings and headings with qualifiers.

Phrase Headings. In the *LCSH* system, compound or complex subjects are generally represented by conjunctive phrase headings or prepositional phrase headings. Conjunctive phrase headings were designed for two purposes: (1) to name affinitives or, in a few cases, opposites which are usually treated together in works, for instance, **Boats and boating; Hotels, taverns, etc.** and **Good and evil**; and (2) to represent relationships, for instance, **Education and state** and **Church and labor**.[3] The Library of Congress has been moving away from the former and now favors establishing each object or concept as a separate heading. In the manual catalog, this separation means access points under each of the subjects. In the online system, although the separation makes little difference in terms of access, it helps to separate material that treats only one of the subjects named in the compound heading and thus contributes to precision. In the case of conjunctive phrase headings expressing general relationships, for instance, **Alcohol and children**, the precoordinated form is the only choice in a manual catalog if one does not wish to have documents treating the relationship interfiled with those treating each subject separately. In the online system, on the other hand, documents treating the subjects in relation to each other can be retrieved either through phrase searching or through keyword searching with a Boolean operation. In fact, in a number of online systems, when a phrase containing the conjunctive "and" is entered, a Boolean operation is performed automatically. In other words, it makes little difference if a document has been indexed under a phrase heading such as **Alcohol and children** or under two separate headings: 1. **Alcohol**; 2. **Children**.

Prepositional phrase headings were designed for three purposes:[4] (1) to express a single concept which cannot be named by a single noun, for instance, **Boards of trade** and **Spheres of influence**; (2) to represent an aspect or facet of a subject, for instance, **Cataloging of art**; and (3) to represent a relationship between distinctive and otherwise independent subjects, for instance, **Religion in literature; Children in pornography; Church work with children**; etc. Few headings belong to the first category. The second function is better handled through subdivision which is the current LC policy. The most common use of prepositional phrase headings is, therefore, to represent relationships. Such headings are different from conjunctive phrase headings in that the preposition often specifies the relationship and therefore renders the heading more specific. For example, the phrases "music and art" and "music in art" have different meanings. Removing the preposition obliterates the relationship. In such cases, the pre-coordinated prepositional phrase heading helps to achieve precision in retrieval, while keyword searching will retrieve irrelevant documents. For example, using the phrase heading **Plants, Effect of poisons on** enables the retrieval of only those documents on how poisons affect plants, while combining the terms "plants" and "poison" results in retrieving documents on poisonous plants as well.

Certain prepositional phrase headings represent relationships between subjects that are unique or unambiguous, for example, the heading **Cookery for cardiacs** and **Self-defense for children**. In these cases, using separate terms with the Boolean operator "AND" in searching yields similar results to using the pre-coordinated terms.

Inverted Headings. Ever since the inception of the LCSH system, inverted headings have been allowed in order to bring the "significant" word forward,[5] for example, **Chemistry, Organic** and **Plants, Effect of light on**. Because there is often no sure way to determine the "significant word" in a multi-word phrase, *LCSH* shows many inconsistencies, an aspect of the system that has drawn frequent criticism. In systems that allow keyword or component word searching, it is a moot question whether one word in a string is more significant than the other or others in terms of accessibility. Of course, word order is still important for an online thesaurus display limited to an alphabetical list of terms without related-term display and cross references. But as online catalogs become more sophisticated, particularly in terms of file indexing and thesaurus display, the significance of word order in headings will diminish even further.

Headings with Qualifiers. In *LCSH*, qualifiers are added to topical headings to distinguish between homographs and to identify obscure or highly technical terms. They are also used with many name headings in accordance with, or in a manner compatible with, descriptive cataloging practice. They appear with the following types of headings:

(1) Topical headings containing homographs, for example, **Cold (Disease)**; **Collisions (Nuclear physics)**; and **Crowns (Dentistry)**.

(2) Topical headings containing obscure or highly technical terms, for example, **Cachets (Philately)**; **Shape theory (Topology)**; and **Rheology (Biology)**.

(3) Music headings specifying instrumental or vocal parts, for example, **Trios (Oboe, harp, violoncello)**; **Rondos (Horn with orchestra)**; and **Sacred songs (High voice)**.

(4) Geographic and corporate headings (with generic, type-of-jurisdiction, geographic, or combination qualifiers), for example,

Generic qualifiers
Royal Oak (Battleship)
Schweppes (Firm)

Type-of-jurisdiction qualifiers
New York (State)
Naples (Kingdom)
Pompeii (Ancient city)

Geographic qualifiers
Rome (Italy)
New York (N.Y.)
Left Bank (Paris, France)
Church of God (Cleveland, Tenn.)

Combination qualifiers
Rhodes (Greece : Island)
Auschwitz (Poland : Concentration camp)
Misti (Peru : Volcano)
Quebec (Quebec : County)

(5) Name headings for gods and goddesses, for legendary, mythological, and fictitious characters, and for other named entities, for example,

Apollo (Greek deity)
Pregnant man (Legendary character)
Draupadi (Hindu mythology)
Snoopy (Fictitious character)
Holmes, Sherlock (Fictitious character)
Dancer's Image (Race horse)

In online systems with keyword or component word searching, a qualifier may provide additional access to the subject represented by the main heading. A heading with a generic qualifier, a qualifier that gives the context for the main term of the heading, for example, **Shape theory (Topology)**, is in effect a reversed classed entry. Headings of this type provide a bi-level approach in online retrieval—in our example, from the topic (shape theory) to the subdiscipline (topology).

Headings with qualifiers representing different facets, used most frequently with music headings, enable the gathering of material based on different criteria. For example, headings such as **Concertos** or **Sonatas** qualified by the names of instruments enable retrieval by both form of music and medium of performance.

Headings with geographic qualifiers provide bi-level access, to the place in question and to the larger place used as the qualifier. In some cases, a heading may contain more than two levels; for example, **Left Bank (Paris, France)** and **Chinatown (San Francisco, Calif.)** each containing three levels: the city section, the city, and the country or first order political division. Headings that contain both a geographic and a generic qualifier provide yet another dimension of access point, for example, **Auschwitz (Poland : Concentration camp)**.

Using a qualifier as a gathering device works well in the current system when headings in a particular category are regularly and consistently qualified, as are headings for local places, headings for mythological, legendary, and fictitious characters, and headings for musical forms. However, most topical headings receive qualifiers only to resolve conflicts or identify obscure terms; qualifiers used for such purposes have less value as gathering devices.

Subdivisions

Subdivisions have two functions, to increase the specificity of headings and to subarrange large files.[6] Information retrieval is essentially a function of file partitioning. The searcher begins with a large file or database from which a relatively small file of relevant records are retrieved by eliminating irrelevant records. Cataloging and indexing provide means of organizing the large file into subfiles. Searching is a process of selecting the particular subfile that contains relevant documents. In the manual catalog, one begins with a particular letter of the alphabet, thus eliminating those files under the other letters. Then, one selects the name of the appropriate subject and thereby eliminates other subjects beginning with the same word. This process goes on until a file of relevant documents is identified. Subdivisions contribute greatly towards this process. The citation order of subdivisions is important in a manual catalog because the searching process proceeds letter-by-letter and word-by-word, following the order in which the heading has been pre-coordinated. In online systems, on the other hand, a searcher does not have to wade through each word or subdivision as pre-coordinated; any of the words or subdivisions in the heading may be used for collocation. Thus, in online systems, terms in subdivisions provide additional access points and means of gathering, and citation order only matters when it determines or affects the meaning of a heading.

Certain online searching capabilities enhance or support some of the functions of subdivisions as originally designed. In this respect, let us consider topical, geographical, period, and form subdivisions.

Topical Subdivision. Topical subdivision contributes towards the identification of individual concepts in a complex subject. Since subdivisions are individually tagged as subfields in the MARC record, they facilitate access to individual component concepts of a subject, and are particularly useful in online systems that provide access to subfields but have no individual keyword searching capability.

Geographic Subdivision. A distinctive and almost unique feature of geographic subdivision in *LCSH* is indirect subdivision, the interposition of the name of a larger place between the main heading and the local subdivision. This particular form is tantamount to classed entry in which terms in the inclusion relationship appear in the same heading. Its justification, as stated by David Judson Haykin, is:

> Indirect subdivision assumes that the interest and significance of certain subjects are inseparable from the larger area—the country or state—or that the study of subordinate geographic areas is best considered as contributing to the study of the larger area.[7]

In other words, indirect subdivision has long been considered to have the advantage of enabling collocation on a broader level of geographic area than the specific place in question. Direct subdivision, on the other hand, has the double advantages of ease in application and ease in use. Furthermore, current Library of Congress policy regarding indirect subdivision has come under a great deal of criticism because of its many exceptions and inconsistent application over the years.

In online systems, the advantages of both direct and indirect subdivision may be realized by using direct subdivision in all cases. The reason this is so is that *AACR2* and Library of Congress cataloging policies require that headings containing local place names be qualified by the names of larger areas, for instance, **Munich (Germany), San Francisco (Calif.)**, and so on. Thus, qualifiers may be used as a gathering device in online retrieval in much of the same way as the interposing elements in indirect subdivision. Currently, with a few exceptions, the same areas are used in indirect subdivision as are used for qualifiers. Using direct subdivision and relying on qualifiers for collocation would enable the same search statement to be used whether a given geographical entity appears in main or subordinate position in a heading. This cannot be done with a single statement now because of the abbreviations used in many qualifiers.

The Geographic Area Code (GAC) of the MARC format may also be useful in online searches involving place. The GAC was developed by the Library of Congress "as an aid to area specialists taking a subject approach to the material" and the codes are "applied to works for which the assigned subject heading contains a geographic term in any form or position or when the text of a work has a geographic orientation."[8] Although the GAC is not yet used as an access point in many of the online systems, it has great potential as a feature of online subject access, particularly when used in combination with other fields or as a limiting device. GAC's normally show country or first order political division and so are on the same level as indirect geographic subdivision. Thus, the GAC provides a very efficient means of gathering documents relating to a broader geographic area than the local place subdivision. A particular advantage of using the GAC is that it often shows geographic orientation even when subject headings are not geographically subdivided.

Period Subdivision. Two kinds of period subdivisions are used in *LCSH*. Historical subdivision, by far the most common, brings out the period covered in the content of the document. The less common type represents date of publication. One example is the subdivision **—Early works to 1800** found under many scientific and technical headings; another is the practice of using dates or date spans under certain voluminous headings to partition the files by *when* the material appeared—for instance, **Education—1945-1964**.[9] This latter feature is particularly useful to someone scanning large files in a manual catalog. In an online system, however, the same screening can be accomplished by limiting by date. This approach is machine-efficient because fixed-field codes can be used. It is particularly effective because it can be applied to all subjects and any year or span of years, not just in cases where pre-coordinated headings have been assigned.

Form Subdivision. Haykin defined form subdivision as "the extension of a subject heading based on the form or arrangement of the subject matter in the book. In other words, it represents what the book is, rather than what it is about."[10] As such, it occupies a rather peculiar place in *LCSH*. It does not relate directly to the subject content of the document but, like the form subheadings used previously in descriptive cataloging, it serves to subarrange large files as well as to provide searchers with useful screening information. Identifying documents by form has become a function of subject headings probably because no other aspect of the card catalog performs it.

The MARC record carries coded information on many common document types: periodicals, bibliographies, biographies, indexes, and so on. Thus, in online systems, some of the functions normally allotted to form subdivision may be fulfilled by searching or limiting by document or publication type. Using such information is machine-efficient. Furthermore, it supplements the form subdivisions in *LCSH* because, by tradition, in Library of Congress practice, certain form subdivisions are not further subdivided by other form subdivisions even when applicable. For example, the form subdivisions **—Congresses** and **—Directories** are not further subdivided by the subdivision **—Periodicals**.[11]

Language Subdivision. Language subdivisions are provided under a small number of headings to indicate the language of the document. Like form subdivision, language subdivision represents something other than subject content, for example, **Mathematics—Dictionaries—German**. The usefulness of this type of subdivision is currently limited because it has not been used extensively in *LCSH* probably due to the fact that the Library of Congress collection originally contained mostly English language books. Yet, as more and more foreign language materials are collected by the Library of Congress and as the number of multi-lingual databases increases, the ability to separate materials in different languages on a subject becomes important. In online systems, this can be done by using the MARC language code, an approach that is particularly effective because it is not limited to the small number of headings with language-of-document subdivisions.

Cross References and Other User Aids

Cross references and other user aids have been the most neglected aspects of manual catalogs, and it appears that the same thing can be said for online systems providing subject access based on *LCSH*. Few systems offer online vocabulary display of *LCSH*; and not all of those include cross references. Let us now ask how well *LCSH* can serve, structurally, as a base for online vocabulary display and other user aids such as synonym operation.

For thesaurus display, the answer is, *LCSH* will serve quite well for initial-word access to headings and cross references, and fairly well for a keyword list. For the latter, however, because of redundancy, considerable editing might be required to ensure a workable product.

Synonym operation, which functions as an invisible lead-in device from the searcher's input terms to the valid subject headings, can be based on the *see* references in *LCSH* as they currently stand. Another useful online feature which serves as a lead-in device is truncation which can be used to collocate terms stemming from the same root or those with variant spellings.

The *see also* references in *LCSH*, as they stand now, are a long way from being usable as a base for hierarchical or other related-term display. Because of the lack of rigorous rules or policies in the past, the current syndetic structure of *LCSH* does not display hierarchical structures consistently. It is good to note that the Library of Congress has recently made a move in the right direction by tightening the structure of hierarchical and related-term references. A properly constructed syndetic structure can be a powerful tool in online searching because it enables scaling up and down the hierarchy and facilitates the broadening and narrowing of search results.

Recommendations

With the increasing availability of MARC records for online searching, LC subject headings are assuming greater significance as an online retrieval tool and so are attracting increasing professional attention. Much has been said about the need to improve and enhance the vocabulary. This paper has pointed out the parallel importance of reconsidering the structural aspects of *LCSH* in the context of online retrieval, and has shown how various *LCSH* features can be used in conjunction with online searching capabilities to improve performances.

Improving the controlled vocabulary is only one of several factors contributing to effective subject retrieval. Of equal importance is online systems design with respect to the methods and policies of file indexing and the availability of retrieval features. These aspects are outside the scope of this paper, but must be taken into consideration in contemplating the future of *LCSH*. In this regard, I wish to note that the timing for implementing any potential change of *LCSH* may be crucial. Some of the proposals made here are contingent on the availability of quite sophisticated online features. Not all online catalogs have such features at the moment. A given change may enhance both efficiency and effectiveness on sophisticated systems but be detrimental in online catalogs not possessing the particular feature or features and in manual searching. It is important, therefore, that the Library of Congress tailor its changes not only to the needs of highly sophisticated systems, but also to those of other systems. Given the rapid development in hardware and software in computer technology, it is perhaps reasonable to hope that what seems highly sophisticated or unfeasible now will soon become commonplace in online catalogs.

In contemplating the structural aspects of *LCSH* in terms of online retrieval, I would like to summarize the possible changes suggested in this discussion:

(1) Adopt natural word order for phrase headings.

(2) Eliminate duplicate entries which have been made in the past in order to bring various elements in a heading to the filing position, for instance, **United States—Foreign relations—China** and **China—Foreign relations—United States**.

(3) Rely more heavily on post-coordination for complex subjects by establishing various elements in a compound or complex heading as separate headings, for example, the two headings, 1. **Federal aid**; 2. **Health maintenance organizations** in place of the heading **Federal aid to health maintenance organizations.** This should not be done, however, in cases where the meaning of the

heading would be affected by the separation, as in the case of **Children in pornography**. Pre-coordination could be reserved for cases where it is needed because citation order or linking words affect the meaning of a heading.

(4) Adopt consistent patterns of citation order between topic and place.

(5) Adopt direct geographic subdivision on all levels of places.

(6) Eliminate subdivisions whose functions can be fulfilled by information in other fields of the MARC record. These include major form subdivisions representing document types, period subdivisions for imprint dates, and language subdivisions indicating the language in which the document is presented.

Some of my recommendations have the effect of reducing the length of the indexing string. This is an aspect of heading structure which has not been discussed much in print but is very important in online searching and file indexing. Although most headings in the Library of Congress system are relatively short, there are many very long ones, most particularly those with several subdivisions. Currently, many systems limit the length of the search string; some allow only forty characters. In such systems, long headings are often truncated in the vocabulary display, and later elements in the heading may not even be indexed for access. And, irrespective of system constraints, long index strings are difficult for users to handle: for one thing, they must depend on the thesaurus; for another, long headings increase the chances of making typing errors on input. Recent catalog studies have shown that most users enter relatively short search terms, and that they have difficulty matching Library of Congress subject headings and their subdivisions.[12] In online retrieval, it is no longer necessary to always rely on pre-coordination and long headings in order to achieve specificity.

Conclusion

The Library of Congress subject headings system is a viable tool in online subject retrieval. Many of its current recognized shortcomings are mitigated not exacerbated by the properties of online information processing systems. How successfully *LCSH* will fare in the online age depends on how well the system adapts to new requirements of online searching and how well online systems design capitalizes on the special features of *LCSH* and the unique capabilities of sophisticated online retrieval. The structural aspects of *LCSH*, as well as its terminological aspects, must be re-examined and re-evaluated. In this re-examination, we must consider not only the vocabulary of *LCSH* itself, but also how we can best make use of the opportunities afforded by modern information retrieval.

Notes

[1] Pauline A. Cochrane, "Modern Subject Access in the Online Age," *American Libraries* 15: 80-83, 145-150, 250-255, 336-339, 438-442 (1984); Karen Markey, *Subject Searching in Library Catalogs Before and After the Introduction of Online Catalogs*, OCLC Library, Information, and Computer Science Series, 4 (Dublin, Ohio: OCLC, 1984); and Carol A. Mandel with the assistance of Judith Herschman, "Subject Access in the Online Catalog" (Report prepared for the Council on Library Resources, 1981).

[2] Pauline A. Cochrane and Monika Kirtland, *1. Critical Views of LCSH—The Library of Congress Subject Headings; A Bibliographic and Bibliometric Essay*; *2. Analysis of Vocabulary Control in the Library of Congress List of Subject Headings (LCSH)* (Syracuse, N.Y.: ERIC Clearinghouse on Information Resources, 1981).

[3] David Judson Haykin, *Subject Headings: A Practical Guide* (Washington, D.C.: Government Printing Office, 1951), 24.

[4] Ibid., 22-23.

[5] Charles A. Cutter, *Rules for a Dictionary Catalog*, 4th ed. (Washington, D.C.: Government Printing Office, 1904), 72-74; Haykin, *Subject Headings*, 22; and Lois Mai Chan, *Library of Congress Subject Headings: Principles and Application* (Littleton, Colo.: Libraries Unlimited, 1978), 54-59.

[6] Haykin, *Subject Headings*, 27.

[7] Ibid., 30.

[8] Library of Congress, MARC Development Office, *Books: A MARC Format: Specifications for Magnetic Tapes Containing Catalog Records for Books*, 5th ed. (Washington, D.C.: Library of Congress, 1972), 29.

[9] Library of Congress, Subject Cataloging Division, *Subject Cataloging Manual: Subject Headings*, prelim. ed. (Washington, D.C.: Library of Congress, 1984), H1085.

[10] Haykin, *Subject Headings*, 27.

[11] Library of Congress, *Subject Cataloging Manual*, H1460; and "The Subdivision 'Periodicals'," *Cataloging Service Bulletin* 3:14-15 (Winter 1979).

[12] Markey, *Subject Searching in Library Catalogs*, 67, 72.

"The Period Subdivision in Subject Headings"

Lois Mai Chan

According to the Library of Congress Subject Headings *list and the* Sears List of Subject Headings, *there are at least six different forms in which period subdivisions under main subject headings are constructed, some with verbal designations, others with numerical dates. The diversity in form creates tremendous problems in the filing, especially by machine, and use of the catalog cards bearing such headings. A modification of the various forms into one uniformed type has been proposed in the Hines-Harris computer filing code. This paper attempts to examine this revised format with reference to the basic nature and function of the period subdivision in subject headings and with regard to its use from the catalog user's point of view.*

In recent years, largely due to the problems encountered in filing by machine, there has been frequent discussion in library literature regarding the formation of period subdivisions under subject headings. The basic problem involves the interfiling, in chronological order, of period subdivisions formed by words or phrases and those formed by numerical dates. Of the various solutions recommended, the most feasible seems to be the consistent formation of period subdivisions by dates, as proposed in the Hines-Harris computer filing code.[1] However, there seems to be a certain hesitation in accepting this revision outside of the computer field, as pointed out by Kelley L. Cartwright, "If LC were to change the heading 'U.S.—History—Civil War' to 'U.S.—History—1861-1865 (Civil War),' then that majority of libraries that have, and for some time to come will continue to have, card catalogs, would legitimately object to the necessity of interfiling headings so different in form."[2]

This paper attempts to determine whether there are logical or inherent reasons for resisting the proposed revision of period subdivision in subject headings. The discussion will be based on an examination of the most widely used subject headings lists in this country—*Subject Headings Used in the Dictionary Catalogs of the Library of Congress*, and the *Sears List of Subject Headings*.

Reprinted by permission of the American Library Association, "The Period Subdivision in Subject Headings" by Lois Mai Chan from *Library Resources & Technical Services*, vol. 16, Fall 1972, pp. 453-59; copyright © 1972 by ALA.

The various subdivisions under subject headings do not represent a logical development of the dictionary catalog. As Paul S. Dunkin has pointed out, "Subdivision is the mark of the alphabetico-classed catalog" and was adopted by Cutter on the basis of "arrangement rather than on theory of entry."[3] The proliferation of library material must have necessitated the subdivisions as a convenient means of arranging the cards.

Since certain subject areas, such as history, the politics and government of individual countries, music, and national literatures, lend themselves to historical or chronological treatment, the period subdivisions were introduced. Each of these subjects requires a different division of historical or chronological periods. As stated by David Judson Haykin, "The period subdivisions used should either correspond to generally recognized epochs in the history of the place or should represent spans of time frequently treated in books, whether they possess historic unity or not."[4] It is impossible to apply a uniform division of periods to all countries or to all subjects. The history of a country is subdivided by the ruling houses and important events or significant dates, and national literatures are usually subdivided by literary movements or trends.

However, there is also diversity in the formation of period subdivisions for which there is little apparent logical reason. According to both the LC and the Sears lists, there are at least six ways of constructing a subject heading with period subdivisions. The Sears list differs from the LC list only in the degree of subdivision in period subdivisions, not in form. The examples used throughout this paper are taken from the 7th edition of the LC list.

(1) An inverted "noun, adjective" heading, for example:

>Sculpture, Ancient
>>Baroque
>>Gothic
>>Medieval
>>Renaissance
>>Rococo
>>Romanesque[5]

Modifiers such as "Ancient," "Renaissance," "Rococo," and "Modern" denote both period and subject characteristics. Such headings are not true period subdivisions, and therefore are interfiled alphabetically with other subheadings that have no period connotation.

However, in certain cases, some of the same adjectives are used as period subdivisions, instead of as modifiers, for instance:

>Music—History and criticism—Ancient
>Music—History and criticism—Medieval.

The *ALA Rules for Filing Catalog Cards* are quite explicit on this point:

>The divisions ANCIENT, PRIMITIVE, MEDIEVAL, RENAISSANCE, BAROQUE, MODERN, etc. are arranged alphabetically, not chronologically, even when followed by a date (e.g., HISTORY, MODERN—20th CENTURY), except when used as further divisions of the subdivisions HISTORY or HISTORY AND CRITICISM (e.g. MUSIC—HISTORY AND CRITICISM—ANCIENT).[6]

Note that in the latter case, the headings are filed chronologically.

This type of subdivision is usually not followed by dates. The filer and the user are assumed to know the proper sequence of these divisions, e.g. "Medieval" comes between "Ancient" and "Renaissance" or "Modern." Although this creates problems in filing by machine, to the manual filer, and the catalog user, at least, it poses relatively few problems, since most of these terms, such as "Ancient" and "Modern," are indicative enough.

(2) A main subject heading with a subdivision in the form of a noun or phrase (without any dates) clearly denoting a chronological period or historical event, such as,

> English drama—Early modern and Elizabethan
> English drama—Restoration
>
> American literature—Colonial period
> American literature—Revolutionary period
>
> U.S.—History—Colonial period
> U.S.—History—Revolution
> U.S.—History—Civil War

In filing, according to both the ALA Rules and the order in which they appear in the LC *Subject Headings* list, these subdivisions are arranged chronologically (instead of alphabetically with the other forms of subdivisions); that is, "U.S.—History—Revolution" is filed as if written "U.S.—History—1775-1783," and "U.S.—History—Civil War" as if written "U.S.—History—1861-1865."

This peculiarity creates a number of problems. The difficulty in instructing a machine to file these headings in the proper chronological order is obvious and has often been commented on in print. The manual filer must mentally translate the period subdivision into dates, for these headings are arranged chronologically without chronological (i.e., numerical) designation. If the filing rules in this particular regard create numerous problems for the librarians, for the average reader they must be close to a mystery. Moreover, even if the reader's awareness of the filing rules is taken for granted, it must also be assumed that he has a familiarity with the chronological order of the events under that particular subject in order to find the headings in the proper places. This means the reader also must insert the dates mentally in the headings. Haykin, recognizing this problem, made the remark: "The date ... makes the sequence of periods in the catalog clear, while the name, if used alone, would make it difficult, sometimes perhaps impossible, for the reader to find." He offered an explanation for the use of such subdivisions in the LC *Subject Headings* list: "Because terminal dates are not always easy to establish, or because there is disagreement about them, or because certain periods and events are familiar to readers, they are sometimes omitted. This practice should, however, be avoided as far as possible."[7]

Most of the headings with period subdivisions of this type occur under American history and American literature. This fact clearly shows a national bias in the early principles of forming subject headings, as stated in the preface to the ALA *List of Subject Headings for Use in Dictionary Catalogs*, a forerunner of the LC *Subject Headings* list:

> The general principle of decision is that the heading should be that under
> which it is supposed that the majority of educated Americans will look.[8]

It is probably true that "the majority of educated Americans" know when the Civil War or the American Revolution took place and can mentally supply the dates to the headings when they use the catalog. However, in the case of many others, especially foreign readers, one cannot assume a similar degree of familiarity. One cannot expect them to be able to always recall the dates of these events and to place them in the proper chronological sequence. With the increasing international scope in the use of Library of Congress catalogs and cards, this national bias should not be retained.

(3) A main heading with a subdivision containing the name of a historical period or event followed by dates.

> English literature—Middle English (1100-1500)
> English literature—Early modern (to 1700)
>
> Great Britain—History—Wars of the Roses, 1455-1485
> Great Britain—History—House of York, 1461-1485
> Great Britain—History—Modern period, 1485-

This form is a modification of type 2. The period subdivisions of this type, when used with headings for history of foreign countries, almost always contain dates after the name of the period, probably with the assumption that the average American reader is less familiar with historical facts of foreign countries. The filer and the user, when dealing with this type of heading, need not supply the missing dates, but still must transpose the name of the period and the dates in order to place the headings in the proper sequence. In other words, the heading "Great Britain—History—Wars of the Roses, 1455-1485" is located in the catalog as if written "Great Britain—History—1455-1485, Wars of the Roses."

(4) A main heading with the name of the century as a subdivision.

> English fiction—19th century
> English fiction—20th century

These subdivisions are arranged as if written "1800-1899" (for nineteenth century), "1900-1999" (for twentieth century), etc. This type of subdivision usually occurs when there is a lack of a distinctive name for the period or event and in cases where a longer period of time than a single event or movement has to be covered.

(5) A main heading with a period subdivision constructed with the preposition "to" followed by a date.

> Great Britain—History—To 1485
> Great Britain—History—To 1066
> Great Britain—History—To 449

Although this type of heading may cause difficulty in filing by machine, it presents little problem for the manual filer and the user. These headings usually precede all the other period subdivisions, i.e., as the beginning period subdivision under a subject.

(6) A main heading (often with aspect subdivision) with dates alone as period subdivision.

> English language—Grammar—1500-1800
> English language—Grammar—1800-1870
> English language—Grammar—1870-

  Great Britain—History—1714-1837
  Great Britain—History—1760-1789
  Great Britain—History—1789-1820

Among the different forms listed above, this is the most logical and straightforward.

  From the examples cited above, it is obvious that there is no consistency or uniformity in the formation of the period subdivisions. The various forms often appear simultaneously under the same main heading. U.S. and British history will serve as examples:

U.S.—History
 —French and Indian War, 1755-1763
 —Revolution
 —1783-1865
 —Confederation, 1783-1789
 —Constitutional period, 1789-1809

* * * * *

 —War of 1898
 —20th century
 —1919-1933

Great Britain—History
 —To 55 B.C.
 —Roman period, 55 B.C.-449 A.D.
 —Anglo-Saxon period, 449-1066
 —1066-1687

* * * * *

 —Commonwealth and Protectorate, 1649-1660
 —1660-1714
 —Restoration, 1660-1688
 —Revolution of 1688
 —1689-1714
 —18th century

  There are no apparent logical or inherent reasons why the period subdivisions should be formed in six different ways, for they all serve to give the subject a chronological or historical treatment. The diversity in form creates numerous problems while serving no useful purpose. On the other hand, the revised form proposed for use in the computer filing code appears to be a logical and the most practical one. If all the period subdivisions were formulated in one format:

Main heading—(subject subdivision, if any)—dates (name of period or
 event, if desired)

the problems discussed above with regard to both filing and using these headings could be largely eliminated. The period subdivisions adopted by the Canadian Library of Parliament for use with Canadian history in the French catalogue follow precisely this format:

e.g. Canada—Histoire
— 1534-1763, Régime français
— 1534-1701
— 1701-1763

* * * * *

— 1812, Guerre de
— 1837-1838, Rébellion
— 1841-1867
— 1866-1870, Invasions fénianes[9]

One can see little reason for objecting to this revision, except a tenacious adherence to tradition or habits; for, in fact, subject headings with period subdivisions are being filed as if they were constructed according to the above format, e.g., "U.S.—History—Civil War" filed as if written "U.S.—History—1861-1865 (Civil War)." The revision will affect the outward forms of the headings only, and will not disturb the order of the cards already filed in the catalog. On the other hand, it will facilitate both the filing and the using of the cards, as the filers and the users are no longer required to supply the dates mentally, or to transpose them to the proper place.

Notes

[1] Hines, Theodore C. and Jessica L. Harris, *Computer Filing of Index, Bibliographic, and Catalog Entries*, Newark, N.J.: Bro-Dart Foundation, 1966, p. 35. Also, Harris and Hines, "The Mechanization of the Filing Rules for Library Catalogs: Dictionary or Divided," *LRTS*, 14:509 (Fall 1970), and Jessica Lee Harris, *Subject Analysis: Computer Implications of Rigorous Definition*, Metuchen, N.J.: The Scarecrow Press, 1970, p.171, 185.

[2] Cartwright, Kelley L., "Mechanization and Library Filing Rules," *Advances in Librarianship*, ed. Melvin J. Voigt, 1:83 (1970).

[3] Dunkin, Paul S. *Cataloging U.S.A.*, Chicago: American Library Association, 1969, p.71, 72.

[4] Haykin, David Judson. *Subject Headings: A Practical Guide*, Washington, D.C.: U.S. Government Printing Office, 1951, p.33.

[5] U.S. Library of Congress. Subject Cataloging Division. *Subject Headings Used in the Dictionary Catalogs of the Library of Congress*, 7th ed., Washington, D.C., 1966.

[6] American Library Association. *ALA Rules for Filing Catalog Cards*, 2d ed., Chicago: 1968, p.176.

[7] Haykin. *Subject Headings*, p.34.

[8] American Library Association. *List of Subject Headings for Use in Dictionary Catalogs*, 2d ed. rev., Boston: Library Bureau, 1905, p.iv.

[9] Canada. Parliament. Library. *Répertoire des Vedettes-Matière; Subject Headings Used in the French Catalogue*, Ottawa: 1963, p.40.

Subject Catalogues:
Headings and Structure

Eric James Coates

Library of Congress Practice

In an earlier chapter it was pointed out that the system of connective references, and the manner in which compound subjects are handled, together determine the essential character of an alphabetical subject catalogue. We may now take in turn each of these aspects of the Library of Congress list. We shall notice that the two aspects are not independent. Reference structure influences the manner in which compound subjects are treated and *vice versa*. Underlying ambiguities in both lurks that hesitancy in applying the principle of specific subject entry which springs from Cutter's attempt to distinguish 'established' subjects. D. J. Haykin recognised that the specific entry principle is applied in a limited fashion in Library of Congress practice, but added no further explanation beyond claiming that the non-specific entry policy is based on the experience of assisting readers. One suspects that the accumulation of a large amount of material on a generically entered subject often leads to a change to specific entry. Such a policy would be closely in line with Cutter's use of subdivisions to break up large numbers of entries under the same heading.

It has already been suggested that the effectiveness of a system of connective references depends upon the extent to which it is a system; that is to say upon the extent to which it is based upon a map of subjects symbolising their mutual relationships. A scheme of classification is just such a map, and we find that the Library of Congress list does appear to stem from such a classificatory background.

There seem to be two distinct and separate layers of relational references in the list. The first layer comprises a more or less complete network of downward directed hierarchical references and horizontally directed co-ordinate references, apparently based upon a classification scheme which often reveals the lineaments of the Decimal Classification. Superimposed upon this is a second layer of references, the content of which is unpredictable and apparently unrelated to any

---

Reprinted, by permission, from Eric James Coates, *Subject Catalogues: Headings and Structure* (London: Library Association, 1960), 69-79.

underlying principle. It would appear, according to Library of Congress reasoning, that a connective reference system based on classification alone does not suffice for a dictionary catalogue.

Miss Pettee, perhaps the most articulate expositor of the American type of dictionary catalogue, reveals a curiously ambivalent attitude to the whole question of the relationship between classification and subject cataloguing. On the one hand she affirms that the classificatory "horse" pulls the logical load of the alphabetical subject references in a dictionary catalogue, on the other she refers to the power of the dictionary catalogue to express relationships in several dimensions at once as its supreme advantage over the classified catalogue. Miss Pettee is right in stressing the multi-dimensional nature of subject relationships, but wrong, it may be thought, in supposing that the freedom of the alphabetical subject catalogue to set up multi-dimensional connective references is necessarily an advantage. Knowledge that such a miscellany of undefined relational dimensions exists is of no help to the subject cataloguer, whose whole task is to select a few of the possible lines of relationship to be embodied in 'see also' references. What the subject cataloguer requires above all are some principles defining and limiting those relationships which are to be expressed in references. Such questions are in current dictionary catalogue theory and practice put on one side in favour of casual selection in Miss Pettee's multi-dimensional continuum.

The multi-dimensional theory is evidently represented in Library of Congress practice by the superimposed or secondary layer of references mentioned above. A single example from the list will illustrate the two layers. At the heading 'Drawing', the following connective references are given:

Drawing
    See also *Anatomy, Artistic
            Architectural drawing
            Blackboard drawing
            Brush drawing
            Caricature
            Charcoal drawing
            Crayon drawing
          *Design, Decorative
            Drawing books
            Drawings
            Figure drawing
            Geometrical drawing
          *Graphic methods
          *Human figure in art
          *Illustration of books
            Landscape drawing
            Map drawing
            Mechanical drawing
            Military sketching
            Painting
            Pastel drawing
            Pen drawing
            Pencil drawing
          *Perspective
          *Projection, Art
          *Proportion, Art
          *Shades and Shadows
            Topographical drawing

and   Art
Design, Decorative
Illustration of books
Manual training
Perspective
    See also   Drawing

The items here asterisked are neither subordinate nor co-ordinate references. They are in fact the superimposed layer corresponding to the multi-dimensional linkages mentioned by Miss Pettee. It is worthwhile pausing to try and define the relationships of some of the asterisked headings to the concept 'Drawing'.

The idea to which they all have a common affiliation is that of Art. Drawing is a particular kind of Art which involves the placing of materials such as charcoal, crayon, etc. on a surface. Artistic Anatomy, Human Figure in Art, and Shades and Shadows are related to Art in a different manner. They are examples of what may be depicted in Art (not only in Drawing). Yet another kind of relationship with Art is suggested by the quartet Design, Decorative; Perspective; Projection, Art; Proportion, Art. Here we have neither a kind of Art nor what is depicted in Art, but some principles belonging to artistic activity and technique (again not limited to drawing alone). Finally we have Illustration of Books which is an example of a particular kind of Art being applied to an extraneous object. Here, then, we have four relational 'dimensions' radiating from Art and tentatively designated as Kind, Subject depicted, Principle of Activity, and Application. These are what Ranganathan would call separate 'facets' of the subject Art.

Now each of these topics is related to others in the other facets of Art indirectly through the common concept (Art) from which they spring. Any system of 'See also' references which tried directly to connect all these subjects would collapse under its own sheer volume. The Library of Congress list links together merely an indeterminate selection. Fortunately it is not necessary to represent indirect relationships by direct reference links.

Direct linkage between topics in different facets occurs when a compound subject (such as Perspective in Drawing, or the Human Figure in Book Illustration) is formed. But by its very nature a compound subject poses no problem of subject relationship which requires 'see also' references. It merely needs a set of references from each of those parts of the heading not used as entry word in the subject heading. Thus the heading 'Perspective, Drawing' and the supporting references from 'Drawing, Perspective' provide everything that is required to signal the relationship between Drawing and Perspective. 'See also' references are needed only to show relationships between those subjects which cannot (because they are in the same facet or in hierarchical relationship) form compound subjects. Why has this simplification of the pattern of 'see also' references evaded the compilers of the Library of Congress list? The reply to this question is to be found in the fact that except for a few special categories to be detailed later the list avoids compound subject headings as much as possible. This policy in turn stems back to Cutter's refusal of specific entry for non 'established' subjects. Semantically compound subjects are certainly, by and large, less 'established' than simple ones, and the general effect in Library of Congress practice is that a compound is often entered under one or more simple generic headings. Thus 'Perspective, Drawing' cannot apparently be admitted as an 'established' subject and books on this subject may expect to receive two generic entries under 'Perspective, Art' and 'Drawing' respectively. But double entry makes no contribution to signposting the relationship between Perspective and Drawing, hence it is necessary to make cross-references between the two headings. Undoubtedly many of the superimposed references compensate for the absence of compound subject headings.

A further consequence of the generic entry of 'unestablished' topics is that it is possible to have 'see' references from an unused specific term to a used generic one. Apparently there is a half-way condition of 'establishment' which warrants a reference but not an entry in the list. Thus we have 'Kneejerks see Reflexes', 'Public Libraries see Libraries', 'Dungeons see Prisons'. The opposite situation can also occur. 'See' references are made from certain generic terms which for unexplained reasons are not used as subject headings. Examples are 'Exports see Commerce' and 'Exports see Tariff'.

Not all terms listed as subject headings are included explicitly in the reference network. Names of concrete objects and materials are frequently not signalled by references from the generic headings which logically contain them. To a certain extent access to material on such subjects is made possible by the use of general references in the form:

Materials.   For special materials see under their names.

Such general references offer the possibility of vast economies both in respect of the actual size of the catalogue as well as in the tracings which need to be maintained. They fail, however, to provide for the collective enquiry which demands access to all the library's resources within a particular subject field. Probably their use in the Library of Congress list is confined to cases where intelligent anticipation suggests that collective enquiries are not likely to be made. As an aid to enquirers whose approach to a specific subject commences by resort to a generic term, the general reference is satisfactory provided that its use is limited to subjects of concrete character. To invite an enquirer to seek headings on 'the various aspects, kinds and applications' of say Biology would certainly fall short of reasonable subject catalogue service. Rather remotely allied to the general reference in Library of Congress is the scope note. This defines the range of meaning of a particular heading, and includes general directions for the finding of subjects which might conceivably be sought under the heading concerned but are in fact entered elsewhere.

Two further ways in which the reference-system of the Library of Congress list departs from the pattern outlined in Chapter III may be mentioned here. The reference pathway leading down from the generic to the specific does not always modulate. A direction may be given not only to the next subordinate term in the hierarchy, but also to a further subordinate term, one or more further stages down in the hierarchy. Thus we have both 'Economics see also Finance, Public', and 'Economics see also Taxation'. This practice is authorised by Cutter, but once again it is difficult to detect any rationale underlying its employment in some cases but not in others. It is not unknown for intermediate subordinate terms to be omitted altogether from the chain of references. Thus there is no reference linking Carving with Ice carving. The second peculiarity in Library of Congress practice is that 'see also' references between collateral subjects are sometimes unaccountably made in one direction only. Thus, we have 'Rime see also Rhythm', but not 'Rhythm see also Rime'.

Perhaps the chief lesson to be drawn from the referencing system in the Library of Congress list is that it is not enough for the purposes of the alphabetical subject catalogue to lay down the rule that collateral or co-ordinate subjects are to be linked by references. It is necessary to define with more precision just what collateral subjects are, otherwise the collateral relationship may be invoked to justify indiscriminate reference linkages. Examples of such false collateral references have been mentioned already in connection with the discussion on the heading 'Drawing' and its associated references. There are many others. Hygiene and Air are not a collateral pair, nor are Publicity and Journalism, nor Book Industries and Trades and Publishing and Publishers, nor Aesthetics and Classicism. The only possible closer definition of collateral relationship appears to lie within the concept of faceted classification.... Tentatively we may say that collateral relationship is restricted to terms which lie within the same facet of a given generic subject. The relationship between such a pair as Aesthetics and Classicism is almost always to be expressed by a compound subject heading (such as Classicism, Aesthetics). We shall now proceed to ascertain why this rarely happens in the Library of Congress list.

Compound subject headings are admitted in the list provided that they can be regarded as 'established'. Following Cutter, the Library of Congress usually enters phrases as they stand, inversion being an exceptional procedure. According to D. J. Haykin, every effort is made to avoid subheadings because they amount to 'indirect entry' which is supposedly incompatible with the specific entry principle. Some subjects are designated in ordinary language by a combination of words. We can, indeed we must, use such a combination as a subject heading in the alphabetical subject catalogue, and provided that the idea signified in the subject heading corresponds to that covered by the document in hand, we have specific subject entry. Such compound headings as 'Personnel Management' (phrase form) and 'Personnel, Management' (subheading form) are equally direct and specific for a document on personnel management. As it was pointed out in an earlier chapter, most subject headings with subheadings are really inverted phrases with the connecting preposition omitted. No doubt the dual reluctance of the Library of Congress to use either the inverted phrase form or the subheaded form springs from a common source. With regard to D. J. Haykin's appeal to directness it is difficult to see in what sense 'Air, Hygiene' is less direct than the two generic headings 'Air' and 'Hygiene' which would presumably replace the single compound heading in Library of Congress practice. The exact contrary would seem to be true. One objection to subheadings voiced both by Haykin and Margaret Mann suggests that their use is appropriate only to the alphabetico-classed catalogue. This is erroneous. The alphabetico-classed catalogue does provide indirect entry *via* a generic term, according to the scheme of subdivision and main classes adopted, irrespective of whether the subheading term standing alone could in fact represent the subject. This is an entirely different matter from the use of subheadings in cases where there is no single word or phrase which denotes the subject. It is hardly an exaggeration to say that the reluctance to use subheadings is the greatest contributory factor to the deficiencies of the Library of Congress Catalogue as a reference tool.

In an effort to avoid the reproach of either non-specific entry or the use of subheadings, the Library of Congress sometimes uses phrase headings which from no point of view can be regarded as established. We find, for instance, 'Medicine, Magic, Mystic and Spagiric'. Another form of phrase without currency outside the list and its derivatives is the conjunctive form employed as a means of distinguishing homonyms. 'Files and Rasps' is an example of a phrase heading of this type. The second term 'Rasps' is a substitute for a qualifying subheading such as 'Tools' which is required to differentiate the files from the office equipment bearing the same name.

In the more recent editions of its list, the Library of Congress has found itself obliged to relax, to some extent, its veto on subject subheadings. D. J. Haykin says that the purpose of these subheadings is "not to limit the subject but to provide for its arrangement". This is a mere play upon words; in the alphabetical subject catalogue the degree of subject specification and the mechanics of arrangement are simply two aspects of a single operation. One decides upon a particular heading and by the same token determines the position of the entry in the catalogue. Where such subject subheadings appear in the list, there is sometimes confusion because the same entry word is also part of one or more phrase headings. Thus we have

Aeroplane racing

but

Aeroplanes - Piloting

This weakness also appears in the Australian subject heading list of Sherrie and Jones, which has

> Animal ecology

but

> Animals - Behaviour

and

> Aeroplane engines

but

> Aeroplanes - Design

It is probably necessary to include both phrases and subject subheadings in dictionary catalogues, but there is a field of choice in deciding whether to use phrases whenever possible or subheadings whenever possible. The Library of Congress and those under its influence have chosen the former method for entangled reasons, which include intractable though indefinite reservations about the specific entry principle and what can only be emotional aversion from the superficial appearance of the alphabetico-classed catalogue. The alternative preference for subheadings with only a residuum of phrase headings was discussed and recommended in Chapter III.

The Library of Congress list also permits the use of form, chronological, and locality subheadings. The form subheadings, which include *subjects* such as societies and law, which classification schemes have for some time placed among common subdivisions, can be applied to any heading in the list. The time and place subheadings can only be used as headings where permission for their use is given. Haykin explains the procedure followed when literature occurs giving local treatment to a topic precluded in the list from taking a locality subheading. For example 'Gnatcatchers' is a term for which locality subheadings are not authorised. A book on 'Gnatcatchers of California' is given double entry as follows:

(1) Gnatcatchers
(2) Birds — California

The rule here appears to be that a second entry is made under the nearest generic term at which locality subheadings are allowed. It is hard to see what advantage is to be found in double non-specific entry over a single specific entry

> Gnatcatchers — California

with inversion reference

> California — Gnatcatchers. *See* Gnatcatchers — California

No doubt in evading specific subject entry in this fashion the Library of Congress Catalogue achieves a superficial appearance of simplicity. Under the generic heading or headings books covering the whole generic subject field are interspersed in random order with books on various sections of the field which possess no "established" subject name. Such lack of specification impedes the enquirer, whether he is seeking generic or specific subject material.

It may be useful to complete this chapter by mentioning a few further details of Library of Congress subject cataloguing practice which will serve to pin-point some minor practical problems not hitherto discussed.

The subheadings for historical periods in Library of Congress practice normally consist of verbal headings followed by dates: the latter are, however, the arranging symbols. The subheadings represent *ad hoc* historical eras worked out for particular subjects. Presumably historical specification in any field awaits the accumulation of a large amount of material under the heading. Historical episodes are normally entered under the place.

The form of geographical heading or subheading has exercised a great deal of the attention of Library of Congress cataloguers. In the first place there is the distinction to be made between ethnic adjectives and the names of places as such. The ethnic adjectives are used to name national schools in many of the fine arts, literature and philosophy. Usually they appear as the second word of an inverted phrase heading, e.g. 'Painting, English'. But in topics connected with language and literature the ethnic adjective is the first word, the phrase in this case not being inverted. The Sherrie and Jones list usefully treats some religious and period adjectives in exactly the same way as ethnic adjectives. Two further problems arise in connection with geographical headings proper. The first is concerned with the possible conflict between geographical names and the names of states. Library of Congress regularly prefers geographical names to political names on the ground of permanency. Against this must be placed the fact that political names are almost always better known, that they are usually more precise in meaning than geographical ones, and some denote areas which have no purely geographical name. The second problem is concerned with whether a locality subheading denoting an area within a country should be given directly or subordinated under country, giving such an entry as

Agriculture — France — Coutances

Directions for direct or indirect subordination are given in the list under each heading for which geographical subdivision is permitted. It is not possible to discern any controlling principle. The indirect method of subordination is contrary to specific entry and the result is a true alphabetico-classed entry. The motive for this practice is undoubtedly to link, say, 'Agriculture in France' with 'Agriculture in Coutances'. The alternative mechanism would of course be a 'see also' reference.

Agriculture — France, see also Agriculture — Coutances.

Any system of subheadings poses this problem, which is not peculiar to Library of Congress methods. Rigorous linkage of subheadings under the same heading by means of 'see also' references would be prohibitive for most catalogers and indexers. Perhaps here the general reference, reminding the enquirer in effect that the alphabetical subject catalogue does not physically group related topics, may come into its own. Thus the direction

Agriculture — France. See also names of parts of France amongst these subheadings under Agriculture

would appear to meet all reasonable needs provided that the number of subheadings under the particular heading is not too great for scanning by the enquirer.

A situation which seems to challenge the whole principle of alphabetical arrangement arises when subheadings representing forms, periods, places and subjects appear together under a particular heading. Few dictionary catalogues are so firmly wedded to thoroughgoing alphabetical arrangement that they would arrange all subheadings in a single sub-sequence. Conventional practice attempts grouping of kinds of subheadings and arrives at some such arrangement as the following:

HEADING
References from Heading
Subheadings
    —Forms
    —Periods
    —Places
    —Subjects

Library of Congress, in its current annual subject catalogues, adopts a simpler scheme, namely:

HEADING
References from Heading
Subheadings
    —Forms, Periods (introduced by the term 'History') and Subjects
      in one sequence
    —Places
Heading as first word of an inversion

With this final passing glance at a particular sector of the alphabetical catalogue structure, at which the alphabetical principle appears to be insufficient, we conclude the survey of this form of catalogue considered mainly from the point of view of heading language. Reference has been made from time to time to the relevance of classification for all forms of subject catalogues; its importance as the foundation of attempts to signal subject relationship has been underlined, though not treated in any detail.

"Classification as an Online Subject Access Tool: Challenge and Opportunity"

Pauline Cochrane

Projects as early as 1965-66 demonstrated that searching a classification schedule online could result in a helpful array of related items during the browsing portion of a search and successful results could be obtained from selecting class numbers and using them as search "terms." Projects using the MARC Pilot Project tapes demonstrated that DDC and LCC class numbers, used in conjunction with the *Library of Congress Subject Headings* (*LCSH*) and title keywords, could bring recall up to and over 90%, when no subject access field could do so well alone. Operational online public access catalogs (OPACs) studied by Hildreth in 1981 showed half of them with a "call number" search capability, sometimes truncated. If all this evidence points toward subject access via classification, why are we asking the question? In my opinion it is because the library world does not seem ready for classification to be used as an online subject access tool. To be ready implies more than a mere list of call numbers from MARC records which can be scanned online. To be ready means re-examining the work of classification and the impact of online access on that process; it means viewing the role of classification efforts from the online searcher's point of view and reviewing what can be done to improve his/her satisfactory searching and results. My analysis of this challenge parallels the work Karen Markey and I did for Central ERIC when they asked us to review the impact of online searching (especially free text searching) on the ERIC database (ED 180432). We had to separate suggestions for improvements into three groups, depending on who the initiator for improvements would be. As in that case, I think we must review the role and efforts of:

1. Classification makers and maintainers (DDC and LCC);
2. OPAC designers (at LC, RLG, WLN, CLSI, and a myriad of libraries, including NLM, OSU, Northwestern, etc.); and
3. OPAC users as represented by library staff (public and technical), and typical "end" users.

Reprinted, by permission, from a paper presented at a Subject Access meeting sponsored by the Council on Library Resources (Dublin, Ohio, June 1982).

To be ready, as I said earlier, means more than listing LC call numbers and DDC class numbers from the MARC records. It means linking class numbers with subject headings (something promised as early as 1927 in the *LCSH* introduction). Several persons outside LC have tried to do this—to mention only a few: Mannheimer, Williams, and Daily; Nancy Olson; Bowker in their *Subject Authorities*. Because few online searchers will care to check all the LC schedules to learn what their favorite class numbers mean, or the Dewey numbers, either, some attempt will have to be made to "translate" these numbers and develop table look-ups for online display, perhaps similar to the *LC Classification Outline*.

The comparable effort for DDC would be a publication of all DDC summaries. Any effort like this, of course, must be viewed as a publication for the online searcher, or a "table" for the online system to display when needed. If it is not viewed as a user's tool, we will create something only useful for the classifiers and catalogers, the intended audience for all of the above-mentioned attempts to combine subject headings and class numbers.

Issue 1: Shelf arrangement problems have served as a brake on revising classification schedules or on demonstrating their utility as a subject access tool. Can we divorce shelf arrangement as a process from classification as a subject access process so that we can create useful, systematic browsing displays online which would provide a helpful order of items, avoiding the problem of the inherent order of alphabets?

Both Michael Gorman (*American Libraries*, September 1981, p. 498-9) and Nancy J. Williamson (*Library Resources & Technical Services*, April/June 1982, 122+) have addressed this issue briefly.

The preliminary results of the CLR-sponsored OPAC User Evaluation studies have shown that users need assistance when their search results are either too few or too many. They also request viewing "terms related to their search." System designers are perturbed about response time when terms which are "too common" are used. Can class numbers in MARCs record be explained by classification schedules in auxiliary online files? Retrieval system designers will have to be creative in this area, more so than presently evidenced. Perhaps some developmental effort needs to be supported again, as was done in 1965-66 (AIP Project AUDACIOUS, funded by NSF). Beyond using the EXPLODE command via MeSH's tree structures, a quasi-classification, there do not seem to be any ingenious uses of classification to broaden or narrow searches, or to improve response time by translating common terms entered into a system message to prompt the user to narrow his/her search, etc.

Issue 2: Can a combination of OPAC designers, researchers, and classification owners and maintainers come up with some ingenious uses of class numbers to improve response time online, to guide users to better search strategies, etc.?

Issue 3: What useful links can be forged between *LCSH* and LCC or DDC which will be helpful online in various OPACs?

This is an issue related to both Issue #1 and #2 because most people have missed the value of these links. NLM has not, interestingly enough, in that the schedule they use for CATLINE (Class W) is indexed using MeSH terms as much as possible. Has that day come for LCC? If it did, what would we do with the result online? The data in the Bowker publication could be of some use for such a study, but taken alone, it can not yet show what the potential is online. Even NLM in writing the specifications for Medlars III has not incorporated any use of their Class W Schedule online, even though it is maintained in machine-readable form.

Subject authority control can be viewed as a problem for one system of subject headings or a single classification system, or it can be viewed as a problem of users who search in multiple files, each with their own unique vocabularies or classification systems. If viewed as the latter, something needs to be done to integrate, if not make compatible, the various systems which might be searched. All through the 1960's attempts at compatibility were made, but we have not yet seen any results in this area which have changed the life of online searchers. Retrieval system vendors like SDC, DIALOG, and BRS have attempted multiple-database vocabulary indexes online, but these are the lowest common denominator, simply a merger of lists of terms from database records, with no attempt to show the syndetic structure of each vocabulary or to group these terms into broad related groups. The *Integrated Energy Vocabulary* and the Battelle Switching Vocabulary System are examples of things to come. The application of BSO (Broad System of Ordering; a UNISIST project) is another way to proceed. Which way will lead to the biggest payoff from the least investment?

Issue 4: Are there automatic means for achieving online switching between subject vocabulary and classification systems? Does an effort like BSO have to be imposed before multiple files can be searched adequately online with the least user effort? Is a transparent translation from a user's search terms to the system vocabularies in an OPAC feasible and practicable?

All of the above discussion assumes that we would not get bogged down by the idiosyncracies of our present systems which have tried to accommodate shelf arrangement, format considerations, and interpolation problems. In other words, if we start off assuming classification can serve a useful purpose online, what might these purposes be and how can we get there from existing records, existing schedules, and existing systems?

* * * * *

Discussion

One participant mentioned that the authority format allows the use of notes that could help the user know where to look for what he is seeking. Participants in some of the focused interviews conducted as part of the online public access catalog evaluation project have talked about the idea of a "knowledge tree," which could help a user broaden or narrow a search.

"LCSH-EVP Notebook of Procedures" and "Using LCSH as a Subject Access Tool in Online Public Access Catalogs"

Pauline Cochrane

Notebook of Procedures

LCSH ENTRY VOCABULARY PROJECT—
Form for Suggested Cross Reference with some instructions

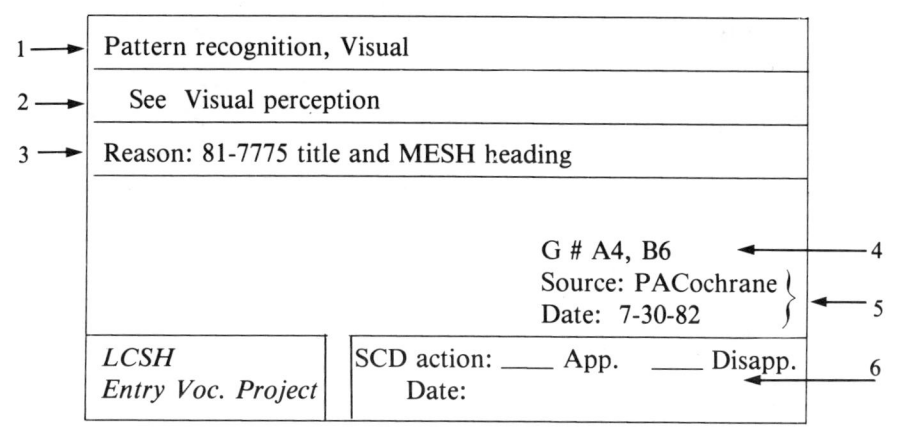

```
1 →  Pattern recognition, Visual
2 →  See  Visual perception
3 →  Reason: 81-7775 title and MESH heading

                              G # A4, B6          ← 4
                              Source: PACochrane
                              Date: 7-30-82       ← 5

     LCSH              SCD action: ___ App.  ___ Disapp.
     Entry Voc. Project    Date:                         6
```

Explanation of Form

1. *Space for suggested lead-in heading.* (See LCSH and supplements to verify that cross reference does not now exist in LCSH; review Guidelines and LC-SCD Policy Statement H373, revised to check on the legitimacy of such a cross reference.)
2. Space for:
    See (*LCSH heading* which has been checked for accuracy)

(Explanation of form continues on page 152.)

Reprinted, by permission, from *LCSH Entry Vocabulary Project*. Final report to the Council on Library Resources and to the Library of Congress (March 1983), ED 234 780.

Explanation of Form—continued

3. *Reason* for suggested cross reference, e.g., better patron access, user problem, new terminology noticed in newspaper, etc.

    also

    Space for LC Card Number (if a given title was being handled when idea for new cross reference occurred.)

4. (optional). *Record of EVP Guideline* which suggested cross reference follows.
    (See separate sheet of guidelines)

5. *Initials of person and date*

6. *SCD action information*; approved or disapproved, with date.
    (If suggestion is disapproved, reason will be given on reverse side before card is sent back to suggestor.)

GUIDELINES
with
Examples

See references are not necessarily statements of equivalence; they simply indicate to catalogers and catalog users that a particular word or concept does not have a separate file but is entered under another heading.

See references are made from synonyms, variant spellings, variant forms of expression, and alternative constructions of headings. Headings consisting of more than one word frequently have *see* references from the words not chosen as the entry element. *See* references are not normally made in this list from abbreviations, nor are they made from foreign language equivalents. Others may wish to make these references if they seem to be useful.

—Introduction, LCSH, 9th edition, 1980, ix

Policies for "See" References appear in the Subject Cataloging Manual of the Library of Congress. The main policy is H 373, Revised November 7, 1981. It is attached. Beside this policy are more than forty other policies which contain some elaboration of this main policy for particular cases such as transliterated names, ancient cities, literary authors, airports, nationalities, family names, etc. The manual and the files at the Library of Congress can help the cataloger at the Library of Congress, but these tools are not readily available elsewhere. For this reason the main policy has been elaborated on below and reorganized to show by example the different types of *See* references which can be found in LCSH. It is hoped that these guidelines will help the person who is some distance from the Subject Catalog Division of the Library of Congress know that they can make suggestions for new see references and expect them to be approved if they are sent in to the Library of Congress *if* they have followed the main policy or found a precedent for their suggestion in and among these guidelines.

The procedure for sending in to the Library of Congress suggestions for new see references is explained below. It has purposely been kept simple, knowing that the least effort may keep the suggestions coming long past the start-up time of this project (Spring and Summer 1982). The form on which the suggestions should be made is simple too. If the supply provided by this project runs out, a blank 3x5 card will do as long as it follows the style of the LC-EVP card.

At the outset, several libraries will serve as local or regional centers for collecting suggestions for see references. They will also serve as conduits for distributing information about this project and the procedures to follow. As time goes on, libraries may want to send their suggestions directly to the Subject Catalog Division of the Library of Congress. There is nothing to preclude this arrangement. All library staff are encouraged to participate in this project, but it is assumed that original catalogers who are handling new titles and checking LCSH for subject headings will be the most enthusiastic of suggestors and reference librarians working with the public at card catalogs or online public access catalogs will be the next most enthusiastic about sending in suggestions and helping us improve the entry vocabulary to LCSH.

TYPES OF SEE REFERENCES IN *LCSH*

Lead-in vocabulary (i.e., *see* references) are needed in any subject heading list because the subjects and topics in items being cataloged or indexed may be expressed in many different ways but only one way will be the approved heading. Oftentimes concepts may be described at different levels of abstraction and the cataloger or indexer who is trying to name the subjects in an item will be hard pressed to fit the author's scope exactly into the levels of abstraction of the subject heading list. For these and many other reasons, lead-in terms are added to the subject heading list to improve the chance of catalog users finding what they are looking for. There are four obvious *types of see references* which when made will improve access:

A. Lead-in references for *Multi-term Headings*, changing the order of the terms for access.

B. Lead-in references for *Alternative Forms of Heading*

C. Lead-in references for *Grammatical Variants*

D. Lead-in references because *related terms* are to be found elsewhere in the list or because a broader or narrower term is being used.

The following examples have been grouped into these four categories and further subdivided to typify the variety in each group. This is not an exhaustive sampler of LCSH *see* references, but it should help someone who does not feel that the main policy in the Subject Cataloging Manual covers the instance where they want to suggest a reference.

A. Word-order Changes which can increase access

1. *Inversion of multi-term headings*:
   Chinese aesthetics
      see
   Aesthetics, Chinese

   American national characteristics in
         motion pictures
      see
   National characteristics, American, in
         motion pictures

2. *Possible insert (or deletion) of term in multi-term heading*
   Acoustic stapedial reflex
      see
   Acoustic reflex

3. *Subdivision vs. phrase heading*
   Evolution and religion
      see
   Evolution—Religious aspects

(Categories continue on page 154.)

4. *Topical subdivision which could be lead-in term*
Arabs—Palestine
see
Palestinian Arabs

5. *Title of painting as lead-in to uniform title heading*
Baptism (Painting)
see
Francesca, Piero della, 1416?-1492. Baptism

6. *Modifier or qualifier as lead-in reference*
Animals—Abnormalities
see
Abnormalities (Animals)

7. *Synonym for term within a multi-term phrase*
School theatricals
see
College theater

B. Alternative forms of heading which can increase access

1. *Lead-in for Popular or technical term*
Tingidae   Blood component separation
  see   see
Lace bugs   Hemapheresis

2. *Translation of Foreign Language term*
Great Poland (Poland)
see
Wielkopolska (Poland)

3. *Synonym* (see also A7)
Auditory reflex   Vermilion Sea (Mexico)
  see   see
Acoustic reflex   California, Gulf of
                          (Mexico)

4. *Change from old to new term* (sometimes handled only by a note in LCSH supplement)
Workmen's compensation
see
Workers' compensation

5. *Acronym or full name as heading*
Instruction Set Processors (Computer
   program language)
see
ISP (Computer program language)

GOS (Meteorology)
see
Global Observing System (Meteorology)

6. *Alternative coined phrases used synonym*
Devils Triangle   Triangle of Death
  see   see
Bermuda Triangle Bermuda Triangle

7. *Possible to use synonymous subdivisions*
Embassy buildings—Sieges
see
Embassy buildings—Takeovers

C. Grammatical variants

1. *Spelling differences*
Wrisley family   Philo-Semitism
  see   see
Risley family   Philosemitism

2. *Singular or plural form*
Ant
see
Ants

3. *Adjectival or noun form*
Book rarities   Surviving skills
  see   see
Rare books   Survival skills

D. Need for Access near Related Terms found elsewhere or access point is broader or narrower

1. *Upward "see" reference to point to heading used*
Occlusal bite plane splints
see
Splints, Bite plane

2. *Downward "see" reference to point to heading used*
   Territorial behavior
       see
   Human territoriality

3. *Lead-in near a related general term*
   Sleep speech
       see
   Sleeptalking

4. *Quasi-antonym for lead-in near related term*
   Cholesterol inhibitors
       see
   Anticholesteremic agents

5. *Lead-in cluster term to show related terms used*
   Field relations
       see
   Operational rations (Military supplies)
   Survival and emergency rations

Using LCSH as a Subject Access Tool in Online Public Access Catalogs

As the LCSH Entry Vocabulary Project was seen as an effort to improve LCSH for use in online catalogs and not as an effort to improve LCSH *per se*, it is considered worthwhile to review the expected use of LCSH in that context. Not many online catalogs were initially designed with a subject authority in mind, not to mention suggestive prompts built into browse displays which would lead the naive catalog user through the maze of cross references and related terms, main and topical, geographic, and chronological subdivisions used in the subject tracing on MARC records. Since the results of the recent Council on Library Resources OPAC User Survey report a preponderance of subject searching online, many system designers are enhancing their original online catalog designs with subject access features. Ohio State University's LCS system will soon have such a browsing display:

SUB/Black Americans
...
14   1   Bka-rgyud-pa (Sect)-- Rituals
15   Black Americans
16   SEE   Afro-Americans
17   1   Black Art--Addresses, essays, lectures
...
TBL/16
         AFRO-AMERICANS   (307 titles)
01   Owens, Don Benn.   The Most controversial American.... .... FBR
02   Jones, Marcus E.   Black migration in the United States 1980 FBR
03   Wilder, Margaret G.   Black assimilation in the urban env. 1979 FBR
...
SUB/Afro-Americans
11   1   Afro-American youth--New York (N.Y.)
12   2   Afro-American youth--Pennsylvania--Philadelphia
13   3   Afro-American youth--Psychology
14   1   Afro-American youth--Religious life
15   307 Afro-Americans   7 sa
...
ENTER TBL/AND LINE NO. FOR TITLES; SAL/ and LINE NO. FOR SEE ALSO REF
SAL/15
     307   Afro-Americans
     see also: 7
        3   Afro-Americans and libraries
        1   Associations, Institutions, etc.--Membership, Afro-American
       25   Freedmen
...

MELVYL, the online catalog at the University of California, now permits a browse display, with no results reported, of all subject headings with the keyword to be searched. They are exploring ways to incorporate cross references into their displays, perhaps in a way similar to how they handle cross references from the Name Authority File (e.g., Mark Twain is also known as....).

On SCORPIO at the Library of Congress, LIV (Legislative Indexing Vocabulary), not LCSH, can be displayed online using a command called LIVT. Here is the display one could see if "LIVT Biomass energy" was entered:

BIOMASS ENERGY
        (Energy produced by conversion of vegetable matter. Technically feasible processes
        to generate fuels from biomass include fermentation to produce methane and alcohol,
        chemical processes to produce methanol, and pyrolysis to convert waste to low Btu
        gaseous fuels and oils.)
    Used for:
        Microbial energy conversion
    Broader terms:
T01   ALTERNATIVE ENERGY SOURCES
T02   FUEL
T03   POWER RESOURCES
    Related terms:
T04   REFUSE AS FUEL
READY FOR NEW COMMAND:

If the online user had entered "LIVT Microbial energy conversion" instead, SCORPIO would have shown the same display with a new header:

"Microbial energy conversion is indexed under...."

In two of these systems the subject authority file, with *see* references, is being used to re-direct the user to the established heading and related references. In one case the user's effort is minimal; in the other additional keying is necessary. In neither case is the user prompted to consider the main headings plus subdivisions, although these can be displayed, if one knows how to do it.

The variation we can expect in online catalog subject access tools is probably limitless, but as always it will depend on what is provided in the subject authority file. Already a plea is being heard from the library profession to make LCSH in machine-readable form as complete as possible. (See the "Holley report," LC Subject Authority Control: Scope, Format, and Distribution; a Final Report by the Ad Hoc Subcommittee submitted to the Subject Analysis Committee, CCS, RTSD, ALA on July 12, 1982). As the second major function of LCSH is seen to be the provision of a cross reference structure which links related terms and which directs one from unused to used terms, the second recommendation of this report calls for "a machine-readable subject authority file which includes all subject headings and cross references which are created by the Subject Cataloging Division" and the seventh recommendation calls for the inclusion of "the reference structure for commonly used subdivisions" which now only appears in a separate publication entitled "LCSH: a Guide to Subdivision Practice". The cross reference structure of LCSH and the use of free-floating subdivisions seem to be recognized at the outset as two areas where LCSH will have to change to be most useful in the online catalog environment. It is suggested that if the machine-readable form of LCSH does not include all the headings (and references) which appear on MARC records, we will not have a complete subject authority file which can be used to enhance online subject access.

There are other problems and considerations which were not addressed by the Holley report but which are seen to create a less than optimum environment for the online subject searcher. The display of all the subdivisions under a main heading can take up to 20 CRT screens to display (see Cochrane article in *Research Libraries in OCLC,* January, 1982)! No one has yet focused on the solution to this problem except, perhaps Charles Goldstein in the experimental version of ILS at Lister Hill/NLM. The display of *see* references, if limited to those created for the card catalog and printed in "the Red Book" (meaning LCSH 9th) may not include the most useful directional signals for the online catalog user. Catalog use research is turning up some interesting case studies and typologies of subject searching. We should be incorporating some of those findings into online subject access features, and the Subject Catalog Division of the Library of Congress may have to take a careful look at how online catalog design will impact on the current practices and policies relating to LCSH cross reference structure and subdivisions (freefloating, etc.). Pattern headings, for example, may have to be specifically tagged in order to guide the online user through all the headings of a certain type, something not done specifically in the "Red Book". General reference notes may have to be redesigned and incorporated into the machine-readable LCSH as special records. Some notes on the currency of headings may have to be incorporated to allow use of the machine-readable LCSH with older files, such as REMARC.

There are groups such at AAT (Art and Architecture Thesaurus) group who feel that the cross reference structure of LCSH will never allow adequate online subject access. They propose to replace it with the tree structure of MeSH which can provide the linkages between terms which are logical, consistent, and displayed in a helpful array.

Many system designers think the formal pre-coordinated LCSH string should be freely accessed, word by word, or permuted, as in MELVYL, using a KWIC-like word-in-context display. Still others feel a basic index of all subject-bearing words should be created from the

MARC records and that that will be enough for browsing lists, Boolean searches, and the like. This latter group sees no value in mounting a separate subject authority file like LCSH on an online catalog. They would place the burden for thinking of synonyms on the user and the burden for finding related terms might be placed on some algorithm in the computer for defining relatedness. Synonyms are not the only problems facing online catalog searchers. Until the entry vocabulary of LCSH is vastly improved, and because of the vagaries and inconsistencies in LCSH, it will behoove any OPAC designer to build in some user aids which will prompt their users to look at their subject search statements in a variety of ways. A report of our analysis of the functions of *see* references in LCSH may help design those user aides. We discovered at least four types of lead-in vocabulary to redirect the user and help improve access:

A. *Word-order changes* caused by inversion of multi-term headings, subdivision or phrase headings, parenthetical qualifiers, etc.

B. *Alternative forms* such as popular or technical terms, foreign or English language terms, old or new terms, alternative coined phrases, synonymous subdivisions.

C. *Grammatical variants* such as spelling, singular or plural forms, adjectival or noun forms.

D. *Related term scattering* with need for point of access to more general terms (sometimes called "upward" see references), quasi-antonyms, cluster terms, etc.

Given all these developments, what might the providers of LCSH, namely the Subject Catalog Division of the Library of Congress, do? The answer to that important question is outside the purview of this project, but it is my opinion that this is one of the most important questions facing LC/SCD today. The question will not go away and the need to improve LCSH for use in online catalogs will become greater as time goes on. The task can not be done at LC/SCD alone. The series of LCSH Institutes now being held around the country, this EVP project, and the workshops being sponsored by the Council on Library Resources to bring LC Personnel together with library researchers, online catalog designers, and library managers to focus on online subject access should have a very positive effect on future efforts.

The entry vocabulary project may expand into a larger cooperative effort between the Library of Congress and other research libraries. Some of the other recommendations in the Mandel report should also be pursued. Bibliographic database producers, be they abstracting and indexing services or libraries, should be contemplating ways to integrate and link their vocabularies as all the signs point to further efforts to cross-file search facilities online. Who better than the keepers of the vocabularies of these files to plan such developments?

The Grammar of Subject Headings:
A Formulation of Rules for Subject Headings Based on a Syntactical and Morphological Analysis of the Library of Congress List

Jay E. Daily

The subject headings in the Library of Congress list, fifth edition, 1948, were analyzed to determine the function of each grammatical form in the structure of the list. The main headings in the list, at least 21,451, were grouped together according to the form of the heading, the marks of punctuation employed, and the inflections of words in the list. Considerable variation of form was found, but the headings in the list may be summarized as being 31.5 per cent one-word headings; 5.5 per cent proper names of more than one word; 5.5 per cent "events" which are distinguished from other forms in that the heading contains a date and usually the words "Battle", "War", etc.; 6 per cent one-word headings followed by one or more words in parenthesis, 4.5 per cent headings which would be counted as two-word headings except that the Library of Congress list retains a hyphened form. The remaining headings consist of two or more words, about 47 per cent of the main headings in the whole list. The two-word headings are 34 per cent of the total number of headings in the list; 3 per cent of the headings are of three or more words without using a preposition, conjunction, or definite article. The remaining 10 per cent of the main headings use one or more of these function words, about 4 per cent include the word "and", about 5 per cent include the prepositions "in, of, with", and approximately 1 per cent include other prepositions. Only a few headings include the definite article, and only one was found which included the indefinite article.

There are significant variations in the use of certain grammatical forms with suggested Library of Congress classifications, but the analysis revealed a pattern of usage such that a sample of headings based on a subject area would not lead to valid conclusions about the whole list.

Reprinted, by permission, from Jay E. Daily, *The Grammar of Subject Headings: A Formulation of Rules Based on a Syntactical and Morphological Analysis of the Library of Congress List* (Doctoral diss., School of Library Service, Columbia University, 1957), 1-3, 74, 152-61.

Three principal uses for marks of punctuation, other than the hyphen, and for the conjunction and prepositions were suggested by the analysis: the grouping of headings together so that the entry word is the same in various modifications, the dispersal of headings so that entry words differ but the same word is used after the mark of punctuation, and the explanation of headings so that the context of the entry word is shown.

A comparison of the grammatical forms used in seven special lists indicated that a single area of usage could be determined for each mark of punctuation, and on this basis rules for use of grammatical form were devised. The problems of grouping and dispersal of headings suggested the need for a classified guide to supplement the alphabetic listing of headings and suggested the use of a mark of punctuation instead of prepositions and conjunctions. A special subject heading list for materials on the desegregation crisis was developed to show the application of the rules. It was not the intention of the study to revise the Library of Congress list of subject headings.

. . . .

Major Forms of Headings by Suggested
Library of Congress Classification
Expressed as Percentage of Total Number 21,333

Classification		One Word	Proper Names	Events	Gloss Words	Hyphen Words	Two Words	Three Words	Function Words	Total
None		4.77	2.06	.65	2.17	.51	6.42	.55	2.41	19.54
Model							.66	.20	.65	1.510
A	General Works	.07			.005	.005				.080
B	Philosophy	2.68	.50	.21	.77	.16	1.20	.06	.75	6.330
C	Auxiliary	.21	.03	.005	.04	.03	.26	.01	.07	.655
D	Universal	1.78	.19	2.49	.22	.02	.46	.02	.12	5.300
E	American	.08	1.66	1.35	.01	.03	.10	.02	.02	3.310
F	Am. History	.16	.79	.47	.01	.01	.12	.01	.06	1.630
G	Geography	1.38	.06	.16	.50	.43	.86	.02	.27	3.680
H	Social Science	1.54	.12	.12	.07	.21	2.06	.20	.78	5.100
J	Political Science	.51	.15	.04	.06	.02	.44	.04	.21	1.470
K	Law								.015	.015
L	Education	.13	.005		.03	.05	.31	.02	.21	.755
M	Music	.50	.01		.41	.10	.84	.19	.84	2.890
N	Fine Arts	.92	.005		.06	.18	.99	.02	.39	2.565
P	Literature	.84	.02	.005	.21	.06	7.26	.35	.84	9.585
Q	Science	8.29	.02	.03	.60	.76	4.02	.13	.80	14.650
R	Medicine	2.23			.12	.19	1.45	.04	.50	4.530
S	Agriculture	1.71	.02		.14	.74	1.76	.29	.24	4.900
T	Technology	2.88	.01	.02	.42	.81	3.36	.30	.70	8.500
U	Military Science	.24	.05		.05	.09	.50	.22	.12	1.270
V	Naval Science	.15			.03	.10	.27	.01	.10	.660
Z	Bibliography	.33	.005		.04	.06	.45	.04	.15	1.075
		31.400	5.705	5.550	5.965	4.565	33.790	2.740	10.285	100.000

. . . .

Rules for the Formation of an Alphabetical Subject Catalogue.

1. Take as the heading the term used in the literature, such as the users of the library would expect to find, subject to rules for the form of heading below.

2. Specify the exact use of the term in such a way that it can serve to indicate the definition of the heading under which works will be found. In using a heading for a certain work, apply that one whose definition best describes the subject approach of the work, as a whole or in part.

3. All one-word headings and the head of two or three word constructions are to be mass nouns. If the term in the literature is a count noun in the singular, add the necessary indication to make it a mass noun. For words in which no distinction is to be made between the singular and the plural form of the word, employ the plural form. If a distinction is to be made between the singular and the plural, employ the definite article with the singular form of a count noun to indicate that it is used as a mass noun. For example, "Discrimination" is a mass noun. "Hotel" is a count noun. The former will fit the pattern "An example of _____", the latter will fit the pattern "An example of a _____". Employ the former term as it is given *Discrimination*. Make the latter term plural, *Hotels*. To distinguish between "Church" as an organized body and various kinds of churches, use the definite article, for example, *The Church*, for the former definition and *Churches* for the latter. Employ the definite article with the noun form of adjectives (substantives).

4. Use the gloss to indicate the general area from which a word has been taken, for instance, *Projection (Psychology)*, but do not use the gloss to distinguish between terms that are identical but are employed in different fields, *e. g.* "Projection (Motion pictures)". Where a homonym would have to be employed, choose another form of the heading, as "Motion picture projection".

5. Employ the hyphen between two-word specifiers in three-word constructions. When the hyphen is customarily used in the general authority taken (as in a standard, modern dictionary), retain it.

6. Take as headings compounds of more than one word, whether or not hyphens are used. Do not invert any words or phrases in the headings taken, but avoid terms which are not compounds but only nonce formations, such as "Discrimination in employment". Do not include phrases in which the specification is not essential to the understanding of the term, as "Attorneys at law", for which the heading *Attorneys* is sufficient. However, some headings which have become customary usage even though a preposition is included may be given as found, for instance *Incitement to riot*.

7. Rearrange two or more word headings so that the most significant element is the entry word unless it is necessary to add an inversion mark of some sort. Do not employ a heading in which an inversion comma or other mark is supposed to indicate a grammatical change, for instance, *Richmond, Virginia, Public School System*, in which the comma is needed for clarity, but not "*Schools, Public*".

8. When a definition is indicated both by a compound and by a single term, take the most explicit but briefest term that will fit into the catalogue. If the word or words other than the entry words are used as near synonyms of the whole phrase, make a *see* reference from those terms to

be one used. If a choice must be made between two different terms of practically equal semantic value, near synonyms, make a *see* reference from the term not chosen to the one that is used.

9. Indicate with a dash (--) subdivisions by geographic area, by historical period and by form of work after a main heading, if these subdivisions are not used as main headings. Do not confuse indication of ethnic group with geographic subdivisions; "English language" is not capable of subdivision as "Language--Great Britain."

10. Make a classified guide of subject headings by listing all main headings according to the general area that their definitions have in common. Number each heading by some system that will provide sufficient space to show like headings together providing several to the page but will not be wasteful of space. For instance, the letters of the alphabet, A through Z, provide for 26 variations. Excluding both A and Z, 24 variations are possible, and employing the 9 arabic numbers followed by the twenty-six letters 5,616 variations are possible. Each subdivision after a dash does not need to be given an individual number, but the standard subdivisions should be listed, preferably as A or as Z to give each kind of subdivision one location.

11. When certain headings tend to be used frequently together or when a heading is reasonably a subdivision of another heading, so far as a certain work is concerned, use the colon ":" to indicate this relationship and list with the term, other than the entry word in the classified guide. For instance, "Employment" and "Discrimination" in such phrases as "Discrimination in employment" may be listed in the catalogue as *Employment : Discrimination* and listed in the classified guide under *Discrimination*. Do not carry this grouping beyond two headings. For a third relationship make two headings.

12. In making subdivisions show the extent of time as exactly as possible, in numerals, not by some word like "modern", "ancient", and so forth. Make a *see* reference from such terms to the heading used. If subdivision by time is not a general feature of the list, such a heading as *Reconstruction, U. S.* may be preferred to *U. S.: History--1865-1877*.

13. For the names of individual persons and corporate bodies, follow the rules for the entry of authors' names, with the provision in filing that all subject headings are listed together in next alphabetic order to the main entry.

14. In applying subject headings, do not use more than one with the same first two numbers of the classified guide. The other headings are understood to be useful in the work simply by the indication [in that group] of [the] one heading.

15. The filing rules for the catalogue would be: File word by word and letter by letter within words. Disregard all marks of punctuation except the dash (--) and file letter by letter after a dash. Arrange chronological entries by date beginning with the earliest and ending with the latest. Disregard articles wherever they occur. When subject headings and main entries are identical, file each, separately in alphabetic order of choice.

Conclusion. The rules developed are basically effective only for the English language, but if the general principles which underlie their formulation are observed, subject heading practice in any language would be the same. The general rule that the heading itself must be taken from the literature of the subject which it will indicate is inescapable and requires a study of authorities in the field. The general rule that the whole definition of the heading, not the word itself, will be considered in the subject cataloguing of a work is meant to obviate the possibility of confusing homonyms and to insure that the broadest possible application will result in the use of any heading. The general rules for the use of marks of punctuation insure that these will be treated as constructive mechanisms each with a definite area of usage such that the grouping involved in the use of the dash and the dispersal made possible by the colon cannot be confused. The requirement that terms in a gloss be purely explanatory insures that gloss terms need never be considered in the alphabetizing of headings. Variant spellings can be shown in a gloss as well as the area of meaning in which the heading is used, but the gloss is not to be considered a substitute for a scope note.

The principle of the classified guide as the meta-language is an inescapable necessity if objective methods are to be used for the formation of a "syndetic" catalogue. If every heading must have its location in the classified guide, then there is no possibility of having headings lost in the catalogue with references neither to nor from the term. All words in a language are related, and all terms in a subject field have some kind of relationship. The classified guide removes the hazards of setting up a large number of synonyms which have ill defined areas of meaning, and equally, it provides for maximum ease in the alteration of headings without extensive cataloguing. Beyond that, its value is like that of a thesaurus to both subject cataloguer and researcher, for it reminds them of other headings and of the areas of usage of each heading.

The rules that deal specifically with language, such as Rule 3, can be translated into general terms to be used with any language. What is required is that the most general term be employed and that the grammar of the language be used in such a way that the heading is not limited in a way that the definition fails to indicate. If a language does not have the grammatical category of partitiveness, indicated in English by the distinction between mass nouns and count nouns, there is no necessity for providing a rule that mass nouns shall be used. All language have peculiarities which the subject heading list will reflect, and Rule 7 prohibiting the inversion of terms for the purposes of grouping the headings is meant to avoid the practice of changing the language of subject headings away from the language used by persons investigating the literature. The subject cataloguer must follow the language of the subject field with which he deals, because he cannot be the arbiter of usage.

The noun rule[1] and Cutter's rules[2] are alike in being basically *a priori* rules for the choice of headings. What relationship these rules have had to the actual language has hitherto been unknown, but this study has suggested what problems the rules of grammatical form should solve so that only choice of the preferable term must of necessity be based not on rules but skill acquired by long experience. The rules seek to prevent the requirements of grammatical form influencing the actual choice of the heading when there are no synonyms. They are such that any two persons independently following these rules must come to the same decision about the form of the heading, except that the same heading in two different lists cannot be expected to have the same location in a classified guide. The value of a classified guide is that the heading is located somewhere not that two people agree on the exact location since all classification is arbitrary. The rules are such that subject heading lists of whatever breadth or variety may be constructed following these rules. Finally, these rules are such that other rules for special needs may be devised without altering the basic structure of the general rules. It is, of course, obvious that no additional rule should be made unless its use can be completely justified; for instance the coordination of headings by using the colon may be dropped or its use extended by an additional mark, say the ampersand, to indicate that a heading is a nonce formation of such importance it will be listed under both headings as an entry word. Though dispersed headings using a colon are entered in the classified guide under the second term, such nonce formations would not be entered in the classified guide.

These four principles were also given in the introductory chapter as the test of objectivity of this study. They are given here as the test of objectivity in the formulation of rules for subject cataloguing. Applying this test to the Library of Congress subject headings, which, in effect, has been done, leads to the conclusion that the cataloguers of the Library of Congress are guided in their choice of the form of heading, by accumulated decisions and the skill they need to fit headings into the list. It is beyond the scope of this study, however, to use these rules to revise the present Library of Congress list of subject headings. Yet it is possible, by objective methods, to summarize the decisions made and to simplify them so that future decisions may follow along certain lines. This would occur without specific direction, since the headings used are ultimately derived from a changing natural language, but there is an advantage in knowing in what ways the language may tend to change and in providing that these changes will not require the undoing of previous cataloguing, with the resultant great expense.

Since the subject heading list developed in Appendix III is for a relatively small and discrete collection, there remains to be tested the extent to which the rules given above could be applied to the formulation of a subject heading list for a large, general library. A further test would be the result of applying the rules as a means of revising the Library of Congress list and providing a classified guide to the headings.

Notes

[1] Prevost, Marie, "An Approach to Theory and Method in General Subject Headings," *Library Quarterly* 16 (1946): 144-51.

[2] Cutter, Charles A., *Rules for a Dictionary Catalog*, 4th ed. (Washington: Government Printing Office, 1904).

"Scope Notes in *Library of Congress Subject Headings*"

Alan M. Greenberg

ABSTRACT. Scope notes from *Library of Congress Subject Headings* are examined for 1) adherence to principles enunciated in the introduction to the list; 2) peculiarities of subject headings associated with such notes; 3) the structure of the notes; and 4) typical patterns associated with certain categories of subject headings. Scope notes are shown to enable catalogers to apply subject headings consistently and readers to distinguish related headings knowledgeably.

Lois Mai Chan's *Library of Congress Subject Headings: Principles and Application* has been received by the library profession as a successful "attempt to re-examine the basic principles [of subject analysis] in light of recent developments and changes and to describe current practice at the Library of Congress."[1] Her book is the obvious successor to Haykin's *Subject Headings: A Practical Guide.*[2] It is not the intention of this paper to examine in detail the similarities and differences, much less the comparative merits of the two works. Rather the writer simply desires to fill a small gap in Chan's otherwise impressive book.

The gap consists in the author's general omission of one of the more interesting features of *Library of Congress Subject Headings* (LCSH): the 1,898 scope notes in the eighth edition.[3] The table of contents, the index and the glossary of Chan's book are silent on the subject. She does define both the "explanatory reference" and the "information card" in the glossary, and discusses the latter in detail in her coverage of the names of corporate bodies. Scope notes are mentioned (with examples) in her discussion of the distinction between headings for the history of a discipline in a place and headings for the actual conditions in the place.[4] Haykin, on the other hand, devotes about a page to scope notes and supplies a glossary definition as well.[5]

This study does not address itself to the adequacy of the number of scope notes provided in LCSH, but rather examines the characteristics of the scope notes that do exist. It remains for another investigator to determine why **Central Europe**, **Christian giving**, and **Optics** require scope

---

Reprinted by permission of The Haworth Press, 28 East 22 Street, New York, NY 10010, "Scope Notes in *Library of Congress Subject Headings*" by Alan M. Greenberg from *Cataloging & Classification Quarterly*, vol. 1, 1982, pp. 95-104; copyright © 1982.

notes whereas **New Thought, Sandwich construction,** and **Open and closed shelves** apparently do not. Nor does the present study treat of the notes given under "Most Commonly Used Subdivisions," these not being typical of the scope notes in the main list of subject headings.[6] Notes in the "Annotated Card Subject Headings List" are also excluded.[7] In addition to the eighth edition of LCSH, the supplementary lists through January-March 1979 were perused for revised and new scope notes. All "catalogers' notes" were examined. These may be defined simply as directions for the primary or sole use of the person applying the subject heading to a work (the cataloger) rather than the person using the heading to retrieve information from the catalog (the reader).

The introduction to LCSH offers a functional definition of the scope note:

> Scope notes are provided when needed to ensure consistency of subject usage by specifying the range of subject matter to which a heading is applied in the Library's catalogs, by drawing necessary distinctions between related headings, or by stating which of several meanings of a term is the one to which its use in the Library's catalogs is limited. These notes appear in the list immediately following the headings with which they are used. A typical example may be found under the heading **Civil service**.[8]

Of the three functions of scope notes described in LCSH, the first, "specifying the range of subject matter to which a heading is applied," appears to be the desired end, the other two functions constituting the means.

"Drawing necessary distinctions between related headings"

Activities and Disciplines

Scope notes enable the reader to distinguish works about an activity or discipline from works about the result of the activity or the object of the discipline:

Bacteria
  Here are entered works on biological studies of
    bacteria. Works on the science are entered
    under the heading **Bacteriology**.

Citation of legal authorities
  Here are entered works on the method of citing
    legal authorities. Compilations of legal
    citations such as citation books are entered
    under the heading **Annotations and citations
    (Law)**

Literature, Drama, Music

Similarly LCSH commonly employs notes to differentiate critical/historical works about a literary, dramatic or musical form and examples of that form. Sometimes the note indicates that works about the form are entered under a heading different from the one under which examples of the form are entered. In other cases the note shows that both kinds may be entered under the same heading:

Bible plays
Here are entered works on the dramatization of Biblical events, collections of such dramatizations, and such individual plays as are not entered under the name of a principal character or other specific heading.

Canon (Music)
Here are entered works on the canon as a musical form. Music scores are entered under the heading **Canons, fugues, etc.**

Kabuki
Here are entered general works and those that deal solely with the presentation of Kabuki plays on the stage. The texts of the Kabuki plays and works treating of them from a literary point of view are entered under **Kabuki plays**.

Popular vs. Technical Terms

When a popular term describes a subject as precisely as a more technical equivalent does, LCSH generally prefers the popular term as a subject heading. However, in what superficially appears a violation of the principle of uniform heading, sometimes LCSH establishes both terms as headings, distinguishing their application with a scope note:

Floriculture
Here are entered works on the commercial growing of flowers and ornamental plants. Works on home flower growing are entered under **Flower gardening**.

Scope notes serve to distinguish a botanical plant from its product:

Cacao
Here are entered works on the cacao tree and its culture only. Works dealing with the commercial product are entered under **Chocolate** and **Cocoa**.

and a colloquial term from its legal counterpart:

Stealing
Here are entered works on the ethical and psychological aspects of theft. Stealing as a crime is entered under the heading **Larceny**.

Point of View

In some rare instances, an identical concept seen from different points of view is represented in LCSH by different subject headings. A scope note enables the reader to identify those works presenting the subject from the required perspective:

> **College graduates**
> Here are entered works on college graduates as a socio-economic group. Works on college graduates in relation to their alma maters are entered under **Universities and colleges—Alumni**.

There are apparently no limitations on the number of related headings which may be conjoined in a scope note. Generally there are two headings, but three, four or more may be linked:

> **Arabs**
> Here are entered comprehensive works on the Arabs as an ethnic group. Works on four or more of the Arabic-speaking countries of Asia and Africa, or of Asia only, are entered under **Arab countries**. Works on Arab civilization are entered under **Civilization, Arab**. Works on the nomadic Arabs are entered under **Bedouins**. Works on the Arabs of the Arabian Peninsula as a whole are entered under **Arabia**. Works on the Arabs in an Arabic-speaking country are entered under the name of the place. Works on Arabs outside the Arab countries are entered under **Arabs in foreign countries**, or **Arabs in** [place]

"Which of several meanings of a term is the one to which its use in the Library's catalogs is limited"

Haykin states that the principal feature of the scope note is that "it indicates the limits within which the subject entries under it fall and at what points other headings will serve the reader's needs."[9] It is not surprising then to find that most scope notes limit rather than expand the extent of the subject denoted in the heading proper. Such limitation may be necessary because a word or phrase has both a common meaning and a special meaning in a certain literary, historical or philosophical context. Or the term itself may be unambiguous, but an elucidation may be dictated by a peculiarity of the term's use as a subject heading:

Common Terms, Special Applications

Cancer education
   Here are entered works on informing the public about cancer and its prevention. Works on cancer instruction for medical personnel are entered under **Cancer—Study and teaching**.

Church of Christ, Scientist
   Here are entered official publications of the church, including hymn-books, etc. Other works about the church are entered under **Christian science.**

Enlightenment
   Here are entered works dealing with enlightenment in the sense of the intellectual movement of the 18th century (German Aufklärung). When the work deals with the movement in a particular country or city, duplicate entry is made under name of place, with subdivision **Intellectual life**.

Broadened Meaning

In some instances a scope note informs the reader that the associated heading is broader than he might otherwise surmise. Headings requiring such notes include those under which two discrete subjects are subsumed:

Consumer education
   Here are entered works on the selection and most efficient use of consumer goods and services, as well as works on means and methods of educating the consumer.

Some headings in LCSH carry a national, linguistic or religious connotation not immediately apparent from the bare heading:

Candles and lights
   Here are entered works on the use of candles and lights in religious worship.

Commandments of the church
   Here are entered works dealing with certain precepts of the church, disciplinary rather than doctrinal in character, e.g. to observe Sundays and fast days, to pay tithes, to go to confession, etc. If used for any church other than the Catholic, the name of the denomination is added as a subdivision.

Dialogues
> Here are entered collections of dialogues in the English language. Works on dialogues are entered under the heading **Dialogue**.[10]

Definitions

While a scope note may include the lexical denotation of the word or words in the subject heading, in practice definitions are rare, and actual extracts from dictionaries rarer still. Headings which require definitions include those consisting of a foreign word or phrase and geographic headings demanding precise delimitation:

Central Europe
> Here are entered works on the area included in the basins of the Danube, Elbe, and Rhine rivers.

Devotio moderna
> Here are entered works on the medieval movement initiated by Gerard Groote, which resulted in the founding of the Brothers of the Common Life and the Windesheim Congregation of Augustinian Canons.

Hamsocn
> "The right of security and privacy in a man's home."—Black, Law dictionary, 4th ed., 1951.

Subdivisions

On occasion, the use of common topical or form subdivisions requires clarification:[11]

Bible—Societies, etc.
> This heading is used for societies organized for professional and scholarly study of the Bible. For societies concerned with the publication and distribution of the Bible use the heading **Bible—Publication and distribution—Societies, etc.**

Identical Terms

When very closely related concepts are assigned separate headings, scope notes allow the cataloger to rearrange identical or nearly identical words to produce the several discrete descriptors necessary:

Black Muslims
> Here are entered works on the movement known as the Nation of Islam or Black Muslims. Works on persons of the Black race who are Muslims are entered under **Muslims, Black**.

Pattern Notes

A sizeable number of scope notes falls into more or less uniform patterns associated with certain types of subject headings. These include the "[language] wit and humor" headings:

Danish wit and humor
Here are entered collections from several authors and individual authors who have not written in other literary forms.

the "survey" headings:

Demographic surveys
Here are entered works on the methods and techniques employed, and on reports of individual surveys. For the latter the heading may be subdivided by place; in such cases a second subject entry is made under the heading [Name of place]—**Population**, e.g. 1. **Demographic surveys—Virginia.** 2. **Virginia—Population.** For demographic surveys on a special topic, the additional subject is made under the special topic, e.g. 1. **Rural-urban migration—Virginia.** 2. **Demographic surveys—Virginia.**

and the "organ" headings:

Digestive organs—Amphibians, [Birds, Fishes, etc.]
Works on the digestive organs of a particular class, order, family, genus, or species are entered under **Digestive organs**, subdivided by the larger zoological groups only. When the monograph treats of one of the smaller divisions, additional entry is made under the special subject, e.g. 1. **Digestive organs—Amphibians.** 2. **Frogs.**[12]

Music

The musical pattern headings, of which there are several kinds, include form headings:

Motets
Here are entered musical works composed in the form of the motet. Works on the motet as a musical form are entered under **Motet**.
A second heading for medium is assigned if a specific medium of performance is given in the work.

dance music headings:

Schottisches
This heading is used without specification of instruments. A second heading is assigned if the work is for a medium other than piano (2 hands)

and chamber music medium headings:

Quartets
Here are entered collections of compositions for four instruments belonging to various families and in various combinations; and compositions for four specific instruments belonging to various families, followed by specification of instruments (including the specification: **Unspecified instrument(s)**)
Compositions for four bowed stringed instruments are entered under **String quartets**; for four wind instruments under **Wind quartets**; for four brass instruments under **Brass quartets**; and for four woodwind instruments under **Woodwind quartets**, with or without specification of instruments in each case.
Compositions for piano, violin, viola and violoncello are entered under **Piano quartets**.
Compositions for four plectral instruments are entered under **Plectral ensembles**, except those for guitars and/or harps, which are entered under **Quartets** followed by specification of instruments.
Compositions for four percussionists are entered under **Percussion ensembles**.
Compositions for four solo voices are entered under **Sacred quartets** or **Vocal quartets**.
Headings with specification of instruments are printed below only if specific cross references are needed.

"Cataloger's Notes"

As illustrated above, "cataloger's notes" usually form an integral part of the text of a scope note, though they may occur alone. Among the more common "cataloger's notes" are those which direct the cataloger to make a duplicate entry under a related heading:

Abnormalities (Plants)
Works on abnormalities in a particular plant are entered here and also under name of plant, e.g. 1. **Abnormalities (Plants)**. 2. **Podophthalmia**.

American literature (Irish)
　Duplicate entry is made under **Irish literature—
　　American authors.**

The note may require the cataloger to subdivide the heading in question by subject:

Cipher and telegraph codes
　Subdivided by subject, e.g. **Cipher and telegraph
　　codes—Astronomy; Cipher and telegraph codes—
　　Bankers and brokers.**

by geographical entity:

Cookery, American
　Subdivided by states or sections, e.g. **Cookery, American—
　　Virginia.**

or by date:

Comets
　Subdivided by date, e.g. **Comets—1935.** Periodic
　　comets are entered under the name of the
　　discoverer, e.g., **Halley's comet.**

　Certain notes warn the cataloger that the associated headings are "used only with subdivisions." Others simply refer him to the scope note and pattern of subdivision of a similar heading by means of a "cf." note, e.g. **Ballad operas.** Marshall states that "these notes should be converted to full *here are entered* notes in a public catalog."[13]

　If, as Chan maintains,[14] many libraries are no longer able (or have never been able) to maintain a complete cross reference structure in their catalogs, it might be heartening to reflect that the insertion of applicable scope notes into the local catalog can provide a serviceable compromise. Libraries planning to close their card catalogs in 1981 can link old and new headings by incorporating "heading discontinued [date]" and "heading used beginning [date]" information into LCSH scope notes. The Library of Congress has already adopted the policy of "split files" in parts of its catalog where large numbers of cards are involved in subject heading changes:

Negroes. This heading discontinued February 1976.
　See **Afro-Americans** for later materials on the
　　permanent residents of the United States. See
　　Blacks for later materials on persons outside
　　the United States.[15]

　In conclusion, scope notes contain information indispensable both to catalogers and to library patrons. Further research should be undertaken to determine if there exist subject headings presently without scope notes which ought to be provided with them, and if so, which ones.

Notes

[1] Lois Mai Chan, *Library of Congress Subject Headings: Principles and Application* (Littleton, Colo.: Libraries Unlimited, Inc., 1978), p. 17.

[2] David Judson Haykin, *Subject Headings: A Practical Guide*, The Library Reference Series: Librarianship and Library Resources (1951; reprint ed., Boston: Gregg Press, 1972).

[3] This number, arrived at by actual count, includes in addition to scope notes strictly defined all cataloging directions ("cataloger's notes") in the list other than the formal x, sa and xx references. It excludes explanatory references attached to x and sa references.

[4] Chan, *Library of Congress Subject Headings*, pp. 84, 105-112, 206-209.

[5] Haykin, *Subject Headings*, pp. 18-19, 102; see also J. C. M. Hanson, "The Subject Catalogs of the Library of Congress," *Bulletin of the American Library Association* 3:385-397 (Sept. 1909); Margaret Mann, *Introduction to Cataloging and the Classification of Books*, 2nd ed. (Chicago: American Library Association, 1943), pp. 145-146; Joan K. Marshall, *On Equal Terms: A Thesaurus for Nonsexist Indexing and Cataloging* (New York: Neal-Schuman Publishers, 1977), p. 15.

[6] U.S., Library of Congress, Subject Cataloging Division, *Library of Congress Subject Headings*, 8th ed., 2v. (Washington: Library of Congress, 1975), 1:xviii-lxxii.

[7] Ibid., 1:lxxvi-lxxxi.

[8] Ibid., 1:ix.

[9] Haykin, *Subject Headings*, p. 18.

[10] These scope notes would be modified or obviated by the substitution of the following for the existing subject headings: **Candles and lights (in religion, folklore, etc.); Commandments of the Catholic Church**; and **Dialogues, English**.

[11] Chan, *Library of Congress Subject Headings*, p. 84.

[12] The last two kinds of notes are characterized by provision for duplicate entry.

[13] Marshall, *On Equal Terms*, p. 15.

[14] Chan, *Library of Congress Subject Headings*, p. 153.

[15] U.S., Library of Congress, Processing Department, *Cataloging Service* 119 (Fall 1976): 24; see also Gregor A. Preston, "Coping with Subject Heading Changes," *Library Resources & Technical Services* 24 (Winter 1980): 64-68.

Subject Headings:
A Practical Guide

David Judson Haykin

Scope Notes

An important element in helping the reader orient himself in the catalog are the scope notes. They may be defined as statements which indicate the subject matter covered by a given heading, usually with reference to related, more particularly, overlapping headings. It partakes of the nature of a definition on the one hand and a "see also" reference on the other. It may, in fact, include both definitions and references. Its principal feature, however, is that it indicates the limits within which the subject entries under it fall and at what points other headings will serve the reader's needs.

An example of a simple scope note, unemcumbered by distinctions or references of any kind, is the following:

Education, Cooperative.
    Here are entered works dealing with the plan of instruction under
        which students spend alternating periods in school and in a
        practical occupation.

The term "cooperative education" does not make clear the sense in which it is used; neither do such of its synonyms as "study-work plan," "work-study plan," "work experience in education." For that reason a scope note is necessary.

The scope note for the heading *Industrial relations* illustrates the type which includes references to specific related subjects:

Industrial relations.
    Here are entered works dealing with employer-employee relations in
        general. For special aspects of this relationship, *e. g.*, Arbitration,
        Industrial; Collective bargaining; Employees' representation in
        management, etc., *see* those specific subjects. For the legal aspects

---

Reprinted from David Judson Haykin, *Subject Headings: A Practical Guide* (Washington, D.C.: U.S. Government Printing Office, 1951), 18-19, 69-71, 92-94.

of industrial relations *see* Labor laws and legislation. For the technique of personnel management and relations from the employers' point of view *see* Employment management. For works descriptive of the social and economic conditions of labor *see* Labor and laboring classes.

The scope note which embodies a general reference is illustrated by the following:

Commodity exchanges.
    Here are entered works on commodity exchanges in general. For works on exchanges dealing in a single commodity or class of commodities, *e. g.*, cotton, grain, tobacco, *see* Cotton trade, Grain trade, etc.

In general, a scope note is necessary when general dictionaries and dictionaries in special subjects fail to agree completely, and when usage does not offer a sufficiently precise definition of the subject. Under these circumstances, it limits the scope of the subject as used in the catalog, thereby helping the reader to determine to what extent the heading covers the material he seeks and making it possible for the cataloger to maintain consistency in the assignment of the subject heading.

. . . .

Subject Catalog vs. Shelflist

Besides serving as an inventory record of the library's classified collections, the shelflist can be used, within limits, as a classified, or systematic, catalog. However, as in the case of any classed catalog, it can be approached only through an index of some sort, since it is arranged according to the symbols of the classification system which the library employs. The relative index of the classification and the indexes to its individual parts may be used as an index to the shelflist. To a certain extent the subject headings for the books in the classified collections may also be used for this purpose. The limitations on this use of subject headings point, on the one hand, to the fact that the shelflist as such cannot take the place of the alphabetical subject catalog and, on the other hand, to the possibility of using the shelflist as a complement to the catalog in such a way as to reduce the growth of the catalog without impairing the subject approach to the classified collections.

Since, for the purpose of shelving, only one class number can be assigned to the physical book, the number must obviously represent the subject matter of the book comprehensively, if possible, or the first or major part of the book, if it deals with diverse subjects. In the case of a set of books, that is, a collection of monographs, it may be desirable to keep the set intact, rather than scatter individual monographs throughout the collection by classifying each monograph separately. Classifying it as a collection of monographs is, in fact, inevitable when the complete monograph occupies parts of more than one volume. This limitation does not, however, apply to subject headings. If the subject matter of a book represents a systematic treatment of it and can be expressed by a single term, then one subject heading will cover it adequately. When this is not the case, as many subject headings may be used for the book as the distinct topics treated in it require. A single subject heading may be applied to the collection of monographs, if the collection as a whole represents a comprehensive treatment of a single subject. On the other hand, regardless of the fact that the collection is kept intact on the shelves, as many subject headings may be assigned to it as the individual monographs require.

In view of these facts, it is obvious that the shelflist ordinarily presents under any class number not all the works in the library which deal with the subject to which the number applies, but only those which deal primarily with it and those not included in a collection under a broader number. A full-fledged classed catalog includes entries under as many class numbers as are needed to represent the subjects treated in the physical volume or in the individual monographs in a series kept as a unit on the shelves. A shelflist serves the purpose of a classed catalog only within the limits indicated.

Nevertheless, for a considerable number of books on the library's shelves on any subject there is a direct correspondence between subject heading and class number. Under most broad subject headings many of the books will bear the same class number, for the reason that classification systems provide class numbers for broad treatments of a subject.

If the shelflist is available to the public and is not too far removed from the catalog, a reference from the subject heading to the corresponding class number in the shelflist will take the place of many entries, yet guide the reader to most of the material on the subject. It will, furthermore, give the reader an insight into the significance of the number. The reference must, however, be worded to show clearly that only part of the material is to be found in the shelflist and that the rest is entered under the same heading immediately following the reference.

There are areas of subject matter, such as sports, in which specific topics are most frequently treated in detached monographs rather than in encyclopedic works or series. The correspondence between subject heading and class number is very nearly complete. The use of a reference to the shelflist in such instances is, however, to be limited to topics on which the number of books is large, since the only justification for directing the reader to the shelflist is economy in the preparation of entries and of space in the catalog.

The following examples will illustrate the use of a reference from the subject heading to a class number in the shelflist both for broad subjects and specific topics.

> Geology—Uruguay.
>   For works devoted exclusively to this subject as a whole, *see*, in addition to those cited under this heading, the following number in the shelflist:
>   QE249
>
> Skating.
>   For works on this subject, *see*, in addition to those cited under this heading, the following number in the shelflist:
>   GV849

An examination of the entries under the headings *Geology—Uruguay* and *Skating* will show that few of the entries bear class numbers other than QE249 and GV849 respectively. Those that do bear other class numbers are either analytical, that is, they cover parts of books, or articles in periodicals, or are used for works in which the given subject heading is a secondary one, the classification being based on another, more important aspect of the work.

At the Library of Congress the device of referring from subject heading to class number was used to a limited extent before the shelflist and the public catalog were placed so far apart that access to the shelflist on the part of the public became difficult. The device of referring to the shelflist does emphasize the relationship between subject heading and class number and represents one way of reducing the large number of entries under some headings without eliminating the reader's approach to them altogether.

. . . .

Authority File

Bearing in mind that usage is, in the main, the decisive factor in the choice of subject headings, the cataloger must be aware of changing usage and continually bring the headings in the list and in the catalog up to date. This is possible only if the cataloger maintains a complete record of the headings showing, for each, which references have been made from it to related headings, from other headings to it, and on what sources of information the choice of the heading is based. To distinguish it from the lists of headings to which a cataloger might resort in choosing new headings, a list of headings and references limited to the catalogs of the library is often spoken of as a subject authority list or file.

The subject authority list will obviously resemble a general list in its principal features. It will show under each heading:

1) the coordinate related headings found in the catalog to which "see also" references have been made;
2) the less comprehensive, subordinate headings to which "see also" references have been made;
3) the broader, more comprehensive headings from which "see also" references have been made to the given heading;
4) the coordinate related headings from which such "see also" references have been made;
5) the synonymous terms, and, in general, terms equivalent to the given heading, from which "see" references have been made directing the reader to the chosen heading;
6) scope notes defining the heading and distinguishing it from other headings, in those instances where one of two or more meanings of the term has been chosen for its use as a heading, or where a distinction must be drawn between the given heading and others closely related to it;
7) the citation of appropriate sources in which the term to be used as a heading was sought, with an indication of the differences found;
8) the citation of the work which occasioned the establishment of the new heading.

Many libraries depend upon a standard, generally accepted list of headings, checking in it the heading and references which they have used in their catalogs and inserting the headings and references which they have themselves developed or drawn from other sources. Some libraries, on the other hand, though they depend on a standard list, prefer to keep on cards a list of the headings and references they have used. This form of an authority list is almost inevitable, if the record of references made is to be kept complete against the possible need of changing headings and references. Standard lists, for example, indicate methods of subdivision, but, for reasons of economy of space and facility in consultation, they avoid listing under each heading the subdivisions used. However, some subdivisions require references applicable solely to a given heading followed by a given subdivision. Changes in such headings accompanied by subdivisions become necessary at times. The lack of a record of the references in such instances makes it difficult, if not impossible, to find and change the references and may result in the retention in the catalog of misleading references or blind ones leading nowhere.

Thus, for example, a list is likely to include the heading *Agriculture* with an indication that it may be subdivided by place, but not specifically the headings *Agriculture—France* or *Agriculture—Ukraine*. Yet in order to serve the needs of the reader who will seek information on the agriculture of France or the Ukraine under the name of the country, it is necessary to make reference to those headings from *France—Agriculture* and *Ukraine—Agriculture* and, by the same token, to maintain entries in an authority list on which the references might be traced. Obviously, authorities need be cited only for the main heading, except in those instances where the heading followed by the subdivision is used in lieu of a phrase heading for the purpose of fitting it into an existing pattern.

It is desirable that the authority card should as far as possible correspond in form to the list of headings which is mainly used by the library. The form of the entries in the fifth edition of *Subject Headings Used in the Dictionary Catalogs of the Library of Congress* is illustrated in the following example:

Offenses against property (Direct subdivision)

  sa Arson; Burglary; Embezzlement; Extortion; Forcible entry and detainer; Forgery; Fraud; Larceny; Malicious mischief; Poaching; Receiving stolen goods; Robbery

  x Crimes against property; Property, Crimes against; Property, Offenses against

  xx Criminal law

ABC 25 May 1948

Face of authority card

Authorities:

°Black

✓Bouvier (Offences against private property)

✓Wharton, Treatise on criminal law. 10th ed. 1896, v. 1, p. 618

Book cataloged: Gutiérrez Anzola, J. E.
Delitos contra la propiedad. 1944.

Back of authority card

Only the face of the card represents the entry in the list. The symbols used have the following meanings:

> *sa* = make "see also" references to
> *x* = make "see" references from
> *xx* = make "see also" references from
> ° = not found in authority cited
> √ = found in authority cited; if form found differs from form used, form found is enclosed in parentheses following the citation.

The initials of the cataloger who established the heading, followed by the date, appear at the foot of the obverse of the card.

Authority cards prepared solely for the purpose of showing the references made need cite no authorities. If a special form is used, it may bear the statement "For tracing references made."

The preparation of an authority card is but a first step. The references from synonymous terms and the "see also" references must be checked against the list to make certain that the headings from which and to which they are to be made are actually in the catalog. If an established heading is canceled or altered, not only must the authority card be canceled or revised accordingly, but new "see" references must be substituted for the old ones and the heading canceled or altered in all the "see also" references traced on the authority card.

"Online Classification Number Access:
Some Practical Considerations"

Janet Swan Hill

For centuries there have been individuals whose pleasure or life's work it has been to attempt to devise methods whereby the whole of human knowledge can be logically arranged. One of the earliest major figures was Aristotle, who is credited with creating a classification framework "designed to aid the mental plotting out of the universe of thought and objects," and with working out a definite system of arranging books that was afterward adopted by the "Kings of Egypt."[1] Nineteen centuries later in "On the Advancement of Learning," Francis Bacon devised a classification scheme that also had considerable impact in the fields of both logic and librarianship.[2] Many classificationists have spanned the years in between and since. The most influential of this century is S. R. Ranganathan.

The impulses for classification study are varied. Aside from philosophical questions such as "What is the proper order of things, and the relationships among them?" and the diversion supplied by approaching classification as a logical or mathematical problem, other concerns such as the need to communicate precise information across language barriers,[3] the need to provide a useful framework for published bibliographies or catalogs, and the need to devise methods for reliable and rapid machine query, have had immediately identifiable practical purposes that could be appreciated by even the most pragmatic minds.

Present Classification Climate

The classification impulse with which most librarians are familiar or sympathetic is that which arises from the need to organize the universe of knowledge as represented by materials in a library in a physical way so that the materials can be conveniently maintained, added to, and used.[4] Although Melvil Dewey's work retained a strong connection to the philosophical framework of Bacon and his successors,[5] and was arranged to fit into a theoretical model, Dewey himself was struggling with the practical difficulties of arranging books in a particular library when he devised his Decimal Classification system. In describing his scheme some years later, Dewey emphasized his concessions to the needs of practicality, observing that

---

Reprinted, by permission, from *Journal of Academic Librarianship* 10 (March 1984), 17-22.

> ... everywhere filosofic theory and accuracy hav yielded to practical usefulness. The imposibility of making a satisfactory clasification of all knowlej as preserved in books, has been appreciated from the first, and theoretic harmony and exactness hav been repeatedly sacrificed to practical requirements.[6]

The Library of Congress carried Dewey's practical trend many steps further, and a theoretical basis for library classification was specifically eschewed when in 1900 Librarian Herbert Putnam decided that the Library of Congress should devise its own classification scheme, designed to fit its own particular collections and service needs.[7] The classification system which resulted is based on literary warrant, and reflects the actual holdings of the Library of Congress. It is almost totally enumerative, and devices for expansion of printed numbers are not based on a uniform theoretical model, but vary according to convenience from one class to another.

Call Number as Location Device

It's no wonder then, given the warning of the creator of one of the United States' two most used classification systems, and the clearly declared nontheoretical nature of the other, that call numbers are viewed by many librarians who assign them as means to the end of arranging and locating books, and not primarily as precise and intellectual representations of the subject content of the works classified. But the thought that the formulation of the perfect call number is a great good pursued uniformly by library processing staff no matter what the cost is an idea that dies hard, and some librarians continue to regard the assignment of the right classification number as a kind of crusade.[8] The very complexity and length of the tools involved in assigning numbers (the Library of Congress schedules occupy more than six linear feet of shelving, and the 19th edition of the Dewey Decimal Classification is nearly 3,400 pages long) would seem to support this perception, since it is difficult to imagine that so much time and trouble would be spent devising call numbers that are only close approximations of the subject content. There is no doubt that to make today's predominantly open stack libraries more usable, librarians do go to great lengths to arrange collections, primarily via call number, in a semblance of subject order. The perception is mistaken all the same.

In addition to the nontheoretical nature of the classification schemes themselves, there are other reasons why the "call number as location device" view is the one which holds sway in today's operational arena. A prime reason has to be the difficulty experienced by classificationists in devising a universal, usable, flexible, generally acceptable, updatable scheme for the classification of knowledge. Despite considerable efforts directed toward this end, even dedicated groups such as the British Classification Research Group (CRG), and the Committee on Classification Research of the International Federation for Documentation (FID/CR) have eventually turned toward creating smaller schemes with specialized applications. A general system has yet to be designed or acclaimed. Some would say that Ranganathan's Colon Classification comes close, but even its admirers are slow to claim that it is simple to use when applied fully, especially in regard to shelving and shelf browsing.[9] Classification schedules whose primary aim is to organize library materials along subject lines, however, have been devised. Each such system has weaknesses, but in schemes that do not claim to be ideal, some flaws can be tolerated.

Economic Pressures

Another explanation for the current role of classification is actually a concatenation of reasons that can collectively be called economic pressures. Even in the fair economic climate of the 1960s, work to be done in libraries exceeded the staff available to do it to perfection. Increasingly, traditional activities have been examined in terms of costs, cost/benefit, and cost effectiveness. These considerations have aided the development and spread of practices such as "mark and park" (acceptance without revision of call numbers assigned by some other agency, usually the Library of Congress); nonrevision of call numbers when class numbers are revised; arbitrary shortening or simplification of classification numbers to meet the needs of computer systems, printing capabilities, etc.

Use as a Shelflist

A final reason may be both cause and effect: For more than 100 years in the United States and many other countries, the primary avenue for subject retrieval of materials in a library collection has been an alphabetically arranged dictionary or subject card catalog, where the emphasis is on subject headings, titles, and other entries.[10] The classed catalog, once a rather common and highly regarded means for public access to subject information, has become today's shelflist, and is now largely an internal file, usually unavailable to the public. Its primary use is in inventory control. Even the call number searching capability in many of today's online catalogs is a thinly disguised shelflist access. Very few systems incorporate a call number or shelf browsing capability, so although they work well for item searches, their use in a true subject search is limited.[11]

Increased Potential for Classification Retrieval

The strong entrance of computer technology into libraries in the 1960s sparked renewed interest in classification, as the capabilities of earlier machines led many to seek avenues for machine query that were easier to handle than words and text strings. The availability of online searching of remote bibliographic databases also gave rise to new consideration of classification schemes as tools for enhancing retrieval. Since the early 1960s, the Universal Decimal Classification (UDC) system has been used in a computer context to assist in the production of bibliographies and subject indexes, and in Selective Dissemination of Information (SDI) services.[12] Several information retrieval databases have their own computer-related uses for class numbers, although notations are usually devised for the specific database or are derived from the discipline being searched, rather than being assigned from a widely used library classification system.

Perhaps because such databases are often the province of commercial bodies that must consider profitability and their own often narrow goals, they have seemed to be beyond librarians' power to influence. A more recent development in library use of computer technology strikes closer to home.

The Online Catalog as an Operational Reality

From its position as a theoretical possibility discussed as part of a moderately distant future in the mid-1970s, the online catalog has emerged in the early 1980s as an operational reality, and one which librarians feel competent to comment on and to mold. Although the primary concern in developing online catalog technology has been the provision of satisfactory retrieval of bibliographic records via the verbal access points of author, title, series, and subjects, the possibility of using classification numbers in subject searching has also received some attention. Online access via call number or classification[13] was one of the topics afforded major consideration at the 1982 Council on Library Resources' special conference on subject access.[14]

Librarians are only now attempting to assimilate the reality and potential of online catalog access via subject headings and subject terms, so it is not surprising that some are reluctant to turn their attention to another type of subject access at this time. But although verbal representations of subject content such as subject headings, keywords, and other descriptors have received most of the United States' subject analysis attention in recent decades, verbal and notational depiction of the subject content of individual works are merely two aspects of the same problem, and it is increasingly difficult to leave untended the topic of notational classification.[15] Classification theorists typically find it difficult to think about one without the other, and often use some of the same terminology to discuss both.

It is not classification experts, however, who will initially determine how or whether online catalogs will incorporate class number searching. It is more likely to be catalog and information access generalists who will have the greatest impact. Generalists and specialists alike cannot but recognize that in addition to the traditional views of catalog data searched and organized by verbal headings, online catalogs have the capability to provide through computer manipulation of records another valuable arrangement of information—the classed catalog. The library profession effectively jettisoned the classed catalog from its complement of bibliographic access tools in the last century, not because the classed catalog was unuseful, but only because it was less useful than the dictionary catalog that replaced it and even without the classed catalog the shelves continued to provide classified subject access to the patron willing to browse. While libraries were bound by the limitations of the card technology, they could not afford to supply both types of catalogs. Online technology can potentially supply both and more.

Effect of Past and Present Practice on the Effectiveness of Class Number Access

Despite the advantages that may accrue from adding another technique to the arsenal of search strategies available from online catalogs, class number access is not without defects and potential handicaps, especially in light of today's and yesterday's practices in assigning call numbers. To proceed with designing online classification access in a rational way, with realistic expectations, and a decent understanding of what remains to be done, librarians need to recognize some of the problems inherent in past and present classification practice.

Classification Schemes Are Not Easy for Users to Figure Out

It is difficult to tell what patrons think about call numbers assigned to library materials, but regardless of whether a user believes that the classification number reflects the precise subject content of a work, it is a rare user who knows how to interpret any but the most basic parts of a number. Less common still is the user who can manufacture a class number on his own. One of the commonly held tenets for online catalogs is that they should be directly usable by patrons, and that they should not require an "expert" intermediary in the way that other information retrieval databases do. For class number access to meet this aim, a system of user aids would need to be devised and made available. Even then, it is likely that class number access would be used by fewer people than could profit by it, and would be used badly by some.

Without understanding the classification system, and lacking user aids, a user can still obtain a class number to search from a work already known to be on the desired subject. A similar widely recommended tactic instructs catalog users to consult subject heading tracings present on relevant records in the catalog, and to use the headings found to refine or broaden a search. A class number search performed along these lines could be quite helpful, but because the user's grasp of the meaning of the numbers may be close to nil, the search could also yield unsatisfactory, unexpected, or even bewildering results.

Classification Numbers Have Not Remained Static

Classification numbers have changed as fields of knowledge have changed. Although most classification schemes try not to re-use old numbers for some period of time, and generally resist wholesale relocation of subjects, re-use and relocation nevertheless happen frequently. Between the 14th and 17th editions of the Dewey Decimal Classification, for instance, nearly 2,400 numbers were relocated, and the process of revision continued unabated through the 19th edition.[16] The Library of Congress uses more than 400 pages a year to issue revisions to its own schedules, and a significant portion of revisions are changes in the scope of numbers and in the location of subjects. Added to the problem of number relocation is the matter of increasing complexity and detail in classification schedules. Topics that were once general divide and subdivide, and material that used to belong in an umbrella number now gets a class number of its own.

It is an uncommon library of significant size that can afford to reclassify all previously cataloged materials just to reflect changes in the classification schedules. Since reclassification can involve intellectual steps as well as physical handling, even the computer's ability to alter every occurrence of a particular character string will still leave "reclassified" items marked and shelved as before.

The availability in machine-readable form of classification schedules and correlation tables, and references between old and new numbers, and among different schemes could provide the initial resources that would enable a computer to retrieve relevantly classified material regardless of the age of the cataloging, and regardless of the classification schedule used,[17] while still leaving the items themselves with their original markings. Although such a capacity would ease the retrieval of differently classified material, it would probably not signal freedom to reclassify whole collections, since the confusion of patrons searching one number in the catalog, and retrieving another number from the shelves could be considerable.

Classification Numbers Are Sometimes Inconsistently Assigned within a Library

They may be consistent with themselves while being at variance from general practice. For example, area collections may choose to emphasize geography over topic in call numbers while the remainder of the library classifies topic over place; Special Collections material may be classed with locally developed schemes; some departments may use Dewey while others use LC; previous standards for minuteness of classification may have had to be revised to fit with card printing or computer display capabilities; and major portions of a collection, such as journals or fiction, may be unclassified.

Classification Numbers Grant Only One Opportunity to Portray the Subject Content of a Work

Classification numbers as currently assigned must be broad enough to encompass the subject content of an entire work. A work, however, may have several identifiably different topics which can be denoted by discrete subject headings. As a result of the noncorrespondence between a single call number and multiple subject headings, it might be expected that much less on a particular topic will be revealed through a search under classification number than is actually present in a catalog. Kelley's classic investigation of the usefulness of classification to the library user bore out this expectation.[18] She found that for three selected subject headings (Beaver, Buffalo, Cormorant), only about one-third the number of titles found by a subject heading search would have been found via a search under the specific call numbers.[19] A more recent test in the Northwestern University Library catalog yielded far less tidy results and illustrates an unpredictability of representation that depends on the minuteness of the classification scheme on a particular topic and on the specificity of the related subject headings. In the case of "Beavers," one quarter the number of titles found under subject heading were retrieved by classification number, but because the relevant Dewey number covers all Sciuromorpha, half the items found were on chipmunks and prairie dogs. "Immortality" yielded 180 titles, but a search of the most relevant class numbers brought to light only 5 percent of that number. A search of "Family Size" retrieved five times as many titles under class number as under subject heading, but because of the broadness of the applicable class numbers, which encompassed such topics as marriage and birth control, most items found through the shelflist were irrelevant to the heading. The most that can be concluded from results such as these is that a class number search will find different works than a subject heading search for the same topic, but just how they will differ cannot be reliably predicted.

Gorman has suggested that the dichotomy between the class number as shelving device, and the class number as subject retrieval device could be solved through the assignment of more than one class number to each item. One relatively general number would be used for shelving, while, to enhance the classification retrieval potential of the database, one or more precise class numbers would be assigned as appropriate to express the different subject aspects of a work.[20] Aside from the unavailability of a suitable MARC field for such numbers, a matter that could be remedied, the greatest objection to the proposal could be economic, as library staffs that have already been relieved of even verifying pre-assigned call numbers are asked to assign multiple new numbers. Perhaps it is thought that the Library of Congress could be prevailed upon to assign multiple detailed class numbers (presumably both LC and DDC) on behalf of American libraries, but LC has already shown its vulnerability to economic pressures in the area of enriched subject access in connection with their investigation into the feasibility of assigning PRECIS strings to their records.[21]

Classification Numbers Are Often Not Really Assigned

Economic restraints combined with the wider availability of shared cataloging have resulted in a situation where classification numbers are increasingly assigned by persons remote from the particular library's catalog. In many libraries, call numbers complete with author Cutters, are simply accepted from incoming copy by clerks who neither examine nor understand them. Such acceptance effectively prevents consistent use of local classification schemes or local emphases within a common scheme. Unreviewed acceptance also means that mistakes and differences in viewpoints and practices from an assortment of libraries are incorporated into a single collection without a coordinating effort. Classification inconsistency is thus inevitable in the online catalog using these numbers, and builds potential unreliability into call number searching.

Classification Numbers Are Not Assigned with a View to Subject Searching

Unfortunately, not "every library [is] filled with people debating the finer points of the Dewey Decimal System."[22] As Gorman has observed, librarians in the United States are predominantly uninterested in classification theory, and are instead concerned with storage and retrieval of individual items.[23] This outlook and the widespread acceptance of practices such as "mark and park" and nonreclassification have contributed greatly to a general denigration of care taken in classification. It contributes to inexactitude in classification, which is a problem for the quality of class number retrieval, and to altering the profile of processing staffs in libraries, which is a problem for libraries being able to perform additional or more exact classification. It is an axiom of organizations that once a function has ceased to be performed, or a particular duty has been relinquished, especially if staff have been surrendered or diverted to other tasks, it is difficult to begin it again. Even if classification were immediately and overwhelmingly recognized as a top priority for subject access in online catalogs, there is a considerable inertia of present practice and staffing to overcome in order to achieve the desired end.

Classification Number Structure Is Not So Well Suited to Machine Searching as Might Be Thought

Possibly because classification schemes are composed mainly of numbers and other symbolic devices, and because in spite of our knowledge to the contrary, they seem to be formed on a theoretical basis, it may appear that class numbers are better suited for machine manipulation than are words or text strings. Several factors, however, make computer manipulation less simple than might be thought.

Limited effectiveness of truncation. Many online catalogs allow users to generalize a search or to compensate for insufficient confidence in a search term by means of truncation. Thus a user unsure whether material will be entered under "aeronautics" or "aeronautical" can search a truncated "aeronautic#" (where # signifies a truncation) and retrieve both. The usefulness of truncating words, of course, depends on the words themselves. Not until "aeronautic" is truncated to its first letter, for instance, will it retrieve "airplane" in the same search. Truncation of class numbers might seem to be even more useful than truncation of words, but it too is subject to limitations. The predominant difficulty with the truncation of LC numbers is calling up a far too general result. Off-target retrieval can also be a problem. For example, truncation of the LC call number for volleyball (GV1017.V6) would retrieve first works on other specific minor ball games (GV1017), then polo (GV1010-1011), and no amount of truncation would broaden the search to general works on ball games (GV861). Despite its deceptively more theoretical appearance, truncation of Dewey numbers is even less successful than shortening LC numbers.[24] Satisfactory performance of a subject search using truncated class numbers from either LC or Dewey would require at least a copy of the schedule, and would be greatly assisted by a basic understanding of the structure of the classification scheme.

Inconsistency of character strings. An area in which Dewey numbers might seem to have special advantages in machine searching is in the consistent use of certain strings of characters to denote particular concepts. Unfortunately, although a certain amount of correspondence does exist within the system, it does not hold constant throughout the schedules. For instance, while the 300s do house the social sciences, and persons occupied with the social sciences are denoted with numbers beginning with 3 in Table 7 (Persons), "3s" are used for parts of the Ancient World in Table 2 (Areas), and for Nordic Peoples in Table 5 (Racial, Ethnic, National Groups). The combination 012 is used to indicate classification of philosophy in Tables 1 and 3, but "nonaborigines" in Table 5. LC classification schedules have much less correspondence than Dewey, and notation conventions that may hold constant in a particular class (in G, for example, numbers with a fourth digit of 4 or 9 indicate a city or part of a city, while numbers whose fourth digit is 2 or 7 are for geographic regions or features) are not necessarily repeated in any other schedule or class. While such noncorrespondence of character combinations does not preclude successful class number searching any more than textual searching is precluded by disparately spelled synonyms, it does not constitute any particular advantage of classification searching over subject term searching.

Searchability of numbers. Computer technology has made substantial advances since libraries started using it, and operations that can be performed affordably and seemingly instantaneously by machines within the reach of individual libraries today would have placed significant burdens on some of the largest computers of the early 1960s. In the milieu of older, less competent and more expensive computing machines, exploration of means of information retrieval via terms such as class numbers that employ a limited character set seemed imperative. While it is still true that a computer can more easily perform searches on a restricted list of symbols than it can on the entire ALA character set, the advantage of numbers is not nearly so great as it used to be, and the need to devise an acceptable computer searching method using numbers has lost its urgency.

Proposals for Action

The limitations enumerated above have not gone unnoticed by the proponents of online catalog access via class number, but the view of visionaries is apt to be long, and supporters have made a number of suggestions for actions that would increase the likelihood and effectiveness of class number retrieval in the future.

A first priority for many is making the major classification systems available in machine-readable form, and relating them to each other, to their own previous editions, and to the commonly used subject heading lists.[25] If such data is to be useful to online catalog users, however, it needs to be incorporated into those catalogs, and for this to be possible, a MARC or MARC-like authorities format for classification numbers needs to be revised. Neither the creation of such a format, nor the intellectual coordination of classification numbers, nor the input of data is a matter of a few months' work. A major commitment of funds and staff would be required for original creation of the structure, as well as for its continued upkeep. Incorporation of the resultant data into the online catalog would also pose significant programming challenges.

Another proposal is that there be a differentiation between the use of classification numbers in shelf arrangement and their use as subject retrieval devices, and that numbers be assigned for both purposes. In addition to the finer subject analysis that multiple class numbers would make possible,[26] other reasons for making a distinction between shelf and catalog access include the increasing amounts of materials which may be available only through online retrieval systems, and which therefore do not constitute shelving problems.[27] The multiplicity of media in which information is being disseminated makes classified intershelving a practical impossibility and makes retrieval systems such as the online catalog the only remaining tools for classified access.[28] In fact, browsing the online catalog via call number as an alternative to browsing the shelves seems likely to become almost as much an assumed part of the future of catalog access[29] as Boolean operators have become. But like the siren of Boolean searching, which is widely listened to by designers, but is so far not all that heavily or well used, call number browsing is not necessarily easily implemented, it is not without costs, and it may not be easy to use.[30] At the most basic level, despite the fact that some suggestions for revisions in MARC fields to enhance classification retrieval have begun to be seen, accommodation of extra class numbers would require alterations in the bibliographic formats, and such alterations are generally neither easily nor speedily made.[31]

Conclusion

It is likely that most online catalog designers could bring up some semblance of call number or even classification access relatively soon if the demand for the service were great enough, but it has been seen that mere ability to retrieve an item by its call number has limited usefulness, and unless the problems of past practice, format hospitality, shortage of staff, etc. can be overcome, even the ability to browse the shelflist will have restricted applications. Although Cochrane and others urge that libraries not get "bogged down by the idiosyncracies of our present systems",[32] the future of classification access must take into account not only present and past systems and practices but also libraries' ability to alter them. No matter how willing catalogers might be to provide enhanced subject access through better, and possibly multiple classification numbers, only so much work can be accommodated by existing staff, and no matter how well new class numbers are assigned, the problems of older records will still need to be acknowledged. Some problems, such as the connection of related, though obsolete or "extra-systemic" numbers may be solvable, although at considerable expense, through creation of machine-readable and interrelated classification schemes, and their incorporation into bibliographic databases. Others, such as unrigorous assignment of class numbers, or blind acceptance of numbers assigned by others, may simply have to be lived with.

The automation of library processes and catalogs has developed at an astonishing rate in the last two decades, and with a success record that could lead an optimist to believe that anything is possible. But workable and generally accepted standards for online catalog access to textual entry fields such as authors, titles, and subjects are still far from settled at the national, library, or system level. Given the expense and time that may be involved in completing work on this type of access for which the demand is clear, and whose usefulness is not subject to question, it must be asked if the diversion of attention and funds to online classification searching is wise. The need for it is not so well established, and its ultimate success is so dependent on major expenditures, realignment of cataloging practices and policies, and alteration in staffing patterns.

A minimum requirement for an online catalog is that it afford at least as good access to information as the card catalog. Online subject searching by classification number would offer an approach to information well beyond the capabilities of card catalogs, and it is undoubtedly worth aiming for. Providing this avenue of access should form a part of our long-term speculations and plans, but it presents complex problems of programming, funding, bibliographic instruction, and more. Quick solutions will not be complete. Complete solutions will not be inexpensive. Online classification access belongs on our priority list, but not yet at the top.

Notes

[1] Arthur Maltby, *Sayers' Manual of Classification for Librarians*, 5th ed. (London: Andre Deutsch, 1975), p. 110.

[2] Ibid., p. 117.

[3] Hans G. Schulte-Albert, "Classificatory Thinking from Kinner to Wilkins: Classification and Thesaurus Construction, 1645-1668," *Library Quarterly* 49 (January 1979): 43.

[4] Paul S. Dunkin, *Cataloging U.S.A.* (Chicago: ALA, c1969), p. 124.

[5] Maltby, p. 121.

[6] Dunkin, p. 100.

[7] A. C. Foskett, *The Subject Approach to Information*, 4th ed. (Hamden, CT: Linnet Books, 1982), p. 409.

[8] Sanford Berman, "Consumer, Beware," *Technicalities* 2 (May 1982): 9-10.

[9] Ingetraut Dahlberg, "Major Developments in Classification" in *Advances in Librarianship*, v. 7, ed. Michael Harris (New York: Academic Press, 1977), p. 73.

[10] Ibid., p. 59.

[11] Charles R. Hildreth, *Online Public Access Catalogs: The User Interface* (Dublin, OH: OCLC, c1982), p. 131.

[12] Dahlberg, p. 76.

[13] In this paper, a distinction is made between access via class number—that is, via the segment of the call number that has subject significance, and access via the entire call number.

[14] *Subject Access: Report of a Meeting Sponsored by the Council on Library Resources, Dublin, Ohio, June 7-9, 1982*, compiled and edited by Keith W. Russell. (Washington: CLR, 1982), pp. 34-39, 59-60.

[15] That is, subject analysis represented by symbols rather than by words.

[16] Dunkin, p. 109.

[17] Dahlberg, p. 78.

[18] Grace Kelley, *The Classification of Books: An Enquiry into its Usefulness to the Reader*. N.Y.: H. W. Wilson, 1937.

[19]Dunkin, p. 18.

[20]Michael Gorman, "The Longer the Number, the Shorter the Spine," *American Libraries* 12 (September 1981): 499.

[21]Library of Congress Subject Cataloging Division "PRECIS Project" (January, 1978). Mimeographed. p. 5.

[22]Emma Lathen, *Ashes to Ashes*, (New York: Pocket Books, c1971), p. 89.

[23]Gorman, p. 498.

[24]Dahlberg, p. 78.

[25]Pauline Cochrane, "Classification as an Online Subject Access Tool: Challenges and Opportunity," in *Subject Access: Report of a Meeting Sponsored by the Council on Library Resources, Dublin, Ohio, June 7-9, 1982*. Compiled and edited by Keith W. Russell (Washington: CLR, 1982), p. 36.

[26]Gorman, p. 489.

[27]Nancy J. Williamson, "Is there a Catalog in your future? Access to Information in the Year 2006." *Library Resources & Technical Services* 26 (2) (April/June 1982): 133.

[28]Tor Henriksen, "Classification and Subject Cataloging in the 1980s: IFLA's Role," *International Cataloging* 10 (4) (Oct/Dec 1981): 47.

[29]Elaine Svenonius, "Use of Classification in Online Retrieval," *Library Resources & Technical Services*, 27 (1) (January/March 1983): 79.

[30]Charles R. Hildreth, "To Boolean or not to Boolean." *Information Technology and Libraries* 2 (3) (September 1983, June 1983): 235-237; Walt Crawford, "Long Searches, Slow Response: Recent Experience on RLIN." *Information Technology and Libraries* 2 (2): 179, 182.

[31]Arnold S. Wajenberg, "MARC Coding of DDC for Subject Retrieval." *Information Technology and Libraries* 2 (3) (January/March 1983): 246-251.

[32]Cochrane, p. 39.

Analysis of Vocabulary Control in Library of Congress Classification and Subject Headings

John Phillip Immroth

Development of the Argument for Analysis of Relationship Between L. C. Subject Headings and L. C. Classification

Introductory Summary

The following 206 subject headings which were derived from three groups of samples are analysed from three different approaches. First the structure of the subject headings and the parallel classification and index headings are examined graphemically, morphologically and syntactically. It is hoped that this structural analysis will discern the parallel linguistic forms of these three approaches to subject analysis. Not only are the perfect matches or identities considered but also the variants of a perfect match are treated. The second analytical approach deals with the semantic parallels of the different headings. Pertinent headings are analysed for lexical meaning. Examples of contextual meaning are also isolated if possible. The third approach is an analysis of the classification numbers attached to the subject heading entry.

The structural analysis consists of three parts. These are graphemic analysis, morphologic analysis and syntactical analysis. The graphemic analysis consists of matching the shapes of the subject headings with the shapes of the classification and index headings. There are three possibilities which may result from graphemic analysis: match, partial match or no match. Match means that all of the symbols or graphemes making up a subject heading are present in the same order in the other heading being examined. Partial match means most of the graphemes are present but not in the same order or not in the same quantity. No match means that there is no parallel graphemic structure between the subject heading and the other heading. The

---

Reprinted, by permission, from John Phillip Immroth, *Analysis of Vocabulary Control in Library of Congress Classification and Subject Headings* (Littleton, Colo.: Libraries Unlimited, 1971), 83-88, 90-101, 107-8.

morphologic and syntactical analysis follows directly from the graphemic analysis. A listing of partial matches begins this phase of the structural analysis. If the partial matches are represented symbolically, they may then be listed and tabulated. Those partial matches which appear to form paradigmatic classes are considered to be morphologic. If paradigmatic classes do not appear, the structure of the partial matches is considered to be syntactical. The use of any function word in the subject heading causes the heading to be considered as syntactical. It may be noted here that examples of repetitive syntactical structure occur very frequently in the subject heading list and only once in the sample covered.

Three groups of subject headings were analysed for graphemic structure. The first group contains forty-nine subject headings. The second group consists of eleven headings; and the third group contains one hundred and forty-six headings. The unevenness of these three groups results from the large number of subject headings contained in the syndetic structure of particular headings. The first group was generated from five random numbers and their appropriate headings. The first two headings generated only a total of five subject headings. The third heading 'Heraldry' generated thirty-four headings. The second group of four headings contained eleven headings and the last group (separated necessarily from the second group) contains all the subdivisions under the heading "Shakespeare". As these three groups total 206 subject headings, no further groups were generated. The author considers this sample to be large enough to test the methodology of this study.

	Classification	Index
Group 1 (49 SH)		
match	10	10
no match	21	17
partial match	23	27
Group 2 (11 SH)		
match	2	4
no match	4	2
partial match	6	3
Group 3 (146 SH)		
match	38	n.a.
no match	65	n.a.
partial match	50	n.a.

The index headings were not counted for group 3 as Shakespeare has only five index headings. These are:
    Shakespeare: PR 2750-3112.
       Authorship: PR 2937-2961.
       Biography: PR 2900-2936.
       Criticism: PR 2885-3088.
       Works: PR 2750-2875.
There is one additional entry in the Additions and Changes:
       Oxford, Edward De Vere, 17th earl of: PR 2947.
There are no entries for Bacon or anyone else involved in the Shakespeare authorship controversy.

	Classification	Index
TOTAL (206 SH)		
match	50	14 (of 60)
no match	65	19 (of 60)
partial match	79	30 (of 60)

In the first group of forty-nine headings 20% appear in identical shape in both the classification schedules and indexes. 43% do not appear at all in the classification schedules while 35% do not appear in the index. Partial matches make up the largest section of this group with 47% in the classification and 55% in the indexes. Similar patterns appear in groups two and three. However, it should be noted that in group three there are more 'no matches' than 'partial matches'. The total tally shows 25% of the classification and 23% of the index headings matching the subject headings. 35% of the classification headings do not match while 32% of the index headings do not match. 40% of the classification headings are partial matches and 50% of the index headings are partial matches. The graphemic analysis shows that about one-fourth of the sample of subject headings match perfectly with the classification and indexes. The size of the sample may preclude the possibility of drawing any further conclusions from these figures.

The second phase of the structural analysis considers the morphology and syntax of the same headings. Of the ten matches in the first sample, nine are direct matches of one word for one word in the classification. Similarly six matches in the index are direct matches of one mass noun for the same mass noun. The other matches in the first group each have a different pattern. These are 'word dash word', 'adjectival word', and 'word/word'. The term 'word' is used generally in these examples to mean a noun in mass form. The no matches of the first group have a very similar pattern. It appears then that the mass noun form is likely to occur in both groups more frequently than any other form. The partial matches show the greatest variety of forms. The form of a subject heading qualified by a gloss word in the index occurs seven times in the first group. The pattern of subject heading followed by a conjunctive function word and another word occurs twice in the classification headings and once in the index. All other forms in the first group occur only once. This is a total of twenty-nine different variants appearing only once in the sample. The partial matches show fifteen forms with additional contextual qualifiers and sixteen forms with some contextual qualifiers of the subject heading not present. The following charts show symbolically the varieties of form in the first sample. In these charts W means a noun in mass form, W_a an adjectival word, F a function word, F_c a conjunctive function word, f an article function word, SH a subject heading, and (sp) a spelling variation.

	Classification	Index
Chart 1 — Matches		
W	9	6
W–W	1	0
W_aW	0	1
W, W_a	0	1
W/W	0	1
WFWF_cW	0	1

	Classification	Index
Chart 2 — No match		
W	6	5
W (W)	1	1
W, W_a	1	0
W_a W	1	1
W F W	1	1
W F_c W	1	1
W_a W, W F f	1	1
W_a W W_a W F W, date–date	1	1
–W	3	3
–W F_c W	2	2

Chart 3 — Partial match	Classification	Index
SH (sp)	5	4
Partial matches with additional contextual qualification		
SH (W)	0	7
SH, W_a	0	1
SH F_c W	2	1
SH F W	0	1
SH, W F_c W	1	0
SH/F W F W	0	1
SH (W_a W)	1	0
W F_c SH	1	0
W F SH	1	1
W (SH . . .)	1	0
SH/ F W	0	1
SH/ W	0	1
W F f SH	1	0
SH, W F	0	1
Partial matches with some contextual qualification missing		
SH — ($\cdot Z_1$)	1	0
SH — ($\cdot Z_1$) (W F W)	0	1
SH —f —sh (W)	0	1
SH, —sh_a (F f W)	1	0
SH, —sh_a F W	0	1
-sh +W SH	1	0
—sh —f SH	1	1
SH (—sh)	1	1
SH — ($\cdot Z_1$) (—sh)	1	0
SH (—sh), W_a	0	1
SH —F —sh W, W, . . .	1	0
SH —sh —F	0	1
SH ($\cdot Z_1$) —W	1	1
SH —F —f —W	0	1
—W SH, W	1	0
(W, SH —f —sh)	1	0

Because of the great number of variations occurring in the first group and the apparent likelihood of this continuing as a seemingly endless list, the second and third groups were not analysed in this fashion. The only paradigmatic classes which appear to be present are the identities which require no transformation and the pattern of SH transformed to SH (W) in the index. The other classes may or may not be paradigmatic. The structural relationship between the subject headings and the classification headings or the index headings does not appear to be consistent in the transformations found in the sample.

The second approach used in this analysis is an attempt to isolate certain semantic features. Lexical meanings are isolated by using a dictionary meaning. This device allows synonyms and near synonyms to be discerned and classified. Further contextual meanings are isolated whenever possible and useful. This method shows that many subject headings apparently rely on the context of the subject heading list for their specific meaning. This context is often provided by a classification number, a scope note or syndetic devices. The area of semantics which the author has not yet been able to isolate deals with the conceptual meanings or the deep structure of the subject heading.

In the first group of samples, which were the only ones treated in this phase of analysis, there are twenty-five discernible semantic variants. All of these variants will be examined in the following section dealing with specific examples. The variants may be summarized as one instance of wrong contextual meaning, one instance of limited contextual meaning, one instance of expanded or redundant contextual meaning, eighteen instances of the contextual meaning contained in the classification number, two possible titles listed as subject headings, one instance of unclear conceptual meaning, and five classes of near synonyms involving twenty subject headings isolated by lexical meanings.

The last approach to analysis deals with the assigned classification numbers. The first sample includes four areas of inconsistency in these numbers. There is one instance of an apparently wrong class number, six number ranges that are too broad, four ranges that are too narrow, and five instances of unused appropriate class numbers. This is a total of sixteen classification inconsistencies in a sample of forty-nine headings or 37% of the headings in this group. In addition there are fourteen headings referring to more than one class number. These headings may apparently be considered as ambiguous in the sense of the classification system. Besides the first sample, the third sample dealing with Shakespeare shows many classificatory inconsistencies. Following the detailed discussion of the first sample, these Shakespeare headings will be rearranged in classified form and compared to the section of the classification dealing with Shakespeare. The only conclusion to be drawn at this point as a result of the summary of the classification number analysis is that the amount of inconsistency seems to be very great.

. . . .

The third random number, 17594, directed the author to page 586 four inches down the second column. This leads to the subject heading 'Heraldry'. This heading has twenty-four sa references, five x references and sixteen xx references. There are also three subdivisions listed. Ten of the xx references also occur as sa references so that there are only thirty-four total to deal with as well as the five x references. The depth of this syndetic structure although initially distressing to the author proves to be most useful. It is in this sample that five classes of near synonyms are isolated. Also there are fourteen instances of contextual meaning contained in the classification.

SH 3	CH 3 CR	IH 3
Heraldry (National, CR; National: theory, JC 345)	Heraldry	Heraldry: CR
	—Political theory —Symbolism, emblems of the state: Arms, Flag, Seal, etc. —General works. Theory. JC 345	Heraldry, National/ Theory: JC 345 Practice: CR

The parent heading of this large family is checked in two different schedules as two different class numbers are given. In CR there is a graphemic match in both the schedules and the index. Its structure is a consistent single mass noun. Semantically this term is defined as

The art or science of a herald; now esp. the art or science of blazoning armorial bearings, of tracing and recording pedigrees, and of deciding questions of precedence.[1]

The lexical meaning for this term may be used to demonstrate the first class of near synonyms. This includes blazonry, pedigrees, and precedence. Two of those terms appear as x references to heraldry which seems to acknowledge the near synonymity of the three lexical senses. Precedence, however, is itself a subject heading listed in heraldry's sa references. The class number CR for the entire subclass devoted to heraldry is appropriate. In the second class number attached to heraldry there is no graphemic match in the classification and a partial match in that index. Its symbolized structure is SH, W_a. It should be noted that the qualification 'National' in the index may also be found in heraldry's class numbers but not with the heading itself. This is a good example of contextual meaning contained in the class number.

sa 3 : 1	CH 3 : 1	IH 3 : 1
Achievements (Heraldry) (CR 41.A)	—Heraldry —Special —Special branches, charges, etc., A-Z.	(∅)

The first sa reference in this family is very interesting in this same sense. 'Achievements (Heraldry)' is the only Heraldry reference which used the gloss word 'Heraldry'. There is no graphemic match for this heading. Morphologically this is a W (W) for which there is no match in the classification or index. Lexically we may discover a second class of near synonyms. The heraldry sense of this word is

An escutcheon or ensign armorial, granted in memory of some achievement. (In this sense corrupted to hatchment.)[2]

Escutcheon and hatchment are also sa references.

sa 3 : 2	CH 3 : 2	IH 3 : 2
Badges (Heraldry, CR 67-69)	CR 67-69 Devices and badges 67 General works. 69 By country, A-Z.	Badges (Heraldry): CR 67-69

Badges is the second sa reference under heraldry. It appears as a partial match in both the classification and the index. The form of the partial match is different however. CH = W F_c SH; IH = SH (W). The lexical meaning of this term introduces class 3 of the classes of near synonyms. There are a total of ten members of this class. Badge is defined as

A distinctive device, emblem, or mark.[3]

Contextually the qualification that badges refers specifically to heraldic badges is contained in the classification gloss and not in the subject heading gloss.

sa 3 : 3	CH 3 : 3 CR 79	IH 3 : 3
Battle-cries (Heraldry, CR 79)	Battle cries. War cries.	Battle cries: CR 79

The third sa reference shows a spelling variation between the subject heading and the classification. Also its contextual meaning appears to be contained in the classification gloss. Certainly there can be battle cries in history, literature, etc.

sa 3 : 4	CH 3 : 4 CR 4501-6305	IH 3 : 4
Chivalry (CR)	Chivalry and knighthood (Orders, decorations, etc.)	Chivalry: CR 4501-6305

Chivalry appears as a match in the index and a partial match in the classification. The partial match is SH F_c W. This heading may be seen a member of class four of heraldic near synonyms. The other member is 'Knights and knighthood'. Again the contextual meaning is found in the classification number. It may also be observed that the classification number is too broad. CR 4501-6305 would seem to be more appropriate than simply CR.

sa 3 : 5	CH 3 : 5	IH 3 : 5
Color in heraldry (no CN)	(∅)	(∅)

This heading is not found graphemically in the classification or index. Its structure is W F W. It appears that it might be a possible title used as a subject heading. It is an approach outside of the structural treatment of heraldry in the classification system. (In the following examples only different variations will be cited.)

sa 3 : 6	CH 3 : 6 CR 55-57	IH 3 : 6
Crests (CR 55-57)	Crests 55 General works. 57 By country, A-Z.	Crests (Heraldry): CR 55-7

Crests is a member of class 3 as its lexical meaning states that it is "A figure or device".[4] Devices is also a sa reference.

sa 3 : 7	CH 3 : 7 CR 4501-6305	IH 3 : 7
Decorations of honor (CR 4501-6305; Military, UB 430-435)	Chivalry and knighthood (Orders, decorations, etc.)	Decorations (Heraldry): CR 4501-6305

This is also a member of class 3 as decorations are defined as "A star, cross, medal or other badge conferred and worn as a mark of honour."[5] It would also seem that the phrase 'of honor' is an instance of expanded or redundant contextual meaning.

sa 3 : 8	CH 3 : 8	IH 3 : 8
	CR 67-69	
Devices	Devices and badges	Devices (Heraldry):
(Heraldry, CR 67-69)	67 General works.	CR 67-69
	69 By country, A-Z.	
	[see CH 3 : 2]	

Devices also belongs to class 3. Its lexical meaning also shows another near synonym.

> An emblematic figure or design, esp. one borne by a particular person, etc., as a heraldic bearing, etc.: usually accompanied by a motto ME.; also, a motto or legend borne with or in place of such a design.[6]

Mottoes is also a sa reference under heraldry.

sa 3 : 9	CH 3 : 9	IH 3 : 9
Emblems	(∅)	(∅)
(Art, N 7740;		
Christianity, BV 150-		
155; Comparative		
religion, BL 603;		
Heraldry, CR;		
Literature, PN		
6349-6358)		

Emblems which is a no match in regard to heraldry is also a member of class 3 of near synonyms. One of its lexical senses states, "A figured object used symbolically, as a badge."[7] It may also be noted that the classification reference to the entire subclass CR is too broad. In fact the number of classification references to various sections of the classification system may be interpreted as ambiguous from a classificatory sense. Certainly one may say that this particular subject heading must bring together material separated by the classification; but the value of such an ambiguous assemblage is questionable.

sa 3 : 10	CH 3 : 10	IH 3 : 10
Emblems, National	[see CH 3]	Emblems of state:
(no CN)		JC 345

Morphologically the partial matches of this heading are 'Emblems of the state' and 'Emblems of state'. The first of these partial matches seems to be an acceptable transformation of the subject heading. In fact 'of the state' appears to be substitutable for 'National' without requiring the inversion in the subject heading. The second partial match from the index is questionable from a grammatical sense. The omission of the article does not seem correct. Further in a classification sense it appears that there is an unused appropriate class number for this heading. JC 345 could be used as a classification reference.

sa 3 : 11	CH 3 : 11 CR 91-93	IH 3 : 11
Escutcheons (CR 91-93)	Shields and supporters 91 General works. 93 By country, A-Z.	(∅) Shields (Heraldry): CR 91-93 Supporters (Heraldry): CR 91-93.

Escutcheons which has already been cited as a member of class 2 has no graphemic match in the classification or index. It is defined as

> The shield or shield-shaped surface on which a coat of arms is depicted; also, the shield with the bearings; a representation of this. A hatchment.[8]

From this lexical description a closeness between classes 2 and 3 of near synonyms may be seen. The contextual meaning shows that this subject heading is being used as a synonym for the classification heading 'Shields and supporters'; however, neither of the other members of class 2 refers to CR 91-93. Thus lexically all members of class 2 are near synonyms but contextually they are not. This seems to show a weakness in the classification headings as well as the subject headings.

sa 3 : 12	CH 3 : 12 CR 345-347	IH 3 : 12
Flags (Emblems of state, JC 345-7; Heraldry, CR 101-115; Merchant marine signaling, VK 385; Military science, U 360-365, UC 590-595; Naval science, V 300-305	Symbolism, emblems of the state: Arms, Flag, Seal, etc. CR 101-115 Flags, banners, and standards	Flag (Emblem of state): JC 345-347 Flags/As emblems of government: JC 345-7 Heraldry: CR 101-15

This heading with six classificatory references (two of which are considered under heraldry) is apparently ambiguous and too generic. Further the contextual meanings given by the classificatory references appear to be too limited.

sa 3 : 13	CH 3 : 13 CS	IH 3 : 13
Genealogy (CS)	Genealogy	Genealogy: CS

This is the fourth subject heading in this sample to pass all four analytical tests. It is the name of an entire subclass, CS, in the classification schedules.

sa 3 : 14	CH 3 : 14	IH 3 : 14

Hatchments
(no CN)
	—Heraldry
	  —Special
	    —Special branches, charges, etc., A-Z.
	CR 41
	[example incl. hatchments]
		Hatchments
		(Heraldry): CR 41

Hatchments already listed as a member of class 2 is defined as "An escutcheon or ensign armorial; = ACHIEVEMENT."[9] Further there is an appropriate class number for hatchments that is not used.

sa 3 : 15	CH 3 : 15	IH 3 : 15
	CR 4480	
Insignia	Royalty. (Insignia.	Insignia of royalty:
(Jeweled, NK 7400-7419; Military, UC 530-535; Naval, VC 345; *Royalty, CR 4480;* Secret societies, HS 159-160)	Regalia, crown and coronets, etc.)	CR 4480

Insignia is another apparent ambiguous heading with limited contextual meanings. It is a member of class 3 of near synonyms.

> Badges or distinguishing marks of office or honour; emblems of a nation, person, etc.[10]

sa 3 : 16	CH 3 : 16	IH 3 : 16
Knights and knighthood (CR)	Chivalry and knighthood (Orders, decorations, etc.) CR 4501-6305	Knighthood: CR 4501-6305

Knights and knighthood appears to be a near synonym of Chivalry and has a classificatory reference that is too broad.

sa 3 : 17	CH 3 : 17	IH 3 : 17
	CR 4701-4775	
Military religious orders (CR 4701-4775)	Military-religious orders	Military-religious orders/ Heraldry: CR 4701-75 Numismatics: CJ 1691-7 Seals: CD 5545-51

This heading which contains another spelling variation has a limited contextual meaning in its classificatory reference. The index to Class C shows additional uses of this phase under both Numismatics, CJ, and Seals, CD. It would seem that either this heading should be further qualified to incorporate these other senses or it must be interpreted as limited only to military religious orders in heraldry. The lack of references to Classes B, Philosophy and Religion, and U, Military Science, is also questionable.

sa 3 : 18	CH 3 : 18	IH 3 : 18
	CR 73-75	
Mottoes (PN 6309-6318; Heraldry, CR 73-75)	Mottoes 73 General works.	Mottoes (Heraldry): CR 73-5

Mottoes has already been listed as a member of class 3 but its lexical meaning shows that it is also related to class 2.

1. Orign., a word, sentence, or phrase, attached as a legend to an 'impresa' or emblematical design. Hence, more widely, a short sentence or phrase inscribed on some object, and expressing an appropriate reflection or sentiment; also, a proverbial or pithy maxim adopted by a person as his rule of conduct. b. spec. in Her. A significant word or sentence usually placed upon a scroll, occas. having some reference to the name or exploits of the bearer, to the charges upon the shield or to the crest, but more often expressing merely a pious aspiration or exalted sentiment.[11]

sa 3 : 19	CH 3 : 19	IH 3 : 19
Nobility	(Ø)	Nobility (Heraldry):
(Political theory,	Titles of honor, rank,	CR 3499-4420
JC 411-417; Social	precedence, etc.	
classes, HT 647-650)	CR 3499-4420	

The index heading gives an unused appropriate class number for this seemingly ambiguous heading.

sa 3 : 20	CH 3 : 20	IH 3 : 20
	CR 4501-6305	
Orders of knighthood	Chivalry and knighthood	Orders of knighthood and
and chivalry	(Orders, decorations,	knighthood and
(CR 4501-6305)	etc.)	chivalry: CR 4651-6305
	—Orders, etc.	
	CR 4651-6305	

This heading which may be considered a member of class 5 of near synonyms along with the above listed Nobility and the following heading Peerage but it may also be interpreted lexically as a member of class 3 and graphemically as a member of class 4. Further it is closely related to Military Religious Orders. And finally it has the same classificatory reference as Decorations of Honor.

sa 3 : 21	CH 3 : 21	IH 3 : 21
Precedence	Order of precedence	Precedence, Order of,
(CR; JX 1678-9;	CR 3575	see Order of precedence
Diplomatic,	[also subdivision 8 in	Order of procedence [sic]
JX 4081)	Table I]	General: CR 3575
		By country: CR 3600-4420,
		Subdivision 8, Table I

Precedence has already been cited as a member of class 1. Further its classificatory reference is apparently too broad.

sa 3 : 22	CH 3 : 22	IH 3 : 22
	CD 5001-6471	
Seals (Numismatics)	Seals	Seals/
(CD 5001-6471;	—Theory. Method, etc.	General: CD 5001-6471
National, JC 345-7)	5037 Relation to heraldry.	Seals and heraldry: CD 5037
	5041 Relation to	Seals and numismatics:
	numismatics	CD 5041
	Symbolism, emblems of	Seals, National: JC 345
	the state: Arms, Flag,	
	Seal, etc.	
	JC 345-347	

The first classificatory reference for this heading is too broad. CD 5001-6471 refers to Seals in general not seals and numismatics. Apparently from the index headings there should be such headings as *Seals, *Seals (Heraldry) and Seals (Numismatics). Only the third heading exists in the subject heading list although there are the following headings: Seals (Animals), Seals (Christmas, etc.), and Seals (Law).

sa 3 : 23	CH 3 : 23	IH 3 : 23
Titles of honor and nobility (CR 3499-4420)	CR 3499-4420 Titles of honor, rank, precedence, etc.	Titles of nobility: CR 3499-4420

This heading also belongs to the apparently ambiguous class 5. There appears to be no precision of meaning for such terms as nobility, honor, rank, precedence, etc. in either the subject heading list or the classification schedule.

sa 3 : 24	CH 3 : 24	IH 3 : 24
Visitations, Heraldic (CS 410-497)	—Genealogy —By country —Great Britain and England CS 410-499	Visitations, Heraldic/ Great Britain: CS 419 County: CS 437

Lexically this heading means "A periodic visit made to a district by heralds to examine and enrol arms and pedigrees."[12] The classificatory reference refers only to British heraldic visitations. The inversion of this heading does not seem necessary. *Visitations (Heraldry) or even *Visitations would seem to have the same lexical meaning.

> also subdivision Heraldry under subjects, e.g. Book industries and trade— Heraldry; Popes—Heraldry; also particular heraldic devices, e.g. Collar (in heraldry), Coq gaulois (Heraldic device), Eagle (in heraldry), Elephant (in heraldry), Fleur-de-lis

The above note separating the sa references from the x references demonstrates the use of Heraldry as a subdivision. Only a census of the list could demonstrate this use fully. Heraldry as a subdivision is not considered in this paper. The examples of particular heraldic devices are somewhat disconcerting. The gloss may be (in heraldry) or (heraldic device). The latter seems to be a wiser choice as it does not involve the function word 'in'. Further there is no apparent reason why there are some heraldic devices listed as sa references, e.g. Achievements and Hatchments, and others such as Collars, Eagles, Elephants, etc. are not. It may also be noted that the x reference Gryphons would seem to fit into this group.

x 3 : 1-5	CH 3 : 25-29	IH 3 : 25-29
Arms, Coats of	(∅)	Arms (Heraldry), see Heraldry
Blazonry	(∅)	(∅)
Coats of Arms	(∅)	(∅)
Gryphons	(∅)	(∅)
Pedigrees	(∅)	(∅)

Four of the five x references are quite appropriately members of classes of near synonyms. Blazonry and Pedigrees are members of class 1 and Arms, Coats of and Coats of Arms are members of class 3. There is no apparent reason why Gryphons is listed as a see reference to

Heraldry. Lexically gryphon is listed as the supposedly dignified spelling of griffin.[13] As already mentioned Gryphons or Griffins would seem to fit more logically in the group of particular heraldic devices. Surely a fabulous animal having the head and wings of an eagle and the body and hind quarters of a lion is not meant to be synonymous with heraldry.

xx 3 : 1	CH 3 : 30	IH 3 : 30
	CC	
Archaeology	Archeology	Archeology: CC
(CC; Art, N; Indian		By country: D-F
and other American		
antiquities, E-F;		
National antiquities		
other than American,		
DA-DU; Prehistoric		
antiquities, GN; Social		
antiquities, manners,		
and customs: general,		
GT)		

This would be a match if the spelling variation did not exist.

xx 3 : 2	CH 3 : 31	IH 3 : 31
	CT	
Biography	Biography	Biography: CT
(CT)		

This is the fifth heading to pass all the analytical tests.

xx 3 : 3	CH	IH
Chivalry	[see CH 3 : 4]	[see IH 3 : 4]
xx 3 : 4	CH	IH
Crests	[see CH 3 : 6]	[see IH 3 : 6]
xx 3 : 5	CH	IH
Decorations of honor	[see CH 3 : 7]	[see IH 3 : 7]
xx 3 : 6	CH	IH
Devices	[see CH 3 : 8]	[see IH 3 : 8]
xx 3 : 7	CH	IH
Emblems, National	[see CH 3 : 10]	[see IH 3 : 10]
xx 3 : 8	CH	IH
Genealogy	[see CH 3 : 13]	[see IH 3 : 13]

The above six xx references have already been analysed as sa references. The varieties of generic and specific meaning that they represent demonstrates the obvious problems in the syndetic structure of the subject heading list.

xx 3 : 9	CH 3 : 32	IH 3 : 32
History	(0)	(0)
(D: History and In-		
ternational law, JX		
1253; History and liter-		
ature, PN 50; History		
and philosophy, B 61;		
History and political		
science, JA 78; History		
and sociology, HM 36)		

Although there are six classificatory references for this heading, heraldry is not listed.

xx 3 : 10	CH	IH
Knights and knighthood	[see CH 3 : 16]	[see IH 3 : 16]
xx 3 : 11	CH	IH
Nobility	[see CH 3 : 19]	[see IH 3 : 19]

These two xx references are also circular references.

xx 3 : 12	CH 3 : 33	IH 3 : 33
Peerage	Peerage (Baronage)	Peerage/Great Britain:
(HT 647; Gt. Brit.,	CS 421	CS 421-3
CS 421-3)		Other countries: CS 80-2209

Peerage is a member of class 5 along with the previously mentioned Nobility and Titles of honor and nobility. Its classificatory reference is apparently too narrow according to the index heading.

xx 3 : 13	CH	IH
Precedence	[see CH 3 : 21]	[see IH 3 : 21]

Precedence has already been covered as a sa reference.

xx 3 : 14	CH 3 : 24	IH 3 : 24
Signs and symbols	CR 29 Symbolism	Symbolism/In
(no CN)		heraldry: CR 29

This is the second heading under heraldry that would seem to be a possible title used as a subject heading. The heraldry classification and index headings are probably more appropriate for the following subject heading, Symbolism.

xx 3 : 15	CH 3 : 35	IH 3 : 35
Symbolism	CR 29 Symbolism	Symbolism/In
(Christian, BV 150-		heraldry: CR 29
165; Civilization, CB		
475; Comparative		
religion, BL 600-620;		
Occult sciences, BF		
1623.S9; Psychology,		
BF 458)		

Symbolism does have an unused class number in heraldry as stated above. The contextual meaning given by the present classificatory references appears to be limited.

xx 3 : 16	CH	IH
Titles of honor and	[see CH 3 : 23]	[see IH 3 : 23]
nobility		

This is the tenth circular reference under heraldry.

−3 : 1-3	CH	IH
−Law and legislation	(∅)	(∅)
−Poetry	(∅)	(∅)
−U. S.	(∅)	(∅)

These three subdivisions are all no matches. Apparently these must be examples of possible subdivisions as there is no other apparent reason for their presence under this subject heading.

From the analysis of the subject heading Heraldry at least four important concepts may be discerned. First the use of lexical meaning has isolated five classes of near synonyms. These are

Class 1	Class 2	Class 3	Class 4	Class 5
Heraldry	Achievements	Badges	Chivalry	Nobility
Precedence	(Heraldry)	Decorations	Knights and	Titles of honor
xBlazonry	Escutcheons	of honor	knighthood	and nobility
xPedigrees	Hatchments	Devices		
		Emblems		
		Emblems, National		
		Crests		
		Seals (Numismatics)		
		Mottoes		
		Flags		
		Insignia		
		Orders of knighthood and chivalry		
		xArms, Coats of		
		xCoats of Arms		

Second there are at least sixteen instances of the contextual meaning of a subject heading being contained in the classificatory reference. Third the use of several classificatory references under a single subject heading may cause an ambiguous assemblage to result. Fourth the syndetic structure of a generic heading such as heraldry is somewhat inconsistent. There are cases of circular unequal headings. The examples of particular heraldic devices are inconsistent. And there is one completely ambiguous or perhaps irrelevant see reference (Gryphons).

. . . .

Interpretations and Conclusions

Of the 206 subject headings tested graphemically, about one-fourth match perfectly with both the classification and index headings. 40% of the classification headings are partial matches and 50% of the index headings are partial matches. The morphological-syntactical analysis shows a single noun in mass form to be the only recurring perfect match in the first group of 49 subject headings. The partial matches of the first group form 31 different variants with only two forms recurring. The only paradigmatic classes which appear to be present are the identities which require no transformation and the pattern of SH transformed to SH (W) in the index which occurs seven times in the partial matches of the first group. In the first group there are 25 discernible semantic variants. These variants may be summarized as one wrong contextual meaning, one limited contextual meaning, one expanded or redundant contextual meaning, eighteen contextual meanings contained in the classificatory reference, two possible titles used as subject headings, and five classes of near synonyms isolated by lexical meanings. There are four different inconsistencies in the classificatory references of the first group. There is one instance of an apparently wrong class number, six number ranges that are too broad, four ranges that are too narrow, and five instances of unused appropriate class numbers. The Shakespeare example shows many subdivisions referring to the same number or range of numbers, fifteen unused appropriate classificatory references and an inconsistent use of sub-subdivisions. When the results of the structural, semantic and classification tests are combined, only five headings or 10% of the first group pass all the tests. In the second group of eleven headings only one passes all the tests.

The size of the sample limits the interpretation to specific statements about the sample and only general statements about the entire list. It appears that the sample covered is only coincidentally related to the classification system. One cannot positively state that the samples used are truly representative of the entire list but there is no reason to state that they are not. The sample clearly demonstrates cases of near synonyms, ambiguous headings and redundant headings. Further the existence of three vocabularies appears to be proved in the sample. There is the vocabulary of the classification schedules, a different vocabulary of the subject headings, and even a third vocabulary of the classification index.

Another major value of this chapter is the success of the methodology. It appears that the methodology will show several levels of inconsistency. These levels are structural on both graphemic and morphologic-syntactical approaches, semantic on both lexical and contextual approaches, and classificatory. The value of the additional tests beyond the graphemic matches may be proved by the 50% reduction of the perfect matches in the first group when the other tests are applied. The graphemic display of the Shakespeare sample shows the value of the classificatory test applied in isolation. Both ambiguous headings and redundant headings may be readily observed in this fashion. In addition cases of near synonyms may be predicted as well as isolating unused classificatory references.

The results of this chapter lead directly into the third hypothesis of this investigation. If the testing methods used in this chapter and the previous one demonstrate inconsistent use of vocabulary, can a chain index solve this problem? An experimental model of chain indexing could be developed from a parent heading such as Heraldry or Shakespeare. Such a model would have to follow strict structural and semantic rules to integrate the vocabularies of the chain index, the classification schedule, the classification index, and the subject headings into one vocabulary. This model could then allow the index to be the list of subject headings. Further this model would allow the classification schedules to be fully indexed. Inherent in the generation of this model would be the development of rules for chain indexing. These rules would then need to be applied to other examples.

Notes

[1] *The Oxford Universal Dictionary on Historical Principles.* Prepared by William Little, H. W. Fowler, J. Coulson. Revised and edited by C. T. Onions. (3d ed. rev.; Oxford: At the Clarendon Press, 1955), p. 892.

[2] *Ibid.,* p. 15.

[3] *Ibid.,* p. 136.

[4] *Ibid.,* p. 421.

[5] *Ibid.,* p. 465.

[6] *Ibid.,* p. 496.

[7] *Ibid.,* p. 597.

[8]*Ibid.*, p. 632.

[9]*Ibid.*, p. 871.

[10]*Ibid.*, p. 1015.

[11]*Ibid.*, p. 1288.

[12]*Ibid.*, pp. 2363-64.

[13]*Ibid.*, p. 831.

"Integrating Subject Pathfinders into Online Catalogs"

William E. Jarvis

Combining "Pathfinders" and Online Catalogs ... the Possibilities

Pathfinders. Library Handouts, Bibliographic Guides. LC Tracer Bullets. Every academic library has them. Public access online catalogs or PAC's ... more and more libraries are getting them. Isn't it about time the pathfinder meets the online catalog? Not just as three-ring binder specifications sitting *next to* public access catalogs, but as programs *in* the PAC, for display or as offline print. As online library catalogs with integrated functions spread, and pathfinders are produced by word processing technology, the desire to integrate pathfinder information online will grow.

Perhaps not every element of every pathfinder can or should be transferred whole cloth into an online catalog. There is also the issue of "user transparency" *vs.* fully articulated pathfinder texts online, elaborate help screens displaying pathfinder information. Whatever the degree or exact type of display, some sort of pathfinder assistance online is as necessary as any other help screen. In the long haul the choice is, I believe clear; either (somehow) augment PAC's with subject-specific pathfinder-like features or face the prospect that public online catalog users will receive little pathfinder guidance. These valuable guides could remain in vertical files, and not be integrated into the online catalog. Librarians will be losing an opportunity to provide routine subject guidance at the catalog terminal; key titles (journals, handbooks, encyclopedias, data compilations) subject headings, classification numbers, or secondary indexes.

Sorting out such key titles and terms from a welter of possible access points and titles has been the task of library print pathfinders. It may be desirable to weight key titles online, especially if a more "user transparent" approach to the pathfinder function is utilized, where the user sees less of the pathfinder on the screen.

A range of options for the integration of subject pathfinders into an online catalog includes; doing nothing, providing pathfinders in user manuals alongside PAC terminals, putting full text-type pathfinder display online, making online pathfinder functions more "user transparent" (with less detail displayed) or perhaps making pathfinders text available as off-line printouts upon

---

Reprinted, by permission, from *Database* (February 1985), 65-67.

user request.[1] Another method of accessing pathfinders within an online PAC could be to catalog them as bibliographic entries, retrievable as one of many holdings records. Display of the full pathfinder would be a possible option for the user. An essential feature of putting pathfinders online is a keyword accessible list of each pathfinder available in the catalog. It will be relatively easy for reference librarians to edit or delete obsolete pathfinders, or to write new ones into the online catalog.

The pathfinder online concept is obviously possible in a wide variety of configurations, and there are some related concepts currently embodied in online catalogs. Pauline Cochrane noted a feature of PAPERCHASE, a sophisticated online retrieval system developed by Massachusetts General Hospital: an online listing of "... approved lists of authors, title words, subjects, and journal titles ..."[2] This is close to putting a full pathfinder online in a PAC. Geac's provision of authority files for PAC's is a related notion.[3] The Library of Congress's CRS "Issue Briefs," searchable online are also related to the pathfinder online concept. But the concept of straightforwardly transforming traditional printed library pathfinders into online PAC "guideware" is nowhere to be found, at least in the literature.[4]

A Pathfinder Online: An Example

In this brief example, features such as "next screen" or "back to menu" options have not been illustrated. Only first and last entries for journals and annuals lists have been illustrated, in the interests of saving space. Note that the online user could miss treatise-encyclopedia titles, journal lists, and relevant secondary index information.

1. Access to the proper pathfinder: two approaches

A. User selects pathfinder
    List option from Help Menu
    ...
    3. How to print results
    4. How to read bibliographic displays
    5. *See List of Subject Pathfinders*
    6. *Input your own choice of keyword and get a relevant pathfinder*
    7. How to limit searches to one type of; document, one or more language, etc.
       ...

    OR...

B. User retrieves bibliographic entry of a specific pathfinder along with a number of book titles

    User then displays full text of pathfinder online.
    (See Sample of an Online Pathfinder below)

    User then selects appropriate pathfinder from full list of pathfinders or by inputting own choice of keyword
    (See Sample of an Online Pathfinder below)

2. Sample of an Online Pathfinder

Biotechnology: Biochemical Engineering
(Online library pathfinder No. 3)

Relevant Subject Headings Include:
1. biochemical engineering
2. enzymes — industrial applications
3. fermentation
4. immobilized enzymes
5. industrial microbiology

Key Treatises and Encyclopedia Articles:
1. *Biotechnology: a comprehensive treatise in 8 volumes.* Weinheim: Verlag Chemics, 1981-.
2. *Encyclopedia of chemical technology* ("Kirk-Othmer") 3rd ed., 1978-. Relevant articles include; "Fermentation," "Enzymes, Immobilized," "Fuel From Biomass," etc. See esp. index.
3. Weisman, A. *Handbook of enzyme biotechnology.* Chichester, Eng.: Halsted Press, 1975.
4. *Prescott & Dunn's industrial microbiology* 4th ed., Westport, Conn. AVI Pub. Co., 1982.

Annual Reviews:
1. *Advances in Applied Microbiology.* Vol- , 1959-.
2. *Topics in Enzyme and Fermentation Biotechnology.* Vol-, 1977-. *Journals*
1. *Applied and Environmental Microbiology* V. 31-, 1976-.
2. *Trends in Biotechnology.* Vol-, 1983-.

Abstracts, Secondary Indexes, External Online Databases:
(Use for subject access to biotechnology journal articles)
1. *Biological Abstracts*, also online as BIOSIS. "Fermentation" is divided among a number of sections.
2. *Chemical Abstracts*, also online (without abstracts) as CASEARCH. For general biochemical engineering see the Section Heading "Fermentation and Bioindustrial Chemistry" (Applications areas are often under different sections headings.)
3. *Life Science Collection Database*
   Available only online (at this library.)
   See especially:
   Subfiles 01 *Applied & Industrial Microbiology*
   Subfile 30 *Biotechnology Research Abstracts*

Conclusion

Useful features of subject pathfinders can and will be integrated into online public access catalogs. Such integrated features could be: within the PAC, offline user guide manuals, remotely printed upon user request, or online as saved searches displayed in help screen format. Excerpts of one such pathfinder display for biotechnology are presented. Although there is a felt need for sophisticated subject and especially syndetic access to online public access catalogs, no one heretofore has formulated the concept of integrated library automated systems supplied with classic pathfinders (or their equivalent). This idea could become a significant enhancement to online library catalogs.

Notes

[1] Offline print option is a suggestion by Pauline A. Cochrane, personal correspondence, May 25, 1984.

[2] P. A. Cochrane "Friendly catalog forgives user errors," *American Libraries*, Vol. 13, No. 5, May 1982, pp. 303-306.

[3] See the Geac entry in S. B. Epstein's survey "System at ALA Midwinter," *Library Journal*, March 1, 1984, pp. 454-455.

[4] For example, J. R. Mathews' *Public Access to Online Catalogs: A Planning Guide for Managers*, Weston, CT: Online, Inc., 1982, (distributed by Neal Schulman, New York, NY) a survey which exhibits a variety of screens from different online public access catalogs, shows nothing like "pathfinders online." The complex needs of online subject access are elaborated in P. A. Cochrane's six part series "Modern Subject Access in the Online Age" which appeared in *American Libraries* February through July/August 1984.

Subject Cataloging Manual:
Subject Headings

Library of Congress,
Subject Cataloging Division

H373
Revised 7 November 1981

"See" References

Reference: This instruction sheet replaces in part the former H 370, dated Jan. 25, 1978. It also includes information from D&P4-1, p. 2; WL75-6; WL76-42; and WL81-22.

Background: H 370 indicated that *see* references are not normally made in those cases where a heading exists in LCSH which can be made an *xx* reference instead. The purpose of this memo is to indicate when *see* references should be made.

Procedures:

1. After deciding which term or phrase is to represent the concept in question when formulating a new heading, add other equivalent terms and phrases as *see* references to the new heading.

    > Bait fishing
    >   x Bobber fishing
    >   Float fishing, British
    >   Leggering (Fishing)
    >   Livebait fishing

2. In addition to the above *see* references, manipulate the new heading and its alternative forms so that additional *see* references are provided under each significant word in the file position, as long as the resulting combination of words represents an

---

Reprinted from Library of Congress, Subject Cataloging Division, *Subject Cataloging Manual: Subject Headings* (Washington, D.C., 1984), H373, H400, and in supplement, H370.

expression which a person might logically be expected to search under. The standard means of accomplishing this is by inverted references, although phrase equivalents of the inverted forms are also used, e.g.

    Truck driving
        x Driving, Truck

    Christian sects
        x Christian denominations
            Denominations, Christian
      xx Sects

    Breakwaters, Mobile
        x Mobile breakwaters

    Light sources
        x Sources of light

Do not add an *x* reference if the same result can be accomplished by means of an *xx* reference (see *Sects* in the example above). For an exception to this rule, see Par. 8 below.

3. If alternative spellings are possible, including singular and plural forms, alternative word endings, etc., make additional *see* references covering these possibilities, e.g.

    Door knobs
        x Doorknobs

    Cluster housing
        x Clustered housing

    Glamour photography
        x Glamor photography

    Historic farms
        x Historical farms

    Serial publications
        x Serials (Publications)

    Buses — Vandalism
        x Bus vandalism

4. *"See" References from Cancelled Headings.* If a heading is cancelled in favor of an alternative form, make a *see* reference from the cancelled form, if such a reference is consistent with current policy. If it is not, submit a request to the subject editor to prepare a 699 note explaining the cancellation.

5. *Upward "See" References.* It is sometimes appropriate to make *see* references from other than synonymous terms or phrases in order to inform the catalog user that a particular concept is entered under another, usually broader, heading, e.g.

    Single parents
        x Single fathers
            Single mothers

    Bait fishing
        x Worm fishing

Make references of this type only in those cases where it is clearly impractical for LCSH to provide separate headings for each possible concept.

6. *Abbreviations, Acronyms, Initials, etc.* Do not normally provide *see* references from such forms to headings spelled out in full. References of the following type normally are not made:

    American Road Race of Champions
        x ARRC

Subject Cataloging Manual   215

Exception: In those cases where a concept may also be well-known to the general public as an abbreviation, acronym, etc. (e.g. SST, UFO), provide *see* references from the abbreviated form.

However, concepts that are known primarily in an abbreviated form may be established as such, e.g. DDT (Insecticide).

7. *Foreign Terms.* As a general rule, do not make *see* references to *topical* headings from their equivalents in foreign languages. References of the following type normally are not made:

    Underground literature—Soviet Union
      x   Samizdat

Note: This provision does not apply to *named entities*, for which reference from the vernacular form are regularly provided when the name has been established in English.

8. *Headings Qualified by Nationality, Ethnic Group, or Language.* Always provide a *see* reference from the alternative form in the case of any heading established with a qualifier designating ethnic group, nationality, or ethnic group.

If the heading is inverted, provide a *see* reference from the straight form; if it is straight, provide a *see* reference from the inverted form. Contrary to the general rule cited in Par. 2 above, *see also* references normally are not made to or from such headings, unless the pattern file specifically requires otherwise, e.g.

    Art, French   Mexican American arts
      x   French art   x   Arts, Mexican American

. . . .

H400
Revised 22 November 1983
Scope Notes

BACKGROUND: Scope notes generally serve to limit the scope of a heading as used in the catalog, thereby helping readers to determine to what extent it covers the material they seek, and making it possible for catalogers to maintain consistency in assigning the heading to new works being cataloged. Scope notes are especially useful under headings that represent new concepts or that employ terminology not yet firmly established in the language. Catalogers are encouraged to be generous in providing scope notes when proposing new headings of this type.

PURPOSE: To describe the various types of scope notes used in *LCSH* and the procedures for submitting proposals to add scope notes to new or existing subject headings.

TYPES OF SCOPE NOTES USED IN LCSH:

1. **A single heading defined without reference to any other headings.** This type of note is required in situations where various reference works consulted in doing authority research fail to

agree completely, and usage does not offer a sufficiently precise definition. It is also necessary when no dictionary definition of the heading is readily available and the meaning of the heading is potentially ambiguous, e.g.

> **Artists' preparatory studies**
> Here are entered works dealing with studies or sketches by artists preparatory to executing works of art in any form.

> **Southwest, New**
> Here are entered works on that part of the United States which roughly corresponds to the old Spanish province of New Mexico, including the present Arizona, New Mexico, southern Colorado, Utah, Nevada and California.

This type of note may also be included, even if *Webster's* gives a definition, if the note will serve a useful purpose. Do not include esoteric or obvious definitions.

2. **A single heading described with reference to more specific headings.** This type of note is used in those occasional situations where it is deemed necessary to state explicitly that the heading in question is used for a topic in its most general sense, and that more specific aspects of the topic will be found under more specific headings, e.g.

> **Commodity exchanges**
> Here are entered works on commodity exchanges in general. Works on exchanges dealing in a single commodity or class of commodities, e.g. cotton, grain, tobacco are entered under Cotton trade, Grain trade, etc.

Note that it is more common to use a general see also reference or specific see also references in situations of this type.

3. **A single heading with explanation for special cases.** This type of note provides not only a description of the scope of the heading but also instructions both to catalogers and to users as to the various subject entries that are made for any work in hand dealing with special aspects of the subject, e.g.

> **Health surveys**
> Here are entered works on the methods and techniques employed in conducting health surveys, and reports of individual surveys. For the latter the heading may be subdivided by place; in such cases an additional subject entry is made under the heading Public health--[local subdivision], e.g. 1. Public health--United States. 2. Health surveys--United States. For health surveys on a special topic, the additional subject entry is made under the special topic, e.g. 1. Youth--Health and hygiene--United States. 2. Health surveys--United States.

(This scope note should serve as the pattern for all headings for specific types of surveys.)

4. **Two or more closely related or overlapping headings.** This type of note provides contrasting information regarding the scope and usage of superficially similar headings.

> **Life on other planets**
> Here are entered works on the question of life in outer space. Works on the prospective use of the science of anthropology in dealing with intelligent beings in outer

space, or establishing earth colonies on extraterrestrial bodies are entered under Extraterrestrial anthropology.

Extraterrestrial anthropology
Here are entered works on the prospective use of the science of anthropology in dealing with intelligent beings in outer space, or establishing earth colonies on extraterrestrial bodies. Works on the question of life in outer space are entered under Life on other planets.

When one heading is defined or described with reference to one or more other headings, reciprocal notes are provided under all other headings to which the original note refers. The wording of the reciprocal note should be a "mirror image" of that of the original note, and the two notes should be composed using the format "Here are entered works on [description of heading A]. Works on [description of heading B] are entered under [heading B]." The second sentence of these notes should not be in the form "For works on [description of heading B], see [heading B]."

5. **Special instructions, explanations, referrals, etc.** This type of note, rather than defining the scope of the heading, provides information such as instructions to catalogers for making additional subject entries, notices to catalog users, or generalized references, e.g.

Economic forecasting
When this heading is subdivided by place, a second subject heading is assigned for the name of the place with subdivisions such as Economic conditions, Economic policy, etc., e.g. 1. Economic forecasting--United States. 2. United States--Economic policy--1981-

Shakespeare, William, 1564-1616
The subdivisions provided under this heading represent for the greater part standard subdivisions usable under any literary author heading and do not necessarily pertain to Shakespeare.

Moving-pictures--Plots, themes, etc.
Films on specific topics are entered under specific headings, e.g. Horror films; War films; Children in motion pictures; Death in motion pictures.

Ocean waves
This heading may be subdivided by bodies of water, e.g. Ocean waves--Atlantic Ocean.

School prose
For works limited to one school, the heading is qualified by nationality and subdivided by place, and an additional subject entry is made under the name of the school.

PROCEDURES:

1. **Proposing a scope note for a new heading being established.**

   a. Type the note on a white or buff scratch card, approximating the following style and spacing:

> Mail art
>
>   Here are entered works on art created collaboratively by using the postal service to transport a work in progress from one artist to another, and usually incorporating postal paraphernalia such as stamps, cancellations, etc. into the work.
>
>   ABC/sc   1-22-83
>   XYZ/sc   1-22-83

    b. Submit the card together with the subject heading proposal card and associated material to the Subject Headings Editorial Section.

2. Adding a scope note to an existing heading. Type the note, as above, on a white or buff scratch card, initial-date stamp the card, obtain section head approval, and submit it to the Editorial Section. Indicate in the upper right corner of the card the number of records to be changed as a result of the proposal ("0 changes," if none). If the proposal has not been generated by a new work being cataloged, write "no book" in the upper right corner of the card.

3. Changing an existing scope note. This procedure consists of cancelling the existing scope note, and proposing a new note as a replacement:

    a. Prepare a substitute scope note card containing the text of the existing note, either by making a Coronastat of the card from the old OCat and labelling it "Substitute," or by typing, on a white or buff scratch card labelled "Substitute," the text of the existing note as it appears in *LCSH*.

    If you wish to alter a scope note that was originally established in connection with the cataloging of an AACR 2 work and is therefore represented by a card in the In-Process File, pull that card from the file, rather than preparing a substitute.

    b. Draw a line across the face of the card, mark it "Cancel," initial, and date it.

    c. Type the new scope note on a white or buff scratch card, as described in para. 1 above. Indicate in the upper right corner of the card the number of records to be changed and whether no book accompanies the proposal, as in para. 2 above.

    d. Submit as a unit both the cancellation and the new note to the Editorial Section.

                                   . . . .

H370
Revised 29 July 1985
See Also References

NOTE: This instruction sheet deals exclusively with making *see also* references to individual headings. In order to determine the full set of references to be made to any given heading, it is necessary also to consult H 373, *See references*.

GENERAL PRINCIPLES: See also references for headings in *LCSH* are created according to the following principles:

1. <u>Hierarchical references.</u> A see also reference is made to a given subject heading from the next broader heading so that terms are arranged in a hierarchy. This type of link is the equivalent in *LCSH* of the BT (broader term) and NT (narrower term) link commonly used in thesauri.

   The following relationships are considered hierarchical in *LCSH*:

   Genus/species (or class/class member):

   Apes
      xx(BT)   Primates

   Women executives
      xx(BT)   Executives

   Dental anthropology
      xx(BT)   Physical anthropology

   Buildings, Prefabricated
      xx(BT)   Buildings

   Cinematography
      xx(BT)   Photography

   Whole/part:

   Toes
      xx(BT)   Foot

   Ethnology
      xx(BT)   Anthropology

   Instance (or generic topic/proper-named example):

   Whitewater Lake
      xx(BT)   Lakes--Wisconsin

   (Whitewater Lake is an instance of a lake in Wisconsin)

   Verdun, Battle of, 1914
      xx(BT)   World War, 1914-1918--
               Campaigns--France

   (The battle of Verdun in 1914 is an instance of a campaign in France during World War I)

2. <u>Related term references.</u> In order to link two headings that are neither broader nor narrower than each other, a see also reference is made from each to the other. This type of link is the equivalent in *LCSH* of the RT (related term) link commonly used in thesauri. *Examples:*

   Rugs
      xx(RT)   Carpets

   Athletes
      xx(RT)   Sports

   Carpets
      xx(RT)   Rugs

   Sports
      xx(RT)   Athletes

Even though headings linked in this way are not hierarchically related, they are mentally associated to such an extent that the link is made explicit in order to reveal alternative headings that might be of interest. In order to avoid subjective judgments, a general guideline for making related term reference links in *LCSH* is that one of the headings should be strongly implied, according to the frames of reference of *LCSH* users, whenever the other is considered. Frequently the concept represented by one of the headings is a necessary complement in the definition of the other. For example, **Birds** is a necessary part of the definition of **Ornithology**.

PROCEDURES:

1. **Hierarchical references.**

    a. **General rule.** When establishing a new heading, follow the principle described above in creating its reference structure, making see also references from broader headings to narrower headings. The notation xx is used in *LCSH* to trace the link between the two headings, as follows:

    [narrower heading]
       xx   [broader heading]

    Example:

    | Hot dog rolls | narrower heading |
    | xx Bread | broader heading |
    | Bread | narrower heading |
    | xx Baked products | broader heading |

    Make at least one hierarchical xx when establishing a new heading. Make this xx even if both headings begin with the same word, e.g.

    Roads, Gravel
       xx(BT) Roads

    Exceptional situations in which hierarchical xx's are not made:

    (1) **"Orphan" headings.** "Orphan" headings, i.e. headings having no hierarchical xx, are generally prohibited in *LCSH*. There are, however, a limited number of situations in which "orphan" headings are permitted, including the following:

    --Headings that are "top terms," i.e. the broadest topic in a given hierarchy, e.g. **Science**.

    --Headings for geographic regions

    --Headings for family names

    --Headings for industries

--Inverted headings qualified by names of languages, nationalities, or ethnic groups when the only appropriate broader term is the identical heading without the qualifier, e.g. **Art, French** does not have the xx **Art**.

Note however that references are routinely made, especially for belles lettres headings of this type, from broader terms with the qualifier in the initial position, e.g. **Short stories, German** has the xx **German fiction**.

(2) "Subdivision-to-subdivision" references. In general, do not make a see also reference from one heading with a subdivision to a narrower heading with the same subdivision. Instead, make the reference link at the level of the unsubdivided headings, e.g.

> Lamas
>   xx(BT)   Priests, Buddhist

[*not* Lamas--Lineage
   xx(BT)   Priests, Buddhist--Lineage]

(3) General see also references. Do not make see also references between individual headings in situations where a general see also reference is appropriate and has been, or should be, made (see H 371).

b. Number of references to be made. Most single-concept headings belong to only one hierarchy and require only one xx. Some headings may incorporate more than one concept in more than one hierarchy and require additional xx's, but rarely more than three. Link a new heading only to the next broader heading in the logical hierarchy by means of an xx, e.g.

> Automobiles   [*not* Automobiles
>   xx(BT)   Motor vehicles   xx(BT)   Motor vehicles
>   Vehicles]

If a new heading is a member of more than one hierarchy, link it to the next broader heading in each hierarchy, e.g.

> Women college administrators
>   xx(BT)   College administrators
>   Women executives
>   Women in education

c. Establishing headings to fill hierarchical "gaps". When establishing a new heading, establish also the next broader heading to use as an xx, if it has not already been established.

Follow this rule in situations where the missing heading comes readily to mind or becomes apparent after checking dictionaries, other thesauri, etc. These situations are generally fairly obvious in the sciences, but less obvious in the humanities and social sciences.

d. Revising existing reference structures. When establishing a new heading that is an intermediate term in a hierarchy, make see also references from the new heading to all appropriate existing narrower headings, and cancel any xx's that link the existing headings to headings broader than the newly-established intermediate term. *Example:*

When the heading **Specialty stores** was established with the xx **Stores, Retail**, see also references were made to the existing headings **Jewelry stores** and **Museum stores**. The xx's linking the latter headings directly to **Stores, Retail** were cancelled, resulting in the following hierarchy:

Specialty stores xx(BT) Stores, Retail	[The hierarchy *before* **Specialty stores** was established had been:

Jewelry stores
   xx(BT)   Specialty stores
	Jewelry stores
	   xx(BT) Stores, Retail

Museum stores
   xx(BT)   Specialty stores
	Museum stores
	   xx(BT) Stores, Retail

    e. <u>**Complex situations.**</u> Many headings in *LCSH* are of the type that incorporate more than one concept, and therefore do not generally lend themselves to strict hierarchical reference treatment. These include headings modified by prepositional or conjunctional phrases, headings constructed with subdivisions, and headings with certain parenthetical additions. As a general rule, when establishing a new heading of this type, make an xx from the generic heading for the term that is the second element in the heading even though the reference may not be truly hierarchical. *Example:*

        Hydrogen as fuel
           xx(BT)   Fuel

As a result of experience gained in the initial period of application of the principles of this instruction sheet, a number of different complex situations have been identified for which special decisions regarding the required xx's have been made. These decisions are recorded in the Pattern File located in the Subject Headings Editorial Section. The following are examples of some of these decisions.

    (1)   <u>**[...] and [...] headings.**</u> Make an xx from the heading (or its equivalent) that follows the word **and** (cf. H 310).

    (2)   <u>**Subdivisions.**</u>

        (a)   <u>**Subdivisions that follow the general rule.**</u> Make an xx from the heading that corresponds to the subdivision, e.g.

           [...]--Contracting out   [...]--Election
              xx(BT)   Contracting out   xx(BT)   Elections

           [...]--Transliteration
              xx(BT)   Transliterations

Note: In some instances this rule is followed only when there is no more specific heading available for use as an xx, e.g.

           [...]--Diagnostic use
              xx(BT)   Diagnosis   [or more specific type of diagnosis, if established]

(b) Free-floating subdivisions. Some subdivisions that are normally free-floating are occasionally established because of special circumstances. In such situations, make no xx. For example, when **Prisoners--Education** (Indirect) was established in order to establish **Prisoners--Education--Law and legislation** (Indirect), no xx was made under **Prisoners--Education** because **--Education** is normally free-floating.

(c) Non-free-floating subdivisions for which no xx's are made. Certain subdivisions must be established each time they are used. For the following subdivisions of this type, make no xx's, since there is no generic term for the concept represented by the term in the subdivision:

[...]--Abuse of
[...]--Application
[...]--Complications and sequelae
[country]--Foreign relations--[period subdivision]
[...]--Programs
[...]--Religious aspects
[...]--Utilization

Note: Although no xx's are made in these situations, x's are required in some cases by the Pattern File, which must be consulted.

(d) Topics subdivided by other topics. Certain topics are constructed in the form of a single heading subdivided by various other topical headings, e.g. **Advertising--[topic], Conflict of laws--[topic], Selling--[name of product], Strikes and lockouts--[group of workers], Trade-unions--[group of workers]**, etc. In such situations, make no xx, e.g.

Advertising--Bus lines
[no xx]

Note: Although no xx's are made in this situation, the Pattern File requires that an x be made from the reversed form, e.g.

Advertising--Bus lines
   x Bus line--Advertising

(3) Prepositional phrases.

(a) Phrases that follow the general rule. Make an xx from the heading that corresponds to the term(s) following the preposition, e.g.

Sex instruction for [group of people]
   xx(BT) [group of people]

Church work with [group of people]
   xx(BT) [group of people]

Communication in [specific field]
   xx(BT) [specific field]

[...] in interior decoration
   xx(BT) Interior decoration

(b) Special situations involving prepositional phrases. Case-by-case pattern reference decisions have been made and recorded in the Pattern File for several types of headings constructed with prepositional phrases, e.g. diseases or psychological concepts in children. The following is a representative sample of these decisions:

[group of people] in medicine
   xx(BT) Medical personnel

[name of sport] for women
   xx(BT) Sports for women

[...] in the Bible
   [no xx]

(4) Parenthetical qualifiers for legal systems. Make an xx from the general heading for the legal system, e.g.

[...] (Roman law)
   xx Roman law

2. Related term references. In order to focus emphasis on hierarchical references, in order to simplify future special projects to revise references in *LCSH*, and in order to reduce the size and complexity of *LCSH*, extremely restrictive rules have been formulated for making related term references. The intended effect of these restrictions is to reduce the number of related term references to almost none. The rules are as follows:

a. Do not link two headings as related terms if they begin with the same word or word stem. For example, do not link **Public libraries** and **Public librarians** or **Handpress** and **Hand-printed books** as related terms.

Exception: Two such headings may be linked as related terms if they are "top terms," i.e. if they stand at the top of the hierarchy of a discipline. For example, **Libraries** and **Librarians** may be linked as related terms.

b. Do not link two headings as related terms if, at any level of the hierarchy, they have a common broader term.

Exception: Two such headings may be linked as related terms if the relationship is so close either that their meanings overlap considerably, or that one is needed to define the other, or that they are frequently used interchangeably. For example, **Carpets** and **Rugs** may be linked as related terms even though they have the common broader term **Floor coverings**. Such close relationships between terms rarely occur, however.

c. Do not link two headings as related terms if terms are higher levels of either of their respective hierarchies are linked as related terms. For example, do not link **Poverty** and **Almshouses** as related terms, since **Poverty** is linked as a related term to **Charities** and **Charities** is at a higher level in the hierarchy for **Almshouses.**

Make related term references only in the following three situations, and then only if not prohibited by one of the above rules:

--To link two terms with meanings that overlap to some extent, or terms used somewhat interchangeably, e.g.

    Boats and boating   Ships
       xx(RT)   Ships   xx(RT)   Boats and boating

[*not*

    Search dogs   Rescue dogs
       xx(RT)   Rescue dogs   xx(RT)   Search dogs

since both headings have the broader term **Working dogs**]

****

--To link a discipline and the object studied, e.g.

    Ornithology   Birds
       xx(RT)   Birds   xx(RT)   Ornithology

[*not*

    Masks   Mask making
       xx(RT)   Mask making   xx(RT)   Masks

since both headings begin with the same word]

****

--To link persons and their fields of endeavor, e.g.

    Medicine   Physicians
       xx(RT)   Physicians   xx(RT)   Medicine

[*not*

    Banks and banking   Bankers
       xx(RT)   Bankers   xx(RT)   Banks and banking

since both headings begin with the same word stem]

"Subject Catalogers— Equal to the Future?"

Manuel D. Lopez

The subject analysis of library materials, the theory and the lack of it, the clerical and physical procedures necessary to such analysis and the possibilities of mechanization have been the focus of general dissatisfaction, evaluation, and criticism. The most important component, in the process of subject analysis, the subject cataloger, has often been ignored. The assumption seems to be that the cataloger of today and tomorrow is capable of: (1) contributing to, comprehending and evaluating the developing corpus of theory, (2) applying and adapting new systems in a uniform, systematic, and consistent manner.

Such attributes are as desirable and necessary now as in the future, and they will be required for the intelligent and logical application of the developed theories and systems and the manipulation of the mechanical or electronic devices to produce the desired results. Unfortunately, such capabilities cannot be simply ascribed and then prophetically projected into the future. However, a modicum of reassurance could be derived from evidence that those qualities are presently manifested in the processes of subject cataloging.

In an attempt to establish the existence of such evidence an analysis of eight library card catalogs was made to determine:

(1) the number of identical books that received identical subject headings.
(2) the number of identical books that received different subject headings.
(3) use of the elements of the system
    (a) scope or definition card
    (b) "see also" cards used
        1) the number of titles "lost"[1] due to inadequate "see also" references.

Reprinted by permission of the American Library Association, "Subject Catalogers—Equal to the Future?" by Manuel D. Lopez from *Library Resources & Technical Services*, vol. 9, Summer 1965, pp. 371-75; copyright © by ALA.

To minimize the effects of a diversity of public served, scope of collection, and purpose of function, the card catalogs of public and special libraries were excluded from the survey. Eight library collections were selected on the basis, as far as existing conditions allowed, of function and level of content. Seven libraries are associated with academic institutions offering a master's degree in one or more subject areas. The eighth library's function is to provide materials to other institutions rather than to an individual directly. Consequently, its own staff, professional research personnel, scholars, and academically-sophisticated students compose its clientele. Library of Congress catalog cards were utilized in the card catalogs, and all the libraries involved followed the *Subject Headings Used in the Dictionary Catalog of the Library of Congress* as the source of their subject headings. It should be noted here that the use of LC cards was considered, for the purposes of the analysis, as indicative of the suggested subject headings. Of the number of titles included in the preliminary sample only nine required original cataloging. It is interesting that they, with one exception, were consistently described with the test term.

The procedure of the analysis included the following operations:

(1) The subject heading, COMMUNICATION, was selected as the test term. The card catalog of each library was searched for this heading and, for titles found under this subject heading, the following information was recorded:

(a) Author
(b) Title
(c) Publisher
(d) Edition
(e) Date

The initial technique of using the subject approach defined the quantity of the sample. A total of 124 titles, which had been described with the test term, was located in the eight selected libraries. No individual library collection contained all of these titles, but copies of different titles in the sample were located in two or more of the libraries included in the survey. This method, the subject approach, also indicated that the test subject heading COMMUNICATION had been consistently assigned to copies of 55 different titles which were available in two or more libraries.

Using the author entry of the 124 titles located by the subject approach, each card catalog was searched once again. This technique located 21 additional copies of the titles in the sample which had not been assigned the test term COMMUNICATION.

This combination of techniques further refined the sample to include only those titles (a total of 76) available in more than one library. Of that total the test subject heading had been consistently assigned to only 55 titles. Considering the criteria for the inclusion of the libraries in the survey, could the low rate of consistency (72%) be justified on the basis of modification for local users?

It must be emphasized that the consistency rate is simply an indication of a comparison of the skills of all the subject catalogers employed by the libraries surveyed. The rate of consistency (72%) which was computed on the basis of this survey cannot be ascribed to the individual libraries included in the survey. No attempt was made to evaluate the consistency rate for the individual libraries; however, a careful review of the data of Table I may provide the necessary basis for reasonable assumptions regarding the subject cataloging of a book in the subject area of COMMUNICATION added to any one of the collections. For example, a high degree of consistency might be expected from libraries G and H and, conversely, a lower degree of consistency could be expected from libraries A, B, and C.

"See also" references as a test element were selected, because the interdisciplinary nature of communications made it unlikely that any one individual would be familiar with all its aspects and relationships to other subject areas; consequently, "see also" cards would be a necessity.

Table I. Summary of the Analysis of the Elements in the
Subject Heading Systems of Eight Libraries

	Libraries							
	A	B	C	D	E	F	G	H
Scope Note used	No	No	No	No	Yes	No	No	No
"See also" Card used	No	Yes	No	No	Yes	Yes	Yes	Yes
No. of Titles lost due to inadequate references	247	120	100	59	32	11	5	0
No. of Books in Subject Area of COMMUNICATION	27	18	14	13	96	35	27	12
No. of "possible" Subject Headings not referred to	7	8	6	6	1	1	2	0

Table II. Possible "See Also" References Not Referred to
on "See Also" Cards

Possible "see also" references	Libraries							
	A	B	C	D	E	F	G	H
Communication and traffic	X	X	X	X			X	
Communications research	X	X					X	
Cybernetics	X	X	X	X				
Information theory	X	X	X	X				
Intercultural communication				X				
Language and languages	X	X	X	X				
Leaflets dropped from aircraft		X						
Oral communication			X					
Popular culture	X							
Semantics (Philosophy)	X	X	X		X	X		
Symbolism in communication		X						
Visual aids				X				

The procedure for the evaluation of "see also" references consisted of the following steps:

(1) From the 6th edition of *Subject Headings Used in the Dictionary Catalog of the Library of Congress* and its supplements a list of suggested "see also" references was compiled:

> Communication and traffic
> Communication in science
> Communications research
> Cybernetics
> Information theory
> Intercultural communication
> Knowledge, Sociology of
> Leaflets dropped from aircraft
> Language and languages
> Oral communication
> Persuasion (Psychology)
> Popular culture
> Science news
> Semantics (Philosophy)
> Symbolism in communication
> Visual aids

(2) In each library the "see also" card for the test term COMMUNICATION was compared with the list of possible "see also" references. The number of subject headings on the checklist which were used in the card catalog but not referred to on the "see also" card was determined. The number of titles located under such "possible" references was tabulated. Table I summarizes the result of this approach.

Another element of the subject classification system selected as a test item was the scope note for COMMUNICATION. Such scope notes are included in the printed list of subject headings of the Library of Congress only when special subject dictionaries and general dictionaries fail to agree and when usage has not produced a definition of practical use and precision. Functionally, scope notes indicate the limits and scope or, if you will, define the subject heading and are useful in maintaining the consistency in the assignment of subject headings and aiding the library patron in determining the extent of the coverage of a particular subject heading. Table I indicates that only one library out of eight included the test scope note in its catalog. Consider the scope note and its function:

> Communication
>   Here are entered works on human communication including both the primary techniques of language, pictures, etc., and the secondary techniques which facilitate the process, such as the press and radio. Works dealing with individual means of communication are entered under the headings Language and languages, Printing, Telecommunication, etc. Works dealing collectively with the industries concerned are entered under the heading Communication and traffic.

This analysis did not attempt to establish a correlation between the lack of scope notes and inaccurate subject classification, nor did it attempt to quantify the errors and confusion of library users who were without the aid of the guidance of such a device; but it would appear self evident that such a special definition requires inclusion in the card catalog.

Limited to the analysis of one subject heading in the card catalogs of eight libraries in one geographic location, the results of this survey would hardly qualify as representative; and the conclusions must be regarded as little more than tentative. In fact, this brief study simply complements Ann Painter's investigation of the convertibility problem at the government Office of Technical Services.[2]

Initially, this survey of library catalogs was to verify the present existence of those qualities necessary for subject catalogers. Unfortunately, the limitations of the study do not provide refuge from the probabilities suggested by the results. There seems to be little appreciation for the function and utility of scope notes. And there is a somewhat less than systematic use of "see also" references. The low rate of consistency (72%) in subject cataloging has already been discussed. It is interesting that Miss Painter noted in her larger study that "We are left with the fact that, in spite of the variables, there is a 62 to 72 percent consistency in indexing. This means that 28 to 38 percent of the indexing is inconsistent, or that the documents indexed will not be retrieved."

Miss Painter suggests that the level of consistency can be raised in four ways: "ensure the adequate training of the indexers before they index at all, i.e., subject training; give opportunity for experience in the art of indexing; standardize the indexing code or rules being followed; closely supervise the input to each system."

Sound suggestions. However, they appear to describe the function of the subject cataloger's graduate education, apprenticeship, and daily professional experience. Perhaps the education and training of subject catalogers should be reexamined and/or other measures should be considered to assure that future subject catalogers will be as intellectually sophisticated as the evolving body of theory and as systematic as the new mechanical systems being developed.

Notes

[1] Books, due to inconsistent subject cataloging and inadequate "see also" references, are considered "lost" to the user of the catalog who only looked under the subject heading COMMUNICATION.

[2] Painter, Ann. "Convertibility Potential Among Government Information Agency Indexing Systems." *Library Resources & Technical Services*, 7:274-281. Summer 1963.

"Enriching the Library Catalog Record for Subject Access"

Carol A. Mandel

This paper analyzes proposals for augmenting library bibliographic records for improved subject searching in online catalogs. Possible fields for enrichment are described and their likely value assessed. The assessment determines that the main value of enriched records would be to provide access to parts of books. The paper presents arguments for and against adding book content indexing to the online catalog and analyzes the feasibility of eleven alternatives for providing such information.

We can view subject access in the online catalog as a system with four interdependent components: (1) the design of the online catalog, (2) the bibliographic records acted upon by the catalog, (3) the users who bring subject searches to the catalog, and finally, (4) the tools we can load into the catalog to facilitate subject searches, such as an online authority file or an online classification schedule. The components of each part interact and interlock, like the pieces in a three-dimensional jigsaw puzzle, with the placement of each one affecting the shape of the other.

The pieces of this puzzle considered here are those derived from the catalog record itself. Specifically, this paper examines ways of enhancing the record to improve the overall system. The record is the most expensive and most difficult part of that system to improve. While creating sophisticated software and online aids is neither easy nor inexpensive, the bulk of such development work is essentially a onetime investment. Record creation is ongoing and requires major continuing expenditures. The magnitude of this effort demands that we take a very hard look at the usefulness of our records in the online catalog and an even harder look at suggestions for expanding these records. We need to address two questions: Can we enhance our standard records to improve online subject searching? And, even if we can, should we?

Reprinted by permission of the American Library Association, "Enriching the Library Catalog Record for Subject Access" by Carol A. Mandel from *Library Resources & Technical Services* (Jan./March 1985), pp. 5-15; copyright © 1985 ALA.

The concept of enriching standard machine-readable catalog records with additional subject information has been a topic of discussion for at least a decade, yet little new work has been done in this area since Pauline Atherton Cochrane completed her landmark Subject Access Project in 1978.[1] Cochrane developed an efficient method for adding terms from back-of-the-book indexes and tables of contents to MARC records and demonstrated that these enriched records could serve to improve subject retrieval in online searching. The Subject Access Project (SAP) technique extracts an average of thirty terms from each book according to criteria aimed to ensure that both significant subjects and useful search terms are chosen. The method has been tested in an online database at Lund University in Sweden[2] and applied in a database of Swedish government reports,[3] but has yet to be tested in an operational online library catalog.

In 1982, the Council on Library Resources (CLR) brought together twenty-three individuals who had a special interest in subject access and asked them to consider means for improving subject searching for monographs in bibliographic databases. Included among the group's top-priority actions is the recommendation to "identify and evaluate ways to augment and enhance subject access in newly created bibliographic records."[4] Several possible methods of enhancement were identified by the conference participants, who also cautioned that "any alternative record enhancement strategy should be pursued only after assessing the cost/benefit to be expected from such enhancements."[5]

Two years have passed since the CLR group met, and action has been taken on a number of its recommendations. However, we are still not much further along in our thinking about the value and feasibility of augmenting library bibliographic records. This paper aims to advance our consideration of enriched records by seeking answers to several basic questions. The paper describes what an enriched record might contain and assesses the value that is added by such enrichment; it then considers both the desirability and feasibility of providing enhanced records online to library users.

What Are Enriched Records?

The fields that can be used for subject searching in standard MARC records are shown in figure 1. Essentially, we are talking about three kinds of information: (1) classification, (2) keywords in various parts of the record, and (3) subject headings selected from a controlled list or controlled vocabulary. A review of the literature reveals suggestions for enriching or expanding all three kinds of subject information.

1. Classification: LC call number; Dewey number; Local call number; Other class numbers

2. Keywords: Titles; Notes (including contents notes); Series statements; Added entries; Juvenile literature summaries.

3. Controlled subject headings: LCSH; MeSH; AC (Annotated Card) headings for children's materials; headings from locally maintained list.

Fig. 1. Subject Information in Standard MARC Records

First, in the area of classification, suggestions have been made to include fuller, more specific classification notations in records and to add additional class numbers covering multiple aspects of the book's subject coverage.[6] Standard classification practice has been criticized as inadequate for subject access because we treat class numbers only as location devices and we fail to revise classification assignments when class schedules are changed.[7]

Second, our existing records have been criticized for their paucity of descriptive subject words:[8] not all titles are descriptive, contents and other subject-related notes are rarely added, and foreign-language materials present an obvious problem. Suggestions for adding keywords or uncontrolled terms to the record have included adding words from the table of contents or index; adding descriptors selected by scanning the material; or adding an abstract or annotation to the record, such as the contents summaries created for the children's literature Annotated Card Program.[9]

In the third area, controlled subject headings, writers have suggested adding more LC headings to standard records and adding terms selected from specialized thesauri.[10] These suggestions result from concerns that too few controlled headings are found on standard records—the average in the OCLC database is only 1.4 LC subject headings per record[11]—and that LC headings are often not specific enough to satisfy a reader's inquiry.

What Would Enriched Records Provide?

Before we pursue any of these suggestions for augmenting records, it is essential that we step back and ask ourselves precisely what we really want from a database of expanded MARC records. It was noted earlier that record creation is, in the long run, the most expensive component of our subject access system. For example, in 1982 the Library of Congress classes and assigned subject headings to approximately 160,000 titles. If the subject work, including LC and Dewey classification, on each title costs $15,[12] we are looking at an ongoing annual cost of $2.4 million dollars at LC alone. Therefore, it is important that we do *not* increase the effort and expense of record creation unless we are gaining enhancements that cannot otherwise be achieved through good online catalog design or through improvements in our subject access tools. We also must distinguish a real need for expanded records from problems which could simply be solved by more careful implementation of our standard library practice. In other words, we should not create enriched records to compensate for improvements better made in the other parts of our whole subject access system.

A number of us have looked to enriched records as a means for correcting a variety of existing limitations in online subject searching. Let us take a look at the four problems in subject searching that are cited most often.

The first is the need to match the searcher's natural inquiry language to terms indexed in the online catalog. One could achieve this by putting as many terms as possible into each record, but this is not the most cost-effective solution, nor is it the one likely to yield the most precise search results. Instead, this problem is best solved by creating a thorough up-to-date entry vocabulary, by keeping the controlled vocabulary as full and as timely as possible, by employing systems such as the National Library of Medicine's CITE, which lead the user from keywords found in one record to controlled terms attached to other relevant records,[13] and by permitting subject keyword searches so that exact phrasing and word order are not required of the user.

A second problem often noted is the need for redundant headings, since users often miss relevant materials that are assigned headings broader or narrower than the term used in the search. Rather than loading broader and narrower terms into each record, it is more efficient to enable users to select broader and narrower terms from an online thesaurus or a subject index, to browse a classification schedule and search by class number (using truncation to broaden the search), and to perform a subject keyword search, pulling together the same term used in subdivisions and inverted headings.

A third problem is the need to refine meaning or aspects of a subject to make search results as precise as possible. While extra subject information could help here, we can also do more with standard records by using the Boolean AND to couple a standard subject heading with a class number, with a title word, or with an additional subject term.

The fourth problem, closely related to problem three, is the oft-cited need for more precise or specialized terms than those supplied from the LC list. In responding to this need, we must distinguish between problems in subject analysis policy and problems in practice. It is standard library policy to provide subject headings which are coextensive with topics covered by the entire book. The *Library of Congress Subject Headings* list (LCSH) can include any term—no matter how specialized—that is needed to describe the subject matter of an entire book. If the specialized term is inconsistent with LCSH editorial policy, it can be used as a cross-reference instead. LC is working to add new headings and references more quickly through its Entry Vocabulary Project.[14] While the case can be made to add subject headings from lists geared to special audiences, such as children, in theory it should not be necessary to enrich standard MARC records just to achieve greater specificity in describing an entire book. Instead, we must add the most precise headings possible when we create a standard MARC record.

If enriched records will not do much to help us retrieve a monograph devoted to the subject we seek, why might we ever want to add more subject terms to bibliographic records? We would if these terms analyzed the *contents* of books. After all, journal articles of less than ten pages are typically given four or five subject headings in a periodical index.[15] Yet one hundred or more pages of monographic text are accessed by only one or two subject terms. Do monographs contain so much less useful information than journal articles? Many of the suggestions for enriching records seek ways to add back-of-the-book index terms and table of contents terms to MARC records. The new information provided by these terms is information about subtopics covered within the book—or book content indexing. Providing access to parts of books in the library catalog would be a considerable change from current library policy. Does responsible implementation of the online catalog demand such a change?

Should Library Catalogs Provide Access to Parts of Books?

Before we can answer that question, we need to explore two issues. The first is to what extent do library users—and of course these users include everyone from schoolchildren to Novel laureates—need new access tools for discovering information within monographs? The second issue is, even if new tools are needed, does book content indexing belong in the online library catalog? In the hope of stimulating that discussion, either today or in the future, this paper poses some of the arguments on both sides.

Perhaps the most persuasive argument one can make *against* developing new tools for access to parts of books is the market theory argument. That is—if there were a demand for a book index tool, we would have one. While this sounds a bit like "if-God-had-intended-man-to-fly" sort of reasoning, we must hasten to note that all kinds of special index tools do exist. For example, we do have the *Essay and General Literature Index* for collected works. Journal indexing is neither cheap nor easy, yet we have developed an elaborate system for providing it. Some journal indexes are even commercially profitable; others are supported by the disciplines that rely on them. So it is not unreasonable to wonder why we are not indexing books to a greater extent. A corollary to this argument is that the overall topic of most monographs provides adequate subject collocation. Perhaps even individual journal articles would not need specialized indexing if each journal issue were devoted to a special topic and could be given subject headings as monographs.

There is also a case to be made for the other side. In response to the supply-and-demand argument, one could suggest that online searching is beginning to stimulate the demand now. Just one year ago, the commercial database publsher Superindex, Inc., made a combined reference book index in science and technology available through BRS. The publisher reports that Superindex has moved from ca. four hundred to ca. eight hundred library subscribers in the first year and that plans are under way to expand coverage to include professional reference works in the social sciences.[16]

While it will take a good bit of real market and library use research to resolve the demand question, we can point to special situations in which book content indexing would clearly fill a need. One example is the case of access to remote collections. Users accomplish their own book indexing now by going to the shelves and thumbing through likely materials. An online tool could substitute for physical handling. Further, many books contain the kinds of concise information users seek in journal indexes—for example, criticisms of individual works of art or literature, or statistical data. An emerging field of research or a new focus on a topic that is coalescing from interdisciplinary work may be discovered only as sections within books for several years until basic monographs are published on the topic. It should be possible to define criteria for selecting monographs that merit fuller content analysis. One estimate that has been forwarded is that four to five thousand of the more than eighty thousand English-language titles cataloged annually by LC would be candidates for content indexing.[17]

Perhaps these arguments have convinced some of you that there is an important, unmet demand for online databases of book index information, at least in selected subject areas. But why would we want to put this information into the library catalog? Information overload and "false drops" are already becoming significant problems in online catalog searching. Why further clutter search results with index entries?

For over a century, library users have sought information in specialized abstracts and indexes; children are taught to use the *Readers' Guide to Periodical Literature* along with the library catalog. Many abstracting and indexing services already cover selected monographic literature. If there is a demand, shouldn't A & I services simply expand their coverage? As noted by Lucia Rather and Mary Kay Pietris, "The purpose of subject headings is to serve as a finding device to locate items in a [local] collection."[18] Library cataloging need not duplicate the function of abstracting and indexing services.

The counterargument to this position is that the nature and potential of the online catalog are forcing a fundamental change in the role of the library catalog. Free of the physical limitations of the card catalog, our records can contain more access points. Linked to external databases by a variety of telecommunication technologies, our online catalog terminals can serve as gateways to other catalogs and to abstracting and indexing databases. Our users are, in fact, asking for indexing information in the library catalog. Respondents to CLR's Online Catalog User Study ranked access to book indexes and tables of contents as the second most desired enhancement to the online catalog.[19] Convinced of the computer's omnipotence, users are also hoping to find journal articles in the catalog. Law and medical librarians in the University of California system are looking at ways to provide access to legal and medical periodical indexes through MELVYL, the university's online union catalog. If their proposals are approved, their studies will help us gauge the likelihood that the online catalog will grow from a single store into a bibliographic shopping center.

Alternatives for Book Content Indexing

We can add another dimension to our consideration of enriched subject access to books by examining whether there are at least viable alternatives for producing and distributing book content indexing information. We also need to consider which alternatives hold the most promise.

Both in the literature and in professional discussions, a considerable number and variety of means have been suggested for providing access to the subject content of books. We can characterize these methods in terms of two aspects: the first aspect is the technique used to derive the index terms; the second is the way in which the records are made available to users. To help analyze the methods, we can form a simple matrix for describing the various alternatives and outline a few basic categories (figure 2).

	CREATE SEPARATE DATABASES	INCLUDE IN LC MARC RECORDS	ADD TO UTILITY DATABASES/ ONLINE CATALOGS
CONTROLLED VOCABULARY	1. Include books in current A & I coverage. 2. New indexing databases for monographs.	5. LC does content indexing for select set of monographs.	8. Create book index tapes which can be loaded into MARC databases. 9. Specially funded and/or cooperative projects to index subsets of monographs, adding terms to utility databases.
UNCONTROLLED VOCABULARY	3. SUPERINDEX 4. Use SAP technique to create specialized databases.	6. LC uses SAP technique on select set of monographs. 7. Publishers supply analytic abstracts which LC includes in bibliographic records.	10. Create MARC-compatible book index tapes using SAP technique. 11. Specially funded and/or cooperative projects to use SAP technique to add terms to utility databases for select set of monographs.

Fig. 2. Alternatives for Producing and Distributing Book Content Indexing.

There are essentially two categories for describing techniques for deriving the subject terms—controlled vocabulary indexing on the one hand, and on the other, selecting terms drawn from the books themselves, that is from indexes, tables of contents, or abstracts. These are shown along the left-hand side of the matrix. The methods for record distribution can also fall into two neat categories: either the records are included in MARC format library catalog databases, or they are not. However, in looking at the alternatives pragmatically, it is useful to further subdivide the former category into suggestions for enriching MARC records at the source (i.e., those alternatives requiring action by the Library of Congress) and suggestions for enriching MARC records after LC tapes are distributed. These three categories are shown across the top of figure 2.

Let us look first at the possibilities for creating separate databases of book index information. While these databases would not directly enhance the library catalog, their existence might well obviate the need to augment the MARC records used by libraries. And, if the online catalog of the future becomes a gateway to a variety of abstracting and indexing databases, a separate book index database could supplement searches at the catalog terminal.

The first alternative listed is simply to include monographs in existing abstracting and indexing tools. This already occurs to some extent, but such coverage would have to be greatly expanded before we could say that the content of most appropriate monographic works is as accessible as information found in the journal lilterature. An obvious advantage of this option is that it builds on our existing system of access to printed information, which does seem to work. It would also place responsibility for selecting the monographs to be covered in the hands of organizations that already serve special groups and subject disciplines.

The next three alternatives are to create a separate new tool, or several tools, to index selected monographs. Like existing journal indexing products, these might be commercially produced or supported by discipline-based organizations. They would be made available through existing database vendors and perhaps eventually linked to online catalogs.

The alternatives are categorized by the different means for creating the index databases. The first of these is to use subject terms selected from a controlled list—the choice of thesaurus would depend upon the coverage of the book database. LC subject terms are even a possibility. This is a labor-intensive way to create the database, but would provide a product comparable in quality to existing journal indexes.

The other two methods rely on terms taken from the tables of contents and indexes of the books themselves. The most direct method is simply to reproduce in a searchable database all such terms from a very select set of monographs. This is the approach taken by Superindex. A well-designed study of the effectiveness of Superindex searches is needed before we can evaluate this method. The fourth alternative suggests using Cochrane's Subject Access Project (SAP) technique to provide content coverage of a selected set of monographs.[20] While a SAP-derived database has never been compared to Superindex, the greater selectivity of the SAP application suggests that it would produce search results superior to the catchall Superindex technique. Of course, both methods are limited by the adequacy of back-of-the-book indexes. A study by Cochrane and others revealed that many books, even scholarly monographs, are not indexed at all; others are poorly indexed.[21]

The SAP method was actually developed to enhance MARC records for use in an online catalog. The remaining seven alternatives shown on the matrix suggest options for creating enriched MARC records and for making them widely available to the library community. Some advocates of enriched records have called for LC to produce enhanced MARC records as part of its national record distribution program. They argue that while this approach would be costly for LC, it would be cost effective on a national scale.

Alternatives five through seven describe three different methods for adding book content information to LC records. Controlled vocabulary indexing, using LCSH, would be the most labor-intensive option but would add ten times the number of meaningful LC subject headings to at least a select group of MARC records. A likely side benefit—and cost—would be the addition of more specialized terms to the LC subject headings list.

The next alternative, numbered six on the chart, would also have LC select a group of monographs for content indexing, but proposes the use of the SAP technique rather than actual subject analysis. This option would be less costly to LC, since SAP can be applied more quickly than traditional subject analysis and does not require that the indexer have special subject knowledge. However, it would require that online catalogs be designed to index and retrieve a new set of uncontrolled descriptive terms. The MARC field 653 should be able to accommodate these terms.

Option seven has been put forward as one that would demand little extra labor of LC staff. This is the suggestion that publishers be asked to supply the library with analytic abstracts that could be keyed into a special note field in the MARC record. This could be a quick and easy way to stuff subject information into MARC records, but it is difficult to predict whether more than a few publishers would be persuaded to supply useful abstracts. Like alternative six, this method would require online catalog designers to devise effective ways to manipulate new kinds of catalog information since many online catalogs do not index the notes field.

A question central to considering any of these three alternatives is, Should we expect the Library of Congress to provide book content subject indexing as part of its record distribution service? A reallocation of the LC budget to produce such augmented records would represent a major shift in the policy and mission of LC's Processing Services. The library's MARC records are created to describe and provide access to bibliographic entities which are, for the most part, physical items that must be stored and retrieved. The records are distributed to help other libraries play the same role. While some may view provision of access to the content of these same items as part of that mission, that position is arguable. We cannot expect LC to take a radically new view of its bibliographic records—especially a view with large dollar signs attached—unless we can present it with a well-documented case for change and a strong demand from the library or library-user community. The hard research evidence needed to make such a case for enriched MARC records does not yet exist.

The critical next step, then, would be to build enriched online catalog databases and test their value to a variety of library users. The four alternatives numbered eight through eleven are possibilities both for developing text databases and for maintaining ongoing distribution of enriched MARC records. They are grouped together because each method would add book content information to MARC records *after* the records leave the Library of Congress. The first option is one that has been suggested by Brett Butler in his proposal to establish the Book Indexing Group (BIG) project.[22] Briefly, BIG would develop a separate MARC format database of content indexing for a set of selected monographs. The database would use LC subject headings and would be designed to load and merge with MARC databases in online catalogs, matching the individual MARC records by LC card number or ISBN. The indexing could be done by a cooperating group of libraries or through a specially funded project. As online catalogs proliferate, sales of the BIG databases might even make it self-supporting. Butler suggests that the first test development of BIG would be in a narrowly defined subject area so that the database could be as complete as possible for the subject targeted.

The tenth alternative suggests an effort similar to BIG, using uncontrolled descriptors derived from applying the Subject Access Project technique. Options nine and eleven are plans for similar enhancements of MARC records—either with LC term indexing or SAP-derived terms—but the options propose that the enhancement be done online to one or more bibliographic utilities. Libraries could then elect to have enhanced records added to the tapes produced for their online catalogs. A successful model for such enhancement of records in shared utility databases is OCLC's work with the Association of Research Libraries Microform Project, predicting that these two alternatives are workable.

However, it is probably premature to establish the technical and political apparatus necessary for altering records maintained on the bibliographic utilities. We would first want to observe expanded records *actually used* in operational online catalogs. Creation of a separate, fully MARC-compatible database for loading into selected library catalogs could be a manageable project, particularly if the subject coverage were narrowly restricted. With regard to the last four alternatives, the most logical next step would appear to be a test of the BIG project. At the same time, further testing and application of the SAP method is warranted—anyone about to build a special database of monographic materials should give this method serious consideration. If we move forward on both of these fronts, we can begin compiling the data needed to answer responsibility to our users' requests for book content information in the online catalog.

This paper has been an exploration of two questions: Can we, and should we, provide book content indexing in the online catalog? The verdict is still out. Eventually the decision will be made by a jury of library users. But the librarian's role is not passive. The possible alternatives suggested in this paper need to be tested and weighed against cost-effectiveness and need. Should we enhance the MARC record to improve subject access? We won't know until we try.

Notes

[1] Pauline Atherton Cochrane, *Books Are for Use: Final Report of the Subject Access Project to the Council on Library Resources* (Syracuse, N.Y.: Syracuse Univ. School of Information Studies, 1978).

[2] Irene Wormell, "Factual Data Retrieval according to SAP Technique," *International Forum on Information and Documentation* 8, no. 3:13-15 (1983).

[3] _____, "SAP—A New Way to Produce Subject Descriptions of Books," *Journal of Information Science Principles & Practice* 3:39-43 (Feb. 1981).

[4] Keith W. Russell, ed. *Subject Access: Report of a Meeting Sponsored by the Council on Library Resources, Dublin, Ohio, June 7-9, 1982* (Washington, D.C.: The Council, 1982).

[5] Ibid., p. 71.

[6] Michael Gorman, "The Longer the Number the Smaller the Spine; or, Up and Down with Melvil and Elsie," *American Libraries* 12:498-99 (Sept. 1981).

[7] Janet Swan Hill, "Online Classification Number Access: Some Practical Considerations," *Journal of Academic Librarianship* 10:17-22 (Mar. 1984).

[8] Carol Mandel and Judith Herschman, "Online Subject Access—Enhancing the Library Catalog," *Journal of Academic Librarianship* 9:148-55 (July 1983).

[9] Russell, *Subject Access*, p. 71.

[10] Monika Kirtland and Pauline Cochrane, "Critical Views of *LCSH*—Library of Congress Subject Headings, a Bibliographic and Bibliometric Essay," *Cataloging & Classification Quarterly* 1, no.2/3:71-94 (1982).

[11] Edward T. O'Neill and Rao Aluri, "Library of Congress Subject Heading Patterns in OCLC Monographic Records," *Library Resources & Technical Services* 25:63-80 (Jan./Mar. 1981).

[12] Cost figure based on estimates provided informally by Mary Kay Pietris, Chief of LC Subject Cataloging Division ($10 to $11 per item, including routine development of new class numbers) and Julianne Beall, Decimal Classification Specialist, LC Decimal Classification Division ($4 to $5 per item for total DDC classification costs).

[13] Tamas E. Doszkocs, "CITE NLM: Natural-Language Searching in an Online Catalog," *Information Technology and Libraries* 2:364-80 (Dec. 1983).

[14] Pauline Atherton Cochrane, "LCSH Entry Vocabulary Project: Final Report to the Council on Library Resources and to the Library of Congress" (Unpublished report, 1983).

[15] Charles R. McClure, "Subject and Added Entries as Access to Information," *Journal of Academic Librarianship* 2:9-14 (Mar. 1976).

[16] B. J. Starkoff, Presentation made at annual meeting of the Society for Scholarly Publishing, May 30, 1984, Washington, D.C.

[17] Brett Butler, "Book Indexing Group: A Database Creation Project to Enhance and Complement Traditional Library Cataloging" (Redwood City, Calif.: Information Access Corp., Business Development Group, unpublished paper, 1982).

[18] Pauline A. Cochrane, "Modern Subject Access in the Online Age," *American Libraries* 15:336-39 (May 1984).

[19] Joseph Matthews, Gary Lawrence, and Douglas Ferguson, *Using Online Catalogs: A Nationwide Survey, a Report of a Study Sponsored by the Council on Library Resources* (New York: Neal-Schuman, 1983), p. 134.

[20] Cochrane, *Books Are for Use*.

[21] Bonnie Gratch, Barbara Settel, and Pauline Atherton Cochrane, "Characteristics of Book Indexes for Subject Retrieval in the Humanities and Social Sciences," *The Indexer* 11:14-23 (Apr. 1978).

[22] Butler, "Book Indexing Group."

"Helping LC Improve LCSH Only Constructive Approach"

Carol A. Mandel

Bates is right about the need to take an imaginative look forward. There are (at least) two ways to bring library subject access into the online age, and we must move on both of them. One is to take advantage of the computer's ability to carry out search strategies using key words found anywhere in a bibliographic record. Following this route could mean changing the MARC format by adding a field for uncontrolled subject descriptors or other subject-related text we want to include in the MARC record.

The second route, which Bates is emphasizing, is that of modernizing our existing controlled vocabulary system. Doing this is less a matter of altering the MARC formats or MARC records than of restructuring LCSH from a printed thesaurus into a tool for the users of online catalogs. In creating this new tool, it is important not to waste our time and intellect attacking LCSH (we will all be old and out of fashion some day) or wishing we could start an entirely new system. There are millions of LC subject headings embedded in our catalog databases and we are converting hundreds more to machine-readable form every day. Besides, subject analysis is expensive; libraries are dependent upon LC-supplied subject cataloging.

The only constructive approach is to seek ways to work with the Library of Congress in modernizing LCSH. In our July 1983 article in the *Journal of Academic Librarianship* (p. 148-155), J. Herschman and I suggest several ways to do this: restructuring LCSH into a hierarchical thesaurus distributed in machine-readable form and using the resultant thesaurus as an online public access tool; adding entry vocabulary and new headings to LCSH through cooperative projects; and designing systems that enhance access to LC headings in online records by linking the headings to users' keyword searches.

If we are to achieve the transition urged by Bates, we and the Library of Congress must begin to view LCSH not as the cumbersome, always out-of-date "red book," but as a National Subject Authority File Service that represents a cooperative effort among LC and other libraries to maintain, enhance, and distribute a subject thesaurus in machine-readable form. The Name Authority Cooperative (NACO) program now underway provides a model, although a cooperative subject service is likely to require more centralized editing functions than are

---

Reprinted by permission of the American Library Association, "Helping LC Improve LCSH Only Constructive Approach" by Carol A. Mandel from *American Libraries*, May 1984, p. 336; copyright © 1984 by ALA.

necessary for NACO. Ideally, the concept of a national subject authority service would extend to the LC classification schedules, since these too can be important online subject access tools.

To answer Bates's first question: LCSH has much potential for online subject access. But we have work to do.

Subject Searching in Library Catalogs

Karen Markey

6.4.2 Required Features for User Assistance in Online Catalogs

The key to *success* at the subject catalog and in the online public access catalog is the *matching* of the searcher's *expressed topic* with the catalog's *controlled vocabulary*. The two searchers who expressed failure at the catalog (Figures 38 and 40) selected terminology that matched neither their expressed topic nor the catalog's controlled vocabulary. However, both encountered two sources of assistance provided by the library and the library catalog (i.e., cross-references and reference assistance). The *Library of Congress Subject Headings*, another source of assistance, was not consulted by the searchers.

Hildreth's (1982b) study of ten operational OPACs disclosed that no OPACs presently provide cross-references for subject headings, although The Ohio State University's LCS began to implement this feature shortly after the CLR-sponsored research projects on online catalogs were concluded (see Figure 7, which includes a "see" reference). MELVYL provides a cross-reference capability for author names, but fails to report that it has also retrieved items written by the requested author but published under a different name. Hildreth (1982b, 119) recommends that OPACs either obtain the searcher's permission or inform the searcher when retrieving cross-references, particularly "see references," so that the searcher is not confused by the system's apparent independent action. Underscoring the need for cross-references in OPACs, Hildreth also indicates that "online catalogs that do not provide 'see' and 'see also' references for term selection deprive users of aids that they may already have grown accustomed to (and benefited from) when searching the card catalog" (Hildreth 1982b, 121).

Reprinted by permission of OCLC from Karen Markey, *Subject Searching in Library Catalogs* (Dublin, Ohio: OCLC, 1984), 108-17.

```
         S: Life.
1A..................
        DC: OK. You're looking for life after death, right?
         S: It might be too hard. I just want to see what I can find on it ....
            I don't think there is anything on it.
        DC: "Life Science," "Life Spirit," "Life Saving."
3B..................
        LA: You might try "Mortality."
5..................
        DC: She suggested looking under "Death" when she started out? Now which
            part of the card are you looking at, the first lines?
         S: No, the next line down.
        DC: OK. So it's the title. Why did you not like that one?
3C..................
        LA: Try "Future Life."
5,1C..................
        DC: Now are you just looking at the first lines?
         S: Now I'm looking at everything—but it just says "death and dying."
3J..................
            I might write it down.
7H..................
        DC: Those are just about death and stuff.
         S: Maybe that one ...
        DC: "The Hour of Death"? It's fiction.
3C..................
         S: No. Darn! There's another one here too .... She [library aide] suggested
4I,3C..................
            "Immortality." That's the same one we had before. That's the only one
            there is.
1C,3C,8A..................

Key:
   S = Searcher
  DC = Data Collector
  LA = Library Aide
  1A = Access point, partial representation of expressed topic (i.e., "Life")
  3B = Scan, subject headings
   5 = Librarian assistance
  3C = Scan, titles
  1C = Access point, different from expressed topic (i.e., "Future Life")
  3J = Scan, full bibliographic information
  7H = Record, unknown
  3C = Scan, titles
  4I = Interactive refinement, negative keyword (i.e., "Fiction")
  3C = Scan, titles
  1C = Access point, different from topic (i.e., "Immortality")
  8A = Exit, to stacks
```

Fig. 40. Coded protocol of a subject search (with librarian assistance) for "Life after Death."

Not one of the 189 searchers consulted the printed volumes of *LCSH* during their subject catalog searches, and only 15 sought the librarian's assistance. Their reluctance to consult the *LCSH* or the librarian might have been due to the method of data collection in this study. Since the data collector followed searchers and prompted them to give voice to their thoughts, the inclusion of another person or written source in a usually solitary activity might have been awkward. Since searchers' problems with the selection of controlled vocabulary will undoubtedly continue after OPACs are introduced, both librarians and the printed volumes of *LCSH* should be nearby and accessible to OPAC searchers.

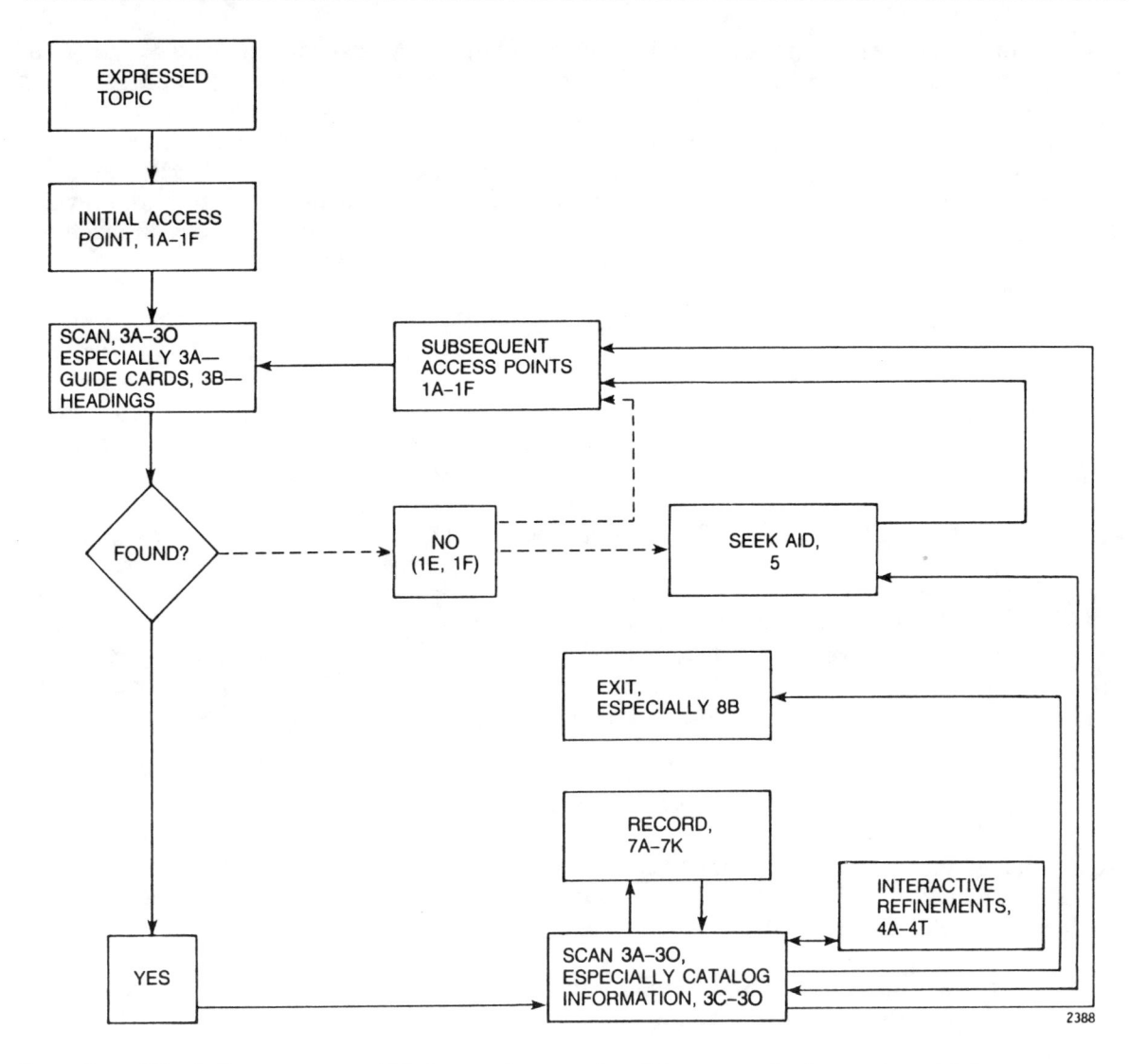

Note: Dotted line indicates process which frequently occurs but did not occur in the search modeled.

Fig. 41. Ad hoc process model of a subject search with librarian assistance.

6.4.3. Multiple Access Points and Assistance in Subject Searches

Online catalog users were asked in the CLR-sponsored survey to select from a list of 14 options four improvements to online catalogs. The most-selected option was the "ability to view a list of words related to my search words." Focused-group interview participants frequently cited the need for related-word lists. Moreover, the capability of placing the OPAC in locations other than the library or its branches (e.g., dormitories and university or city offices) and accessing it from remote locations via cable television or dial-in access underscores the need for assisting the searcher *while he is using the online public access catalog.* Online aids for finding, browsing, and selecting controlled vocabulary are *imperative.*

The top priority action from the CLR-sponsored Subject Access Meeting held May 1972 in Dublin, Ohio, was the production and distribution of the *Library of Congress Subject Headings* in machine-readable form. From this LCSH, OPAC systems designers would be able to implement related-word lists in online catalogs. However, production of this machine-readable LCSH has been impeded by other priorities at the Library of Congress (Russell 1982), and it will not be available as soon as anticipated. In the meantime, it behooves us to study the revised MARC format for subject authorities and to plan for incorporation of this LCSH in machine-readable form in online catalogs (Library of Congress 1981a).

Subject-rich fields of the revised MARC authorities format are enumerated in Table 52. When these fields are linked to subject-heading entries in the *printed volumes* of *LCSH* in Figure 42, we are surprised by the fact that LC's production of *LCSH* in machine-readable form will *not contain all the information detailed in the printed LCSH*! It will not contain "see also" references, i.e., subject headings that are traditionally considered narrower than the main subject heading.

Much of our previous research into subject catalog use (before and after the introduction of online catalogs) tells us that library catalog searchers consult a heading in the catalog that is broader in concept than what they really are looking for. (See chapter 4; see also Cochrane and Kirtland 1981; Bates 1977b; Knapp 1944.) As produced by LC, the machine-readable LCSH will not detail "see also" references (i.e., subject headings that are more specific than the one entered or consulted by patrons). Instead, it will detail the exact opposite—"see also from" references which are usually *broader* than the subject heading that the searcher entered. Sinkankas' conclusion from a study on the syndetic structure of *LCSH*, that the searcher is not guided well through a subject area, but rather "led out it, and very quickly" (1972), appropriately describes what is going to happen if the machine-readable LCSH produced by LC is simply dumped into OPACs by system designers.

If "see also" references were either included in the machine-readable LCSH produced by LC or processed into this LCSH by OPAC system designers, an online feature for this LCSH such as the example given in Figure 43, could be implemented into online public access catalogs. When patrons make exact matches of assigned headings or LCSH cross-references, instead of obtaining a list of alphabetically arranged subject headings, they would obtain a list of *related* subject headings. The related-term list would include at least:

- Main, assigned subject heading entered by the patron or cross-reference with a message informing him of the preferred heading
- "See also" references
- "See also from" tracings
- Number of items assigned to the main heading and related references and tracings
- Classification area or ranges where books on the main heading, references, and tracings can be found
- Line-number select capability (so that the patron does not have to retype the subject heading)

Prompts concluding the related-term display should include:

- Selection of listed heading(s)
- Browse forward or backward in the related-term display
- Entry of another subject-search statement

Table 52. Subject-rich fields of LC/MARC authority records.

Tag	Field Name	Subfield	Description
053	LC classification number	a	LC class number—single number or beginning number of a range
		b	LC class number—end number of a range
		c	Explanatory term
083	Dewey Decimal classification number	a	DDC class number—single number or beginning number of a range
		b	End number of a range
		c	Explanatory term
150	Established topical subject heading	a	Topical subject or name of place as entry element
		b	Name following place as entry element
		x	General subject subdivision
		y	Chronological subject subdivision
		z	Geographic subject subdivision
151	Established geographic name subject heading	a	Geographic name or name of place as entry element
		b	Name following place as entry element
		x	General subject subdivision
		y	Chronological subject subdivision
		z	Geographic subject subdivision
260	General explanatory see reference	a	Subject heading
		i	Explanatory text
360	General explanatory see also reference	a	Subject heading
		i	Explanatory text
450	Topical subject see from tracing	a	Topical subject or name of place used as entry element
		b	Name following place as entry element
		i	Text of reference instruction phrase
		x	General subject subdivision
		y	Chronological subject subdivision
		z	Geographic subject subdivision
451	Geographic name see from reference	a	Geographic name or name of place as entry element
		b	Name following place as entry element
		i	Text of reference instruction phrase
		x	General subject subdivision
		y	Chronological subject subdivision
		z	Geographic subject subdivision
550	Topical subject see also from tracing	a	Topical subject or name of place as entry element
		b	Name following place as entry element
		i	Text of reference instruction phrase
		x	General subject subdivision
		y	Chronological subject subdivision
		z	Geographic subject subdivision
551	Geographic name see also from tracing	a	Geographic name or name of place as entry element
		b	Name following place as entry element
		i	Text of reference instruction phrase
		x	General subject subdivision
		y	Chronological subject subdivision
		z	Geographic subject subdivision
680	Scope note	a	Subject heading
		i	Explanatory text
681	Example under/note under	a	Subject heading
		i	Explanatory text

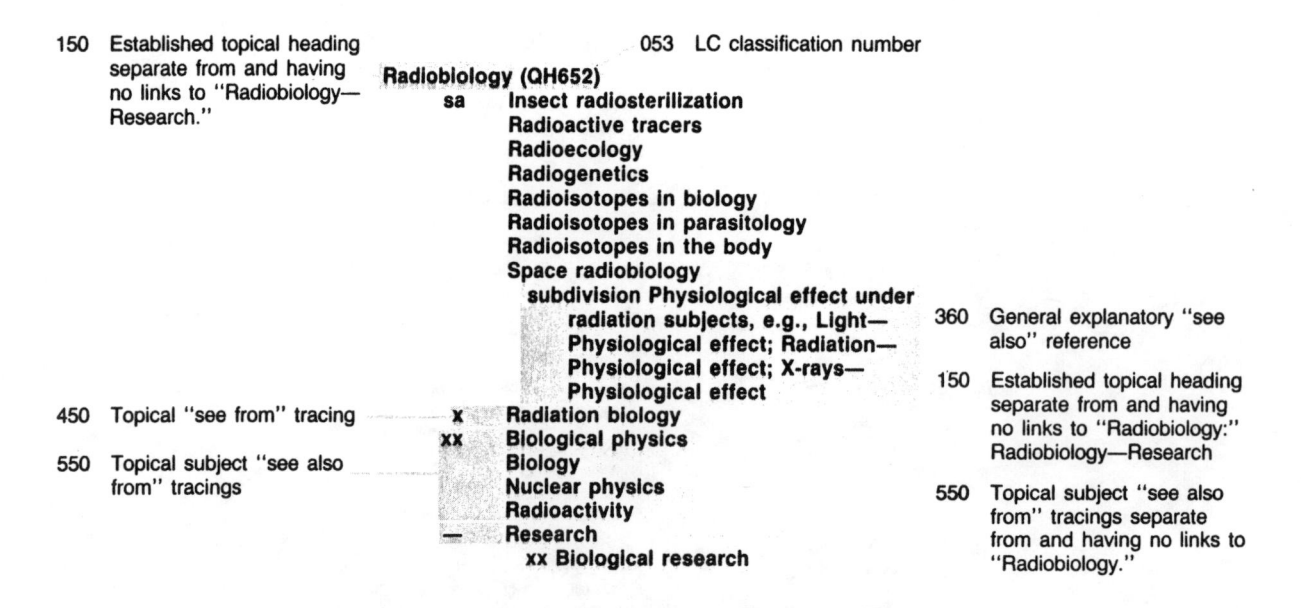

150	Established topical heading separate from and having no links to "Radiobiology—Research."	053 LC classification number

Radiobiology (QH652)
  sa Insect radiosterilization
      Radioactive tracers
      Radioecology
      Radiogenetics
      Radioisotopes in biology
      Radioisotopes in parasitology
      Radioisotopes in the body
      Space radiobiology
          subdivision Physiological effect under radiation subjects, e.g., Light—Physiological effect; Radiation—Physiological effect; X-rays—Physiological effect

		360 General explanatory "see also" reference
450	Topical "see from" tracing	150 Established topical heading separate from and having no links to "Radiobiology:" Radiobiology—Research
	x Radiation biology	
	xx Biological physics	
550	Topical subject "see also from" tracings	550 Topical subject "see also from" tracings separate from and having no links to "Radiobiology."
	Biology	
	Nuclear physics	
	Radioactivity	
	— Research	
	xx Biological research	

Fig. 42. Entry for "Radiobiology" in printed *LCSH* with field tags in machine-readable LCSH.

```
>USER:  Sub/Medieval Art
 OPAC:  Art, Medieval and related subjects are:
```

LINE	ITEMS	SHELF AREA	RELATED SUBJECTS	
				Brief explanation
1	39	N5940-N6311	ART, MEDIEVAL	Main subject heading
2	34		Art, Byzantine	
3	5		Art, Carlovingian	
4	1		Art, Cisterian	
5	15		Art, Gothic	
6	1	N6243	Art, Merovingian	See also tracings
7	1		Art, Ottonian	
8	10	N6280	Art, Romanesque	
9	20	ND2890-ND3416	Illumination of books and manuscripts	

TRY THESE SUBJECTS TOO:

10	1		Archeology, medieval	
11	115	N7810-N8189.6	Christian art and symbolism	See also from tracings
12	114	CB351-CB355	Civilization, medieval	
13	52	CB351-CB355	Middle ages	

```
PAGE 2. - FOR OTHER PAGES, ENTER "PR" AND PAGE NUMBER
        - FOR TITLES ON A SUBJECT, ENTER "LN/" AND LINE NUMBER
        - TO START OVER, ENTER "SUB/" AND SUBJECT HEADING
```

Fig. 43. Related-term display with class areas and "see also" tracings.

Many subject searchers withhold the vocabulary of their expressed topic and access the card catalog with either a partial representation of or terms different from their expressed topic. Rarely do searchers' access points exceed two words. Online vocabulary displays might be a means of stimulating searchers to respecify their access point through the vocabulary of online displays.

For example, the University of California's MELVYL produces a keyword-in-context controlled vocabulary display. Searchers are able to scan a list of *all* assigned subject headings in which their search term(s) is (are) encased. Such an operation is virtually impossible using the traditional library catalog and printed *LCSH*; even to attempt it requires time-consuming effort and "detective" work. MELVYL's keyword-in-context display for "Automobiles" is depicted in Figure 31. Unfortunately, there are no helpful prompts concluding the display to guide the searcher to the next step. The mere length of the display could frighten searchers. Cochrane (1982c) suggests that controlled vocabulary displays, such as the keyword-in-context example, be categorized by subdivisions (e.g., geographical, chronological, or format). Figure 44 is an example of how an online display of "Islam" subject headings with geographical subdivisions would be activated in an OPAC search. The addition of postings and class number areas in both keyword-in-context displays (Figures 31 and 44) would assist bookshelf browsers.

Postcoordination of subject and title words through Boolean operations has already been discussed as a means of refining the output of subject searches and increasing precision. It could also be connected to a feature which tracks the assigned subject headings and class number areas in the output and suggests the same to the searcher based upon subject headings and class number areas common to the greatest number of items in the output (Atherton and Markey 1979). For example, an OPAC search for "FCC" in Syracuse's SULIRS retrieved eight items. Class number areas and subject headings assigned to the eight items and the number of times they occur are as follows:

No. of Items	Assigned Subject Headings and Class Number Areas
3	United States. Federal Communications Commission
3	TK6554.5.S9
2	Broadcasting Policy — United States
2	HE8689.8.C56
1	Radio — Examinations, questions, etc.
1	Radio Operators — United States
1	AS36.R282R1896MF
1	KF2805.A2W44
1	KF2844.L4

Two subject headings and two class number areas are common to five of the eight retrieved items. A suggestive prompt following the display of the eight titles would inform the searcher of subject headings and class number areas in which he might also be interested (Figure 45).

PaperChase, the retrieval system for journal citations at Beth Israel Hospital, already features a link between title terms and *Medical Subject Headings (MeSH)*. PaperChase prompts the searcher when a controlled vocabulary term is available to express the concept (Horowitz and Bleich 1981; Cochrane 1982b). Mischo's idea of rotating title terms in MARC records and producing displays of assigned subject headings in response to title word searches is comparable; however, such an idea would not allow searchers to obtain the results of title keyword searches alone.

```
>Searcher:  BROWSE SU ISLAM
254 subjects found.  Subjects can be listed with:
     1. type of materials, e.g., Bibliography.
     2. geographic areas, e.g., East Africa.
     3. time periods, e.g., Middle Ages.
     4. other subjects, e.g., Sex.
     5. all of the above

Which line above is closest to your interest?

>2
```

```
 1. Communism and Islam—Sudan
 2. Fasts and feasts—Islam—Indonesia—Jakarta
 3. Fasts and feasts—Islam—Indonesia—Medan
 4. Islam—Africa
 5. Islam—Africa—Addresses, essays, lectures
 6. Islam—Africa—Bibliography
 7. Islam—Africa—Congresses
 8. Islam—Africa, East
 9. Islam—Africa—Hisotry
10. Islam—Africa, North
  .
  .
  .
22. Islam—Egypt
23. Islam—Egypt—History
24. Islam—Ethiopia
25. Islam—Gujarat
  .
  .
  .
39. Islam—Upper Volta
40. Islam—Zaire
  .
  .
  .

Which lines above are closest to your interest?
```

Fig. 44. Keyword-in-context display of assigned subject headings (Islam) with geographical subdivisions.

```
                  .
                  .
                  .
                 8.
Call Number:    HE.8689.8.C56
Author:         COLE, BARRY G
                OETTINGER, MAL, 1932-
Title:          RELUCTANT REGULATORS : THE FCC AND THE BROADCAST AUDIENCE
Publisher:      READING, MASS, ADDISON-WESLEY PUB. CO/C1978
Language:       ENGLISH
Availability:   DISCHARGED - ON 4/15/82
Subjects:       1. UNITED STATES. FEDERAL COMMUNICATIONS COMMISSION
                2. BROADCASTING POLICY—UNITED STATES

Try these subjects and class numbers for more books:

     1. United States. Federal Communications Commission
     2. TK6554.5.S9
     3. Broadcasting Policy—United States
     4. HE8689.8.C56

Which lines above are closest to your interest?
```

Fig. 45. Online vocabulary aid suggesting assigned subject headings and class number areas.

Cochrane (1982c, 5) also envisions other features to assist searchers in the selection of vocabulary for subject searching in OPACs:

- Automatic interaction between searcher and computer system so that the best of search terms can be found.
- Automatic display of some retrieved items for relevance, feedback, and iteration of the above feature using different selection rules.
- Automatic display of logical outlines (or classification lists) to select search terms in context—some broader, some coordinate, some narrower. This may help increase the output or sharpen the precision of the search.
- Automatic display of limit options (language, date of publication, etc.). This could help reduce the output of the search.

The logical outlines or classified lists called for by Cochrane are presently available only through OPAC searches using truncated call numbers. This feature simulates searching the library's shelflist. CITE, an OPAC at the NLM, incorporates class numbers into its feedback routine. However, the way in which class number searching is done in an OPAC requires searchers to know the meaning of the class number. In the late 1960s, Freeman and Atherton (1968) experimented with information retrieval through automatic manipulation of the Universal Decimal Classification (UDC) schedules in the AUDACIOUS Project. In view of their findings, Cochrane (1982a, 1982d) now places classification research into the context of the online public access catalog. She has initiated further research to explore the subject retrieval potential from the text, i.e., classification captions of the Dewey Decimal and Library of Congress Classification (DDC and LCC) schedules. Screen displays of the DDC show how the classification's hierarchical structure could lead searchers to topics which are coordinate to or broader or narrower than the vocabulary used to represent their access point (Figure 46). Such hierarchical displays of controlled vocabulary or classification captions are necessary to draw out the expressed topics from searchers, since they are prone to consult a partial, different, or shortened representation of their expressed topic.

Online vocabulary displays can assist OPAC searchers when selecting access points. Such displays were never possible in traditional library catalogs. Technology makes it possible for an OPAC to manipulate assigned subject headings and machine-readable LCSH in many ways to stimulate OPAC searchers. We have covered six online vocabulary displays that an OPAC can provide: 1) cross-references; 2) related subject headings, such as the printed arrays in *LCSH*; 3) keyword-in-context displays of subject headings; 4) keyword-in-context displays of subject headings by type of subdivision (e.g., geographical or chronological); 5) automatic detection of subject headings and class number areas common to the greatest number of displayed or retrieved items; and 6) logical outlines or lists from classification schedules to put topics in context. In a study of human information search strategy, Bates (1979, 208) introduced 11 term tactics to aid online searchers "in the selection and revision of specific terms within the search formulation." These 11 tactics include displays that we have already discussed. Furthermore, each tactic could be implemented in an online catalog to assist users in finding the right search terms to express their topic in the course of their online search. The 11 tactics are:

Term Tactic	Explanation
1. SUPER	To move upward hierarchically to a broader (superordinate) term
2. SUB	To move downward hierarchically to a more specific (subordinate) term
3. RELATE	To move sideways hierarchically to a coordinate term
4. NEIGHBOR	To seek additional search terms by looking at neighboring terms, whether proximate alphabetically, by subject similarity, or otherwise

Term Tactic *(cont'd)*	Explanation *(cont'd)*
5. TRACE	To examine information already found in the search in order to find additional terms to be used in furthering the search
6. VARY	To alter or substitute one's search terms in any of several ways
7. FIX	To try alternate affixes, whether prefixes, suffixes, or infixes
8. REARRANGE	To reverse or rearrange the words in search terms in any or all reasonable orders
9. CONTRARY	To search for the term logically opposite from that describing the desired information
10. RESPELL	To search under a different spelling
11. RESPACE	To try spacing variants

```
SEARCHER:   Browse ISLAM/CT Summary

            297 ISLAM and religions derived from it

            Summary
    297.1   Sources, relationship, attitudes of Islam
       .2   Islamic doctrinal theology (Aqaid and Kalam)
       .3   Islamic public worship and other practices
       .4   Islamic religious experience, life, practice
       .5   Islamic moral theology
       .6   Islamic leaders and organization
       .7   Islamic activities
       .8   Islamic sects and other religions derived from Islam

Which line above is closest to your search topic???_____
```

SOURCE: Cochrane (1982a, "Figure 1. Screen Display with Classification Summary").

Fig. 46. The Dewey Decimal Classification scheme in the online public access catalog.

6.5 Subject Searches and Scans

6.5.1 Description

The term "scan" refers to the reading or perusal of textual information in or near the subject catalog. In only 26 searches were no scans recorded. Table 53 summarizes the number and type of scans which occurred in 189 searches. Fewer than 25% of the subject searches involved more than three scans. In Table 53, the frequencies of scan types indicate that subject searchers overwhelmingly scanned *subject-rich information* found on catalog cards (i.e., subject headings and titles). These two types of information accounted for 74% of the information scanned by subject searchers. However, some textual information scanned by searchers is not always present for every cataloged item (e.g., notes, guide cards, and publication date); thus, it is not surprising that the highest ranked information (i.e., titles, subject headings, and author) is usually enumerated for every bibliographic record in the library catalog.

Table 53. Types of scans (ranked by frequency of occurrence)

Type of Scan		Frequency	Percentage
3C	Titles	316	58.0
3B	Subject Headings	88	16.1
3D	Author	29	5.3
3E	Call Number	22	4.0
3J	Full bibliographic information	19	3.5
3K	Publication date	18	3.3
3G	"See also" reference	15	2.7
3M	Unknown	12	2.2
3F	Tracings	8	1.5
3A	Guide cards	7	1.3
3I	Notes	6	1.1
3L	Library location	3	0.6
3N	"See" reference	2	0.4
3O	Number of pages	0	0.0
3H	*Library of Congress Subject Headings*	0	0.0
	Total	545	100.0%

6.5.2 Required Features for Scanning in Online Catalogs

Since subject catalog searchers are prone to scan subject-rich information, it is recommended that assigned subject headings and titles be included in intermediate subject displays of individual items in OPACs. Tracings should also be included in intermediate displays, and they should be labeled so as to suggest to the searcher that he should incorporate this vocabulary into his search strategy to obtain similar library materials.

Call numbers should also be included at the intermediate display level to accommodate searchers who wish to terminate their OPAC search and browse the bookshelf. Figure 47, an example of such a display, shows how an OPAC can provide a helpful prompt immediately following the system's response to a search argument. It tells the user how to obtain abbreviated or intermediate displays of individual items.

```
42 Results When Looking For Power Resources

1. Title:          The poverty of power: energy and the
                   economic crisis
   Other Subjects: Power (Mechanics)
                   Energy policy – United States
   Call Number:    HD 950 A2 C643 1976

2. Title:          Beyond the age of waste: a report to
                   the Club of Rome
   Other Subjects: Economic History – United States
                   Natural Resources
                   Energy Policy – United States
   Call Number:    HC 59 G231 1981

   Page 1. - FOR MORE TITLES, PRESS "RETURN"
           - FOR PREVIOUS SCREEN, ENTER "PS"
           - TO ENTER MORE SUBJECTS, ENTER "SUB/"
             AND SUBJECT HEADINGS
```

Fig. 47. Example of an intermediate display of a retrieved item in an OPAC subject search.

Abbreviated displays should produce the call number and title; intermediate displays should include call number, title, and assigned subject headings. Call number is a requirement for any and all item displays produced as a result of subject searches, since a predominant number of searchers rely on bookshelf browsing for book selection.

6.5.3 Highlighting Matched Subject Terms in Retrieved Items

Highlighting terms that users match in subject searches with the subject vocabulary in retrieved bibliographic records is a feature that has already been implemented in retrieval systems accessed by end users. CITE (see Figure 37) and LEXIS highlight matched terms through the use of reverse video for library patrons at the National Library of Medicine and for LEXIS searchers, e.g., lawyers, legal researchers, and other individuals. Should machine-readable cataloging records be augmented with additional search terminology, e.g., annotations, tables of contents, etc., highlighting matched terms in these records will enable patrons to view retrieved items quickly online by looking for highlighted matched terms and reading them in context.

6.6 Summary

Protocol analysis of traditional library catalog subject searches has provided us with knowledge about the process of subject searching and the capabilities online catalogs must have if they are to support the search tactics of traditional catalog searchers. An ad hoc process model of subject searching was constructed from the protocol analysis of 189 subject searches. This model is a composite representation of the process of subject searching the library catalog. However, subsets of the composite model reveal paths that subject searchers preferred, paths that are more faithful representations of the process of subject searching than those of the composite model. These subsets both suggest features for an online catalog to support catalog users' search tactics and online user assistance to effect fruitful communication between user and system.

Five subsets of the composite model were presented, described, and discussed in terms of the features *required* of online catalogs and the features that, while not possible in traditional library catalogs, could be implemented in online catalogs. These subsets and features are:

Model 1. Bookshelf Browsing

Required Features:
1. Alphabetical list of assigned subject headings in response to the user's input subject access point
2. Suggestive prompts at the conclusion of this subject headings list informing the user of possible next actions

Future OPAC Features:
1. Online *Subject Guide* in which the alphabetical list of assigned subject headings includes the classification numbers common to the majority of books assigned each heading and the number of books in the particular class area

Model 2. Subject Searches with A Priori Refinements

Required Features:
1. Alphabetical list of assigned subject headings and subdivisions in response to the user's access point
2. Suggestive prompts at the conclusion of this subject headings and subdivisions list informing the user of possible next actions

Future OPAC Features:
1. Rotated (or keyword-in-context) displays of assigned subject headings
2. Option to users to produce keyword-in-context displays by type of subdivision, e.g., geographical, topical, etc.

Model 3. Subject Searches with Interactive Refinements

Required Features:
1. An intelligent, i.e., forgiving and simple, implementation of Boolean search capabilities
2. Limit capabilities accompanied by online user assistance that informs users when it is appropriate to enter limit criteria

Future OPAC Features:
1. User feedback routines, such as ranking of search terms, ranking of search output on a best-match-of-searched-terms basis

Model 4. Subject Searches and Assistance

Required Features:
1. Online cross-references which would lead searchers to the preferred subject heading(s)
2. Proximity of librarian assistance to OPAC searchers
3. Proximity of the printed volumes of *LCSH* to OPAC searchers

Future OPAC Features:
1. Online related-term lists containing "see also" tracings and "see also from" references and prompts directing users to possible next actions in response to users' input subject terms

2. Online links to controlled vocabulary and class numbers providing users with system feedback to find additional relevant library materials
3. Online displays of logical outlines or classified lists, such as classification schedules, to put topics in context and provide browsing capabilities

Model 5. Scanning in Subject Searches

Required Features:
1. Inclusion of subject-rich information, e.g., assigned subject headings, titles, etc., in bibliographic records retrieved as output in subject searches
2. Highlighting terms that users match in their subject searches

An Exploratory Study of Three Subject Access Systems in Medicine: LCSH, MeSH, PRECIS

H. Mary Micco

Abstract

This study examines the see also reference structures (syndetic structures) of three subject access systems in medicine PRECIS, MeSH, and LCSH. It explores differences and similarities in the syndetic structures in an effort to develop the best possible structure using features of all three systems. MeSH has a more clearly defined hierarchical structure with a numeric notation that makes possible the "explode" feature. Here, a search on a given term can be exploded to capture all narrower terms. LCSH is strong in providing series of related concepts assisting the reader in browsing widely. PRECIS makes possible the definition of multi-facetted or narrow complex subjects within a subject class, but it has a minimal network of see also references. Its thesaurus serves only to guide the reader to broader headings.

In this study, five broad subject areas in medicine were selected from a stratified random sample, and then plotted on subject area maps developed from recognized "classic" textbooks. The textbooks were used as a universal standard to determine what should or should not be considered as included in, or related to, a given field. Graphs were also developed to show the nature of the linkages provided in each of the three systems.

Three variables were evaluated:

1. *subject area coverage:* the total number of subject headings provided in a given subject area. This varied considerably in the three systems studied.

Reprinted, by permission, from H. Mary Micco, *An Exploratory Study of Three Subject Access Systems in Medicine: LCSH, MeSH, PRECIS* (Ph.D. diss., University of Pittsburgh, 1980), Abstract, 45-50, 58-60, 82-92, 147-53.

2. *browseability:* the number of narrower linked headings captured when the lead term was exploded.

The ability to browse through the available subject headings is directly related to the number and types of references provided.

3. *flexibility:* the number of separate look-ups required to locate all narrower headings.

This was determined by mapping all relevant subject headings and the linkages provided in each system. Separate unconnected clusters of headings appeared in all three systems, as did orphaned headings.

Maps were developed for the subject headings in each system. When compared against the maps developed from the textbook, gaps in coverage and inconsistencies in terminology control were also readily identified.

It is anticipated that the maps of terms developed in the manner described could easily be converted to computer displays that should do much to improve both precision and recall in bibliographic data bases.

Methodology

2. Textbook Selection

Having selected the subject areas for study and mapping, the next step was to develop a standard against which to measure the extent of the subject coverage provided in each of the systems. It was decided to select a recognized classic textbook in each of the broad areas in which the chosen subjects were to be found. This would provide insight into possible broader and related terms.

In order to standardize the selection of subject headings from the textbooks, headings selected were limited to the chapter and section headings unless another term appeared in one of the systems, in which case, the term was checked in the book index.

The problem of identifying standard texts in the subject areas involved was resolved by utilizing the bibliography of standard medical works distributed to students studying for accreditation from the Medical Library Association and referenced in J. B. Blake's, Medical Reference Books. Whenever two or three textbooks appeared equally appropriate, a random selection was made (and a second text was selected to check the validity of the first choice)....

3. LCSH, PRECIS and MeSH Edition Selection

In order to resolve the difficulty that all three of these systems are growing and changing, it was decided to freeze them as of December, 1979. Freezing the systems at a given point in time would serve adequately for this study, since the focus was on the underlying syndetic structure rather than on the headings themselves. The editions chosen for this study are as follows:

```
LCSH..............8th Edition
MeSH............. 1979 Edition
PRECIS.......... RIN File 06/11/78
```

In MeSH, a question arose as to the use of the Trees in this study. In some cases, particularly in the drug group, the relationships were made explicit only through the tree structures. It was decided since the system was designed as an integral whole, and since the notation does link the two, that the Trees and the subject headings would be combined and treated as one system.

It should be noted that the PRECIS thesaurus used in this study of their syndetic structure is not yet published, but can be obtained in microfiche form, as RIN File 06/11/78 from the Bibliographic Sources Division of the British Library. It should also be understood that this system depends primarily on a permuted key word subject indexing of actual books and, therefore, little emphasis has been placed on the thesaurus. Austin, however, clearly indicates that their thesaurus is organized and intended to reveal the underlying classification. In order to ensure uniformity, only the thesaurus entries were studied and mapped.

4. *Mapping Format*

A vertical display that would serve to clarify the classification inherent in the system would have been the ideal format. However, due to space limitations and the crowding such a display would cause, it was decided to display the hierarchy horizontally from the left (broadest terms) to the right (most specific terms).

5. *Term Selection*

The most critical element in this project was the development of a reasonable and appropriate universe of subject headings mapped in a hierarchical framework against which to measure the performance of each system.

The first step was to draw upon the chapter and paragraph headings provided in the textbook which immediately produced a hierarchical framework of terms. This was used to form the map outline that became the guide to the placement of all the terms identified in any of the systems. This was done to ensure consistency, to identify synonyms, and also, to permit a visual comparison of the four systems.

6. *Related Terms*

In dealing with terms that did not appear in the textbook's chapter and paragraph headings, these were checked in the book index. If found, they were then placed on the map as subdivisions of the appropriate paragraph heading. If a term was not found in the book index, it was considered to be outside the subject area and was placed in the borders as a related term adjacent to the term with which it was connected.

It was found necessary, particularly with LCSH, to define this as a cut-off point. No term was pursued beyond this level in searching out other linkages outside the subject area under study.

From this exercise, a universe of terms was obtained and mapped that could be described as representative of the subject area in question, with an explicit hierarchy of terms, showing any related terms that had actually been used in at least one of the systems.

7. *Generic Headings*

One difficulty surfaced immediately. Most of the textbooks use a number of broad generic headings that are virtually meaningless (as topic subject headings) in their chapter headings e.g., Diseases, Pathology. It was decided to display these terms because they make the hierarchical structure more explicit, with the use of [ ] square brackets. Such terms were not considered as topical subject headings and were not checked.

8. *Linkages*

Having established a universe of subject headings, every term except those in square brackets was checked in all three systems under study and all the linkages displayed.

A problem surfaced in relation to LCSH. In some cases, the linkages are implicit rather than explicit. Briefly stated, the rule is as follows:

> "Do not make a reference from one heading (A) to another heading (B) when the concept designated by heading A (be it a term or phrase) is simply repeated initially in heading B with a modifying term or phrase following.
>
> E.g., Color   )
>   s.a. color in advertising   ) incorrect
>
>   Industrial equipment   )
>   s.a. industrial equipment leases) incorrect"

It was decided to check these implicit linkages in all three systems to ensure uniformity.

Another problem with LCSH occurred because of its nature as a general subject heading system. In the subject area Animals, there were an unmanageable number of closely related terms linked by see also references which were not really relevant to the medical aspects of the subject matter, e.g., furs and fur farming, nor did they appear in the textbook. It was decided to handle this overload problem by showing all these headings in a series of charts, crosschecking the other two systems for any similar headings. Where necessary, the number of subheadings attached to each term was counted and the number posted rather than attempting to list all of them individually.

9. *Directional References*

A number of difficulties surfaced in attempting to map the direction of the references. All of the references in PRECIS are upwards with the result that zero scores are consistently obtained on browseability even though the system contains a number of relevant headings.

In LCSH, on the other hand, there is a very sophisticated network of interconnections, which are used to distinguish between related terms, broader terms, narrower terms and topical subheadings. There is also an intricate network of bidirectional references, as well as many implicit references, e.g., animal remains have an implied link with animals.

MeSH also presented difficulties in that in several cases the linkages are not made explicit in the thesaurus but are found only in the hierarchically structured trees.

. . . .

Scoring the Data

In scoring the data, the following system was used.

a. *Subject Coverage.* The total number of headings in each system was expressed as a percentage of the perfect score, the number of headings on the master.

The number of headings at each level of specificity was counted and expressed as a percentage of the number of headings found in the Master at the same level. The purpose of this analysis was to look for patterns in the distribution of the headings.

b. *Browseability.* This score was obtained by counting all the headings currently linked to the main headings being studied: Lymphoid Tissues, Animals, Esophageal Diseases, Heterocyclic Compounds with four or more rings, Orthodontics. The larger the number of linked headings, the higher the score. Scores were again expressed as percentages of the "perfect" score obtained by the master where all the headings were linked.

c. *Fragmentation.* This score was obtained by counting the number of separate distinct subject clusters used to cover the subject area. Since this measure was designed to reveal the fragmentation of the subject area, a perfect score was 1, meaning that the subject area is covered by one cluster. These scores were expressed as ratios to the Master.

d. *Related Terms.* The number of related terms in each system was counted and an effort was made to evaluate the nature and types of references provided, and to gain further insight into the nature of the syndetic structure provided.

. . . .

Results

Subject Area: Animals

This subject presented a very different problem, since the subject area is not strictly a medical one but rather draws upon the biological sciences, the study of organisms.

1. *Textbook Selection*

Before being able to find a suitable textbook on animals then it was necessary to go to the MeSH classification scheme and it was quickly evident that Animals was considered as a subset of vertebrates. Keeton's classic textbook on *Biology* outlined several methods of classifying the Animal Kingdom—a composite of those headings was drawn up and matched against the three systems. Both the textbook and the backup text, Villee's *General Zoology*, presented a very orderly hierarchy reflecting, as is proper, mutually exclusive categories. The problem is that people do not always classify animals by one set of biological characteristics. This problem was resolved in MeSH by the addition of a small group of headings under animals that provide for different regroupings of the same animals, e.g., a cat can belong to four categories at one and the same time namely, domestic animals, laboratory animals, newborn animals and carnivores.

2. *Limitations*

As a first step in organizing the subject headings, the textbook was used to generate a set of charts comparing the headings used in each system to describe the animal kingdom from a biological point of view. Even in this effort, however, the scientist conflicts with the layman in his view. The layman uses the term invertebrates rather loosely to describe all organisms that are not vertebrates. The scientist, on the other hand, uses the class and phylum names to describe the organisms more accurately. A major confusion occurs in the superimposition of the layman's term invertebrates to group all organisms other than vertebrates, when the biologists have several hierarchical levels involved. The subject heading systems seem to move indiscriminately from lay terminology to scientific names with little effort to connect the two.

In order to work with a manageable universe, it was decided to limit the first set of charts to vertebrates and to focus particularly on mammals. Major headings for groups of Invertebrates were posted but the related references were not included. It was also decided not to look at specific animals' names, since the purpose of this research was not to determine how many specific animals are listed in the systems but rather to examine the underlying syndetic structure— how are the subject headings connected to each other and what groupings emerge.

There were still so many subject headings that dealt with Animals from a variety of different aspects that it was decided to create two additional sets of charts. The second set ... was developed to display the many different groupings of animals available in the three systems other than the biological classes. No one textbook was available that listed all the possible ways to group animals; therefore, it was decided to obtain a master by making a composite of all the headings found in the three systems. There was little overlap between LCSH and PRECIS, where some rather odd groups were featured, such as, "animals which spend time upside down," and "animals living under stones".... In MeSH, which is primarily a medical data base, there was very limited coverage with only 9 out of a possible 69 groupings or 13 per cent. Coverage in PRECIS was strong in this area with 43 headings or 62 per cent of the headings identified; including 14 not found in LCSH. The most interesting point observed was the very large number of loosely related topics linked in LCSH.... Thirty-one related headings in all lead the reader rapidly away from Animals to explore very broad areas such as evolution or agriculture, not to mention the fact that many of the groupings also lead to discussions of applied areas such as the health and welfare of animals and their habits and behaviors. These are complex subjects with many levels of headings in and of themselves. It was decided to map these on a third set of charts.... In other less complex applied areas, e.g., animal industries, the number of headings was simply posted, ... since it would not have contributed much to map out each one of those headings when no similar headings exist in MeSH.

The third set of charts then compared the three systems in two major subject groups, habits and behaviors of, and the health, education and welfare of animals. Again, the coverage in LCSH was much more extensive. Eighty headings were found in this third set, while in PRECIS and MeSH, there were only 9 and 12 headings, respectively.

3. *Subject Coverage*

The first set of graphs on Animals dealt with them from the biologist's point of view. In MeSH, 50.6 per cent of the headings were identified. In LCSH, there were 80 per cent of the terms, and even in PRECIS, there were 62 per cent.

The chart below summarizes the scores obtained by the three systems.

These are not really very meaningful without an analysis of the performance of each system at different levels of specificity.

One of the problems with LCSH, for example, is that its headings do not cascade systematically.

SUBJECT COVERAGE: ANIMALS - SETS I, II, III

SET I	Textbook Actual	%	LCSH Actual	%	MeSH Actual	%	PRECIS Actual	%
Subject Coverage	53	100	40	80	31	56	31	62
Browseability	49	100	26	53	28	57	4	8
Fragmentation	1:1		11:1		2:1		3:1	
Number of Related Terms	---		31		2		3	
SET II								
Subject Coverage	69	100	48	70	9	13	43	62
SET III								
Subject Coverage	88	100	80	91	9	10	12	14

... zoology is connected directly to many different levels of specificity. This results in a completely unmanageable number of see also references under zoology but also results in inconsistencies in that not all subheadings are systematically linked. There is also considerable semantic confusion between overlapping but not synonymous terms such as Vertebrates, Mammals, Fauna, and Animals. Only by displaying the terms in a hierarchical structure of the type proposed do these problems surface, and it becomes possible to establish some sort of order in the chaos revealed.

Many headings at varying levels of specificity are linked to the broad heading zoology. Still others are linked only to the heading animals. One group, fur bearing animals, is also attached to the heading vertebrates, although no others are so linked. The heading fauna is not used but various subsets of fauna are identified and listed. None, however, are linked with animals. Again, 10 of the 13 different types of fauna are directly linked with zoology. In addition, a total of 24 different groupings of animals turned up. Of these, nine are directly connected to zoology.

By way of contrast, in MeSH subkingdoms, phyla and subphyla are linked into a loose group of invertebrates which is considered a subset of organisms. There is no connection made between the phylum chordata and its subphylum vertebrates, even though it is directly linked to organisms four levels higher... little effort is made even in MeSH to cascade the headings systematically through the different levels of specificity as the textbook does.

In PRECIS, the subphylum vertebrates is connected correctly to its phylum chordata, but the latter is not connected to vertebrates. Only three headings appear linked to invertebrates drawn from three different levels. Cephalechordates are shown linked to chordates but there is no recognition of their status as invertebrates. On the fringes of this hierarchy, there is a direct link from zoology to animals which ignores all the levels in between.

Efforts to discover patterns in the distribution of headings at different levels of specificity proved unsuccessful as can be seen from the data summarized in the following chart.

NUMBER OF HEADINGS AT DIFFERENT LEVELS OF SPECIFICITY: ANIMALS

Level	Master Actual	Master %	LCSH Actual	LCSH %	MeSH Actual	MeSH %	PRECIS Actual	PRECIS %
1 — Zoology	2	100	1	50	2	100	2	100
2 — Protozoa	5	100	4	80	3	60	2	40
3 — Radiata	3	100	1	33	0	0	1	33
4 — Chaetognatha	5	100	4	80	2	40	2	40
5 — Urochordata	5	100	4	80	2	40	2	40
6 — Agnatha	10	100	9	90	5	50	8	80
7 — Prototheria	2	100	0	0	0	0	0	0
8 — Monotremata	21	100	17	81	17	81	16	76
Totals	53		40		31		31	

4. *Browseability*

In LCSH, a number of the scientific terms are implicit orphans, linked only by a vague direction, "Zoology see also class, phylum, vertebrates, mammals and names of specific animals." In evaluating browseability, it was decided to ignore this instruction and to count only headings which were specifically linked to others in the system, giving a score of 53 per cent.

The poor score of 8 per cent in PRECIS is due to the fact that neither vertebrates nor invertebrates are linked to Zoology. In MeSH, where there was actually less subject coverage, the score on browseability was higher, because the headings are connected more systematically.

5. *Flexibility*

The number of separate distinct subject clusters found in the system can best be determined by viewing the graphs. The scores were as follows:

```
LCSH      11
MeSH       2
PRECIS     3
```

The large number of clusters in LCSH is largely due to the number of orphans.

6. *Other Comments*

As already mentioned, there was a large number of related terms under the heading zoology in LCSH, 31 altogether. By way of contrast, there were very few in MeSH or PRECIS (only 2 and 3, respectively). In both cases, the reader is referred to closely related fields of study, e.g., microbiology, herpetology, and ornithology.

An Exploratory Study of Three Subject Access Systems in Medicine 265

Table 12.

B: ANIMALS - SET I: SUBJECT HEADINGS: MASTER

1	Microbiology
2	Protozoology
3	
4	Cells
5	SUBK — Protozoa
6	
7	
8	
9	
10	INGD — Parazoa
11	
12	OMS — Mesozoa
13	
14	
15	
16	
17	Animal Colonies
18	SECTIONS — Radiata
19	
20	Protostomia — PHYLUM Chaetognatha
21	Herpetology
22	Ornithology — Echinodermata
23	Organisms
24	Zoology — Pogonophata
25	Animal Kingdom — Hemichordata
26	Acarology
27	Anatomy, Comparative — Metazoa — Deuterostomia — Chordata
28	Biology
29	Embryology
30	Entomology
31	Ethnozoology
32	Evolution
33	Helminthology
34	Hibernation
35	Ichthyology
36	Morphology
37	Natural History
38	Palaeontology
39	Phenology
40	Phylogeny
41	Physiology, Comparative
42	Polymorphism (Zoology)
43	Protozoology
44	Psychology, Comparative
45	Variation (Biology)
46	Zoogeography
47	Zoological Specimens
48	Zoology, Experimental
49	Nature Study
50	Science

INVERTEBRATES (2)
VERTEBRATES

Chordata subgroups: SUBPHYLUM — Urochordata, Cephalochordata, Protochordata

CLASS — Agnatha, Placodermi, Chondrichthyes, Osteichthyes, Pisces, Amphibia, Reptilia, Aves, Mammals, Vertebrates, Fossil

SUBCLASS — Prototheria, Theria

Prototheria → Monotremata (Egglaying Mammals)

Theria orders:
- Marsupiala (Marsupials) (1)
- Insectivora (Moles, Shrews) (1)
- Dermoptera (Flying Lemurs) (1)
- Chiroptera (Bats) (1)
- Primates (Monkeys-Man) (1)
- Edentata (Anteaters, etc.) (1)
- Pholidota (Manis) (1)
- Lagomorpha (Rabbits) (1)
- Rodentia (Rodents) (1)
- Cetacea (Whales, etc.) (1)
- Carnivora (Carnivores) (1)
- Tubulidentata (Aardvark) (1)
- Proboscidea (Elephants) (1)
- Hyracoidea (Coneys) (1)
- Sirenia (Manatees) (1)
- Perissodactyla (Horses, etc.) (1)
- Artiodactyla (Giraffes) (1)
- Pinnipedia (1)
- Animals *
- Fauna *

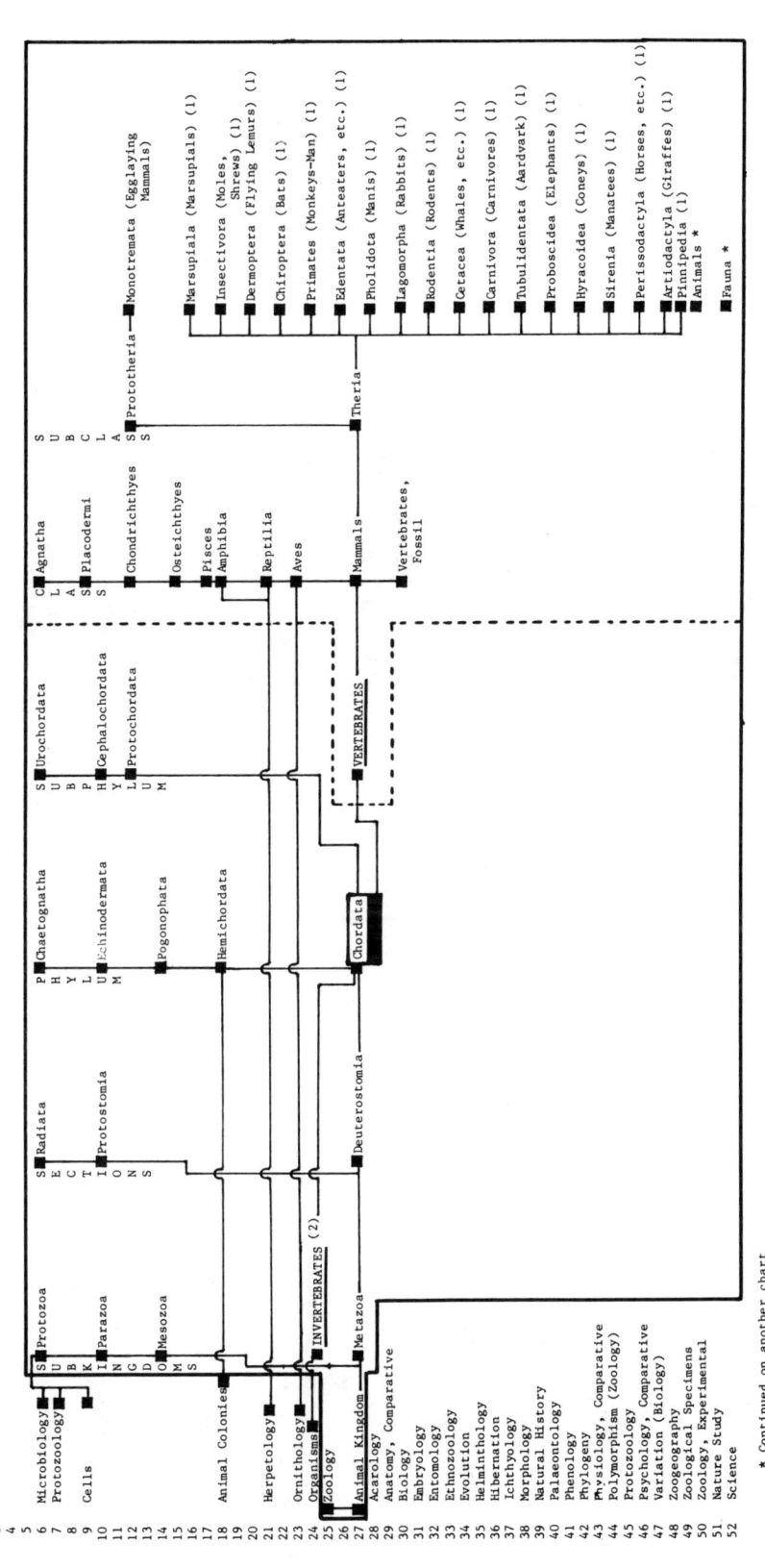

* Continued on another chart
(1) Names of Specific Animals
(2) The term vertebrates designates only a part of phylum-chordates. The rest of that phylum and all other phyla then fall under the heading invertebrates.

Table 13.

B: ANIMALS - SET I: SUBJECT HEADINGS: LCSH

1. Microorganisms ■ ▲ 22
2. Protozoa ■ ▲ 22
3. B
4. U
5. Cells ■
6. K
7. I
8. N
9. G
10. Mesozoa ■ ▲ 0
11. D
12. O
13. M
14. S
15.
16. Animal Colonies ■
17.
18. Herpetology ■
19.
20. Ornithology ■
21.
22. Zoology ■ ▲ (2)
23. INVERTEBRATES ■ ▲ (2)
24.
25. Metazoa ■ ▲ 0
26.
27. Acarology ■
28. Anatomy, Comparative ■
29. Biology ■
30. Embryology ■
31. Entomology ■
32. Ethnozoology ■
33. Evolution ■
34. Helminthology ■
35. Hibernation ■
36. Ichthyology ■
37. Morphology ■
38. Natural History ■
39. Palaeontology ■
40. Phenology ■
41. Phylogeny ■
42. Physiology, Comparative ■
43. Polymorphism (Zoology) ■
44. Protozoology ■
45. Psychology, Comparative ■
46. Variation (Biology) ■
47. Zoogeography ■
48. Zoological Specimens ■
49. Zoology, Experimental ■
50. Nature Study ■
51. Science ■

Radiata ■ ▲ 3
SECTIONS

Chaetognatha ■ ▲ 0
PHYLUM
Echinodermata ■ ▲ 10
Hemichordata ■ ▲ 2

Chordata ■

Tunicata ■ ▲ 0
SUBPHYLUM
Protochordates ■ ▲ 0

VERTEBRATES ■
Chordata, Fossil ■ ▲ 1

Agnatha ■ ▲ 2
CLASS
Placodermi ■ ▲ 0 (Orphan)
SUBCLASS
Chondrichthyes, Fossil ■ ▲ 0 (orphan)
Osteichthyes ■ ▲ 9
Fishes ■ ▲ 21
Amphibians ■ ▲ 8
Reptiles ■ ▲ 17
Birds ■ ▲ 18
Mammals ■
Vertebrates, Fossil ■ ▲ 1

Monotremata (Egglaying Mammals) ■ (1)
Marsupialia (Marsupials) ■ (1)
Insectivora (Moles, Shrews) ■ (1)
Primates (Monkeys-Man) ■ (1)
Edentata (Anteaters, etc.) ■ (1)
Pholidota, Fossil ■ (1)
Rodentia (Rodents) ■ (1)
Cetacea (Whales, etc.) ■ (1)
Carnivora (Carnivores) ■ (1)
Tubulidentata (Aardvark) ■ (1)
Proboscidea ■ (1)
Hyracoidea ■ (1)
Sirenia (Manatees) ■ (1)
Perissodactyla, Fossil ■ (1)
Artiodactyla (Giraffes) ■ (1)
Animals * ▲ 10
Fauna * ▲ 10

* Continued on another chart
(1) Names of Specific Animals
(2) The term vertebrates designates only a part of phylum-chordates. The rest of that phylum and all other phyla then fall under the heading invertebrates.
(3) Zoology includes divisions, classes, orders, etc. of the animal kingdom, e.g. invertebrates, vertebrates, birds, insects, mammals, cetacea, ungulata; and particular animals, e.g. antelopes, buffalos, squirrels, tigers.

Conclusions

Research Findings

The purpose of this research was to develop a methodology for examining the syndetic structures of subject access systems in medicine.

The methodology selected involved comparing the subject headings in each system with those obtained from the textbook and mapped in a hierarchical display developed from the chapter and paragraph headings. This technique proved very effective in pinpointing difficulties and weaknesses in the different systems. It showed up orphans, fragmentation of subject areas, unnecessary redundancies and flagrant omissions....

In studying the samples obtained, it became obvious that there were inconsistencies, weaknesses and major gaps in all three systems. These could be corrected. A much more significant outcome was the development of a technique for making the syndetic structures explicit and readily obvious to the users. Even MeSH, for all its sophistication, involves numerous look-ups to locate all the related terms in a subject area.

As we move into the computer era, it is time to avail ourselves of this sophisticated technology to make a quantum leap forward in creating and displaying our subject access systems. We are no longer limited to linear displays in card catalogues or to bulky and unwieldy printed lists of subject headings.

A computer can readily be programmed to create, at high speed, the types of displays described in any format or combination requested, e.g., all diseases affecting the esophagus or all body parts affected by myasthenia gravis.

The need for such displays was highlighted by the three sets of charts needed to map all the headings available on Animals. By rapidly viewing the three maps, the reader could readily determine the scope and subject matter of the material available, and the correct headings to use to increase the precision of the search....

... it might be helpful to display the scope of a subject even if the headings were not in use, especially in light of the fact that most systems have been criticized for lack of specificity and poor coverage.

One solution to this dilemma might well be to display all the appropriate headings, highlighting the ones actually in use.

The need to improve on existing subject access systems is underscored by the problem that is occurring in most of the major computerized data bases but particularly the ones that provide full text or permuted keywords. The number of "hits" under many headings is overwhelming. Without a graphic display of headings in the system, there is no easy way to render searches more specific. The reader has no idea of the size or complexity of the subject of interest, nor of the headings available.

Much criticism has been made of computerized data bases because they restrict browsing in contrast to open shelf systems. Using the computer to display rapidly maps of the subject area of interest will enable the searcher to clarify his thinking and to zero in on the aspect that is appropriate with the correct terminology. This is a modern, sophisticated way to assist the reader in browsing by providing not the book titles themselves, but first the subject headings.

This research also served to underline the impossibility of developing one hierarchy that would fit every situation. In all five areas studied, difficulties appeared because of differing views on how to classify the information. Each subject may be viewed from many different aspects and the diversity and complexity increase geometrically as one moves to more universal subjects, e.g., animals.

Three sets of charts were necessary to convey the extent and complexity of the headings provided in LCSH for animals....

The solution appears to lie not in abandoning classification, but in using it to produce the sets of maps on demand. The most critical need is to move away from the concept of a rigid hierarchy consisting of mutually exclusive categories to that of overlapping and flexible subject groupings. By mapping the terms in flexible series of hierarchies, they can be realigned readily as needed or whole new sets of maps created on demand.

It seems obvious from the samples studied that all three systems have weaknesses and that the best possible system should draw upon the strengths of all three. In LCSH, there are consistently more related terms to give a wider view of the subject and to reveal important interconnections. In MeSH, there is the "explode" feature, which enables the reader to retrieve all the headings subsumed under the heading of choice without having to list them separately. There is also a built-in classification system which could easily be mapped. In PRECIS, there is a sophisticated permuted alternate title keywording system which adds to search precision once the correct headings have been identified....

In conclusion, the analysis and mapping of the complex headings under Animals could be regarded as the acid test of the methodology. By breaking the subject down into manageable sections and by providing the necessary linkages, it is possible to organize even such complex and complicated subjects as animals, for computer mapping.

"Authority Control in the Retrospective Conversion Process"

Dan Miller

Retrospective conversion of a library's records to machine-readable form in support of automated circulation control, or for an online or COM catalog, is either in process or on the agenda of many libraries. Conversions are typically undertaken because of the improved service and long-range cost savings derived from working in an automated environment. Much has been written on retrospective conversion options with survey articles reflecting the technological innovations over time. Butler et al.[1] reviewed the offerings and procedures when retrospective conversions were first gaining momentum. More recently, Epstein,[2] in a series of articles, brought the subject up-to-date with an exploration of the vendors and methods associated with retrospective conversion and the nuances associated with converting copy-specific information. Secondary concerns relating to duplicate record elimination and holdings consolidation in a single source file at a major academic library are explained by Caplan.[3] Her article details Harvard University's method for consolidating a MARC transaction file, where each record represents a volume and local information resides in various fields, into a database where each record represents a title and local holdings data are consolidated into a single field. McPherson et al.[4] describe the University of California's method for merging records from various sources for the production of an online union catalog.

Why Apply Authority Control?

One aspect of the retrospective conversion process that has not received much attention in the literature is authority control. Most large source files used in the retrospective conversion process contain records in which the heading fields contain data reflecting the rules and practices

---

Reprinted by permission of the American Library Association, "Authority Control in the Retrospective Conversion Process" by Dan Miller from *Information Technology and Libraries*, September 1984, pp. 286-92; copyright © 1984 by ALA.

in effect at the time the records were converted, or at the time the cataloging for the title was originally done. With regard to name and uniform title access points, the implementation of AACR2 has tended to compromise the uniformity of the data, as some records were created prior to implementation of AACR2 and some were created after implementation. For subject access fields, our perpetual redefinition of the world around us along with changes in cataloging rules has resulted in source files in which works for given subjects are likely to be found under various (sometimes archaic) headings. These inconsistencies, coupled with other types of heading errors, impede the colocation of entries in a traditional COM catalog and inhibit access to records in an online catalog. A system for correcting headings in converted records via error-correcting algorithms (like those described by Brown[5] with regard to OCLC's AACR2 edit), or via authority file matching, is therefore required.

B/NA's Authority Control System

The Blackwell North America (B/NA) authority control system has been in operation for more than thirteen years. While subject authority control in support of B/NA-produced COM catalogs was the principal focus of the system for many years, recent activities reflect equal emphasis on both name and subject authority control in support of both COM and online catalogs. The authority control system is a batch mode, offline system. It employs a file-matching approach involving libraries' converted bibliographic files and Library of Congress name and subject authority files. In addition to authority data received from LC in machine-readable form, the subject authority file includes more current records keyed from LC's printed lists of subject headings. Also, the system extracts very new headings from cataloging processed through the system. These headings perform a standardizing function temporarily until replaced by a full authority record provided by LC.

Briefly stated, the system does the following:

- Updates library headings in the MARC format to LC's most recent practices.
- Standardizes the forms of headings for filing purposes and for improved online access.
- Corrects MARC tags and subfield codes based on data content.
- Provides deblinded cross-references for use in COM catalog production or online systems.

The first three capabilities relate to the findings of O'Neill and Aluri, later expanded upon by O'Neill and Vizine-Goetz, concerning the majority of errors found in subject-heading fields of 33,455 OCLC sample records.[6] The authors identify four major categories of errors:

1. Inconsistency in spacing, punctuation, and capitalization.
2. Typographical and minor spelling errors.
3. Invalid form of heading.
4. Incorrect MARC tag or subfield code.

Before explaining in detail how the authority system addresses these errors, I would like to briefly review the structure of authority records (see figure 1). Each record contains a field with the authorized data and, frequently, other fields, such as *see from* fields, containing old or unauthorized forms of the same concept or name. Library headings are matched against *see from* data to determine if upgrading is required and against the authorized form to validate the heading. *See also from* data, which will not be examined here in depth, provides information on

```
150 AUTHORIZED DATA              150 CLARINET

450 SEE FROM DATA                450 CLARIONET

450 SEE FROM DATA                450 PRIMER CLARINET

550 SEE ALSO FROM DATA           550 WOODWIND INSTRUMENTS
```

Fig. 1.

related headings. Understanding how correction of the aforementioned errors is accomplished requires an understanding of the difference between the normalized form of a heading and the catalog form of a heading.

Normalized versus Catalog Form of Heading

The normalized form of a heading is a computer-edited form (see figure 2), where all alphabetic characters are set in uppercase, MARC tags and subfield codes removed, all punctuation and special and diacritical characters deleted, and spacing between words regularized. The catalog form of the heading is the form that we are accustomed to seeing in a full MARC display. It includes full punctuation and capitalization, all special and diacritical characters, as well as MARC tags and subfield codes.

Library Heading

600$aDvorak, Anton,$d1841- 1904

Normalized Form

```
DVORAK ANTON 1841 1904  ◄─────────── AUTHORITY FILE
DVORAK ANTON 1841 1904  ◄─────────── LIBRARY FILE
```

Catalog Form

```
100$aDvořák, Anton,$d1841-1904  ◄──────── AUTHORITY FILE
600$aDvorak, Anton,$d1841- 1904 ◄──────── LIBRARY FILE
```

Fig. 2.

When the authority system passes headings from a library catalog against the authority file, the headings are submitted to a matching test at two levels. First, matches are identified based on comparison of the normalized form of the library heading with the normalized form of the authority record heading. The same headings are then matched using the catalog form of the headings. Any difference in headings at the catalog form match phase is attributed to an error in the library heading, and the system replaces it with the form from the authority file.

In figure 2, the normalized forms of the headings from the authority file and the bibliographic file match, but the catalog forms do not match, as the library heading is missing diacritical marks and the spacing in subfield d is in error. The system replaces the library's heading with the correct form from the authority file.

Error Correction

The first of O'Neill's categories of errors is inconsistencies in spacing, punctuation, and capitalization. As a result of the two-level match between the normalized form and the catalog form of headings, such inconsistencies are eliminated.

O'Neill's second category is typographical and minor spelling errors. B/NA's editorial staff has found that this category constitutes the largest portion of exceptions or nonmatches through the system. These exceptions are easily identified and remedied by the staff of editors because, as O'Neill points out, they are usually simple errors of omission, addition, substitution, or transposition of characters. Once these errors are corrected by the editors, the headings are again passed against the authority file for upgrading to the proper form of the heading or to validate the heading as the correct form.

The third category noted by O'Neill is invalid form of the heading, including incorrect use of qualifiers, inversion errors, and abbreviations (such as "U.S." where "United States" is required). Incorrect use of a qualifier, such as in the heading "Phylogeny (Zoology)," is automatically remedied when this form exists as a *see from* field in an authority record. The system supplants the erroneous form on the library's file with the correct form "Phylogeny."

An inversion error, such as in the heading "Inorganic Chemistry" is automatically changed to "Chemistry, Inorganic" when the erroneous form exists as a *see from* field in an authority record. However, many inversion errors and incorrectly used qualifiers and most abbreviations (O'Neill's third category of form error) do not exist as *see from* data in LC authority records. B/NA maintains a machine-readable file of thirty-five hundred commonly used erroneous abbreviations, inversion errors, and incorrectly used qualifiers that LC has chosen not to include in its authority file. They have been added to B/NA's authority file in a manner that allows the system to supply the correct form of the heading to the bibliographic record without providing a *see* reference from the erroneous forms. Thus, the headings are corrected and at the same time the integrity of LC's cross-reference structure for a given heading is maintained.

O'Neill's fourth category is incorrect MARC tags or subfield codes. Authority file headings contain tags that are similar to bibliographic file headings in that the last two digits of the tag indicate the type of heading. For example, corporate name fields 110, 410, 610, 710, and 810 in bibliographic records all end with 10, while the authorized form of a corporate name in an authority record is tagged 110 (see figure 3). When a data match occurs, a routine compares the last two digits of the MARC tags from the authority file heading and from the library heading and corrects the tag in the library heading field, if necessary, to match the last two digits on the authority heading tag. The headings in figure 3 match, but the last two digits of the tags do not. The system changes the tag on the library heading to 600.

Type of Heading	MARC Tag Suffix
Personal Name	00
Corporate Name	10
Conference Name	11
Uniform Title Subject	30
Topical Subject	50
Geographic Name Subject	51

100$aDvořák, Anton,$d1848-1904 ←— AUTHORITY FILE

610$aDvořák, Anton,$d1848-1904 ←— LIBRARY FILE

Fig. 3.

As matching between library headings and authority file headings involves the two-phased match of the normalized form (in which subfield codes are absent) and the catalog form (where the subfield codes are present), all subfield codes from the authority file heading are imposed on the library heading. This is not unlike the logic that corrects spacing and diacritical errors, as the subfield codes are simply treated as data. In figure 4 the normalized forms of the headings from the authority file and the bibliographic file match, but the catalog forms do not, as subfield code d is miscoded as b. The system replaces the library's heading with the correct form from the authority file, including the correct subfield code. This feature of the system is particularly useful for correcting errors in subject subdivisions where subfields that should be coded y (period) and z (place) are often miscoded as x (general).

Other Edits

A condition not mentioned by O'Neill but addressed by the system is where an existing heading can be changed to more than one heading depending upon the context. For example, "Colonialism" can be changed to "Colonies," "Imperialism," or "World politics." In this case, the records are displayed for review by editors who choose the appropriate heading or headings for assignment to the record.

Library Heading

600$aDvorak, Anton,$b1841-1904

Normalized Form

DVORAK ANTON 1841 1904 ◄──────────── AUTHORITY FILE
DVORAK ANTON 1841 1904 ◄──────────── LIBRARY FILE

Catalog Form

100$aDvořák, Anton,$d1841-1904 ◄────────── AUTHORITY FILE
600$aDvorak, Anton $b1841-1904 ◄────────── LIBRARY FILE

Fig. 4.

If a full heading (including subheadings) is not found on the authority file during the match process, but the main heading and each subdivision exist independently on other authority records, the system views the full heading as permissible. After editorial review, it is added to the authority file as a new valid combination. This "parts match" also operates where the main heading or subheadings exist as *see from* fields in authority records, in which case the heading or subheading is changed to its authorized form before the full heading is deemed permissible. As all matching involves a two-phased match between normalized and catalog forms of the heading, parts matches also correct errors in punctuation, spacing, capitalization, and special or diacritical characters.

Conversion of a library's authority file to machine-readable form is also addressed by the system as it generates a tape copy of all authority records matched or created during the authority control edit. Duplicate records are eliminated from this file, and all *see also from* references are deblinded to correspond to headings on the library's bibliographic file. The provision of this file, in a format compatible with *Authorities: A MARC Format*, along with a copy of the library's edited bibliographic file, completes the library's retrospective conversion process.

Retrospective conversion of a library's catalog to machine-readable form is an important component in the library's preparation for the future. Optimal return on the retrospective conversion investment includes the improved access that authority control provides, whether the file is used for COM fiche or film, or for an online catalog. Just as a misshelved book is a waste of the library's investment in purchasing the volume, so an incorrect heading that results in a patron missing a record is a waste of the library's investment in cataloging the item and in converting it to machine-readable form.

Notes

[1] Brett Butler, Brian Aveney, and William Scholz, "The Conversion of Manual Catalogs to Collection Databases," *Library Technology Reports* 14:109-206 (Mar.-Apr. 1978).

[2] Sue Baerg Epstein, "Converting Bibliographic Records for Automation: Some Options," *Library Journal* 108:474-76 (Mar. 1, 1983); Sue Baerg Epstein, "Converting Records for Automation at the Copy Level," *Library Journal* 108:642-43 (Apr. 1, 1983).

[3] Priscilla Caplan, "Retrospective Duplicate Resolution for the Harvard Distributable Union Catalog," *Information Technology and Libraries* 1:142-43 (June 1982).

[4] Dorothy S. McPherson, Karen E. Coyle, and Teresa L. Montgomery, "Building a Merged Bibliographic Database: The University of California Experience," *Information Technology and Libraries* 1:371-80 (Dec. 1982).

[5] Georgia L. Brown, "AACR2: OCLC's Implementation and Database Conversion," *Journal of Library Automation* 14:161-73 (Sept. 1981).

[6] Edward T. O'Neill and Rao Aluri, *A Method for Correcting Typographical Errors in Subject Headings in OCLC Records*, Report no.: OCLC/OPR/RR-80/3. (Columbus, Ohio: OCLC, 1980); Edward T. O'Neill and Diane Vizine-Goetz, "Computer Generation of a Subject Authority File," *Proceedings of the ASIS Annual Meeting* 19:220-23 (1982). These two articles are hereafter cited as O'Neill.

"Natural versus Inverted Word Order in Subject Headings"

Jessica L. Milstead

In the Library of Congress subject headings inversions may be divided into three groups: (1) ethnonational adjectival phrases; (2) all other adjectival phrases; and (3) complex headings, usually including a prepositional phrase. The choice between natural and inverted word order in adjectival phrase headings appears to be governed by the degree of specification offered by the noun in the phrase. There is a tendency to invert to bring the noun forward unless it is much more common in natural language than the adjective with which it is associated. Major literary forms and certain headings in the social sciences are usually entered directly in ethnonational adjectival phrases, but other headings are inverted. In the light of current practice in other systems, and the lack of predictability in the present LCSH, it is recommended that normal practice should be direct entry for such phrases. Complex headings are leftovers from catch-title entry and classified catalogs and could best be reformulated into phrase or heading-subdivision form, keeping the same word order as at present.

As long as a subject can be expressed in a single word, devising the appropriate index term is relatively easy. However, as soon as the expression becomes more complex, devising the term becomes a two-step process: (1) selecting the words to express the subject; and (2) determining the order of these words.

This paper is concerned with the second part of the process, with primary attention to phrase subject headings in the Library of Congress system.

Such headings were seen as problems by Cutter, whose proposals for dealing with them were ambiguous and apparently unsatisfactory even to him.[1] Practice has more or less followed Cutter, but without any real guiding principles. Meanwhile, practice in modern tools such as thesauri has diverged rather sharply from that in subject heading lists. Since the Library of Congress, and probably many other libraries as well, will be freezing their catalogs in the near future, it is time to examine the problem again.

Reprinted by permission of the American Library Association, "Natural versus Inverted Word Order in Subject Headings," by Jessica L. Milstead from *Library Resources & Technical Services*, Spring 1980, pp. 174-78, copyright © 1980 by ALA.

It is convenient to treat the two major types of phrases, adjectival and prepositional, separately. For purposes of this paper adjectival phrases consist exclusively of nouns and adjectives with an occasional conjunction, while prepositional phrases are of more complex structure. Each may occur in one of three forms: (1) direct natural language order; (2) inverted, using the comma; and (3) dashed subdivisions, in natural language order or inverted.

Inverted Word Order in Library of Congress Subject Headings (LCSH)

Chan[2] summarizes reasoning advanced by such authorities as Cutter, Haykin, and Mann, indicating that inversion is used to emphasize the noun in an adjectival heading, for collocation of headings beginning with the same noun, when the adjective merely differentiates between different aspects of the same subject, or when the reader is assumed to think first of the noun. None of the criteria provided by any of these authors can realistically be described as anything but rationalization; that is, they try to explain what has been done, but no two catalogers applying this reasoning in devising a heading of a new type are particularly likely to come up with the same decision on word order. No "grouping" explanation accounts for the opposite treatment of literature and art, for example, with the former always direct and the latter always inverted.

Adjectival Phrases

It is convenient to consider two groups of adjectival phrases separately:

1. Adjective-noun phrases, direct or inverted, in which the adjective denotes an ethnic, linguistic, national, or cultural emphasis (called ethnonational phrases in this paper); and
2. Other adjective-noun phrases (direct, inverted, or in heading-subdivision form).

The two major attempts to determine empirically if criteria that can be objectively stated exist for word order decisions in LCSH are those of Chan[3] and Harris,[4] both of whom considered only direct and inverted order, not subdivisions. Chan limited her study to ethnonational adjectival phrases, while Harris studied both types.

Ethnonational Adjectival Phrases

Chan attempted to search for patterns in inversion of such phrases. She concluded that inversion is the normal practice, finding categories of exceptions that include:

(*a*) Some literary forms (examination shows these are major ones).
(*b*) Some nouns relating to anthropology, linguistics, history and the social sciences, such as ... *antiquities*; ... *movement*.
(*c*) *Law* when used with ethnonational adjectives to form names of legal systems rather than headings that indicate the laws of specific countries or peoples, e.g., **Roman law**, but **Law, Aztec**.
(*d*) Proper names such as **American Party, Celtic Church**.
(*e*) Names that have lost their ethnonational connotation, such as **Arabian horse, Prussian blue, Aeolian harp**.

Chan found that the adjectives *Jewish* and *Negro* (in LCSH 7) presented an anomalous pattern, tending to be entered directly in situations where other ethnonational adjectives would be inverted. She suggests that, because *Jewish* may have both religious and national connotations, the direct entries may be found where the religious aspect is considered to predominate. She makes no attempt to explain the anomaly found with *Negro*.

Harris' approach was different; her work and that of Chan confirm each other. The frequency in natural language of the words used in a 10 percent sample of LC subject headings was examined on the hypothesis that rarer words were more likely to be used as the access point for a subject heading. Again, with the exception of the adjective *Negro* (*Jewish* did not appear in the sample) the noun in an ethnonational adjectival heading was found to be the determinant of direct or inverted entry. If the noun is a "common" one, (e.g., *literature*, or *drama*) entry is direct (adjective first), while if rarer (e.g., *quatrains*), entry is inverted (noun first). Two clear exceptions to this finding are *art* and *music*, both of which normally appear in inverted form.

The complementary nature of Chan's and Harris' work is clearly seen when some of the social science and anthropological nouns Chan listed are noted (these are entered directly): *children, language(s), people(s), emperors, movement, question, studies*. These are all rather common words, likely to occur more frequently in the English language than the ethnonational adjectives specifying them.

Thus, it is probably the case that, in ethnonational adjectival phrases, the natural language frequency of the noun in the phrase has been a major determinant of word order. Since more words are rare than are common, it is not surprising that inverted nouns appear to outnumber nouns entered directly, although neither the Harris nor the Chan study provides firm data in support of this assumption. The fine arts are an exception, since music and art headings are inverted.

Other Adjectival Phrases

The natural language frequency of the entry word in such headings is usually less than that of the nonentry word, but there is a tendency to invert when the difference in frequency between the adjective and the noun is small. That is, when the cataloger is in doubt, he or she inverts. Presumably, catalogers have felt that nouns are better specifiers than adjectives.

In about 80 percent of main headings followed by both inversions and subdivisions, the latter are used for aspects and forms, while the former are used to designate kinds or subclasses of the subject. Most of the remaining 20 percent deviated only slightly from this pattern, often in cases where the subclass could not conveniently be expressed in an adjectival phrase.[5] Despite a small number of inconsistencies, the use of inversions and subdivisions to produce a classified subarrangement is clear.

Complex Phrases

Such headings as **Animals, Habits and Behavior of**, have not been the subject of empirical research. It does seem relatively safe to speculate that these headings are carry-overs from catchword title entry and/or the classed catalog and many are now being reformulated by LC, usually to a subdivision or phrase maintaining the present word order.

Form of Headings in LCSH Practice

There is considerable evidence that, in complex headings, once the entry word has been selected, the structure of the heading is determined to a large extent by the desire to create alphabetically classed files, usually on the basis of punctuation marks. For example, it has been found that where a given word introduced both an inverted heading and a dashed subdivision, the subarrangement thus created by the punctuation separated facets of the subject (**Grain elevators, Cooperative** and **Grain elevators—Fires and fire prevention**).[6] Such covert arrangements do not serve readers. Interpolation of what amounts to a label identifying the facet becomes more practicable when headings in catalog entries are mechanically produced. **Cookery** is an obvious example. A list including the headings

Cookery—Exhibitions
Cookery, Greek
Cookery (Beets)
Cookery for cardiacs

could just as well read: Cookery—General—Exhibitions; Cookery—Specific cuisines—Greek; Cookery—Specific foods—Beets; Cookery—For special groups—Cardiacs; or something of the sort. A parallel may be found in the Wilson indexes, where such practice is often found, e.g., **Classification—Special subjects—Business**.

Current Trends in Subject Index Vocabularies

The current trend in indexing vocabularies is toward entry in natural word order. The only major thesaurus that uses inverted headings is *Medical Subject Headings* (MeSH). All others use direct entry. Of course, the trend in such vocabularies is toward less complex terms, with reliance on post-coordination. Post-coordination automatically reduces the number of decisions about word order.

Recommendations

First, the easy one. Inversion should never be used for headings containing prepositional phrases. The entry word desired for the concept should be selected, and the heading then formulated into a direct phrase or heading-subdivision form as appropriate.

For adjective-noun headings, more research is needed to determine when, if ever, the user is more likely to look under the inverted form of terms. Such research should, desirably, correct for the bias introduced by the fact that there are few naive users. That is, asking a random sample of library users what form they expect will only show what they think libraries do.

Even though methods of compensating for user experience can surely be found, other approaches should also be investigated. For instance, it would be interesting to learn if narrative texts show consistent usage patterns. Which predominates, "Music of France" or "French music"; "Short stories of America" or "American short stories?"

As long as the needed research is lacking, we should drop the principle of putting things where the user will look first, simply because we don't know where that place is, and are fooling ourselves when we say we do. We have been putting things where the cataloger thought the best array would be produced, an entirely different matter. If this procedure had produced a predictable file, the need to learn how to access it would be acceptable. However, the location of adjectival phrases is only partly predictable, and then only by someone who has gone to a great deal of trouble in studying the subject heading system. Lacking certain knowledge, we should opt for predictability.

Adjective-noun headings should normally be entered directly. Any departures from such a system should be ones that can be clearly and unambiguously explained to a moderately literate library user in such a way as to enable that user to predict reliably whether a desired concept will be entered directly or inverted. This excludes such reasoning as, "where it is assumed the user will look first," or "to bring multiple aspects of the same subject together."

Where headings are now written in an inverted or subdivided style in order to achieve a classified arrangement on the basis of punctuation marks, they should be revised to make the arrangement explicit rather than implicit.

Notes

[1] Charles Ammi Cutter, *Rules for a Dictionary Catalog* (4th ed.: Washington, D.C.: Govt. Print. Off., 1904) p.72-75.

[2] Lois Mai Chan, "American poetry" but "Satire, American": The Direct and Inverted Forms of Subject Headings Containing National Adjectives, *Library Resources & Technical Services* 17:330-39 (Summer 1973).

[3] Ibid.

[4] Jessica L. Harris, Subject Analysis: Computer Implications of Rigorous Definition (Metuchen, N.J.: Scarecrow; 1970), p.62-92.

[5] Ibid., p.81-90.

[6] Ibid.

"Expanded Subject Access to Library Collections Using Computer-assisted Indexing Techniques"

William H. Mischo

Abstract. This paper describes two projects implemented at Iowa State University to provide expanded subject access to reference collection materials and monographic titles. Printed/microform subject indexes have been produced utilizing computer-assisted indexing techniques applied to descriptor strings assigned to reference titles and to Library of Congress Subject Headings and title strings contained in records on OCLC MARC archive tapes. The advantages of the enhanced subject access strings produced by the computer-assisted techniques are discussed and their use as recorded keys in on-line catalog files is explored.

Introduction

Computer-based techniques to generate index entries for printed, card, or microform subject indexes can be characterized as "automatic" or "semi-automatic". Automatic indexing using statistical measures to extract entries from natural language text has been the subject of much research[1,2] but is still in the experimental stage. Semi-automatic or computer-assisted indexing exhibits varying degrees of human intervention and forms the basis for present operational systems. Keen[3] has surveyed and categorized the computer-assisted indexing techniques reported in the literature. The primary function of computer-assisted indexing procedures is to rearrange the elements of ordered multiterm descriptor strings in order to produce multiple access points for an alphabetical index.

Reprinted from *Information Interaction: Proceedings of the 45th ASIS Annual Meeting, Volume 19, 1982.* Edited by Anthony Petrarca, Celianna I. Taylor and Robert S. Kohn. Published for the American Society for Information Science by Knowledge Industry Publications, Inc., 701 Westchester Avenue, White Plains, NY 10604. Reprinted by the permission of the publisher.

This paper describes two projects which utilize computer-assisted indexing techniques to enhance subject access to library materials at Iowa State University. In one, a printed/microform subject index to reference collection materials was produced using phrase manipulation techniques applied to descriptor strings assigned by librarians. The second project was designed to increase access to monographic titles by producing a short-entry subject index with access points generated from OCLC MARC archive tapes by applying term manipulation procedures to Library of Congress Subject Headings (LCSH) and title strings.

Purpose

Because reference collection materials are approached by users who are in most cases not interested in a known item but in finding items that can fill a specific informational need, the subject approach is paramount. Since LCSH are unable to meet these needs and augmentation of LCSH with title words or other data contained in MARC record fields is insufficient, this project explored the use of local subject augmentation, with computer-assisted indexing, in improving subject access to reference materials. A printed/microform index to the more than 6,000 titles in the Iowa State University Library reference collection, currently containing more than 70,000 entries in 1,000 printed pages, has been produced. This project is described in detail elsewhere[4]. The index displays short-entry records and uses custom-designed mechanized indexing procedures to expedite data entry and produce multiple entry points by software manipulation of ordered descriptor strings. (See figure 1.)

Subject Heading	Title	Date	Call Number
Agronomy Index/Abstract Service	Biological and Agricultural Index	V.1,1916+	Table 11
Agronomy Index/Abstract Service	Biodeterioration Research Titles	V.12, 1976+	QP517.B5
Agronomy Periodicals	Botanico-Periodicum-Huntianum	1968	QK1.A1186x
Agronomy Periodicals	NAL Serials Currently Received	Updated	S493.A11U5
Agronomy Serials Catalog	NAL Serials Currently Received	Updated	S493.A11U5
Agronomy Stats Info	McGraw-Hill Encyclopedia of Food, Ag	1977	TX349.M2
Agronomy Stats Info	Agricultural Statistics	Annual	Ref Desk
Agronomy-USE ALSO 'Soil Science', 'Crop Science'			
Agronomy-Corn	Bibliography of Corn	1959-1968	SB191.C8
Agronomy-Meetings Index/Abstract Serv I	Agronomy Abstracts	1955+	S591.7.Am
Agronomy-Millet	The Millets: A Bibliography	1930-1969	SB191.M5
Agronomy-Sorghum	Sorghum: A Bibliography	1930-1969	SB235.A11
Agronomy-Wheat	International Bibliography of Rice	1951-1961	SB191.R5
Agronomy-Wheat	Bibliography of Wheat	1959-1968	SB191.W5
AID Societies	National Directory of Addresses & Tel	Updated	Ref Desk
AIM-ARM Index/Abstract Service	**Abstracts of Instructional & Research	V.1, 1967+	Table 11
Air Conditioning Dictionary	Air Conditioning Heating & Refrigera	1977	TH7007.Z87

**This Abstracting or Indexing Service can be searched by computer. Inquire at the Reference Desk.

Fig. 1. Reference collection index.

The same descriptor phrase manipulation techniques have been applied to LCSH and title phrases in order to provide expanded subject access to general monographic works. These procedures are used in the production of a short-entry subject and title derivative index in printed and COM format presently covering over 60,000 Iowa State University titles on OCLC MARC archive tapes. While these measures by no means solve the problem of subject access to monographs, they do assist subject retrieval in several ways. The incorporation of multiple subject access points for monographs by providing entries under all significant elements of composite subject headings helps to overcome the inconsistent phrase constructions of LCSH. It also addresses the problem of lack of user perseverance in subject catalog searches, as documented by several studies showing that between 66% and 77% of users in academic libraries searched at one entry point and then discontinued the search[5]. Providing title word access with abbreviated records that include the LCSH tracing allows retrieval of garbled references, access to terms more specific or current than are used in LCSH, and, through the LCSH tracings, the determination of the proper form of subject headings assigned to works with specific title words or phrases. In addition, catalog use studies have suggested that the failure rate for known item searches can be reduced by the addition of permuted title entries to the catalog[6].

Procedures

Subject descriptors are assigned to reference titles by librarians following a prescribed form of data entry and subject term selection procedures. Phrase manipulation software rearranges the component terms of n-element strings according to the positioning of embedded phrase manipulation symbols assigned by the indexer.

Several optional phrase manipulation symbols are available to the indexer. The symbol "#" produces a cycling operation in which the phrase elements following the "#" are brought to the lead position; a dash is then inserted and the elements preceding the "#" are added. For example, an input string of the form A#BC will yield ABC and BC-A as entries. Any number of manipulation symbols may be coded. The string A#B#C yields ABC, BC-A and C-AB. In addition, any string with two or more of the "#" symbols, such as in the above example, will produce two additional articulated string entries generated by (a) combining the elements preceding the first "#" with those following the final "#" and subdividing with the remainder of the string, and (b) bringing the string elements following the final "#" to the lead, inserting the elements between the first and last "#" symbols, and following with the elements preceding the initial "#" symbol, with the three sections separated by hyphens. Thus, in the case of A#B#C, the two additional entries AC-B and C-B-A are generated by articulation. None of the phrase manipulation symbols will appear at the output stage.

As an example, the input string GERMAN-ENGLISH#PHYSICS#DICTIONARY generates the lead terms:

GERMAN-ENGLISH PHYSICS DICTIONARY
PHYSICS DICTIONARY – GERMAN-ENGLISH
DICTIONARY – GERMAN-ENGLISH PHYSICS
GERMAN-ENGLISH DICTIONARY – PHYSICS
DICTIONARY – PHYSICS – GERMAN-ENGLISH

The use of the manipulation symbol " + " causes a similar cycling operation, but a hyphen is inserted in the original string in place of the space. For example the string WOMEN + LITERATURE produces the two lead terms:

WOMEN – LITERATURE
LITERATURE – WOMEN

The articulation symbol "@" produces an entry string generated by combining the single term following the symbol with the terms preceding it and then subdividing by the remaining terms. Thus, the string AB@CD produces, in addition to the original string, the entry C – AB – D.

Similar phrase manipulation procedures have been applied to MARC record data in the personal name (600 tag), corporate name (610 tag), conference or meeting (611 tag), uniform title (630 tag), topical heading (650 tag), and geographic names (651 tag) subject fields. Entries from these fields are examined for subfield codes and manipulation symbols "#" are automatically inserted by the software before all ≠a(name), ≠z(geographic), ≠k(form), ≠x(general), and ≠t(title) subfield code elements. A study by O'Neill and Aluri over a sample of the OCLC database showed that 67% of the LC subject headings in the OCLC monographic records contained at least one subfield[7]. However, many of the form subdivisions ≠k, e.g. History, Congresses, were judged to be unsuitable as lead terms and these rotations are not made. In addition, the general subdivision (≠x) contains both form and topical entry elements, so that data in these subfields must also be checked for desirability as lead terms.

The LC subject descriptors are processed in the manner described above. For example, the subject heading LIBRARIES≠zGREAT BRITAIN≠xAUTOMATION is manipulated to yield the five headings:

LIBRARIES—GREAT BRITAIN—AUTOMATION
GREAT BRITAIN—AUTOMATION—LIBRARIES
AUTOMATION—LIBRARIES—GREAT BRITAIN
LIBRARIES—AUTOMATION—GREAT BRITAIN
AUTOMATION—GREAT BRITAIN—LIBRARIES

Phrase manipulation has also been performed on those LCSH in inverted order, such as CIVILIZATION, MEDIEVAL, to produce the entry MEDIEVAL CIVILIZATION. This type of rotation is, in the above instance, indispensable since only a general cross-reference "Medieval Archaeology, Architecture, etc. see Archaeology, Medieval; Architecture, Medieval; etc." is given in LCSH.

Multiword subject descriptors appearing as the first (≠a) element have been articulated so that WATER IN LANDSCAPE ARCHITECTURE yields LANDSCAPE ARCHITECTURE—WATER IN.

The term manipulation procedures used on LCSH produce conflicts with already existing cross-references in LCSH. However, most college and research libraries (including Iowa State University) do not have their catalog cross-references in a machine readable form nor do they have the LCSH cross-reference structure in a form that allows interfacing to a microform or on-line catalog. For these institutions, the term rotation entries will not conflict with LCSH cross-references and, in fact, could be used as preferred form or "see" cross-references rather than as entries. This might produce a more systematic syndetic structure, since Harris[8] and others have shown that LCSH cross-references are inconsistent and incomplete. In the project described here, we chose to provide catalog entries under each component of a multiterm string rather than cross-references because of the short-entry format and the problem of lack of user perseverance noted above. Some provision still needs to be made for RT, BT, and NT cross-references. Work has begun on interfacing the LC Subject Authority tapes into the system.

Access to title word phrases using a left-justified KWIC format allows fast retrieval of specific items such as titles containing the phrase "California's Proposition 13" which can be retrieved by subject only through the LC subject heading REAL PROPERTY TAX—CALIFORNIA.

Applications

The two projects described in this paper differ in that the reference collection index requires indexer-assigned terms to augment the standard bibliographic information while the monographic collection subject index contains entries generated by format recognition software using data from MARC record fields. The monographic collection index, by providing expanded access points utilizing only standard MARC record data, differs from Pauline Atherton's Subject Access Project in which MARC records were augmented by humanly assigned descriptor terms from the table of contents and index of the work[9]. An on-line catalog with boolean search capabilities using an inverted file configuration would of course obviate any need for manipulation of either multiterm LCSH or assigned descriptors by allowing access to combinations of individual terms either taken from different subject strings or within the same string regardless of word order. However, it is not clear, at present, if college and research libraries will be able to support the hardware requirements for an on-line catalog or, perhaps more importantly, if constraints in disk storage space for on-line catalogs will prevent the maintenance of large inverted file systems needed for boolean searching[10]. If the storage medium constraints will not permit an on-line file structure in which boolean searches can be performed, then the multiple lead terms produced by subject descriptor manipulation techniques could serve as discrete recorded keys in an on-line catalog. Increasing the number of retrieval keys in this manner would expedite subject retrieval and, in some measure, simulate a boolean search capability. Thus, computer-assisted indexing techniques, whether operating on LCSH or used to rearrange indexer-assigned descriptor strings, can greatly increase search success in printed or COM format indexes and may also play a significant role in on-line catalogs by increasing the number of catalog recorded keys.

Acknowledgements

The projects reported in this paper were supported by grants from the Council on Library Resources and the Iowa State University Research Foundation.

Notes

[1]Harter, Stephen P. "Statistical Approaches to Automatic Indexing." Drexel Library Quarterly, 14:2 (April 1978) 57-74.

[2]Jones, Karen Sparck. "Automatic Indexing." Journal of Documentation, 30:4 (December 1974) 393-432.

[3]Keen, E. Michael. "On the Generation and Searching of Entries in Printed Subject Indexes." Journal of Documentation, 33:1 (March 1977) 15-45.

[4]Mischo, William H. "Expanded Subject Access to Reference Collection Materials." Journal of Library Automation, 12:4 (December 1979) 338-354.

[5]Bates, Marcia J. "Factors Affecting Subject Catalog Search Success." Journal of the American Society for Information Science, 28:3 (May 1977) 161-169.

[6]Weintraub, D. Kathryn. "The Essentials or Desiderata of the Bibliographic Record as Discovered by Research." Library Resources and Technical Services, 23:4 (Fall 1979) 391-405.

[7]O'Neill, Edward T.; Aluri, Rao. Subject Heading Patterns in OCLC Monographic Records. Research Report. OCLC, Inc., Columbus, Ohio, August 1979. (OCLC/RDD/RR-79/1).

[8]Harris, Jessica Lee. Subject Analysis: Computer Implications of Rigorous Definition. Scarecrow Press, Metuchen, N. J., 1970.

[9]Atherton, Pauline. Books are for Use: Final Report of the Subject Access Project to the Council on Library Resources. Syracuse University School of Information Studies, 1978, ED 156 181.

[10]Hickey, Thomas. "Searching Linear Files On-Line." On-Line Review, 1:1 (March 1977) 53-58.

"Study of the *See-also* Reference Structure in Relation to the Subject of International Law"

Vaclav Mostecky

Part Three

Tentative Proposal for a Classified Subject Heading List

The principal advantage of alphabetical subject headings is their alphabetical arrangement, which is familiar to every user. Their main drawback is the lack of internal logic in the arrangement. The alphabetical principle scatters related topics throughout the catalog. The present study has tried to demonstrate that the *see-also* references suffer from the same deficiency—the absence of a rational system. We shall attempt, in this concluding section, to suggest a possible remedy and to outline a method for the development of a systematic list of subject headings in the field of international law.[1]

The procedure consists of the following five steps:

(1) First, the discipline of international law must be divided into its component parts, proceeding from the general to the special, or specific. Writings of outstanding authorities and specialists may serve as basis for this classification. Our example follows the general arrangement of Oppenheim's *International Law*, amended from the outline of Hyde's treatise. The resulting list is not a hierarchical classification, but a logical map of the field.

(2) Agreement must be reached on terminology and a decision made on the use of such technical expressions as "Open Sea" vs. "High Seas"; "Territorial Waters" vs. "Marginal Seas"; "Holy See" vs. "Vatican (State)"; "Nationality" vs. "Citizenship"; "Human Rights" vs. "Freedom," "Liberty," "Personal Rights," or "Rights of Man." Again, the consensus of specialists, preferably American authorities, will be the basis for decision for the final choice. All confusing synonyms will be eliminated and *see* references made from the rejected terms to the one which has been adopted.

Reprinted, by permission, from *American Documentation* 7 (1956), 309-13.

(3) Since most terms have been taken from book outlines, tables of contents, and indexes,[2] many will be descriptive in form and unsuitable for use as subject headings. The necessary editorial adjustments will have to be made and a general policy formulated on the use of direct vs. indirect headings, inverted headings, and qualifying sub-headings. In our example, direct headings have been given preference whenever possible.

(4) The final list will actually be a balanced and systematic analysis of the field of international law, presented in the form of subject headings, descending from the most general to the more specialized terms. The degree of analysis will, of course, depend entirely on the size and nature of the collection. A small library may stop at the first level and satisfy its users with the broadest subject headings of INTERNATIONAL LAW; STATES; INDIVIDUALS; OPEN SEA; INTERNATIONAL ORGANIZATION; and INTERNATIONAL TRANSACTIONS. A specialized library, on the other hand, may want to employ such fine distinctions as AMBASSADORS; ATTACHES: NUNCIOS; DELEGATES TO CONFERENCES; COURRIERS; SECRET AGENTS. However, the narrower headings can be added only after the broader terms have been adopted. It is essential that the intermediate links be preserved since their omission would ruin the logical structure of the system.

(5) Finally, *see-also* references will be introduced at all levels throughout the system, both to the nearest broad heading and to the nearest specific or narrow terms. This procedure will correct most of the faults which have been found in the present practice. No subject heading will be left isolated and without connection to its related terms. On the other hand, references from the broadest heading to specialized terms (for example, INTERNATIONAL LAW *see-also* REBUS SIC STANTIBUS) will be eliminated. The reader will be guided systematically, step-by-step, from one subject heading to its nearest logically related term.

Of course the necessary references to other areas of international law and to other fields must be added.

There are two ways in which the resulting arrangement of subject headings may be presented: either (1.) as a simple running list with varying indentions indicating the degree of relationship of the individual headings, or (2.) as a chart.[3] Both should, be provided with an alphabetical index, similar to the standard subject heading lists, or the "relative index" of the Dewey Decimal Classification. Such indexes may well be provided with simple summaries.

Advantages of the proposed system.

(1) *To the cataloger.* At present, the cataloger has very few tools at his disposal to assist him in assigning subject headings. The alphabetical list is of little help since it often fails to link related topics together, primarily because of its poor *see-also* reference structure. Provided with the suggested systematically arranged list, the cataloger should find his work considerably easier, more rewarding, and more scientific. He will abide by the following simple rules:

(a) First, he must decide on the subject field covered by the book, determine the area with which it deals specifically, and choose, from the terms given on the list, the one which describes the subject matter most adequately.

(b) If the book deals with several topics, all related to a broader term, only the more general subject heading will be assigned. For example, ACQUISITION OF TERRITORY will sufficiently describe a book discussing the various modes of acquiring territory; there is no need to enumerate ANNEXATION; OCCUPATION; and CONQUEST.

(c) If, on the other hand, the book treats of a particular aspect of the subject, the cataloger should select the specific heading only; relations to broader topics will be indicated on the *see-also* reference card. For example, if the book discusses the clause *rebus sic stantibus*, it will not be necessary to add TREATIES or INTERNATIONAL LAW to the tracings.

(d) Only if the book touches upon two or more subject areas which are not directly related will the cataloger have to assign several subject headings.

(2) *To the reader.* The reader should be on much firmer ground when consulting the catalog. In particular, he should be reasonably certain that he has not overlooked important material by starting with the wrong subject heading.

(a) *See-also* references from the specific to the broader term, although unorthodox in current practice, are believed to be especially important in this respect. Under CREDENTIALS, the library may have only one or two entries; however, the topic is discussed thoroughly and perhaps more authoritatively by virtually every book on AMBASSADORS; DIPLOMATIC SERVICE; and DIPLOMACY. A *see-also* reference to the nearest broader heading will make it unnecessary to include additional subject cards for each of the three broader terms.

See-also reference cards may be prepared in the following form:

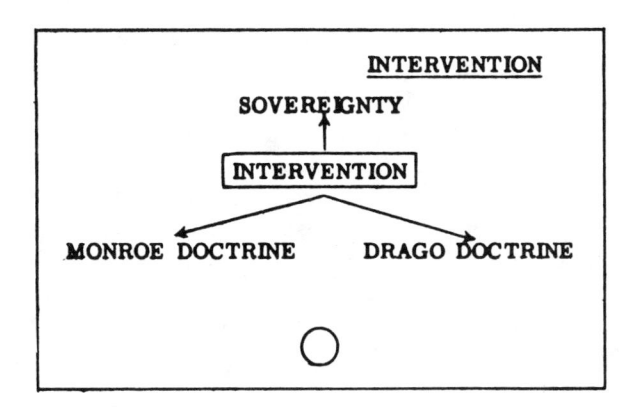

```
                            INTERVENTION
                  SOVEREIGNTY
                       ↑
                  INTERVENTION
                  ↙         ↘
         MONROE DOCTRINE   DRAGO DOCTRINE
                       ○
```

Or:

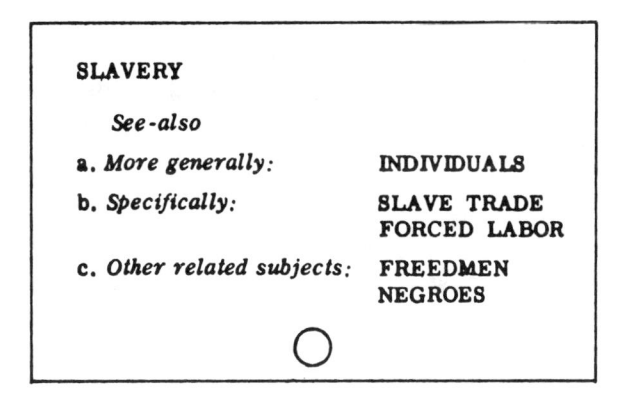

```
SLAVERY
    See-also
  a. More generally:       INDIVIDUALS
  b. Specifically:         SLAVE TRADE
                           FORCED LABOR
  c. Other related subjects:  FREEDMEN
                              NEGROES
                       ○
```

Fig. 3.

(b) By referring to the proposed systematically arranged list of subject headings (which should be made available to the public), the reader should be in a much better position to decide which term corresponds the closest to the topic he is investigating. Much of the present guesswork will be eliminated and the wide differences in the readers' approach to the catalog, demonstrated by Mr. Lilley's control group mentioned earlier, should be reduced, if not entirely eliminated.

(c) Last but not least, the adoption of a consistent and rationally developed terminology, free from the confusion of vague, non-expressive, and synonymous terms, will make the catalog a more dependable finding tool and restore the confidence of the reader.

(3) *Reduction in the size of the catalog.* The preceding discussing has emphasized repeatedly that a logically developed system of subject headings coupled with a rational *see-also* reference structure will result in a considerable reduction in the number of required subject cards, and thus reduce the size of the catalog itself.

The 720 titles of our original sample had been assigned a total of 1,198 subject headings in the Kent Library (or 1.6 headings per title). If the rules suggested above had been followed, only 891 subject headings (or 1.2 per title) would have been needed. This would represent a saving of 307 subject cards, or 27 percent.

It is obvious that the rapidly growing size of the catalog considerably reduces its efficiency as a finding tool. Whenever the number of cards filed under one entry exceeds 500, the patience of the reader is put to a severe test. The librarian should make every effort to reduce the number to a workable proportion either by eliminating unnecessary entries or by dividing broad heading into narrower subdivisions. It has been pointed out that the Kent Library has 1,271 cards under INTERNATIONAL LAW. By the application of our rules, no less than 508 of these (or 40 percent) could be removed. The remaining 763 cards, representing general works on international law, could be arranged by language (the collection contains a high percentage of books in Spanish, Italian, French, and German, which are probably consulted only infrequently) or by date, to emphasize the recent, up-to-date literature, which is, understandably, in greater demand. A more radical solution might be to eliminate the older cards altogether and refer the reader to bibliographies appended to current works. Oppenheim's *International Law* alone carries an excellent and extensive list of general treatises which could be easily located by consulting the corresponding author entries in the catalog.

Comparable savings would be achieved in other broad headings. In the course of our survey, eight such headings have been investigated. Of the 2,708 cards filed under them, 995 (or 37 percent) could be safely eliminated.

Conclusion

It is interesting to note that books, which are generally considered easy to consult, nevertheless provide the reader with guides to their contents: tables of contents and indexes have become standard features of modern works. It would appear only logical that libraries would provide their public with systematic guides to their catalogs which, again by general agreement, are infinitely more complex and intricate.

The plan outlined in the concluding section of this study would not only rationalize the subject heading structure of the catalog; it would also equip the reader — as well as the cataloger — with a key to its arrangement. The practice of alphabetical filing of subject entry cards separates topics which logically should be related. That is why so many critics have been calling, with increasing vigor, for the replacement of the dictionary catalog with a classified catalog. Our proposal is actually an attempt to combine the best features of the former, particularly its alphabetical principle, with the main advantage of the latter, its internal logic.

Since our discussion has been limited to one well-defined subject field, and no attempt at generalization has been made, our task has been relatively easy. However, in dealing with the catalog of a large general library these difficulties would certainly be multiplied many times. But they have been solved by our major classification systems, in spite of the handicaps inherent in the restrictive notation. A systematic list of subject headings would not have to be compressed into a pre-determined number of classes, and there would always be room for expansion. Its outstanding features — simplicity, flexibility, and inherent logic — seem to provide an incentive for a further investigation.

Notes

[1] Attempts at a rationalization of subject headings have been often reported in professional literature, beginning with C. A. Cutter. The Armed Forces Medical Library system is particularly interesting.

[2] Hyde's *International Law* contains a very helpful list of specialized terms in an appendix.

[3] Graphic presentation was used in a discussion of overlapping terminology in the field of economics by Julia Pettee. (*Subject Headings*. New York: Wilson, 1946, p. 75).

PAIS Subject Headings

User's Guide to PAIS Subject Headings

Public Affairs Information Service is a nonprofit organization founded in 1914 for the purpose of indexing library material in the field of public affairs and public policy published throughout the world. The *PAIS Bulletin* covers material in the English language. The *PAIS Foreign Language Index* complements the *Bulletin* by indexing material written in French, German, Italian, Portuguese, and Spanish. PAIS attempts to identify public affairs information likely to be useful and interesting to legislators, administrators, the business and financial community, policy researchers, scholars, and librarians.

SUBJECT COVERAGE

The PAIS printed indexes and databases cover publications on all subjects that bear on contemporary public issues and the making and evaluation of public policy, irrespective of source or traditional disciplinary boundaries. These include the policy-oriented literature of the academic social sciences (economics, political science, public administration, international law and relations, sociology, and demography); professional publications in fields such as business, finance, law, education, and social work; reports and commentary on public affairs from the serious general press; and reference works including statistical compilations, bibliographies, directories, encyclopedias, handbooks, and subject dictionaries. Government documents are included for their value as sources of factual information or their relevance to subjects of current social and political importance, rather than as records of government operations. In addition PAIS covers the economic, social, and political aspects of subjects outside the traditional social sciences. The *PAIS Selection Policy and Periodicals List* is available upon request.

Over the years PAIS has built up an extensive list of subject headings representing a pragmatic collection of descriptor terms reflecting materials actually indexed. PAIS utilizes a subject authority control system. Every subject heading and every heading/subheading combination assigned to a bibliographic entry must find a match in the subject authority file. The

---

Reprinted, by permission, from *PAIS Subject Headings* (New York: Public Affairs Information Service, Inc., 1984), "User's Guide to PAIS Subject Headings" and sample pages.

subject authority control system assures quality and consistency in indexing, facilitates changes of subject headings, and generates cross references (*See* and *See also* references).

For purposes of this publication the PAIS list of subject headings was reviewed carefully. Subject headings, scope notes, and cross references were added, changed, or deleted. Since the subject heading list serves as an access tool to the printed PAIS indexes as well as the PAIS databases, we decided to leave headings in the list that had been used in the printed indexes before PAIS became available online.

This publication is in two parts. The list of main headings is followed by a list of subheadings.

MAIN HEADINGS

Each entry in the PAIS subject heading list consists of the established form and may in addition include notes and references.

1) *Established form.* This may consist of a main heading by itself, a main heading with a subheading, or a main heading/subheading/sub-subheading combination.

Main headings may consist of:

- a single word, e.g. Housing
- a multiple word phrase, e.g. Industrial relations consultants
- an inverted multiple word phrase, e.g. Finance, Public
- a single word or multiple word descriptor with a parenthetical word or phrase, e.g. Contracts (international law)

2) *Notes*

Some items contain one or more notes as follows:

- scope notes explaining intended use of a heading that might otherwise be ambiguous
- indication of geographic subdivision by the *Bulletin* (see section on subheadings for further details)
- indication of permissible subdivision of a heading
- indication of permissible use of a main heading as a subheading

3) *References*

Most items contain one or more references as follows:

See from (SF) references that refer

- from terms not in the PAIS vocabulary to those used by PAIS, e.g. *Robots* SF *Automatons*
- from direct headings to the inverted form and vice versa, e.g. *Banking, International* SF *International banking*
- from a broader term to several narrower terms used to encompass various aspects of the subject, e.g. *Agricultural assistance* SF *Foreign aid*; *Economic assistance* SF *Foreign aid*; *Military assistance* SF *Foreign aid*
- from a narrower term to a broader term under which the more specific aspect of the subject is subsumed, e.g. *Tax collection* SF *Withholding tax*

See references are generated from the *See from* references, e.g. *Automatons* SEE *Robots*; *Foreign aid* SEE *Economic assistance*

See also from (SAF) references that refer

- from broader to narrower terms and/or related terms, e.g. *Occupational mobility* SAF *Labor Mobility*

  See also (SA) references are generated from the *See also from* references, e.g. *Labor mobility* SA *Occupational mobility*

TYPES OF SUBJECT HEADINGS OMITTED

The following categories of main headings used by PAIS have been omitted from this list in order to keep it to a manageable size and to avoid cluttering it with headings that follow a repetitive pattern.

- *Geographic headings*
  These include countries, states, provinces or comparable jurisdictions, regions, metropolitan areas, cities, rivers, etc. However, for illustrative purposes we have included the heading *United States* with its subheadings.
- *Names of individuals*
  These include government officials, business leaders, professional leaders, trade union officials, etc.
- *Names of national or local organizations and institutions*
  These include churches, colleges and universities, academies, foundations, libraries, political parties and organizations, trade unions, etc.
- *Names of governmental bodies, departments, or agencies*
  These include legislative bodies, executive departments, regulatory agencies, etc. For illustrative purposes, however, we have included all headings relating to the federal government of the United States.
- *Names of international organizations*
  These include intergovernmental as well as private organizations. For illustrative purposes, however, we have included the heading *United Nations* with most of its subdivisions and headings for United Nations-related organizations and activities.
- *Repetitive headings that can be freely multiplied*
  These include *Foreign students in [the United States], [Americans] in foreign countries, [Italians] in the [United States], Indians of [Peru], [English] language,* etc. We have, however, included examples of these types of headings, particularly those that involve the words American or United States. Headings for ethnic groups with distinctive names have also been included, e.g. *Mexican Americans.*

MAIN HEADING/SUBHEADING COMBINATIONS

The possibilities of forming main heading/subheading/sub-subheading combinations in the PAIS indexes are virtually unlimited. While every combination ever used in the databases becomes part of the authority control system, no useful purpose would be served by reproducing this voluminous file. Instead we have, in the subheading list, set forth the rules followed in forming subject heading strings.

In the main list we have included only the following combinations:

- Unique combinations in which the use of the subheading is restricted to a specified heading or a small number of headings.
- Main heading/subheading combinations illustrative of subheading use restricted to specified categories of subjects, such as Insurance or Libraries.

- Certain heading/subheading combinations, which would ordinarily have been omitted, have been included to maintain the cross reference structure.

SUBHEADINGS

Broadly speaking, PAIS subheadings fall into two categories:

1) Main headings that may also be used as subheadings
2) Descriptors that can be used as subheadings only

Both categories are included in the subheading list, making for some overlap between the first and second parts of this publication. Notes in both parts indicate which main headings may be used as subheadings.

For each subheading listed, we have indicated not only the permissible use, but also any *See from* (SF) and *See also from* (SAF) references called for.

Subheadings vary in their permissible use as follows:

- Subheadings that may be used under any subject or geographic heading, e.g. *Money supply—Statistics; France—Statistics*

Main Headings

A.I.D. (Agency for international development)
   SEE United States - International development agency

AIDS (acquired immune deficiency syndrome)
   SEE Acquired immune deficiency syndrome

A.W.O.L
   SEE Absence without leave

Abaca industry
   SEE Manila hemp

Abalone industry
   SAF Shell industry
        Shellfish industry

Abandoned buildings
   SEE Buildings, Abandoned

Abandonment of automobiles
   SEE Motor vehicles - Abandonment

Abandonment of family
   SEE Desertion and nonsupport

Abandonment of railroad routes
   SEE Railroads - Abandonment
        Railroads, Electric - Abandonment

Abatement of taxes
   SEE Taxation - Abatement

Abazinians

Abbreviations
   NOTE: May also be used as a subheading where appropriate, e.g. Science - Abbreviations.
   SA Acronyms
   SAF Acronyms

Abduction
   SEE Kidnapping

Ability
   SA Creative ability
      Intelligence
      Learning ability
   SF Talent

Ability grouping in education
   SF Grouping by ability
   SAF Education

Aborigines
   SEE Native races

Abortion
   SAF Birth control

Abortion - Moral and religious aspects
   SAF Church and social problems
       Religion

Abrasive wheels
   SEE Grinding wheels

Abrasives industry
   SA Corundum

Abscam operation
   SEE United States - Federal bureau of investigation - Operation Abscam

Absence without leave
   SF A.W.O.L.
   SAF Military service

Absentee voting
   SEE Voting, Absentee

Absenteeism (labor)
   SA Malingering
   SF Employee absenteeism
   SAF Labor
       Personnel management

Abstract and title companies
   SEE Title companies

Abstracting and indexing services
   SAF Bibliography
       Indexing

Abstracts
   NOTE: May also be used as a subheading where appropriate, e.g. Environmental policy - Abstracts.

Academic achievement
   SA Student aspirations
   SF Achievement, Academic
      Scholastic success
   SAF Education
       Student aspirations
       Success

Academic degrees
   SEE Degrees, Academic

Academic freedom
   SA Scientific freedom
   SF Freedom
   SAF Civil rights
       Education
       Intellectual liberty
       Liberty

Academic year
   SEE School year

Acceleration clause (mortgages)
   SEE Mortgages - Due-on-sale clause

Accelerators, Particle
   SEE Particle accelerators

Acceptances
   SAF Banking
       Credit
       Negotiable instruments

Access roads
   NOTE: May also be used as a subheading where appropriate, e.g. Forests, National - Access roads.
   SF Roads, Access
   SAF Highways

Access to highways
   SEE Highways - Access

Access to solar light
   SEE Solar access rights

Access to the sea
   SF Landlocked countries
   SAF Ports

Accessories (dress)
   SEE Dress accessories

Accessories (motor vehicles)
   SEE Motor vehicle accessories

Accident insurance
   SEE Insurance, Accident

Accident prevention
   SEE Accidents - Prevention

Accident research
   SAF Research

Accidents
   NOTE: May also be used as a subheading where appropriate, e.g. Air transport - Accidents.
   SA Drinking and accidents
      Drowning
      Electricity, Accidents from
      Explosions
      Personal injuries
      Poisons - Accidents
      Railroads - Accidents
      Shipwrecks
   SAF Disasters

Accidents - Prevention
   SA Safety measures
   SF Accident prevention
   SAF Safety measures

Accidents, Home
   SF Home accidents

Accidents, Industrial
   SA Workmen's compensation
   SF Industrial accidents
      Work accidents

Accidents, Industrial - Prevention
   SEE Industrial safety

Subheadings

Abandonment
May be used under the following headings:
Railroads
Railroads, Electric
   SF   Abandonment of railroad routes
Motor vehicles
   SF   Abandonment of automobiles

Abatement
May be used under any tax heading, e.g. Income tax - Abatement.
   SF   Abatement of taxes
         Tax abatement

Abbreviations
Main heading which may also be used as a subheading where appropriate, e.g. Science - Abbreviations.
   SAF   Abbreviations

Abstracts
Main heading which may also be used as a subheading where appropriate, e.g. Environmental policy - Abstracts.
   SAF   Abstracts

Access
May be used under the following headings:
Highways
   SF   Access to highways

Access roads
Main heading which may also be used as a subheading where appropriate, e.g. Forests, National - Access roads.
   SAF   Access roads

Accidents
Main heading which may also be used as a subheading where appropriate, e.g. Air transport - Accidents.
   SAF   Accidents

Account executives
May be used under the following headings:
Advertising agencies
   SF   Account executives

Accreditation
May be used under headings for various types of institutions, e.g. Hospitals - Accreditation.
   SF   Accreditation

Acquisitions
May be used under any library heading, e.g. Libraries - Acquisitions.
   SF   Acquisitions by libraries

Adjustment
May be used under the following headings:
Employees
Executives
   SF   Adjustment (employment)
         Work adjustment

Adjustment of claims
May be used under any insurance heading, e.g. Insurance - Adjustment of claims.
   SF   Adjustment of claims
         Claims, Adjustment of

Administration
Main heading which may also be used as a subheading where appropriate, e.g. Hospitals - Administration.

Admission
May be used under the following headings:
Colleges and universities
   SF   Admission to college
   SAF   Colleges and universities - Entrance requirements

Admission to the bar
May be used under the following headings:
Legal profession
   SF   Admission to the bar

Advisers
May be used under headings for presidents of countries, e.g. United States - President - Advisers.
   SF   Advisers to the President
   SAF   Government consultants

Aerial operations
May be used under headings for specific wars, e.g. Vietnamese conflict, 1961-75 - Aerial operations.
   SAF   Aerial warfare

Age
Main heading which may also be used as a subheading where appropriate, e.g. Motor vehicle drivers - Age.
   SAF   Age

Agricultural assistance program
May be used under geographic headings for donor countries or under headings for international organizations, e.g. United States - Agricultural assistance program; International development association - Agricultural assistance program.
   SAF   Agricultural assistance

Agricultural geography
Main heading which may also be used as a subheading under geographic headings, e.g. Europe, Western - Agricultural geography.
   SAF   Agricultural geography

Agricultural history
Main heading which may also be used as a subheading under geographic headings, e.g. United States - Agricultural history.
   SAF   Agricultural history

Agricultural news
Main heading which may also be used as a subheading under headings for various communication media, e.g. Newspapers - Agricultural news.
   SAF   Agricultural news

Agricultural work
May be used under the following headings:
Missions, Foreign
   SAF   Agriculture
         Agricultural assistance

Aid
May be used under the following headings:
College students
   SAF   Scholarships and fellowships
         Student loans

Aims and objectives
May be used under the following headings:
Education

Air conditioning
May be used under any appropriate heading, e.g. Motor vehicles - Air conditioning.
   SAF   Air conditioning industry

Air force
May be used under headings for individual countries, e.g. United States - Air force.
   SF   Air force

All risk policies
May be used under the following headings:
Insurance
   SF   All-risk insurance
   SAF   Insurance - Policies
         Risk (insurance)

Alumni
May be used under headings for various educational institutions, e.g. Colleges and universities - Alumni.
   SF   Alumni

Amendments
May be used under headings for national and state constitutions or charters of international organizations, e.g. United States - Constitution - Amendments. For a specific amendment to the United States constitution, use that amendment as a subheading, e.g. United States - Constitution - First amendment.

Amphibious operations
May be used under headings for specific wars, e.g. World war, 1939-45 - Amphibious operations.
   SAF   Amphibious warfare

Subject Headings:
The History and Theory of the Alphabetical Subject Approach to Books

Julia Pettee

Definitions and the Analysis of Topical Material

One difficulty common not only to public libraries, but to all libraries, is the lack of definitions in the use of many overlapping terms for closely related material. Take the headings on currency. We have Currency *see* Money, Currency question, divided by country, e.g., Currency question—U.S. We have Money divided by country, e.g., Money—U.S. We have Legal tender, Gold, Silver question, Paper money, etc. How do we distinguish between them? The dictionary definitions are of little help for the writers do not keep within these limits. Without a Library of Congress card we are not sure whether Library of Congress would use Currency question—U.S., Money—U.S., Legal tender, or all three.

These overlapping terms need much further study. For all types of libraries definitions follow and depend upon the logical analysis of the subject. For example let us select a few of the "see also" references under Money to illustrate method. It is not necessary to take them all. We have Money *see also* Bank notes, Barter, Bimetallism, Coins, Counterfeits and counterfeiting, Credit, Currency question, Gold, Legal tender, Paper money, Silver, Silver question, Tokens. Greenbacks and Numismatics, topics in the general alphabetical list, are omitted in the Library of Congress "see also" references but should have been included. Besides these "see also" references we have Money subdivided by country, Currency *see* Money, and Currency question subdivided by country. A diagram helps in the analysis of relationships. See p. 299.

After the subject matter has been analyzed the next step is carefully to define the scope of each topical heading.

Reprinted, by permission, from Julia Pettee, *Subject Headings: The History and Theory of the Alphabetical Subject Approach to Books* (New York: H. W. Wilson Co., 1947), 73-80.

Subject Headings

Topical Analysis of Money and Its Relationships to Other Topics

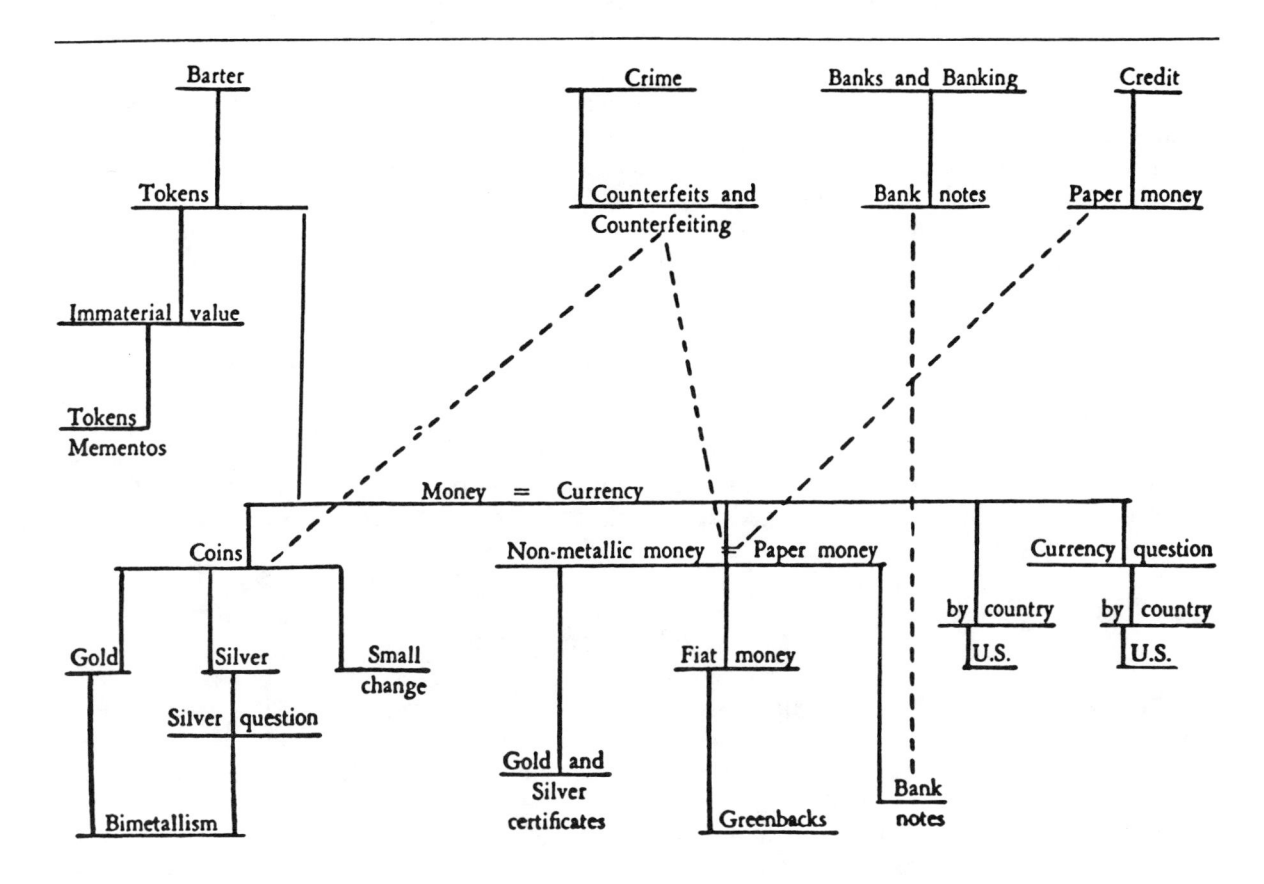

BANK NOTES. Certificates representing money issued by banks.
BARTER. Simple exchange of commodities without use of money.
BIMETALLISM. The use of two metals, gold and silver as standards of monetary value.
COINS. Metallic money.
COUNTERFEITS AND COUNTERFEITING. Imitation of genuine money either metallic or paper.
CURRENCY. The accepted present medium of exchange—money in current use.
CURRENCY QUESTION. Current discussion of money theory and policies.
FIAT MONEY. Money issued by government on government credit alone.
GOLD. This heading includes gold alone as a standard of money.
GREENBACKS. Issue of 1862 of money by the United States Government, not redeemable in gold or silver.
LEGAL TENDER. Money authorized for payment of debts.
MONEY. Authorized medium of exchange—a comprehensive term.
NUMISMATICS. Historical study of coins and medals.
PAPER MONEY. Authorized paper certificates representing money.
SILVER QUESTION. Discussion of silver alone as standard of money.
TOKENS. Symbols representing value, either (1) immaterial or (2) material values which may be exchanged for goods or services.

Keeping these definitions and relationships in mind, checking the number of books in hand, and considering the probable growth of the collection on money, the cataloger is ready to select the headings best suited to his particular library.

Special works on Barter, Tokens (both kinds) and Counterfeits and counterfeiting are not restricted to money alone and, of course, books dealing with these topics should be given these headings.

There is not likely to be much material in a town library limited to Bank notes, a subtopic belonging both to Banks and banking, and to Money. Although this is a good Library of Congress heading it would probably be better not to set up the special topic Bank notes but to treat the single tract or book as a two-topic book making an entry both under Money and Banks and banking.

Coins as commonly used in current transactions are the money of today. The history of coins is quite covered by Numismatics. Do we need to set up Coins as a special heading? For the average public library the cross reference is better, Coins *see* Money; Numismatics.

We already have the cross reference Currency *see* Money. Money may be subdivided by country, e.g., Money—U.S. Do we need to sort out controversial material and set up a new heading Currency question—U.S.? The two headings are so closely parallel the average reader in search of information would be puzzled as to what to expect under each. Currency question as well as Currency can be omitted.

Duplication of Entry Again

Bimetallism, Greenbacks, Gold, Silver question, Paper money, Legal tender, are all subtopics under Money having good subject heading names. Single volumes or pamphlets restricted to these single topics may (1) follow the rule to enter once under most specific topic, or (2) enter under both specific topic and Money, or (3) enter under Money and make a "see" cross reference from the specific topic to the general topic Money.

The choice will depend upon the size of the collection and the clientele. A very small collection would lump these headings together under Money with "see" cross reference from the specific topic. But if the collection attains some importance and there is an active interest in the gold or silver standards or lively discussion on greenbacks, these headings should be sorted out for the convenience of the reader. An active public library in a city of any size will surely need them. Whether a subject card is also entered under Money will depend upon the cataloger's theory as to the desirability of the double entry under both general and specific topic. The Library of Congress' present tendency is to avoid it, but the overlapping of material in the books themselves is so usual that many can be called two-topic books. If the book collection is small the double entries do no harm but the rule for one entry only whenever a specific topic embraced within a more comprehensive topic is excluded from it, is advocated here.

Another Example for Practice in Definition

Peace is a subject which has given trouble to catalogers as well as to politicians. The Library of Congress has recently helped by adding the very useful heading, Conscientious objectors, but the air has not been cleared by its addition of the term Pacifism while it still retains the heading, Evil, Non-resistance to. This latter heading, much to their amazement, formerly included conscientious objectors. If Conscientious objectors and Pacifism are both set up as headings, the books on Evil, Non-resistance to, a heading probably suggested by a literal interpretation of the Bible verse "Resist not evil," could be transferred to Pacifism as a negative part of its program. If Pacifism is omitted, all pacifist works will find a proper place under the several headings:

Peace, War and religion, and Conscientious objectors. Theoretical works on the purely negative method, Gandhi's method,[1] and exegesis of the Biblical verse can go under the old heading, Evil, Non-resistance to. Pacifism seems hardly needed as a separate heading as its chief emphasis is not negative but is on the many positive measures necessary to avoid war, and the purely Pacifist treatises are difficult to identify. The justification for this heading is a theoretical one rather than one arising from the literature itself. The term, Conscientious objectors, however, is needed as there is considerable literature about their treatment.

War and religion: If Pacifism is omitted, all the literature strictly limited to the objections to war, as well as the religious obligation to engage in a just war, can be included here. Some of the objections to war are moral and practical rather than religious but this term will cover. War — Religious and moral aspects is a better heading.

Before establishing the peace headings they should be carefully defined for use in the catalog. Here are suggested definitions:

PEACE. A term which covers all types of theoretical and practical literature intended for the promotion of international comity which will result in the abolition of war.

PEACE MOVEMENT. The New York Public Library uses this term to cover the practical proposals, conferences, etc., for promoting peace, leaving under Peace the more theoretical discussion. Not a Library of Congress heading.

EVIL, NON-RESISTANCE TO. Theoretical or exegetical works limited to non-resistance to evil by physical force.

PACIFISM. A term covering the theory that physical force alone is inadequate to prevent war but that recourse must be made to spiritual values and to the promotion of constructive measures for mutual welfare. It overlaps Peace.

CONSCIENTIOUS OBJECTORS. This term is limited to the treatment of persons refusing to bear arms.

WAR AND RELIGION. Religious or moral arguments for and against engaging in war.

These rather extensive examples are given as a sample of the method of analysis and definition necessary in establishing useful and economical headings.[2]

In ordinary routine work the headings come up one by one. Of course the cataloger can not use this process for each individual heading which he assigns. The headings in his official list have presumably already been analyzed and defined. It is his duty simply to know and consider all the related headings and choose the one or ones best covering the contents of the books.

When a new heading is to be established this method is useful. The cataloger must be cognizant of all the "next of kin," analyze, relate and define all headings in this immediate family group. The analysis can not stop short of this but need not extend beyond it.

Libraries that are reclassing or that are revising large groups of subject headings have the great advantage of being able to survey main groups as a whole. It is far more satisfactory to select subject headings when one is familiar with the total literature of the group than to set up new headings piecemeal. If one is recataloging a whole group it is an excellent practice to hold up the master cards for a final checking until the recataloging of the group is completed and then revise all of the subject headings for the group and write out the necessary cross references.

This logical analysis is absolutely necessary for consistency and uniformity in subject headings, but the interrelationships are so extensive that it is beyond the bounds of practicability to devise a comprehensive analysis covering the whole field of knowledge and including all the multifarious interrelationships. It is one thing to map a logical shelf classification for books with its sharp and definite lines of demarkation and quite another thing to map the many third dimensional criss-crossing relationships of subject headings. Mr. Perkins,[3] in an entertaining article in an early number of the *Library Journal*, promulgated this latter project. He claims that it was Mr. Cutter's original idea and blames him for backing down on it. Citing many of the inadequacies of which we are all aware, he claims that the only remedy is just such an elaborate, comprehensive and complete analysis of every possible relationship suggested by each subject heading. No one seems to have been inspired to devote a life time to this heroic purpose.

It is the nature of the alphabetical subject list to begin with the specific request for information and work backward in its analysis. The subject headings do not assume theoretical completion but are practical aids to actual needs. Therefore, usefulness to the libraries' particular clientele is the test for the entry of any subject word in the catalog. Unwanted topics have no place in it. A law library does not need the topical headings useful for a collection of music.

Notes

[1] Gandhi's method has two aspects. As a protest to civil authority it is civil disobedience for which the Library of Congress heading is Government, Resistance to. As a method of non-violence it is covered by the Library of Congress heading, Evil, non-resistance to.

[2] This method has been excellently worked out by Clyde E. Pettus in her book, *Subject headings in education*. New York. H. W. Wilson. 1938.

[3] Frederic B. Perkins. "Classification in dictionary catalogues." *Library Journal*. 4:226-34. 1879.

"An Approach to Theory and Method in General Subject Headings"

Marie Prevost

Types of Headings Proposed

Good headings are (or should be): (1) arbitrary terms, (2) definite as to coverage, and (3) specific via the subhead. A good list is neither a directory nor a phrasebook. Its intention is to lead the eye as directly as possible to the salient words indicating subjects and their interrelation, using the same method of approach to all subjects and having under each subject a single alphabet of breakdowns, aspects, and juxtaposed subjects. The following are proposed:

A. For subjects other than place or personal names: (1) noun (direct subject); (2) noun (direct subject) plus subhead after dash; plus further subheads after dash if required for breakdown;[1] (3) noun (direct subject) plus qualifying word in parentheses; (4) noun (direct subject) plus qualifying word in parentheses plus subhead after dash; plus further subheads after dash if required; (5) noun (direct subject) plus subhead with preposition in parentheses inserted after the dash (to avoid erroneous or indefinite impression); (6) noun (direct subject) plus subhead with qualifying phrase in parentheses inserted after the dash (to clarify distinct subjects brought into juxtaposition).

B. For names of events, including wars: name of event invariably—with *see also* to history plus dates, as desired.

C. For place names: (1) place; (2) place plus subhead; (3) place plus political unit in parentheses; (4) place plus political unit in parentheses plus subhead; (5) place plus subhead "History,' plus dates; (6) place plus geographic division in parentheses; (7) place plus geographic division in parentheses plus subhead.

To the instinctive objection by many that breakdown by subhead alone will not be adequate, the writer can only submit that it has been found to be so in a list covering, now, some seven thousand headings with a variety of content fairly analogous to a general list, whose principles have served equably and comfortably for seventeen years at the Newark Business Branch and in the transference of its headings to the main library catalog as required.

Reprinted by permission of Univ. of Chicago Press, publisher, from *Library Quarterly* 16 (1946), 144-47, 149-50.

While it is customary to refer to commercial or business service in public libraries as a type of specialization, the material required by a business branch (even more than by a division in the main building) reaches frequently into general subjects. The Newark list covers many industries, trades, and businesses, together with subjects expressing function, as "Salesmanship"; others supplying sidelines of data, such as those needed in advertising; and subjects contributory to business, as "Statistics," "Costs," and so on. Most of the questions concerning breakdown that occur in the construction of a general list apply to it. Each heading was selected, defined, delimited, and co-ordinated in the whole, to meet known reference needs, in the mind of Linda H. Morley, who was then in charge of the branch and giving in person topnotch service to it. Her list, prepared for *2400 Business Books* and its supplement and taken over for the branch catalog, has the integrity and consistency of a one-man job whose maker's ability is too well known to require comment. Her breakdown was entirely by subhead.

It has been rightly said of our general lists that they give little help to the specialist. Therefore, a list which can compass the general and insert without friction, wherever possible, provision for the special seems to be the desideratum which we are all seeking. The needs of a specialist who approaches a general catalog may be expressed as (1) ability to reach all material on his subject in a segregated group and (2) ability to consult this material in full breakdown. It would seem that the general catalog should aim at least to supply his first necessity wholly in spreading before him all it has on his primary subject and to include as much of his second necessity—breakdown indication—as the library's policy of analysis permits. Further subdivision for the nonce we may have to leave to the special librarian; yet, if desired, it is easily open to us. We can, I think, achieve this service merely by following our two already advocated procedures: (1) to break down by formal subhead only and (2) to enter under both "keys" with appropriate subheads, when two key headings (headings having, or fitted to have, subheads) meet in a subject term, never permitting the substitution of a *see* reference for either.

A second objection to the noun approach—that too much material will congregate under given nouns—is bound up with our present concept of the desirability and expectation of finding our material under adjective and in a small compass. This is merely a habit of mind which can be changed. The mind can be trained to seize on the salient subject noun as one crosses to the catalog, expecting to find all its modifications in a single alphabet of subheads; and eye and hand will quickly learn to leap from guide to guide instead of from card to card, as we now automatically adjust our approach to the Webster or the Oxford dictionary. It is a matter of orientation. Once used to it, one has a strong staff to lean upon. "Chemical affinity" will become automatically "Chemistry—Affinity." "Iron trade" will become "Iron—Trade." "Iron age" will become "Age—Iron." And even "Intercultural relations" (a compound adjective hitched to an indeterminate noun) will right itself into "Cultures—Interrelation," unless we agree that "Race" is better than "Culture" for our purpose.

It will be noticed that the proposed rules permit no composite headings and no running headings, except where the name of an event takes a running form. The conjunction "and" rightly should become anathema in headings. Wherever it now appears, it either kills the possibility of definite indication, hitches on a useless appendage, or presents, as Alex Ladenson has put it recently, no real subject area.

While a preposition in a running heading may lead to vagueness, certain current running headings do make good sense. The intention here is to eliminate the running form by recasting it in subhead form after Morley, who found that a preposition in parentheses (to signify "disregard in filing") modifying a subhead was needed for clarity, as in "Salesmanship—(to) Children." Provision for it seems of distinct value in a general list. Also the prepositional phrase invented by Morley to indicate type of reader, rather than content matter, for certain items, as "Accounting" (for its local reference importance and to draw attention to its unusual intention), could well be modified to file in the single-subhead alphabet of a general list as "Accounting—(for the) Executive." In other words, where needed to modify a subhead, a preposition or prepositional phrase may be inserted in parentheses and disregarded in filing—except, of course, to keep itself intact.

Consonant with this disposition of the preposition, the eliminated composite, or "and," heading may be replaced in subhead form by any requisite brief phrase in parentheses (signifying "disregard in filing") that will tie up lucidly the two key nouns, as "Education—(relation to) Democracy"; "Art—(relation to) Morals"; "Railroads—(regulation by) Government"; "Church—(relations with) State."

One particularly bad employment of the "adjective plus direct noun" appears in the present language and literature groups. No less than when it occurs in classification does sharp cleavage between headings for the language and for the literature of a country cause trouble to cataloger and reader. The reason we have no heading for "English" in its present frequent coverage of both language and literature (other than by a third grouping under "Philology," which seems still further to complicate our differentiation troubles) may be laid at the door of our persistent use of the word, and of its sister-words, as adjectives. A shift to the substantive meaning would fill the need for a comprehensive term, enable us to apply our direct-noun approach here also, shorten headings, and give all material in one, instead of several, groups. This would mean that subheads now in use for both language and literature, together with all direct nouns now following the adjective, would be thrown into a single secondary alphabet, thus:

> English
> English—Abbreviations
> English—Ballads
> English—Business
> English—Drama
> English—Essays
> English—Fiction
> English—Grammar
> English—Study

—with further subheads as required. This would also apply to tribal names of American Indians.

Again, beyond everything, we need exactness in our terms, as the astute among us have declared. For a work on the interaction of the dawning peace and another subject, we would not continue to assign two vague headings as "World war, 1939-45—Peace" and, say, "Democracy." The phrase in parentheses would open the door to such clear exactitude as:

> World war, 1939-45—Peace—(affected by) Democracy
> World war, 1939-45—Peace—(effect on) Democracy
> World war, 1939-45—Peace—(affected by) Education
> World war, 1939-45—Peace—(effect on) Education
> World war, 1939-45—Peace—(affected by) Religion
> World war, 1939-45—Peace—(effect on) Religion

and our rule for double entry for a conjunction or juxtaposition of key headings would add:

> Democracy—(affected by) World war, 1939-45—Peace
> Democracy—(effect on) World war, 1939-45—Peace

and so on.

This would be of great assistance in establishing a heading instanter for a brand-new subject. Since the phrase in parentheses is disregarded in filing (except, of course, for the secondary observance of keeping cards on an identical subject together), it would be of no practical moment whatever if the phrasing within the parentheses varied from that employed in sister-libraries, for example, if "influence" or "result" were used instead of "effect." Any one of them would answer equally the purpose of anyone approaching the catalog, for the latter invariably would come holding nothing in mind but the key nouns.

The proposed rule for names of events forces all entries for events under the best-known (generally the only) phrase and forbids its use as a subhead. This phrase may be subjected to breakdown as for noun, though such a breakdown is seldom required.

The proposed rules for place follow current practice in the latter's points 1-6 and reject current practice in the latter's points listed as 6, 7, and 8, in the following respects: (1) Names of events are not to be used as subheads. As desired, they may also be connected with country, subhead "History," plus dates, by *see also* reference from name of event. (2) Geographic division will not be indicated, capitalized, after place name preceded by comma. (3) Geographic division will not precede place name as heading. Thus differentiation in the treatment of geographic divisions to indicate common verbal usage, as "Cape Ann," "Vesuvius (mount)," will be eliminated by the consistent use of parentheses and lower case, even for "Virginia (city)," in the interest of having a single alphabetic line with no filing complications. The only apparent exception (not a real one) is the case in which the word signifying geographic division is not used in its inherent sense, as in "Cape Colony."

Some examples of apparent hurdles in heading shift may be given. Our use of "Natural history" defines it as the consideration of nature in general, which may or may not be presented in the form of history. The long-accepted phrase is bad for its purpose, whereas the area it covers is succinctly expressed in the subject "Nature." "Natural" itself is not too clear, since it may mean "habitual"; and "history" may be a misnomer for any title to which it is applied. The teachers who caused us to establish "Nature study" were clear thinkers, yet in so doing we added to our muddle. We should retain for them "Nature—Study" and recast all "Natural" and "Nature" headings into a single alphabet of subheads under "Nature."

Similarly, in the term "International relations" we are talking about nations, their interrelation, and the heading becomes "Nations—Interrelations." In "International law," two key headings meet. To give specialists in both their leads, we need both "Nations—Law," and "Law—International."

. . . .

GENERAL RULES

1. Be specific, but via the subhead, not the adjective.
2. Be definitive. Vague and ambiguous headings should be either eliminated, delimited by clear definition, or replaced by two or more concrete headings (as for the "ands").
3. Inverted titles are not to be used as substitutes for headings. At present this is officially permitted for a new idea whose area is not yet sufficiently delimitable to permit of establishing a heading. Instead, use a tentative, temporary heading, indexing it in pencil without references, writing it in pencil on catalog cards.
4. Subject takes precedence of place invariably. Where subject subheads under place are desired, as for local needs, make the reverse entry also.

PROCEDURE UNDER A SUBJECT

1. Take a broad subject such as that indicated by the heading "Education," together with its subheads.

2. From its *see also* references take all containing the word "education" and invert to subhead form, thus:

> Agricultural education *to* Education—Agriculture (but indicate, also, Agriculture—Education)
> Coeducation *to* Education—Coeducation
> Education of adults *to* Education—Adult
> Drama in education *to* Education—(through) Drama (but indicate, also, Drama—(in) Education
> Education and state *to* Education—(relations with) State
> Monitorial system of education *to* Education—Monitorial
> Montessori method of education *to* Education—Montessori
> Self-government in education *to* Education—Self-government
> Overpressure in education *to* Education—Overpressure
> Jesuits—Education *to* Education—(of) Jesuits (but indicate, also, Jesuits—Education)
> Feeble-minded—Education *to* Education—Feeble-minded (but indicate, also, Feeble-minded—Education)

and interalphabetize with original subheads. Dig out the actual references now indicated only in blanket form (as "under names of," etc.) and do the same. Blanket references should be eliminated.

3. Examine the remaining *see also*'s critically, to ascertain which should be retained because needed as key headings. Delimit and define such unless clear. Bend backward to keep their number down.

4. Distribute the remaining *see also*'s as subheads under "Education" or under another retained key heading. *See also* references under "Education" will now be reduced to a few key headings—perhaps only to "Schools" and "Teaching." (At present there are seventy-five or more.)

5. Apply the four preceding procedures to the *see also* references under subheads of "Education."

6. Take each of the retained key headings and apply the above procedures to each and to its subheads.

7. Take all subsequent headings beginning with the word "Education" and change to subhead form.

8. Take all subsequent headings beginning with the word "Educational" and invert in subhead form, as "Educational psychology" to "Psychology—Educational," or change to subhead of "Education," as "Educational surveys" to "Education—Surveys."

9. Check all references *to* all headings considered in steps 1-6, to discover subheads appropriate to add to "Education" or to retain as key headings, and then make them.

10. Examine the entire result to remove synonyms and clear up ambiguity.

Conclusion

Of his own rule, opening wide the door to the adjective, Cutter said: "It must be confessed that this rule is somewhat vague and that it would be often of doubtful application."[2] We have been using this rule for over seventy years, and we know no truer word was ever spoken. We have been leaning on a rule which has proved to be a reed. Cutter's objection to the opposite rule of Schwartz admitted that it (the noun rule) "was clear and easy to follow" but was objectionable because it would put subjects "under words where nobody unacquainted with the rule would expect to find them."

Now should the noun rule be adopted, it would not be done *sub rosa*. Every library-school student would assimilate it overnight. At present, according to Cutter, we are expected to be teaching each new approachee to a catalog the rule of specific entry. The mere word "specific" will faze the ignorant; so why should he not be told at once to look for the "*specific noun*"—i.e., if he wants electric motors to look for "Motors" and turn over until he finds "Motors—Electric"? Is it really any harder to grasp?

Then if we follow the further rules suggested here of entry both ways when two key-noun ideas are in conjunction or when two totally different subjects are brought into juxtaposition and if we add our occasional cross-reference from the more dominating type of the adjectival form (though the writer dreads even this concession), it will transpire that very few holes indeed remain through which to slip. And we should have an invariable rule on which to lean with the dependability of a staff. It seems as if the time had come to give John C. Schwartz and the lesser-known brethren who thought and think with him their chance to demonstrate.

Notes

[1] Subheads include noun plus inverted adjective and noun plus inverted qualifying noun, the dash being substituted for the comma to insure one alphabet.

[2] Cutter, Charles A., *Rules for a Dictionary Catalog*, 4th ed. (Washington: Government Printing Office, 1904).

"Cats:
An Example of Concealed Classification in Subject Headings"

Phyllis Allen Richmond

In recent years there have been repeated references to a "concealed" classification in the syndetic section of the subject heading system.[1] Julia Pettee has given an example of this in the case of the term *money*, a very broad subject heading with a complex group of hierarchies whose relationships are best illustrated in a chart.[2] Her chart forms one section of a classification table or map. In elaborating the relationships inherent in the subject heading *money*, however, the index potentialities of a subject heading list are illustrated better than its latent classification. Classification characteristics may be shown more clearly when one is dealing with a simpler subject. For this purpose, the subject heading *cats* has been picked as an example.

Before proceeding to an analysis of the term *cats*, it seems advisable to state plainly the basic premises to be followed in this study. The first fundamental assumption is that there is a classification in the "see also" or syndetic part of the subject headings, thus accepting George Scheerer's view that "every subject heading list presupposes a basis in classification either through category analysis or through reference to a real or ideal classification, because this is the way we organize and clarify our knowledge."[3] The second assumption is that, because of the nature of subject heading structure, this classification is hidden and therefore has not been subjected to the logical criticism which overtakes an open classification. The third basic premise is that in the "see also" references, classification should proceed from the general to the particular, or in the related sequence of the subject's internal classification (chain), and that when there are lateral cross-references these should be made only to terms on the same classification level (array). There should be no references from particular to general.[4] These views run counter to those expressed by Charles A. Cutter and David J. Haykin, who, under certain circumstances, would permit lateral cross-references under less restricting conditions, or even refer from particular to general.[5] While it is possible to have an inductive classification, from particular to general, the analytic method involved is more satisfactory for the classified type of subject heading, which is beyond the scope of this paper.[6]

Reprinted by permission of the American Library Association, "Cats: An Example of Concealed Classification in Subject Headings," by Phyllis Allen Richmond from *Library Resources & Technical Services*, vol. 3, Spring 1959, pp. 102-12; copyright © by ALA.

In general, the "see also" references lead from the term selected to *related* terms which might also be pertinent to the topic being searched. By collecting all the subject headings on cats and the cat family from the Library of Congress list and supplements to date,[7] one may construct a table showing these relationships (Fig. 1). This table has been limited to recognizable cats, and excludes cat-like creatures comprising other branches of the superfamily *Feloidea*, such as civets, mongooses, hyenas, suricates, fossas, and so forth. It may be seen immediately from the table that there are four levels of classification, beginning with the most general, *mammals*, and proceeding to the most specific, *Angora cat, Cacomitl cat, Cheetah*, and others. For the sake of clarity, the "see also from" references leading back from the specific to the general are omitted. This chart, then, gives the classification of the cat family, or some of it, as derived from the Library of Congress subject headings.

1st level	MAMMALS	sa Carnivora [etc., etc.] also names of families, genera, species, etc.
2nd level	DOMESTIC ANIMALS	sa Cats [etc.]
	CARNIVORA	sa names of carnivorous animals
3rd level	CATS x Cat.	sa Angora cat, Cacomitl cat, Cheetahs, Eyra, Lynx, Marbled cat, Siamese cat
	PANTHERS	sa Pumas
	LEOPARDS	sa Clouded leopards
	LIONS	
	TIGERS	
	FOSSIL CATS	
4th level	ANGORA CAT	
	CACOMITL CAT	
	CHEETAHS x Cheetas, Chetahs, Chetas, Chitahs, Hunting leopards	
	CLOUDED LEOPARD x Clouded tiger, Felis nebulosa, Neofelis nebulosa	
	EYRA	
	LYNX x Wildcat	
	MARBLED CAT x Felis marmorata, Pardofelis marmorata	
	PUMAS x Catamounts, Cougars, Mountain lions. sa Panthers	
	SIAMESE CAT	

Fig. 1. Classification of cats in the Library of Congress subject heading list. cf. U.S. Library of Congress. Subject Cataloging Division. *Subject headings used in the dictionary catalogs of the Library of Congress.* 6th ed. (Washington: U.S. Govt. Print. Off., 1957).

The question may be asked: How well does this subject heading classification fit current zoological classification for the same subject? One must admit that in zoological classification there is no hard and fast agreement on the placing of the various members of the cat family. Some zoologists put all kinds of cats in one big group, genus *Felis*. Others make a genus for each cat in creation. This is the pattern followed by Mivart[8] and, to a considerable degree, by Bliss in his classification scheme.[9] George Gaylord Simpson, of the American Museum, whose classification is reproduced here (Fig. 2) uses three genera for non-extinct cats with sub-genera indicated under each.[10] Regardless of which kind of zoological classification is selected, there is reason to believe that the classification latent in the subject headings could be improved by recognizing it as such and by bringing it into line with more accepted scientific forms.

    FAMILY   Felidae Gray, 1821

        SUBFAMILY   [3 extinct subfamilies]
                          Felinae Trouessart, 1885. . . Cats

        GENUS   [3 extinct genera]
                          Felis Linnaeus, 1758

            SUBGENERA and synonyms of *Felis:*
                        Felis (Felis) Linnaeus, 1758. Domestic cat, Old
                          World wild cat
                        Felis (Microfelis) Roberts, 1926. Black footed cat
                        Felis (Lynx) Kerr, 1792. Lynx, bobcat, caracal
                        Felis (Otocolobus) Brandt, 1842. Manul
                        Felis (Liptailurus) Severtzov, 1858. Serval
                        Felis (Prionailurus) Severtzov, 1858. Dwarf "tiger" cat
                        Felis (Pardofelis) Severtzov, 1858. Marble cat
                        Felis (Badiofelis) Pocock, 1932. (Borneo) marble cat
                        Felis (Profelis) Severtzov, 1858. Golden cat
                        Felis (Ziberthailurus) Severtzov, 1858. Fishing cat
                        Felis (Ictailurus) Severtzov, 1858
                        Felis (Leopardus) Gray, 1842. Ocelot
                        Felis (Noctofelis) Severtzov, 1858. Margay, guiña
                        Felis (Herpailurus) Severtzov, 1858. Eyra, jaguarundi
                        Felis (Dendrailurus) Severtzov, 1858. Kodkod, pampa cat,
                        grass cat ("gato pajera")
                        Felis (Puma) Jardine, 1854. Puma, cougar, mountain
                        "lion," (American) "panther."

        GENUS   Panthera Oken, 1816

            SUBGENERA and synonyms of *Panthera:*
                        Panthera (Panthera) Oken, 1816. Panther, leopard
                        Panthera (Leo) Oken, 1816. Lion
                        Panthera (Tigris) Oken, 1816. Tiger
                        Panthera (Jaguarius) Severtzov, 1858. Jaguar
                        Panthera (Neofelis) Gray, 1867. Clouded leopard
                        Panthera (Uncia) Gray, 1867. Irbis, snow leopard,
                        "ounce."
                        [1 extinct subgenus]

        GENUS   Acinonyx Brookes, 1828. Cheetah, guepard, hunting
                        "leopard"

        SUBFAMILY   Machairodontinas Gill, 1872. . . Saber-tooths
                        [10 extinct genera]

Fig. 2. Zoological classification of the cat family. Taken from George G. Simpson, *Principles of classification and a classification of mammals* (Bulletin of the American Museum of Natural History, v. 85; New York, 1945), pp. 119-120.

Comparison of Library of Congress subject heading classification for *cats* and the zoological system of Simpson reveals some strange bedfellows. In the first place, the "Cacomitl cat" is no cat. He is a close relative of the raccoon, as his family tree shows.[11] (Fig. 3) The subject heading *Cacomitl cat* should be changed to *Cacomistle* with "see" references from Ring-tailed cat, and Cacomitl cat.

>   FAMILY   Procyonidae Bonaparte, 1850
>   SUBFAMILY   Procyoninae Gill, 1872
>   GENERA   Bassariscus Coues, 1887. Cacomistle, ring-tailed "cat"
>   Procyon Storr, 1780. Raccoon
>   Nasua Storr, 1780. Coati, coati-mundi
>   Potos Cuvier & Geoffroy, 1795. Kinkajou

Fig. 3. Zoological classification of the Cacomistle (from Simpson).

In the second place, cross-references should not mix levels of classification. Cats which are a species of a subgenus, such as the divisions of *Felis* (*felis*): Angora, Siamese, Manx, domestic shorthair, Old World wild cat and such, certainly should not be entered on the same level of classification as those which are distinct sub-genera in the same line: lynx, eyra, marble cat, etc. This is equivalent to mixing generations, as may be seen from a genealogical-type table. (Fig. 4)

```
[Subfamily]                              Felinae
                        ┌──────────────────┼────────────────────────┐
[Genera]              Felis             Panthera                 Acinonyx
                                                                 (Cheetah)
              ┌────┬────┬──────┬─────┐   ┌────────┬──────┬────────┐
[Subgenera] Domestic Eyra Lynx Marbled Puma Panther   Lion  Tiger  Clouded
             cat              cat           (Leopard)              leopard
              ┌────┴────┐
[Species]  Angora    Siamese
            cat        cat
```

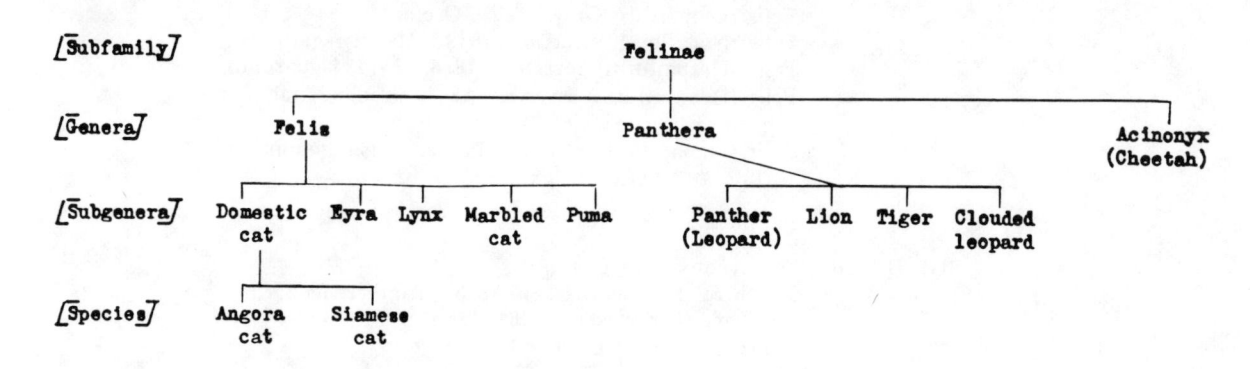

Fig. 4. Abbreviated family tree indicating kinship among cats.

Thirdly, cross-references should not cut across genus lines. Cats which belong to a higher level—those which form a separate genus, such as the cheetah—should certainly not be considered on the same level of classification as species of domestic cats or the subgenera lynx, marble cat and eyra. This point is also illustrated by Figure 4.

Fourthly, cross-references should not be made between cats which stand in the relationship of first cousins. The references from *pumas* to *panthers* and vice versa violate this rule. In this case, as in the Cacomitl "cat," an ambiguity in common names has caused the difficulty, since the puma is sometimes called the American "panther."

Finally, terms which are zoological synonyms, as "leopard" and "panther," should be used as such.

There are at least two ways in which the classification difficulties in the subject heading *cats* may be resolved. One is to use the term "cats" for all members of the subfamily *Felinae*, which would cover all kinds of cats. The addition of *lynx, eyra, cheetahs* and *marbled cat* to the "see also" references from *cats* in the Library of Congress system suggests that this alternative was followed at one time. However, if followed consistently, it would be necessary to add *lions, tigers, panthers, clouded leopards* and similar headings to the "see also" references from *cats.*

Another alternative is to restrict the use of the term "cats" to the members of the genus *Felis.* This would eliminate *cheetahs* from the "see also" references, but would add *pumas.* If this alternative is followed, one would need a heading *Domestic cat* for the common garden variety of pussy. It might even prove advisable to use *cats* for the genus and *cat* for the subgenus. A similar solution would also be necessary for the panther group, genus *Panthera*, unless one took *panther* for the genus and its synonym *leopard* for the subgenus. The cheetah, genus *Acinonyx*, is fortunately unique in the respect that there is no subgenus with the identical name to confuse with the genus name.

Even if one restricts the term "cats" to the genus *Felis*, nine-tenths of the cats in this category are not domestic animals. In fact, most are very much the opposite. Therefore, reference to some general subject heading, such as *Carnivora*, is to be prepared at the upper level, and the heading *Domestic animals* should be limited to the tamer members of cat society: domestic cats and cheetahs.

These suggested revisions of the subject heading *cats*, following the second of the alternatives given above, are outlined in Figure 5. No revision has been suggested for the term *Fossil cats*, which at present covers all pre-historic cats. If needed, however, one could easily work out a classified arrangement by consulting Simpson's classification. The presence of fossil cats has been indicated in Figure 2, but their names omitted.

In summary, the classification of cats in the Library of Congress subject headings leaves something to be desired. The very fact that the hierarchial arrangement is concealed prevents the discovery of such obvious errors as the inclusion of a raccoon relative in the midst of the felines. The less apparent oddities are also hidden until one constructs a chart or makes some similar analysis.

In defense of the concealed classification, one may claim that (1) the subject heading list is only meant to be an index, or (2) subject headings are based on words and not ideas, or (3) subject headings are designed as relatively non-specific topical guides for the general reader, with cross-references added at random as directed by "experience." The first argument would be more potent if the cross-references had been limited to the "see" type. The classification, unfortunately, came inevitably with the addition of the "see also" type. The argument that subject headings are only words and not ideas is more subtle. It explains why Cacomitl "cat" was placed with cats instead of raccoons, and puma with panther. It can lead to ludicrous as well as dangerous errors. The word "cat," after all, has many applications. The variety of meaning in words of the English language makes context a necessity for truly accurate definition.[12] Classification is one way of supplying context. It has proved necessary in both indexes and subject heading lists to use such classifications as:

    Escape (Ethics)
    Escape (Law)

or many modifications of a large topic such as Photography:

    Photography, Aerial
    Photography, Architectural
    Photography, Ballistic [etc., etc.]

or "see also" references. Isolated words are about the weakest reeds upon which to lean.

1st level	MAMMALS	sa Carnivora, Domestic animals [etc., etc.] also names of families, genera, species, etc.
2nd level	CARNIVORA	sa Cats, Panthers, Cheetahs [& other kinds of carnivorous animals]
	DOMESTIC ANIMALS	sa Domestic cat, Cheetahs [& other kinds of domesticated animals]
3rd level	CATS [Genus Felis] sa Domestic cat [etc.]	
	PANTHERS [Genus Panthera] sa Panther [etc.]	
	CHEETAHS [Genus Acinonyx] x Guepard, Hunting leopard, Cheetas, Chetahs, [etc.]	
	FOSSIL CATS [not subdivided]	
4th level	DOMESTIC CAT sa Angora cat, Siamese cat [etc.]	
	BLACK FOOTED CAT	
	LYNX x Bobcat, caracal, wildcat	
	MANUL	
	SERVAL	
	DWARF "TIGER" CAT	
	MARBLE CAT x Felis marmorata, Pardofelis marmorata	
	BORNEO MARBLE CAT	
	GOLDEN CAT	
	FISHING CAT	
	OCELOT	
	MARGAY x Guiña	
	EYRA x Jaguarundi	
	KODKOD x Pampa cat, Grass cat	
	PUMA x Cougar, Mountain lion, Catamount, American panther	
	PANTHER x Leopard	
	LION	
	TIGER	
	JAGUAR	
	CLOUDED LEOPARD x Clouded tiger, Felis nebulosa, Neofelis nebulosa	
	SNOW LEOPARD x Irbis, Ounce	
5th level	ANGORA CAT	
	SIAMESE CAT	

Fig. 5. Suggested revision of the Library of Congress subject heading *cats*. Additions at the fourth level to be adopted as needed. There are many different names for the subgenera of *Felis*, so that many more cross-references undoubtedly would be needed. Except for the domestic cat, a species has been made a direct cross-reference of its subgenus.

The first part of the third argument, that subject headings should be non-technical, may be a valid reason for the treatment given some of the more esoteric branches of knowledge or for advanced sections of the common divisions, but it falls flat as an excuse for illogical references in a mundane subject such as cats. If the subject heading *cats*, when treated logically, thereby becomes too advanced for general usage, what on earth is a simple subject? The second half of the proposition, that cross-references have grown from experience undoubtedly explains what has happened, but it is scarcely an argument in favor of such a haphazard approach.

The method of comparison, which has been used in this study, offers one way of ascertaining whether the relationship tables constructed from "see also" subject heading references are in accordance with current classification practice in the subject field. This method works best for biological subjects or others with a very definite internal classification. Otherwise, the method outlined by Julia Pettee and refined by Vaclav Mostecky,[13] though somewhat more complex, is preferable. In either case, the purpose of the analysis is to achieve a more logical organization in subject heading structure, and thereby to make the cross-references more rational and more useful than they are at present. The results of current language studies should lead to considerable improvement in the matter of terminology.[14] Ultimately, the results of both the classification and linguistic approaches should benefit the user of the subject catalog by enabling him to find things in a more familiar setting.

From the specific example, *cats*, used in this study, several practical suggestions for future application may be implied, though further work should be undertaken before any of these are considered as conclusive. First, it is possible to develop an analytic approach to the problem of making syndetic cross-references in subject headings. This may be either the deductive method utilized in the *cats* case above, or an inductive one as suggested by Prevost and Vickery.[15] Either of these methods should result in a more systematic and logical cross-reference structure, on an acceptable classification basis. If the deductive approach is used, the classification will still be latent.

Secondly, one might seriously consider eliminating the "see also" references altogether. Obviously this is a negative attitude: it would solve the ticklish problem of classification in the syndetic catalog by abolishing the whole system. Such radical surgery of the subject catalog could scarcely be undertaken without a full-fledged inquiry to determine the present effectiveness or ineffectiveness of the "see also" references from the user's point of view. The elimination of syndetic references would leave the subject catalog a mixture of catchword and alphabetico-classed entries, which, in turn, perhaps would be less desirable than either type of entry alone. One could convert the "see also" references to alphabetico-classed subject headings, but this would presuppose that such a list is preferred to a catchword one—again a major decision.

There is one final consideration in the matter of practical application of the logical treatment of cross-reference structure in subject headings. Such a methodical approach is a necessity in the mechanization of the subject catalog, a process which has already begun in some quarters. The creation of a general information system for a machine may be made in several ways. One may proceed through classification *per se*, a procedure advocated by the Classification Research Group in England,[16] or one may use existing subject headings *if there is a logical relationship pattern among them*. The machines cannot function without some kind of patterns of related sequences. One may also attack the problem linguistically through conceptual, transformational, or other analysis of words and phrases. This is now being done to some extent as a by-product of the mechanical translation process.[17] It is difficult to see how any subject approach to a general information system can be made without indicating logical relationship patterns, though the classification involved may not be in a conventional form.

Conclusion

The subject catalog functions on the theory that information on any given subject, stored in books, periodicals or other media, may be extracted by means of key index words or phrases familiar to the major proportion of potential users. There is neither general agreement on what form these words should take, nor on what organization is most effective in displaying them. In the present study, a single word, *cats*, has been demonstrated in one type of organization, the "see also" cross-reference, which has a concealed classification inherent in it because of the very nature of the connective pattern of the references. The organization in the subject heading's cross-references has been compared with a subject norm, and, on the assumption that the cross-reference structure should parallel the subject's internal classification, a logical example has been constructed. It has been suggested that the adoption of classification principles in making "see also" references should result in a more rational and therefore a more functional structure for this part of the subject catalog.

Notes

[1] See, for example: Bradford, S. C. *Documentation*. Washington, Public Affairs Press, 1950, p. 51; Sayers, Berwick. "Classification," *Library Trends*, 2:239, 1953; Vickery, B. C. "Developments in Subject Indexing," *Journal of Documentation*, 11:1-11, 1955; Clapp, V. W. "Subject Controls—Nature and Level of Controls," *American Documentation*, 3:11-14, 1952; Scheerer, George. "The Subject Catalog Examined," *Library Quarterly*, 17:191-194, 1957.

[2] Pettee, Julia. *Subject Headings: the History and Theory of the Alphabetical Subject Approach in Books*. New York, H. W. Wilson, 1946, pp. 3-4, 57-60, 73-80.

[3] Scheerer, George. "Subject Catalog Examined," *Library Quarterly*, 17:192, 1957.

[4] It is possible to view the "see also" cross-reference system as a maze instead of a classification. This presupposes no intentional or logical organization and seeks merely the shortest point-to-point path through the maze by means of a rather simple technique. Cf. Estrin, Gerald. "Maze Structure and Information Retrieval," *Preprints for the International Conference on Scientific Information, Washington, D. C., November 16-21, 1958*. Washington; National Academy of Sciences, National Research Council, 1958. (Hereafter referred to as *Preprints*), Area 6, pp. 115-119. If the lattice idea in subject analysis and classification structure should prove generally acceptable, the views expressed in this paper may be rendered untenable. Cf. Vickery, B. C. "Subject Analysis for Information Retrieval," *Preprints*, area 5, pp. 41-51; "The Structure of Information Retrieval Systems," *Preprints*, area 6, pp. 5-19; Masterman, M., Needham, R. M., and Spärck Jones, K. (Cambridge Language Research Unit) "The Analogy Between Mechanical Translation and Library Retrieval," *Preprints*, Area 5, pp. 111-112, 121; Fairthorne, R. A. "The Patterns of Retrieval," *American Documentation*, 7:65-70, 1956.

[5] Cf. Cutter, C. A. *Rules for a Dictionary Catalog*, Washington, GPO, 1876, p. 15, 48-49; 3rd ed. (1891), p. 57-58; 4th ed. (1904), p. 79-80. Cutter's definition: "Syndetic, connective, applied to that kind of dictionary catalogue which binds its entries together by means of cross-references so as to form a whole, the references being made from the most comprehensive subject to those of the next lower degree of comprehensiveness, and from each of these to their subordinate subjects, and so on. These cross-references correspond to and are an important substitute for the arrangement in a systematic catalogue. [The present author does not know whether this means that they are intended as an alternate form of classification, replacing the multiple entries of a classified catalog, or as an alternative to a classified subject heading list.] References are also made in the syndetic catalogue to illustrative and co-ordinate subjects." (1876, p. 15); Haykin, D. J. *Subject Headings, a Practical Guide*, Washington, GPO, 1951, pp. 14-15.

[6] The rudiments of such a system for subject headings are contained in Prevost, M. L. "An Approach to Theory and Method in General Subject Headings," *Library Quarterly*, 16:140-151, 1946. It is a very short step from the work of Miss Prevost to the process of facet analysis. Cf. Vickery, B. C. "Systematic Subject Indexing," *Journal of Documentation*, 9:48-57, 1953. The inductive approach is ably defended in Morris, Jack. "The Duality Concept in Subject Analysis," *American Documentation*, 5:117-146, 1954.

[7] U. S. Library of Congress. Subject Cataloging Division. *Subject Headings Used in the Dictionary Catalogs of the Library of Congress*. 6th ed. Washington, GPO, 1957, and *Supplements* to Sept., 1958.

[8]Mivart, St. George. *The Cat; an Introduction to the Study of Backboned Animals Especially Mammals*, New York, Scribner, 1881, pp. 390-430.

[9]Bliss, H. E. *A Bibliographic Classification, Extended by Systematic Auxiliary Schedules for Composite Specification and Notation.* New York, H. W. Wilson, 1940, I, 463.

[10]Simpson, G. G. *Principles of Classification and a Classification of Mammals.* American Museum of Natural History. *Bulletin*, v. 85, New York, 1945, pp. 118-121. An equally sophisticated and exhaustive treatment, limited to the genera *Felis* and *Otocolobus*, has been given in Pocock, R. I. *Catalogue of the Genus Felis.* London, British Museum, 1951.

[11]Simpson, *op. cit.*, p. 112.

[12]Chomsky, Noam, "Logical Structure in Language," *American Documentation*, 8:284-291, 1957. An interesting discussion of meaning and an example of a noun "slip" with at least 18 distinct meanings may be found in Singer, T. E. R. "The Need for Imagination and Skepticism in Making Literature Searches." *Record of Chemical Progress*, 8:27-28, 1957.

[13]Pettee, *op. cit.*, p. 73-76; Mostecky, Vaclav. "Study of the *See also* Reference Structure in Relation to the Subject of International Law." *American Documentation*, 7:294-314, 1956.

[14]See Daily, Jay. "Subject Headings and the Theory of Classification." *American Documentation*, 8:269-274, 1957; Williams, Thyllis. "Language Engineering," *in* Shera, J. H., Kent, A., and Perry, J. W. *Documentation in Action.* New York, Reinhold, 1956, pp. 330-337. "Language engineering" here means a process of concept analysis of phrases, *not*, as Joshua Whatmough uses the term, mathematical linguistics; Smith, C. G. "Basic Documentation," *Preprints*, Area 5, p. 272, 277; Koller, H. R., Marden, Ethel, and Pfeffer, Harold "The Haystaq System: Past, Present and Future," *Preprints*, Area 5, p. 340.

[15]Prevost, M. L. "Approach to Theory and Method in General Subject Heading." *Library Quarterly*, 16:140-151, 1946; Vickery, B. C. "Systematic Subject Indexing," *Journal of Documentation*, 9:48-57, 1953.

[16]*Proceedings of the International Conference on Classification for Information Retrieval Held at Beatrice Webb House, Dorking, England, 13th-17th May, 1957.* London, ASLIB, 1957, Appendix 2, pp. 137-147.

[17]Masterman, Needham and Spärck Jones, K., "The Analogy Between Mechanical Translation and Library Retrieval," *Preprints*, Area 5, pp. 103-121.

"Intelligent Indexing and Retrieval"

R. A. Wall

Overlapping Terms

If Related Terms were broken up into:
>overlapping terms (from variant hierarchies)
>coordinate terms (at same level with same Broader Terms)
>associated terms (without hierarchical relationships)

it should be possible to build a thesaurus capable of being fully manipulated by computer. Since one would then be concerned with all relationships and all relevant terms, not with giving prominence to "preferred terms", it should also become possible to show only true relationships between terms. This could facilitate the merging of small thesauri thus constructed. For reasons which are given later, when an updated means of designating overlapping terms is described, the splitting of RT into three groups would require no additional human input.

With regard to the construction rules, BS5723:1979 on thesaurus construction guidelines was published recently. The term link codes offered are as follows:

USE: before preferred term/UF: before non-preferred equivalent
TT: top term in a hierarchy
BT: broader term
NT: narrower or more specific term
BTG: broader term generic
NTG: narrower term generic
BTP: broader term partitive
NTP: narrower term partitive

if one wishes to distinguish between hierarchical and whole-to-part relationships

and, last but not least, *the old favourite*:
RT: related term

The Standard shows a clear case of *generic* relationship determinable by the "some-all" test, which shows *some* members of the class RODENTS are MICE, and that *all* MICE are RODENTS.

Reprinted with permission from *Information Processing and Management*, vol. 16, R. A. Wall, "Intelligent Indexing and Retrieval," copyright 1980, Pergamon Press, Ltd.

```
                    RODENTS
           some  |           ↑  all
                 ↓           |
                    MICE
```

However, it is said:
"This test would usually prohibit the subordination of a term such as MICE to a class such as PESTS. MICE are not PESTS by definition, and this relational situation would be represented by the diagram:

```
                    PESTS
           some  |           ↑  some
                 ↓           |
                    MICE
```

Both terms should then be assigned to the same document".
Unless, it is added, a special PEST CONTROL thesaurus were under construction, when generic relationships could be assumed. However, these two terms are really *overlapping* terms, though the standard does not say so, and each could divide the other.

Example
BS5723:1979 gives the following as an example of a poly-hierarchical relationship:

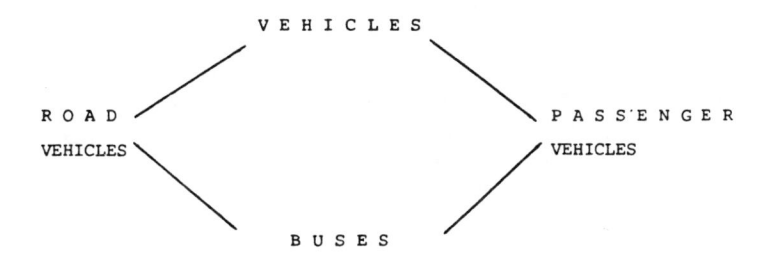

```
                    VEHICLES
                   /        \
           ROAD                PASSENGER
           VEHICLES            VEHICLES
                   \        /
                    BUSES
```

The Standard however suggests no way of defining the different hierarchies, and no cross-link is made between ROAD VEHICLES and PASSENGER VEHICLES. This has been taken as the basis of an example for presentation here to show how the hierarchies might be found definable.

To commence the example, let it be supposed that the terms in Fig. 1 are already present in a thesaurus. The links are shown as though the proposed techniques have been applied. Generic links, using the "some-all" test, are shown simply as BT-NT. To illustrate partitive or whole-to-part links for those who would prefer to distinguish them, they are indicated as BTP-NTP, and the test is "some parts-all parts".

It is proposed that overlapping terms should be determined by the *"some-some"* test and
    XT = Overlapping Term
    NX = Narrower Overlapped Term: this code is not intended to be input manually. The human input would be NT but a computer program, finding a case of subordination to two or more overlapping terms, could alter the NT code to NX. This would seem necessary as an indicator for future use when computer-tracking across hierarchies.

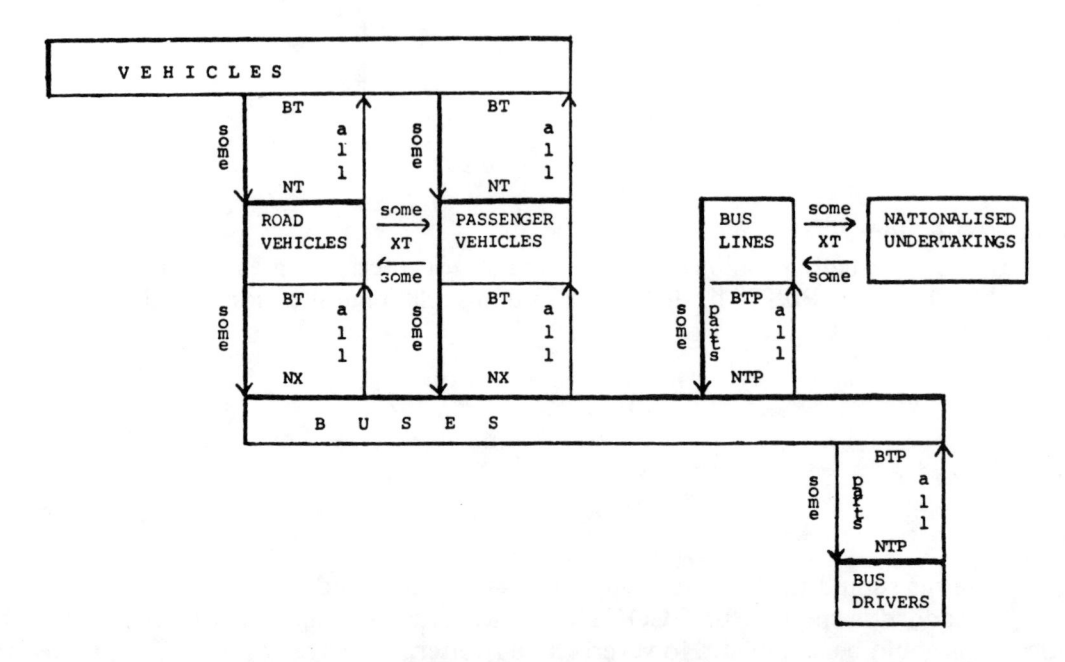

Fig. 1. Example of terms assumed already present in a thesaurus.

Now it is necessary to show how links would be treated in a thesaurus build-up procedure from day to day indexing. Three hypothetical, stepwise additions will be considered. Terms will not be expressed in a formal style. Firstly, a document on ONE-MAN OPERATED BUSES arrives. If that term is more specific than any others in the relevant part of the thesaurus, all the human input would need to do is tack it on to such appropriate broader term(s) as may be *already* present, but just those immediately adjacent. The computer would respond by adjusting entries under the broader term(s); also, if any sister NT's were already present, they would become Coordinate Terms (CT) to the newly added term.

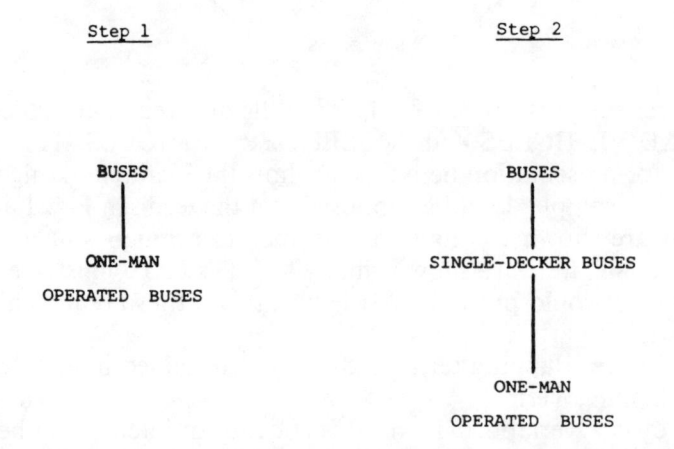

```
       Step 1                        Step 2

       BUSES                         BUSES
         |                             |
       ONE-MAN               SINGLE-DECKER BUSES
    OPERATED BUSES                     |
                                    ONE-MAN
                                 OPERATED BUSES
```

Step 2 is the arrival of a document on SINGLE-DECKER BUSES which, being narrower than BUSES and broader than ONE-MAN OPERATED BUSES, needs to be inserted between them. Human input would show only the relationships of the new term to existing terms. Computer response would change all other entries.

Step 3 is the addition of ONE-MAN OPERATED *VEHICLES*:

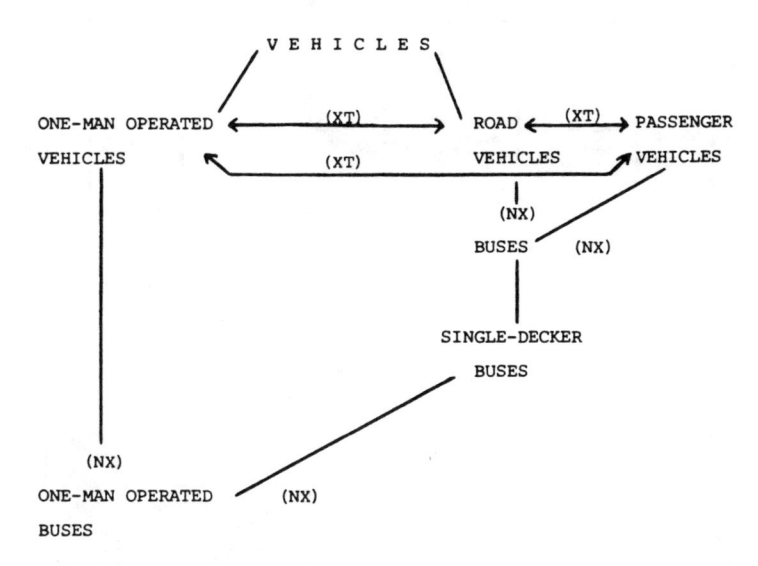

```
                        V E H I C L E S
                       /       |       \
ONE-MAN OPERATED ←──(XT)──→  ROAD  ←──(XT)──→ PASSENGER
   VEHICLES     ↖    (XT)   VEHICLES       ↗  VEHICLES
                              |
                            (NX)
                            BUSES    (NX)
                              |
                         SINGLE-DECKER
                            BUSES
         |
       (NX)
ONE-MAN OPERATED    (NX)
   BUSES
```

When a term is to be *inserted*, at least one relevant existing thesaurus term must be shown as NT, and the computer would show any of its sisters as NT's also.

The input would be as follows:

Step 3

Human input: ONE-MAN OPERATED VEHICLES
        BT   VEHICLES
        NT   ONE-MAN OPERATED BUSES
        XT   PASSENGER VEHICLES
        XT   ROAD VEHICLES

The computer additions illustrate the possible extent of computer aid for this simple example. Hopefully, this also shows how the structure could grow from day to day indexing:

Computer additions:
(VEHICLES):
NT   ONE-MAN OPERATED VEHICLES
(PASSENGER VEHICLES):
XT   ONE-MAN OPERATED VEHICLES
(ROAD VEHICLES):
XT   ONE-MAN OPERATED VEHICLES
(ONE-MAN OPERATED BUSES):
BT   ONE-MAN OPERATED VEHICLES
*(SINGLE-DECKER BUSES):
NX   ONE-MAN OPERATED BUSES
(ONE-MAN OPERATED VEHICLES):
NX   ONE-MAN OPERATED BUSES

(*N.B. by tracking XT across to Passenger Vehicles and down to this term)

It should be noted that the state of development would reflect the documents actually in the system, and the result should be the same if the documents were received in any other order, provided the human input were reliable.

Diagrammatically, the three steps have brought the development to Fig. 2.

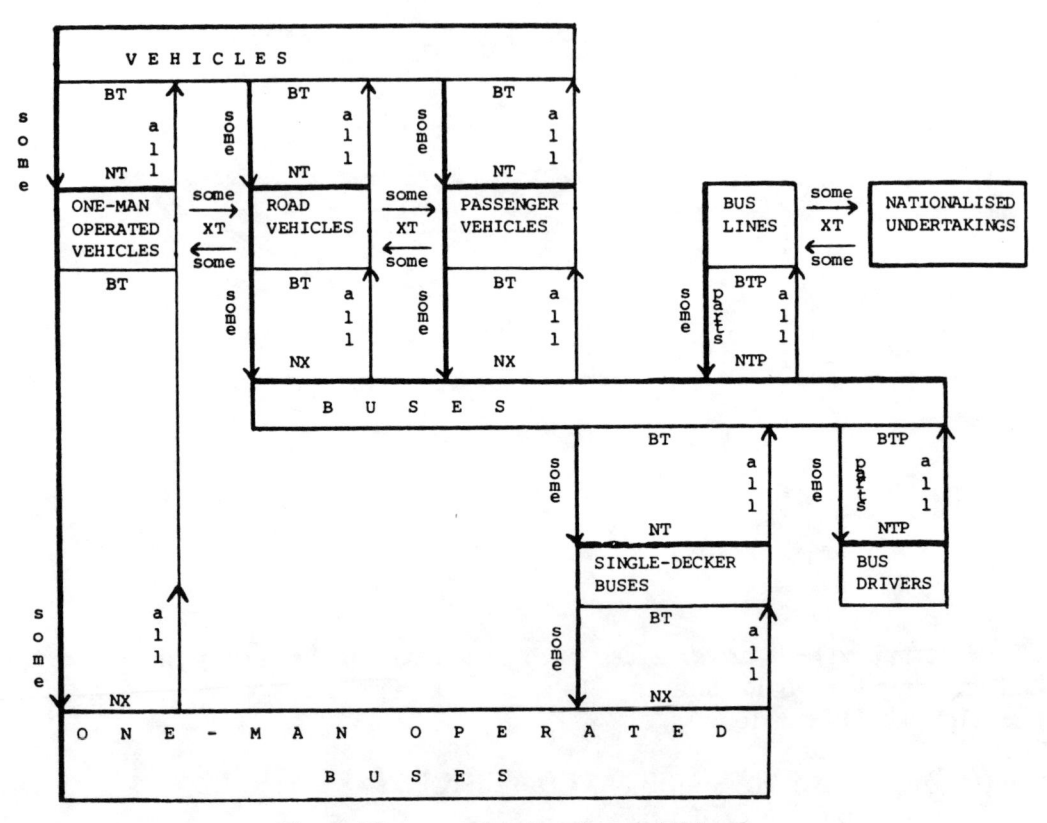

Fig. 2. The example after three additions.

Computer Tracking of Hierarchies

A user would select tracking routes from initial display of adjacent terms, preferably plus class context or Top Terms.

Upward tracking of hierarchies by computer could produce a visual display by tracing out routes as follows:

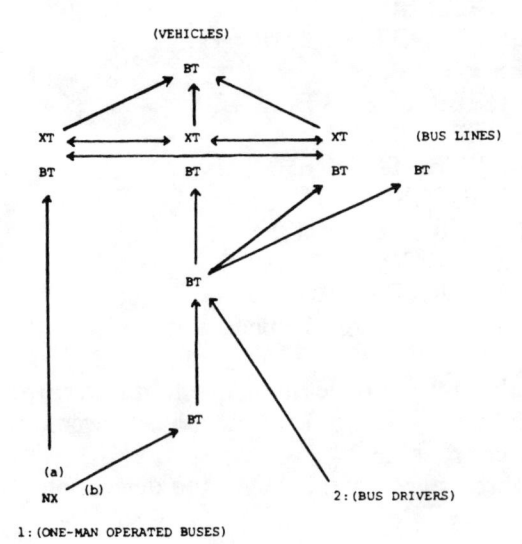

1: (ONE-MAN OPERATED BUSES)
2: (BUS DRIVERS)

Intelligent Indexing and Retrieval

Other links could of course be present at any point. There are three routes from point number (1) ONE-MAN OPERATED BUSES, coded NX, to vehicles as top term. NX could signify in a computer program that:

(i) "there is more than one route of equal validity";
(ii) "NT's at the same level are CT's, but must be separately displayed per BT";
(iii) "NX's of BT's which are *XT-linked* are also CT's when not already linked vertically".

The three routes from (1) to VEHICLES area:
1 (a) 2 steps to VEHICLES as top with crosslinks to 2 XT's
  (b) 2 alternative sub-routes of 4 steps to VEHICLES as top, through 2 XT's.

There are also three routes upward from point (2) BUS DRIVERS:
2 (a) to BUS LINES as top
  (b) to VEHICLES as top, via 2 sub-routes and through 2 XT's

It is important to note that subsets of the XT-linked terms can have their own, separately traceable hierarchies:

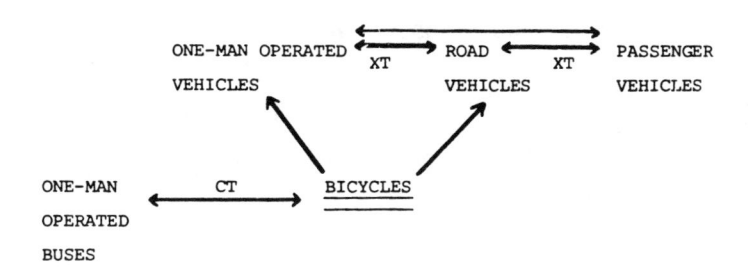

```
ONE-MAN OPERATED  <--XT-->  ROAD      <--XT-->  PASSENGER
VEHICLES                    VEHICLES            VEHICLES
        ↑                      ↑
        |                      |
ONE-MAN        <--CT-->    BICYCLES
OPERATED
BUSES
```

For example, if BICYCLES were in the structure, ONE-MAN OPERATED VEHICLES and ROAD VEHICLES would be BT's, but they are already linked as XT's with PASSENGER VEHICLES. However, BICYCLES would not be displayed as having any relationship with PASSENGER VEHICLES or its NT's, because the computer program would not be able to complete an "across-and-down" route through the link codes of the latter term, and hence would disregard it as a hierarchical trace for BICYCLES.

Of course, XT links do not *have* to be visualised as horizontal—though hopefully that convention aids clarity in these diagrams. In a full thesaurus, all the permutations of division found necessary for indexing would be present, and the XT links would be numerous and would form *nodes* through which related hierarchies would pass.

It should be noted that the division order ceases to have importance when full class display is not needed. The effect of XT in making, say, PASSENGER VEHICLES-ROAD VEHICLES-BUSES as valid a route as ROAD VEHICLES-PASSENGER VEHICLES-BUSES is that BUSES becomes automatically linked with the largest possible Coordinate Term group, as if the route were always the former, which can do no harm: both other kinds of Passenger Vehicle and other kinds of Road Vehicle would be CT's. Just to add a few more, the following could be XT-linked. They are all at the same level, shown as though viewed in plan:

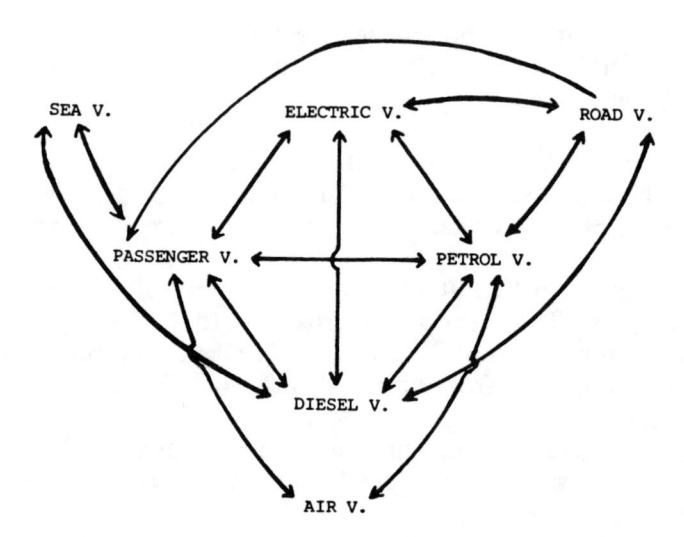

If GROUND VEHICLES were then added as XT, ROAD VEHICLES would be shown as a NT thereto—the computer could interpret this as an instruction to cancel the XT link for ROAD VEHICLES, as well as cope with any other changes. In upward tracking, the subset of XT terms followed would be those stated as BT's to the same NX. Where there are no NX, *all* the above XT linked terms would be shown as the joint starting points of tracking to VEHICLES, TRANSPORT, ENGINEERING, and so on.

Proposed Term Designations

Turning now to the suggested full list of term designations, omitting the British Standard's BTG and BTP etc. as perhaps unnecessary:

```
          ( TERM IDENTIFICATION NUMBER )

          ( USE ) / UF

          ( TT ),  BT ,  NT ,  ( NX )

          XT , ( AT ) , ( CT )
          ─────────────────────
                former RT
```

Notes: (...) means COMPUTER-ASSIGNABLE or SUGGESTABLE

   ─ means MINIMUM HUMAN INPUT

NT: Narrower term (if numerous above a stated limit, computer could give first 3 and refer to a separate array)
NX: Narrower overlapped term
XT: Overlapping term

AT: Associated term, suggestable by computer count of word association frequency (or more sophisticated automatic text analysis techniques) in respect of words having no stated hierarchical relationships, requiring human edit. Alternatively, manually input.

CT: Coordinate (i.e. same level of division) term. Determinable by computer selection of term having the same BT and not already otherwise interlinked.

Of the three categories proposed instead of RT:

XT, AT and CT; only XT should be determined by human intelligence alone. It should be noted that separately designating XT does not increase the human input.

In any event, a by-product might be the avoidance of the inadvertent inclusion of BT's in a group of RT's. For example the Engineers Joint Council in New York published the large thesaurus of Engineering and Scientific Terms (TEST), which includes two BT's among RT's under: *BUSES (VEHICLES)* — as opposed to another entry for BUSES (CONDUCTORS), in electrical conductors

UF School buses (vehicles)
BT Ground vehicles
    Passenger vehicles

suggested instead:

RT	Automobiles	—	CT
	Bus lines	—	BT
	Electric vehicles	—	should not be here — they are
	Military vehicles	—	both XT to Ground vehicles
	Motor trucks	—	CT
	Motor vehicles	—	BT

The VEHICLES example could be developed further, but hopefully it will suffice to show principles of the "learning process" of thesaurus build-up, which would of course require on-line indexing via a Visual Display Unit.

"Language of the Library of Congress Subject Headings Pertaining to Society"

Jan Wepsiec

Existing headings are grouped into twenty-two types, using the syntactic structure of the modifier of the focal noun as the criterion of differentiation. Some semantic types are found to have been expressed by more than one syntactic type. Reasons are given for eliminating certain syntactic types, reducing the total from twenty-two to fifteen, without loss of specificity of the headings.

This paper examines the syntactic structures of Library of Congress subject headings pertaining to society.[1] The analysis centers upon the use of grammatical categories in modifiers of the focal nouns in the headings. The semantic content, or concept, of each syntactic type is then determined, and in some cases it is found that more than one syntactic type corresponds to a given semantic type. This finding raises the question of whether or not certain syntactic types may be eliminated without impairment of the basic requirement, specificity of the headings.

Among studies dealing with aspects of this problem, the following recent works should be mentioned: Steinweg's two papers, one dealing with punctuation[2] and the other with specificity,[3] and Chan's paper on the principle of uniform heading.[4] By limiting the present study to one subject field, that of society, it is possible to attempt a more detailed examination of the syntactic-semantic relationship.

Linguistically, a subject heading is a nominal group including at least one noun. In the majority of cases the noun is modified—by another noun or nouns, by a phrase, by adjective(s), or by another nominal group used as a subdivision. Using the presence or absence of a modifier, and the type of modifier as criteria, one can identify four groups of headings as follows:

A. Without modifier
B. With the principal or focal noun modified by a modifier in parentheses, or by a noun or nouns, occasionally with a preposition or conjunction

Reprinted by permission of the American Library Association, "Language of the Library of Congress Subject Headings Pertaining to Society," by Jan Wepsiec from *Library Resources & Technical Services*, vol. 25, April/June 1981, pp. 196-203; copyright © by ALA.

C. With the principal noun modified by an adjective or adjectives, or by a word or words of some other grammatical category

D. With a nominal group modified by a second nominal group, the latter forming a subdivision

Within each of these four groups more specific types can be discerned, mainly on the basis of the form of modifier. These types are listed below.

1. Headings in group A, e.g., **Sociology**, do not require comment and represent only a small portion of the total body of headings.

Headings within the other three groups are categorized further, according to the structure of the modifier. The types are numbered in one sequence throughout this paper. Turning to group B, in which the modifier is in the form of a noun, or noun as part of a phrase, we recognize:

2. A two-noun heading, e.g., **Mass society**, in which the noun modifier occasionally performs the function of an adjective. The term *mass* in this example limits the meaning of the term *society* to a particular type of modern industrialized society, one characteristic of which is the role of the mass media.

3. A heading consisting of two nouns connected by *and*, e.g., **Religion and sociology**, the first noun denoting a social institution, and the second denoting the study of this institution within a sociological framework.

4. A heading syntactically similar to, but semantically differing from type 3, although it consists of two nouns connected by *and*, e.g., **Art and society**. This heading denotes a relationship between a social institution and society as a whole. Depending upon its application, this relationship, as will be seen later, denotes the impact of art on society or the study of a social institution. In the latter, the sociological perspective, this type of heading resembles type 3.

5. A compound heading consisting of two nouns denoting social categories of comparable conceptual range, connected by *and*, e.g., **Master and servant**. Headings of types 3 and 4 are of the same syntactic structure but they differ in the conceptual range of the focal noun and the modifier. In type 5 there are two nouns of comparable semantic range connected by *and*; the meaning of the heading is the relationship (ascribed or contractual) between two categories of people of different social status.

6. A phrase heading consisting of two nouns related by the preposition *in*, e.g., **Information theory in sociology**, and **Social classes in literature**. Despite the syntactic similarity, there is a considerable difference in semantic type. The first heading denotes the application of a certain method to the study of society; the second relates a social unit to images created by literary means (broadly, aesthetic means, since headings referring to the visual or other arts may be similarly established).

7. A phrase heading consisting of two nouns related by the preposition *of*, e.g., **Conflict of generations**.

8. The same syntactic structure as 7 but in inverted form, e.g., **Knowledge, sociology of**.

9. A heading in which the focal noun is modified by either a single noun or a compound modifier, placed in parentheses, e.g., **Assimilation (Sociology); Polarization (Social sciences)**. The modifier is necessary because a social meaning is not implicit in the focal noun.

10. A noun modified by another noun in a phrase employing an adverb, e.g., **Women as authors**.

11. A nominal group that includes an idiomatic phrase, e.g., **Parents-in-law**, denoting an affinal rather than a conjugal kinship.

Turning to group C, in which adjectives are employed as modifiers, we identify:

12. The focal term denoting the concept of sociology, preceded by an adjective that limits the meaning of the focal term to a specific subfield, e.g., **Industrial sociology**.

13. The same syntactic structure as 12 but in inverted form, e.g., **Sociology, Rural**.
14. The same syntactic structure as 12 and 13 but the focal term is followed by two adjectives, of which the second is placed in parentheses, in order to achieve a higher degree of specificity, e.g., **Sociology, Christian (Baptist); Sociology, Rural (Lutheran)**.
15. The focal term preceded by the adjective *social* to supply the social meaning not carried by the noun, e.g., **Social stability**. One notes that in type 9 the modifier in parentheses performs a similar function.
16. The same syntactic structure as 15 but in inverted form, e.g., **Marginality, Social**.
17. The same syntactic structure as 15 but the adjective *sociological* replaces *social*, e.g., **Sociological jurisprudence**.
18. The focal noun modified by an adverb or participle assuming the function of an adjective, e.g., **Only child; Middle-aged women**.

In group D we discern four types of heading based upon the meaning of the subdivision. In addition to the form subdivisions, one should note the geographic subdivisions introduced in the scope note to **Sociology** (not discussed here).

19. A heading consisting of two nominal groups. The first term denotes the study of society and the second, forming a subdivision, denotes an aspect of this study, e.g., **Sociology—Methodology**.
20. A heading modified by the compound nominal group **Sociological aspects**, e.g., **Hospitals—Sociological aspects**.
21. A heading syntactically similar to type 20 modified by the compound nominal group **Social aspects**, e.g., **Industry—Social aspects**.
22. A one-noun or compound heading subdivided by a compound nominal group other than those mentioned in 19, 20, and 21, e.g., **Family—Caricatures and cartoons**.

This breakdown of headings into twenty-two syntactic types, more detailed than that discussed by Haykin, stems in part from the more detailed analysis of modifiers and in part from inconsistencies that have occurred in the phrasing of the Library of Congress subject headings (LCSH) over the years.[5]

Analysis of Subject Heading Types

A basic difficulty in attempting to analyze the types of headings is the lack of a general, detail code for LCSH. The foundations laid by Cutter in his *Rules for a Dictionary Catalogue*[6] were not developed into a detailed, comprehensive, and consistent code, and, although the LCSH system is the most extensive system for a large, general library, Haykin's *Subject Headings* is far from being a comprehensive code. The individual attempts by Pettee[7] and Prevost[8] provide valuable insights based on differing assumptions, but neither develops a comprehensive code. On the other hand, some studies of selected aspects of LCSH have made useful contributions by opening the way to improvements in that system.[9]

Using present-day knowledge about headings, we now examine the listed syntactic types in relation to the types of concepts they express. The question is whether all the existing syntactic types are necessary, to maintain the all-important conceptual specificity of headings.

Before investigating syntactic structure, one must decide whether to apply the old rule of assigning first place in the heading to the most significant term, or to adopt the natural language. Natural language is now widely accepted by various indexes and by PRECIS, and has been followed by LC in structuring some types of headings. The decision here, therefore, is in favor of natural language and headings using subdivisions.[10]

The types of headings listed above that do not invite questions are not discussed. We begin the analysis, then, with types 3 and 4 and clarify the meaning of the phrases *and sociology* and *and society*. Scope notes do not exist for these headings, so for some indication of the meaning we consult the *see* references from unused terms. There we find one *see* reference from *Sociology and religion* to **Religion and sociology**, and thus must assume that the heading stands for the sociological perspective in the study of religion. But no other heading is provided for the particular aspect of the impact of religion on society, so that in fact the heading **Religion and sociology** is used to denote literature on this aspect also.

The heading **Art and society** (4), judging by its *see from* references *Art and sociology, Art and society,* and *Sociology and art,* denotes both a sociological perspective and the impact of art on society. One may ask why two aspects are denoted by one heading here, and by separate headings elsewhere, e.g., **Sociology, Military** (13) and **War and society** (4); **Industrial sociology** (12) and **Industry—Social aspects** (21). It is clear that literature on two aspects of a subject requires that two separate headings be provided.

When considering the syntactic structure of a heading denoting the impact of a social unit on society, we may follow LC practice and give precedence to the term denoting society or personality which is the subject of the impact, e.g., **Personality and culture**. Following such a practice, the heading denoting the impact of art on society would be *Society and art*. There is, however, the alternative of using a heading with subdivision, a method that will be discussed further during the analysis of types 20 and 21.

Headings of type 8, **Knowledge, Sociology of**, could be phrased in a manner similar to type 3, **Religion and sociology**, or by applying the subdivision **Sociological aspects** (which has a corresponding equivalent, *Sociological perspectives*, in PRECIS). The heading with subdivision seems preferable.

Headings with the modifier placed in parentheses (9) may achieve the natural language structure if the present modifier is eliminated and the adjective *social* is placed before the focal noun, e.g., the present heading **Polarization (Social sciences)** would be changed to *Social polarization* and its meaning would not be changed. This is not to imply that the modifier placed in parentheses would necessarily be eliminated from the entire LCSH system.

Headings employing the inverted form (13) may be rephrased to follow the natural language, e.g., *Rural sociology* as in **Industrial sociology**. Headings with a large part of the nominal group inverted (14) may at first appear resistant to this type of change but in fact do not present difficulties. The heading **Sociology, Christian (Baptist)** requires only the one modifier, *Baptist*, in which *Christian* is implicit, in the rephrased heading, *Baptist sociology*. The heading **Sociology, Rural (Lutheran)**, because the two adjectives belong to two different semantic sets (one community, the other social institution), would retain both adjectives in the rephrased heading *Lutheran rural sociology*. The heading **Marginality, Social** (16) could be changed to *Social marginality*, consistent with **Social structure** (15).

Sociological jurisprudence (17), according to its *see from* references *Law and society, Law—Sociology, Society and law,* and *Sociology and law*, denotes both the study of law applying sociological methods, and the impact of law on society. It could be rephrased in the forms *Jurisprudence (or law) and sociology* and *Sociology and jurisprudence (or law)*; or preferably *Jurisprudence (or law)—Sociological aspects* and *Jurisprudence (or law)—Social aspects*.

The type of heading described in 19 applies subdivisions that pertain to essential aspects of the study of society. Geographic subdivisions introduced in the scope note to **Sociology**, and form subdivisions, are excluded from this discussion. The subdivision **History** is not considered, as it was by Haykin, to be a form subdivision but rather a subdivision denoting an aspect of the subject of the study itself.[11] A similar method of structuring could be applied to any subfield of the study, e.g., **Industrial sociology**. It offers the advantage of proximity of all aspects of the study. Employing a phrase heading such as *Methodology of sociology* would not offer such an advantage.

The meaning of the subdivision in headings of type 20 may be deduced from the references leading to them. The heading **Psychiatric clinics—Sociological aspects** is related to two superordinate headings, **Sociology** and **Social medicine** (the latter with *see from* reference

Sociology of medicine). Thus, the subdivision **Sociological aspects** is clearly justified and the same reasoning is valid in regard to other existing headings that apply this subdivision.

This is an appropriate moment to resume discussion of the type 3 headings. The heading **Religion and sociology** also denotes sociological aspects of religion; thus it would be rational to rephrase it in accordance with type 20. It is desirable to have only one syntactic type for a given semantic type; hence the heading **Religion and sociology** may be eliminated in favor of *Religion — Sociological aspects.*

Headings with the subdivision **Social aspects** (21) require a more detailed analysis. Implicit in this subdivision are two meanings: (a) sociological aspects (implied by the scope note for **Science — Social aspects** and the *see* reference from *Sociology of science*); and (b) the impact of social institutions on society (implied by the scope note for **Technology — Social aspects**). The *see* references to other headings imply that this subdivision generally denotes the impact of a social unit on society. In order to achieve clarity, the duality of meaning should be eliminated and the meaning of this subdivision should be confined to the concept of the impact on society. Assuming that, as suggested above, headings of the type **Religion and sociology** are eliminated in favor of headings with the subdivision **— Sociological aspects**, headings of the type **Art and society** (4) should be rephrased to follow type 21 and apply the subdivision **— Social aspects**. The heading **Art and society** and other headings of this type may need to be replaced (if the existing literature so requires) by two headings, one denoting sociological aspects and the other the impact of a social unit on society. The heading would then be replaced by **Art — Sociological aspects** and **Art — Social aspects**. A check of LCSH reveals a significant number of headings with these two subdivisions. This fact points to the need for clear delineation of the semantic distinction between the two subdivisions.

Type 22 headings, e.g., **Family — Caricatures and cartoons**, may be retained in their present form or, preferably, converted to headings without subdivision, as in **Social classes in literature** (6).

Recommendations

On the basis of this analysis, it is recommended that headings of two major types be retained without change: those employing subdivisions such as **Sociology — Methodology** (19), and those expressed in natural language, as illustrated in the following examples: **Sociology** (1), **Mass society** (2), **Master and servant** (5), **Information theory in sociology** (6), **Conflict of generations** (7), **Women as authors** (10), **Parents-in-law** (11), **Industrial sociology** (12), **Social stability** (15), and **Only child** (18). A second recommendation is that headings of the type: **Assimilation (Sociology)** (9), **Sociology, Rural** (13), **Sociology, Christian (Baptist)** (14),. and **Marginality, Social** (16) conform to type 15, exemplified by the heading **Social stability**; and **Family — Caricatures and cartoons** (22) conform to type 6, exemplified by the heading **Social classes in literature**. A third recommendation concerns the following six types of headings: **Religion and sociology** (3), **Art and society** (4), **Knowledge, sociology of** (8), **Sociological jurisprudence** (17), **Hospitals — Sociological aspects** (20), and **Industry — Social aspects** (21). Here, there is a choice. These headings could conform to the type consisting of a focal noun followed by subdivisions as needed: **— Sociological aspects** (denoting the sociological study of an institution), and **— Social aspects** (denoting the impact of an institution on society), exemplified by the headings just listed. Alternatively, they could conform to the types: **Religion and sociology** (denoting the sociological study of religion) and **Society and religion** (denoting the impact of religion on society). The headings with subdivisions are preferred because the meaning is more clearly brought out; another advantage is that the headings denoting social aspects and sociological aspects would be brought close together in the card or printed catalog.

Present Heading	First Preference	Second Preference
Religion and sociology	Religion—Sociological aspects (Religion—Social aspects)	**Religion and sociology** (Society and religion)
Art and society (in LC, this heading denotes both aspects)	Art—Sociological aspects Art—Social aspects	Art and sociology Society and art
Knowledge, Sociology of	Knowledge—Sociological aspects (Knowledge—Social aspects)	Knowledge and sociology (Society and knowledge)
Sociological jurisprudence (in LC, this heading denotes both aspects)	Jurisprudence—Sociological aspects (The term "law" is now commonly used) Jurisprudence—Social aspects	Jurisprudence and sociology Society and jurisprudence
Hospitals—Sociological aspects	**Hospitals—Sociological aspects** (Hospitals—Social aspects)	Hospitals and sociology (Society and hospitals)
Industry—Social aspects*	**Industry—Social aspects**	Society and industry

*This heading has its counterpart in:

Industrial sociology Industry—Sociological aspects Industry and sociology

which is one of the retained headings. If and when a separate heading is established for society, and **Sociology** is limited to the study of society, this heading should be changed in accordance with the preference.

Existing headings in the matrix above appear in boldface type; proposed headings (when differing from existing ones) appear in normal type. Where there is no existing equivalent heading for one of the aspects discussed, "_____" appears in column one, and headings in columns two and three appear in parentheses.

From this matrix, it may be seen how rules for providing semantic and syntactic consistency should be formulated and so provide the framework of a code for establishing and applying headings.

Notes

[1] Library of Congress, Subject Cataloging Division, *Library of Congress Subject Headings*, 8th ed. (Washington, D.C.: Library of Congress, 1975); *Supplement to LC Subject Headings, 1974-1976; Supplement to LC Subject Headings, Jan-Dec. 1977*.

[2] Hilda Steinweg, "Punctuation in Library of Congress Subject Headings," *Library Resources & Technical Services* 22:145-53 (Spring 1978).

[3] Hilda Steinweg, "Specificity in Subject Headings," *Library Resources & Technical Services* 23:55-68 (Winter 1979).

[4] Lois Mai Chan, "The Principle of Uniform Heading in Library of Congress Subject Headings," *Library Resources & Technical Services* 22:126-36 (Spring 1978).

[5] David Judson Haykin, *Subject Headings: A Practical Guide* (Washington, D.C.: U.S. Govt. Print. Off., 1951).

[6] Charles A. Cutter, *Rules for a Dictionary Catalogue*, 4th ed. rewritten (London: Library Association, 1935).

[7]Julia Pettee, *Subject Headings: The History and Theory of the Alphabetical Approach to Books* (New York: Wilson, 1946).

[8]Marie-Louise Prevost, "An Approach to the Theory and Method in General Subject Headings," *Library Quarterly* 16:140-51 (April 1946).

[9]Jay E. Daily, "The Grammar of Subject Headings: A Formulation of Rules of Subject Headings Based on a Syntactical and Morphological Analysis of the Library of Congress List" (D.L.S. dissertation, Columbia University, 1957); Carlyle J. Frarey, "Subject Heading Revision by the Library of Congress, 1941-1950" (master's essay, Columbia University, 1951); Oliver L. Lilley, "Evaluation of the Subject Catalog: Criticisms and Proposals," *American Documentation* 5:41-60 (April 1954).

[10]S. T. Highcock, "Natural Language Indexing for Automatic Information Systems," in K. G. B. Bakewell, ed., *Classification for Information Retrieval: Papers Presented at an Intensive Course held in September 1967 at the School of Librarianship, Liverpool College of Commerce* (London: Bingley, 1968), p.85-96.

[11]Haykin, *Subject Headings*, p.27-29.

Index

Robert H. Burger

AACR2
  influence on LCSH, 24
AAT. *See* Art and Architecture Thesaurus
ABN. *See* Australian Bibliographic Network
Abstracts, 86. *See also* Notes
  provided by publisher, 237-38
  publisher's analytic, 87
Access point. *See also* Heading
  multiple, 124, 282-83
  single, 124
  word length, 249
Adjectives
  LC list used in phrase headings, 105
ALA Subject Analysis Committee, 48
Alphabetical principle
  drawbacks, 287
Alphabetico-classed catalog. *See* Classified catalog
Alphabetico-classed heading, 109
Alternative form, 46, 158
  see reference use, 113
Aluri, Rao, 270, 284
Amplified heading, 13. *See also* Heading
Analytical entries, 119-20
  as enhancement, 88
Angell, Richard S., 49, 51, 103
Annotated Card Program
  as an example of enrichment, 233
Antonym, 112. *See also* Quasi-antonym
  see reference use, 113

Aristotle, 181
ARL Microform Project, 238
Arret, Linda, 91
Art and Architecture Thesaurus, 51, 77, 157
Associated term, 51, 318
  definition, 325
Association of Research Libraries
    Microform Project. *See* ARL Microform Project
Atherton, Pauline. *See* Cochrane, Pauline
Audacious Project, 251
Audit trail
  of changes in LCSH record, 4
Austin, Derek, 259
Australian Bibliographic Network, 5, 119-20
  use of non-LCSH heading, 32
Authorities Format, MARC. *See* MARC Authorities Format
Authority (evidence)
  for main heading, 178-79
Authority card, 179-80
  symbols used at LC, 180
Authority control
  Blackwell/North America, 270
  different views, 149
  PAIS, 292
  in retrospective conversion, 269-74
Authority file, 55, 178-80
  auxiliary files of, 23
  components, 178

333

Authority file (*continued*)
   development, 4
   local practices, 23
   as online thesaurus, 123
   online use, 157
   related to bibliographic file, 24
   various library practices, 178
Authority record
   absence in libraries, 17
   changed, 9
   control numbers, 9
   coverage, 10-11
   definition, 5
   deleted, 9, 10
   display, 5, 19-22, 88-89
   display of subdivisions, 33
   information excluded from MARC record, 10-11
   new, 9
   relation to subject heading, 14
   structure, 270
Automatic indexing, 281

Back-of-the-book subject index. *See* Book index
Bacon, Francis, 181
Bates, Marcia, 85, 241, 251
Battele Switching Vocabulary System, 150
Berman, Sanford, 31, 85, 121
Bibliographic file
   related to authority file, 24
Bibliographic format, MARC. *See* MARC Bibliographic Format
Bibliographic Retrieval Service. *See* BRS
BIG. *See* Book Indexing Group
Bi-level access, 128
Bishop, William Warner, vii, 31, 36, 46, 51, 54
Blackwell/North America
   authority control system, 270
BLAISE
   browse command, 73
Bliss, H. E., 310
Blume, Edward J., 47
B/NA. *See* Blackwell/North America

Bonnici, Norbert, 32
Book index, 88
   as enhancement, 86-87
   online, 235
Book indexing. *See also* Indexing
   alternative, 235
   databases, 236
   new tools, 237
   in online catalog, 234
   perceived need, 234-35
   produced by LC, 238
   production and distribution alternatives, 236-39
Book Indexing Group, 238
Boolean operations, 124
Boolean searches
   effect of storage medium constraints, 285
Bowker
   Subject Authorities, 73, 75, 149
British Classification Research Group, 182
Broad System of Ordering (UNISIST), 150
Broader term, 19, 47, 48, 51, 113. *See also* Hierarchical relationships
   definition, 112
   in MARC subject authority records, 11
Browse displays, 91
Browseability
   in subject access study, 258, 261, 263
BRS, 149
BSO. *See* Broad System of Ordering (UNISIST)
BT. *See* Broader term
Burger, Robert H., 24
Butler, Brett, 238, 269

Call number
   browsing in OPAC, 188-89
   as location device, 182
   use as a shelflist, 183
Canadian Library of Parliament
   use of period subdivision, 138-39
Caplan, Priscilla, 269
Cartwright, Kelley L., 134
Cat family. *See also* Cats
   classification chart, 310

Catalog
    needs of specialists, 304
    rate of growth, 114
    reduction in size, 290
    size, 114
Catalog records
    enhancements, 82, 86
Catalog use research
    findings, 157
Cataloger's note, 166. *See also* Notes
    as part of scope note, 172-73
Cataloging Manual for Subject Headings
        (Australia), 5
Cats. *See also* Cat family
    suggested revision of LCSH, 314
Central topic
    definition, 112
Chain indexing, 207
    of LCC, 77
Chan, Lois Mai, 7, 33, 36, 55, 57, 123, 134, 165
    on inversion, 277, 278
    on uniform heading, 326
Character strings
    inconsistency, 187-88
Chronological period
    limiting of subject search in OPAC, 33
Chronological subdivision. *See* Period subdivision
Citation order
    consistency, 132
CITE (NLM), 251, 254
Classification
    changing nature, 185
    conflicting pruposes, 70
    criticism of practices, 233
    current role, 183
    enrichment, 232-33
    gloss, 197
    past and present practice, 184
    relation to subject heading, 69, 141
    relocation of numbers, 185
    study of, 181
    suggested uses online, 149
    user interpretation, 184-85
Classification number
    encompassing subject of entire work, 186
    explanation online, 146

    inconsistent assignment of, 185, 186, 196
    linked with subject heading, 73, 149
    poor suitability for machine searching, 187
    relation to subject heading, 72-73, 177
    as search term, 148
    searchability online, 188
    in shelf arrangement, 188
    as subject retrieval device, 188
    two functions of, 186
    unreviewed acceptance, 186
Classification Research Group, 315
Classification schedule
    effect on shelf arrangement problem, 149
    in MARC format, 73
    non-theoretical nature, 182
Classification system
    availability in machine-readable form, 188
Classification theory
    lack of United States interest in, 187
Classified catalog
    LCSH, 75
    rejected in favor of dictionary catalog, 104
    as shelflist, 177
    subdivision in, 144
Classified guide
    as meta-language, 163
CLR. *See* Council on Library Resources
Cluster terms, 50
Coates, Eric James, 7, 33, 49, 51, 140
    on collateral relationship, 114
Cochrane, Pauline, 5, 17, 49, 70, 75, 85, 148, 151, 189
    and Subject Access Project, 232
    and vocabulary selection in OPAC, 251
Collateral relationship, 114
    definition, 143-44
Collateral subjects
    use of see also references, 143
Colon
    use of, 162
Colon Classification, 182
COM catalog
    colocation of entries, 270
Common usage
    as basis for selection of indexing terms, 107

Compatibility
  of LCSH with other vocabularies, 107
  of vocabularies and classification systems, 149-50
Complex subjects
  exposition of, 110-11
  post-coordination, 131-32
Component word searching. *See* Keyword searching
Compound subjects
  influence on reference structure, 140
Compton, Arnold, 90
Computer mapping
  in subject access study, 268
Concealed classification
  defense of, 313-14
  in syndetic section of system, 309-15
Conjunctions
  LC list used in phrase headings, 105
Conjunctive phrase headings. *See* Phrase heading: conjunctive
Contents note, 86. *See also* Notes
Controlled vocabulary
  LCSH as example, 104
Coordinate reference, 140. *See also* Reference
Coordinate term, 51, 318, 320
  definition, 325
Council on Library Resources, 47, 49, 82
  group on enhanced subject access, 232
  OPAC user survey, 155, 235
  special conference on subject access, 184
CRG. *See* British Classification Research Group
Cross references, 45-52. *See also* Reference
  analytic approach, 315
  in COM catalogs, 270
  cutting across genus lines, 312
  deblinded, 270
  deductive method, 315
  effectiveness, 140
  inductive method, 315
  mixed levels of classification, 312
  neglected in manual catalogs, 130
  in OPACs, 243
  in PAIS, 293

  recommendations for improvement, 48
  relation to classification, 69
  types of, 46
Cutter, Charles Ammi, 301
  adoption of subdivision, 135
  avoidance of inversion, 111
  on compound subjects, 144
  definition of cross-references, 316
  on established subjects, 140, 142
  influence, 104
  on lateral cross-reference, 309
  on objects and means, 103
  on phrase headings, 276
  rejection of alphabetico-classed heading, 109
  in relation to language, 163
  rule on adjectives, 307-8
  on specificity, 108
  subject heading code, 328

Daily, Jay E., 32, 33, 51, 52, 55, 56, 57, 70, 73, 77, 149, 159
Dash
  use of, 162
Dates
  in subject headings, 33
DDC, 187
  concessions to practicality, 181-82
  display online, 251
  short version for shelf arrangement, 70
  subject access online, 78
  as subject retrieval tool, 70
  use in online catalog, 70
Definite article
  use of, 161
Descriptor
  vs. subject heading, 23
Descriptor phrase
  manipulation procedures, 283-84
  manipulation techniques, 282
  symbols used for manipulation, 283-84
Dewey, Harry, 45
Dewey, Melville, 181
Dewey Decimal Classification. *See* DDC
Dewey on Catalog Records. *See* DOC
DIALOG, 149
  availability of MARC records, 123

Dialogue modes, 91
Distributed relative problem, 110
DOC
    searching, 79
Double entry indexing. *See* Indexing: double entry
Dunkin, Paul, 108, 111, 135
Duplicate entries
    elimination of, 131

Effect
    used parenthetically in subdivision, 306
English language
    specificity of, 108
Enhancements
    Mandel's matrix, 86
    to subject terminology, 90
    types, 86-87
Enriched records
    definition, 232
Entry Vocabulary Project, 49, 85, 151-58, 234
Epstein, Sue Baerg, 269
ERIC database, 148
ERIC thesaurus, 48
Error
    correction in machine readable file, 272
    incorrect form of heading, 272
    incorrect tagging, 272-73
    in OCLC subject fields, 270
    spelling, 272
    typographical, 272
EVP. *See* Entry Vocabulary Project
Explanatory reference, 165. *See also* Reference
Explode feature (MeSH), 251
Expressiveness
    in place of specificity, 108

Facets, 142
FID/CR. *See* International Federation for Documentation, Committee on Classification Research
Filing rules, 162

Flexibility
    in subject access study, 258, 264
Form subdivision, 57-59, 110-11, 145. *See also* Subdivision definition, 130
Foskett, A. C., 7, 13, 70
Fragmentation
    in subject access study, 261
Frarey, C. J., 107, 108, 114
Free-floating subdivision, 13, 58, 157. *See also* Subdivision
    xx references, 223
Free text searching, 88
Frosio, Eugene, 54
Frost, Carolyn O., 59

GAC. *See* Geographic Area Code
General reference, 143. *See also* Reference
General reference note, 157. *See also* Notes
Generic heading, 259. *See also* Heading
Geographic area code, 57
    advantages, 129
    purpose, 129
Geographical heading. *See also* Heading
    vs. jurisdictional heading, 146
    LC list used as main headings or subdivisions, 105
    problems, 146
Geographical subdivision, 33, 109, 145. *See also* Subdivision
    direct, 57, 129, 132, 146
    indirect, 57, 129, 146
Getty Art History Information Program, 51
Ghikas, Mary W., 24
Gloss, 33, 161
Goldstein, Charles, 157
Gorman, Michael, 24, 70, 149, 186, 187
Grammatical form
    effect on choice of heading, 163
Grammatical variants, 49, 158
Graphemic analysis, 192, 194
Greenberg, Alan M., 36, 165
Guideware, 210

H. W. Wilson Co.
    use of LCSH, 105
Hardy, Mary, 3

Harris, Jessica
   inversion studies, 278
Harvard University
   retrospective conversion, 269
Haykin, David Judson, 7, 13, 14, 17, 33, 36, 69, 72, 104, 165
   on authority file, 178-80
   on avoidance of subdivision, 144
   on form subdivision, 130
   on geographic subdivision, 145
   on inversion, 277
   on justification for indirect subdivision, 129
   on lateral cross-reference, 309
   on LCSH code, 328
   on period subdivision, 135, 136
   on scope note, 168, 175-76
   on shelflist and subject headings, 176-77
   on specific entry principle, 108, 140
   on subdivision, 109, 329
Heading. *See also* Access point; Alphabetico-classed heading; Amplified heading; Generic heading; Geographical heading; Inverted heading; LCSH; Main heading; Multi-term heading; Orphan heading; Pattern heading; Phrase heading; Referred heading; Related heading; Scientific headings; Subject heading; Topical heading
   assignment of two or more, 110
   catalog form, 271
   established, 142-43
   establishment of in LC, 107
   form and structure, 31, 111
   loosely related, 51
   normalized form, 271-72
   principle of uniformity, 125
   principle of uniqueness, 125
   with qualifiers, 127-28
   see also references for related terms, 153, 154-55
   see references for alternative forms, 153, 154
   see references for grammatical variants, 153, 154
   vs. term, 113
Henderson, Judith J., 85
Herschman, J., 241
Hierarchical classification
   compared with thesaurus, 74
Hierarchical references, 140. *See also* Reference
   overcoming weaknesses, 73
Hierarchical relationships. *See also* Broader term; Narrower term
   computer tracking, 322-24
   graphical display, 52
Hildreth, Charles, 91, 148, 243
Hill, Janet Swan, 70, 181
Hines-Harris computer filing code, 134
Historical subdivision. *See* Period subdivision
History note, 4. *See also* Notes
Holley Report, 157
Homographs
   minimizing adverse effects, 125
   use of qualifiers to distinguish, 108, 127
Hyphen
   use of, 161

Immroth, John Phillip, 7, 49, 51, 70, 73, 76, 77, 192
Indexing. *See also* Book indexing; Journal article indexing
   disadvantages of long strings, 132
   double entry, 33, 300
Influence
   used parenthetically in subdivision, 306
Information cards, 4, 47, 114, 165
   use in catalog maintenance, 115
Information overload, 85
Information Retrieval Thesaurus of Education Terms
   use of RT, 114
Integrated Energy Vocabulary, 150
Interactive searching
   refinements, 91
Intermediary language. *See* Switching language

Intermediate displays
   in OPACs, 253-54
International Federation for Documentation, Committee on Classification Research, 182
Inversion, 31
   affected by post-coordination, 279
   empirical studies, 278
   recommendations, 279-80
   solution by noun rule, 111
Inverted forms
   conversion in LCSH, 121
   as see references, 214
Inverted heading. *See also* Heading
   noun, adjective, 135
   purpose, 127, 277

Jarvis, William E., 92, 209-12
Journal article indexing. *See also* Indexing
   compared to book subject analysis, 234
Jurisdictional names
   vs. geographical names, 146

Kanwischer, Dorothy, 31
Keen, E. Michael, 281
Kelley, Grace, 186
Keyword searching, 124
   use of qualifier, 128
Keywords
   enrichment, 232-33
Kirtland, Monika, 5, 17
Knapp, Sara D., 90
Knowledge tree
   in OPACs, 150
Known item searches
   reduction of failure rate, 283
Kochen, Manfred, 51
KWIC
   display in OPAC, 250
KWIC display
   for LCSH, 157

Ladenson, Alex, 304
Language subdivision, 130. *See also* Subdivision
Lawrence, Gary S., 91
LC Tracer Bullets, 209
LCC
   beginning of, 182
   chain indexing, 77
   comparison with LCSH, 76
   contextual meaning, 196
   indexes, 77
   literary warrant, 182
   short version for shelf arrangement, 70
   as subject retrieval tool, 70
LCSH. *See also* Heading
   AAT criticism, 78
   adoption of new heading, 112
   ALA Institutes, 4
   amplification, 104
   auxiliary records, 105
   changes in bibliographic file, 23-24
   changes in x-ref structure, 17-18
   changes resulting from AACR2, 24-29
   classificatory base, 112
   classified, 73
   comparison with LCC, 76
   compatibility with other vocabularies, 107
   components of, 14
   compound subjects, 144
   consistency in application, 226-30
   as controlled vocabulary, 104
   cross-reference structure, 157
   display, 157
   effect of term manipulation on cross-references, 284
   Entry Vocabulary Project. *See* Entry Vocabulary Project
   errors in syndetic structure, 46
   establishment of new heading, 301-2
   exclusion of certain headings, 116
   features of entries, 104
   followed by LCC numbers, 72
   form, 104, 279
   four groups of headings, 326
   function, 157

LCSH (*continued*)
   fundamental principles, 125
   future of, 106-7
   grammar, 159-64
   historical determinants, 104
   inconsistencies, 31, 106
   as index to LCC, 72
   influence on by AACR2, 28
   introduction, 4
   lack of classificatory base, 140
   length of indexing string, 132
   linguistic analysis, 328-30
   linguistic types of headings, 327-28
   machine readable, 3, 248
   main headings' characteristics, 55-56
   maintenance problems, 114-15
   modified by local libraries, 4
   multi-dimensional nature of subject relationships, 141
   need for comprehensive code, 328
   need for machine-readable form, 246-47
   nonsystematic cascading, 262-63
   non-technical, 314
   notes. *See* Notes
   number of MARC subfields, 284
   omitted headings, 104
   online implementation, 131
   for online retrieval, 123-32
   as pre-coordinate vocabulary, 104
   publication of future editions, 116
   recommendation built on linguistic analysis, 330-31
   reference structure, 111-12, 143
   references. *See* Reference
   restructuring into hierarchical thesaurus, 241
   review of existing heading, 112
   rules for assignment, 288
   see also reference. *See* See also reference
   semantic analysis, 195-209
   semantic features, 195-96
   semantic variants, 196
   statistics, 57
   structural analysis, 192-95
   subdivisions. *See* Subdivision
   as subject authority file, 4
   suggested reforms, 121
   suggestions for raising application consistency, 230
   syndetic structure, 46, 246, 326-31
   synonym display online, 131
   terminology, 31-32
   as thesaurus, 23, 24
   thesaurus display online, 131
   tools for assignment, 288
   types of see references, 153
   uniformity, 125
   uniqueness, 125
   use of punctuation marks, 160
   use of thesaurus terminology, 113
   uses, 105-6
   variations in form, 159
   viewed as a national subject authority file, 241
   weakness of, 6-7
Lead in vocabulary. *See* Reference
Lead term, 111
Leads
   definition of, 46
Legislative Indexing Vocabulary. *See* LIV
LEXIS, 254
Library of Congress
   addition of book content information to bibliographic record, 237-38
   main catalog, 105
   OCat. *See* Library of Congress: official catalog.
   official catalog, 105
   online authority display, 62
   printed card service, 105
   Subject Cataloging Manual, 213-25
Library of Congress Classification. *See* LCC
Library of Congress Subject Headings. *See* LCSH
Lilley, O. L., 108
Limiting, 124
LIV, 156
Locality subdivision. *See* Geographical subdivision
Lopez, Manuel D., 226
Lund University (Sweden), 232

Main heading, 13. *See also* Heading
   combined with subheading in PAIS, 294-95
   as distinct from subdivision, 56
   form, 126-28
   PAIS, 293
Mandel, Carol A., 85, 86, 87, 158, 231, 241
Mandel's matrix, 86, 88
Mann, Margaret, 114
   on inversion, 277
   objection to subdivisions, 144
Mannheimer, Martha, 73, 149
Manual retrieval
   difference from online retrieval, 124
MARC Authorities Format, 19, 36, 48
   classification number, 188
   exclusions, 246
   subject field, 246
   260 field, 59
MARC Bibliographic Format
   additional subject field, 241
   language code, 130
   x subfield, 57
MARC Bibliographic records
   enhancement, 237, 238
   identification of document types, 130
MARC Distribution Service
   subject authorities, 9
Mark and park, 183, 187
Markey, Karen, 70, 75, 76, 77, 78, 86, 91, 148
Maxwell, Margaret F., 59
McPherson, Dorothy, 269
Medical Subject Headings. *See* MeSH
MELVYL, 157
   access to periodical indexes, 235
   browse display, 156
   controlled vocabulary display, 249
   cross-references, 243
   KWIC display, 249
Menu-driven system, 91, 92
MeSH, 77
   cascading headings, 263
   see also references, 257-68
   tree structures, 51, 157
Micco, H. Mary, 49, 51, 52, 257

Miksa, Francis, 7
Miller, Dan, 59, 70, 269
Mills, Jack, 108
Milstead, Jessica L., 32, 276
Mischo, William H., 85, 90, 249, 281
Mivart, St. George, 310
Model headings. *See* Pattern heading
Money (subject heading)
   analysis of related headings, 298-300
   subject access through phrase manipulation, 282-83
Morley, Linda H., 304
Morphological analysis, 194-95
Mostecky, Vaclav, 49, 51, 287, 315
Multi-element work
   definition, 110
Multi-term heading. *See also* Heading
   see reference, 153
Multi-word access, 125

NACO, 85, 241-42
Name Authority Cooperative Project. *See* NACO
Narrower term, 19, 47, 48, 51, 133. *See also* Hierarchical relationships
   in MARC subject authority records, 11
Narrower topic
   definition, 112
National Library of Medicine Classification Schedule, 77
National Subject Authority Service
   suggestions for, 84
Near synonym, 206. *See also* Synonym
Newark Business Branch
   list of subject headings, 303-4
Nodes
   presence in hierarchical indexing, 323
Non-free-floating subdivision
   xx references, 223
Notational classification, 184
Notes. *See also* Abstracts; Cataloger's note; Contents note; General reference note; History note; Refer from note; Scope note; See also reference note
   in authority records, 36
   for catalog use, 36
   displayed for searchers, 122
   in PAIS, 293
   use online, 38

Noun rule, 307
   relation to language, 163
NT. *See* Narrower term

OCat. *See* Library of Congress: official catalog
OCLC
   record enhancement, 238
OCLC-Forest Press/CLR Project, 78-79
Ohio State University LCS
   authority display, 62
   browse command, 73
   browsing display, 61, 155
   cross-references, 243
Olson, Nancy, 77, 149
O'Neill, Edward T., 270, 284
Online catalog. *See* OPAC
Online public access catalog. *See* OPAC
Online retrieval
   difference from manual retrieval, 124
OPAC
   abbreviated display, 254
   aids for subject searches, 245
   authority file, 210
   built-in assistance, 83
   capabilities, 83
   class number searching, 184
   display screen characteristics, 62
   enhanced by indexing and abstracting services, 92
   features for user assistance, 243
   integration of pathfinders, 209-12
   intermediate display, 253-54
   KWIC display, 250
   as learning environment, 92
   minimum requirements, 189
   as operational reality, 184
   reports, 74-75
   as shelf browsing tool, 77
   suggested improvements, 245
   vocabulary aid, 250
   vocabulary display, 251
   vocabulary selection, 251
OPAC Interface Adequacy Assessment Guide, 91

ORBIT
   availability of MARC records, 123
Orne, Jerrold, 46, 51
Orphan heading, 85, 220-21.
   See also Heading
Overlapping terms, 51, 298, 318-22
   computer manipulation, 319

Painter, Ann, 229, 230
PAIS, 58, 292-97
   subject authority control, 292
   subject headings, 292
PAIS Bulletin
   coverage, 292
Paperchase (retrieval system), 210, 249
Parenthesis
   used with consistent meaning, 108
Pathfinders
   accessing online, 209-10
   example online, 210-11
   integration into OPAC, 209-12
   online, 92
   user transparent approach, 209
Pattern file
   in LC, 222
Pattern heading, 4, 14, 59, 157. *See also* Heading
   examples, 14-17
Pattern note. *See* Scope note
Peace (subject heading)
   analysis of related headings, 300-301
Period subdivision, 57, 109. *See also* Subdivision
   arrangement, 135-36
   basic problem, 134
   with dates alone, 137-38
   filing, 135-36
   name of century, 137
   name of historical period, 137, 146
   noun or phrase, 136
   with preposition "to", 137
   recommended solution, 134
   types, 130, 135-38
Perkins, Frederick, 301-2
Pettee, Julia, 7, 36, 141, 142, 298, 309, 315, 328

Phrase heading, 276. *See also* Heading
   conjunctive, 126
   drawback, 304
   prepositional, 126
   recommendations, 304
   types, 126, 277
Phrases
   adjective, 277-78
   complex, 278
Pietris, Mary K., 5, 85, 235
Place subdivision. *See* Geographical subdivision
Poly-hierarchical relationship, 319
Post-coordinate indexing
   refinement of searches, 249
Post-coordination
   effect on inversion practice, 279
PRECIS, 186, 328
   cascading headings, 263
   compared to LCSH, 125
   see also references, 257-68
Precision
   in phrase headings, 126
Pre-coordinate indexing system
   factors affecting heading, 111
   form, 111
   structure, 111
Pre-coordinate vocabulary
   LCSH as example, 104
Pre-coordination
   reserved for special use, 132
Prepositional phrase
   to modify a subdivision, 304-5
   see also references, 223-24
Prepositional phrase headings. *See* Phrase heading: prepositional
Prepositions
   LC list used in phrase headings, 105
Preschel, Barbara M., 55
Prevost, Marie, 32, 33, 303, 315, 328
Public Affairs Information Service. *See* PAIS
Punctuation marks
   principal uses in LCSH, 160
   purpose, 163
Putnam, Herbert, 182

Qualifier, 32
   access to, 57
   as gathering device, 128, 129
   for geographic name, 57
   LC list of terms used, 105
   for legal system, 224
   purpose, 104, 108
   types, 127-28
Quasi-antonym, 50. *See also* Antonym

Ranganathan, S. R., 7, 24, 142, 181
Rather, John C., 47
Rather, Lucia, 5, 85, 235
Reciprocal reference. *See also* Reference
   for related headings, 113
Reclassification, 185
Red book. *See* LCSH
Refer from note, 37. *See also* Notes
Reference. *See also* Coordinate reference; Cross-references; Explanatory reference; General reference; Hierarchical references; Reciprocal reference; Related reference; See also from reference; See also reference; See reference; X reference; XX reference
   determining direction, 260
   record of, 178
   use in catalog maintenance, 115-16
Reference materials
   subject access, 282-85
Reference structure
   influence on compound subjects, 140
   revision, 221-22
Referred heading. *See also* Heading
   records for, 19
Related heading. *See also* Heading
   use of reciprocal references, 113
Related reference, 47. *See also* Reference
   definition, 46
Related term, 19, 47, 48, 113, 259
   display in OPAC, 248
   restrictions on references, 224-25
   scattering, 50, 58
   in subject access study, 261
   types of, 318
Related topic, 112
Relative index
   as shelflist index, 69, 176-77

REMARC, 157
Reports
   from online catalog, 74-75
Research Libraries Information Network.
      See RLIN
Response time
   effect of class numbers on, 149
Result
   used parenthetically in subdivision, 306
Retrieval systems
   enhancements, 90-91
Retrospective conversion
   authority control, 269
   matching of normalized and catalog entry
      forms, 271-74
Richmond, Phyllis A., 49, 51, 309
RLIN
   availability of MARC records, 123
   general authority file, 19
   Library of Congress resource file, 19
RT. *See* Related term

SAP. *See* Subject Access Project
Scan
   definition, 253
   types, 253
Scheer, George, 309
Schwartz, John C., 307, 308
Scientific headings
   LC record not included in basic list, 105
Scope note, 4, 36-39, 175-76, 196. *See
      also* Notes
   for activities and disciplines, 166
   adding to existing heading, 218
   broadened meaning, 169-70
   cataloger's note, 172-73
   changing an existing, 218
   common terms, special applications, 169
   for commonly used subdivisions, 38
   definition, 143, 166, 175
   for definition of heading, 170
   extent of use, 36
   gloss as substitute for, 163
   identical terms, 170
   LC policy, 215-18
   LC procedures, 217-18
   limiting effect, 168
   literature, drama, music, 166-67
   in machine authority record, 39
   music, 171-72
   for new heading, 217-18
   in online display, 38
   pattern note, 171-72
   point of view, 168
   popular vs. technical term, 167
   principal feature of, 168
   on printed page, 38
   purpose, 36, 218
   relation to cross-reference structure, 38
   rich in subject content, 38
   for single heading, 215-16
   for special instructions, explanations,
      references, 217
   for subdivision, 170
   as test element in consistency study, 229
   two or more closely relating or over-
      lapping headings, 216-17
   types used in LCSH, 215-17
   use in State Library of New South Wales
      catalog, 37
   value of, 39
Scoping. *See* Limiting
SCORPIO, 156-57
   example of browse display, 60
   full record display, 89
SDC, 149
Sear's List of Subject Headings
   derived from LCSH, 105
   period subdivision, 135
See also from reference. *See also* Reference
   PAIS, 294
See also reference, 17, 51-52, 257-68.
      See also Reference
   basis for structure, 69
   between collateral subjects, 147
   collateral, 114
   complex situations, 222
   displayed for searchers, 122
   downward, 112, 113
   drawbacks, 287
   elimination, 315
   establishing new hierarchical, 220
   exclusion from authorities format, 246
   general, 221
   general to particular classification, 309

See also reference (*continued*)
  in [. . .] and [. . .] heading, 222
  hierarchical, 51, 85, 219
  hierarchical deficiencies, 73
  for hierarchical gaps, 221
  LC policy, 219-225
  legal systems, 224
  linkages, 260
  number to be made, 221
  objections to, 46
  online display, 131
  in OPACs, 243
  as part of reference structure, 111-12
  prepositional phrases, 223-24
  procedures for establishing, 220-25
  prohibitions, 220-21
  purpose, 51
  related terms, 51, 219-20
  revised rules for, 48
  in revising reference structures, 221-22
  as scope note, 175
  from subdivision, 222-24
  for subdivision to subdivision see references, 221
  for subject cataloger, 48
  suggested revision, 307
  as test element in consistency study, 227-29
  two types, 51
  upward, 114
  use by catalogers, 48
  use in non-compound subjects, 142
  user advantages with systematic list, 289
See also reference note, 37
See also reference structure, 257-68
  classification, 309
  in international law, 287-90
See from reference. *See also* Reference
  in PAIS, 293
See reference, 46, 49-50. *See also* Reference
  from abbreviations, acronyms, initials, etc., 214-15
  from cancelled heading, 214
  determination of spelling, 214
  display, 157
  from equivalent term, 213
  from foreign terms, 215
  formation, 152
  from headings qualified by nationality, ethnic group, or language, 215
  from invented form, 214
  LC policy, 152, 213
  made laterally, 113
  in OPACs, 243
  part of reference structure, 111
  procedure for establishing, 152-53
  purpose, 152
  from significant words, 213-14
  types, 49-50, 153, 158
  upward, 50, 214
  use in LCSH reforms, 121
Semi-automatic indexing, 281
Shelf arrangement
  as one purpose of classification, 70
Shelflist
  as classified catalog, 69, 176, 177
  limitations of, 177
  vs. subject catalog, 176-77
Sherrie and Jones list, 146
Simonds, Michael J., 82, 88
Simpson, George Gaylord, 311
Single entry specific, 108
SOC
  searching, 78
Spalding, C. Sumner, 47
Specific entry principle, 140
  as per Cutter, 104
Specificity
  attribute of subject cataloging, 108
  in English, 108
  use of analytical entries, 120
Split files
  disadvantage, 121
  effect on subject heading corrections, 30
Steinweg, Hilda, 32, 326
Stevens, Norman, 92
Subdivision, 54, 55. *See also* Form subdivision; Free-floating subdivision; Geographical subdivision; Language subdivision; Period subdivision; Topical subdivision
  adjective plus direction, 305
  citation order, 128
  commonly used, 38
  Daily's rules, 56
  direct. *See* Geographical subdivision: direct
  display, 157

Subdivision (*continued*)
   distinction from main heading, 56
   for facet of subject, 126
   filing, 146-47
   form. *See* Form subdivision
   free-floating. *See* Free-floating subdivision
   function, 128
   geographical. *See* Geographical subdivision
   indirect. *See* Geographical subdivision: indirect
   language of text, 110
   LC file, 105
   as mark of alphabetico-classed catalog, 135
   need for, 55
   online display of, 59-62
   in PAIS, 294-95
   period. *See* Period subdivision
   purpose, 144
   reference structure, 157
   after subject noun, 32
   topical. *See* Topical subdivision
   types, 13, 104, 109-10
   use of, 32
Subheading. *See* Subdivision
Subject access
   online components, 231
   patron demand, 82
   suggestions for improvement, 83-84
Subject Access Project, 87, 88, 237, 238, 285
   x-reference technique, 232
Subject access study
   conclusions, 267
   method, 267
Subject access system
   essential features, 91
Subject area coverage
   in subject access study, 257-58, 260-61, 262-63
Subject bibliographies
   based on LCSH, 105

Subject catalog
   neglect of maintenance, 4
   rules for formation, 161-63
   vs. shelflist, 176-77
   theory of, 315
Subject catalog searches
   consultation of LCSH, 244
Subject cataloger
   capabilities, 226
Subject cataloging
   relation to classification, 141
Subject Cataloging Manual (LC), 5, 48
Subject guides
   for catalogs, 70-71
Subject heading
   affected by AACR2, 28
   assumptions about users, 136-37
   change impeded by old headings, 85
   characteristics used in consistency study, 227
   and classification number, 69, 72-73, 177
   classified approach to formation, 32
   coextensive with book topic, 234
   controlled by subject authority records, 33
   conversion table for reference designation, 113
   defined linguistically, 326
   definition 5, 13
   vs. descriptors, 23
   display in OPAC, 32-33
   display on catalog record, 32-33
   enrichment, 232-33
   erroneous, 14
   established, 13
   form of, 13, 32
   maintenance, 4, 17
   matched with natural language, 233
   omissions from PAIS, 294
   precision, 234
   qualifier, 32, 33
   redundant, 233
   revision, 307
   rotation of words in, 33
   rules for creation, 306
   rules for general list, 303

Subject heading (*continued*)
  selection from textbooks, 258
  shareable (ABN), 120
  source of meaning, 195-96
  tested for matches with classification and index heading, 206
  two concepts in, 33
Subject heading classification, compared with zoological classification, 310-11
Subject Heading on Catalog Record. *See* SOC
Subject heading string, 54
  construction, 62
  permutation, 62
  possible coding scheme, 63-66
  rotation, 62
Subject relationships
  multi-dimensional nature, 141
Subject retrieval
  as one purpose of classification, 70
Subject searching
  ad hoc process model, 245
  problems, 233-34
  types, 255-56
Subject work
  cost at LC, 233
SULIRS (Syracuse U.), 249
Superindex, 87, 88, 235, 237
Switching language
  purpose, 107
Synonym, 112. *See also* Near synonym
  problems in online searching, 158
  see reference use, 113
  zoological, 312
Synonym operator
  as hidden see reference, 125
Syracuse University
  browse command, 73
  Subject Access Project, 87

Table of equivalences (Bonnici), 32
Tabliaocozzo, Renata, 51
Taylor, Arlene G., 59
Term
  vs. heading, 113
TERM (BRS), 90

Term relation designations, 113-14
Term tactics (online searching), 251-52
Terminology
  British equivalences in LCSH, 32
  consistent and rationally developed, 289
Textbook selection
  in subject access study, 261
Thesaurofacet, 114
Thesaurus
  compared with hierarchical classification, 74
  features of, 23
  guidelines, 318
  online display, 124
  standards, 48
Thesaurus term
  conversion table for reference designations, 113
  proposed designations, 324-25
Time dimension
  specification of in OPACs, 33
Topical heading. *See also* Heading
  definition of scope, 298-300
Topical subdivision, 57-59, 109, 129. *See also* Subdivision
TOSCA, 23
Total Online Support for Cataloging Activities. *See* TOSCA
Tracer Bullets. *See* LC Tracer Bullets
Trees (MeSH), 77
  in subject access study, 259
Truncation
  limited effectiveness, 187
  types, 124

UDC. *See* Universal Decimal Classification
UF, 113
Uncontrolled vocabulary, 85
Universal Decimal Classification
  AUDACIOUS project, 251
  use in preparation of bibliographies, 183
University of Toronto
  browse command, 73
"Use", 113
User aids
  neglected in manual catalogs, 130
User behavior
  models, 91

Vickery, B. C., 315
Vizine-Goetz, Diane, 270

Wall, R. A., 49, 51, 73, 90, 318
Washington Library Network. *See* WLN
Wellisch, Hans, 32
Wepsiec, Jan, 32, 33, 51, 56, 326
Western Library Network. *See* WLN
Wiberley, Stephen E., Jr., 85
Williams, James G., 73, 149
Williamson, Nancy J., 149

WLN
    availability of MARC bibliographic records, 123
Word adjacency, 124
Word order changes, 49
    see references, 158
Word proximity, 124
Wynar, Bohdan, 7

X reference, 19
XX reference
    instead of see reference, 213

SOUTHEASTERN MASSACHUSETTS UNIVERSITY
Z695.C646 1986
Improving LCSH for use in online catalog

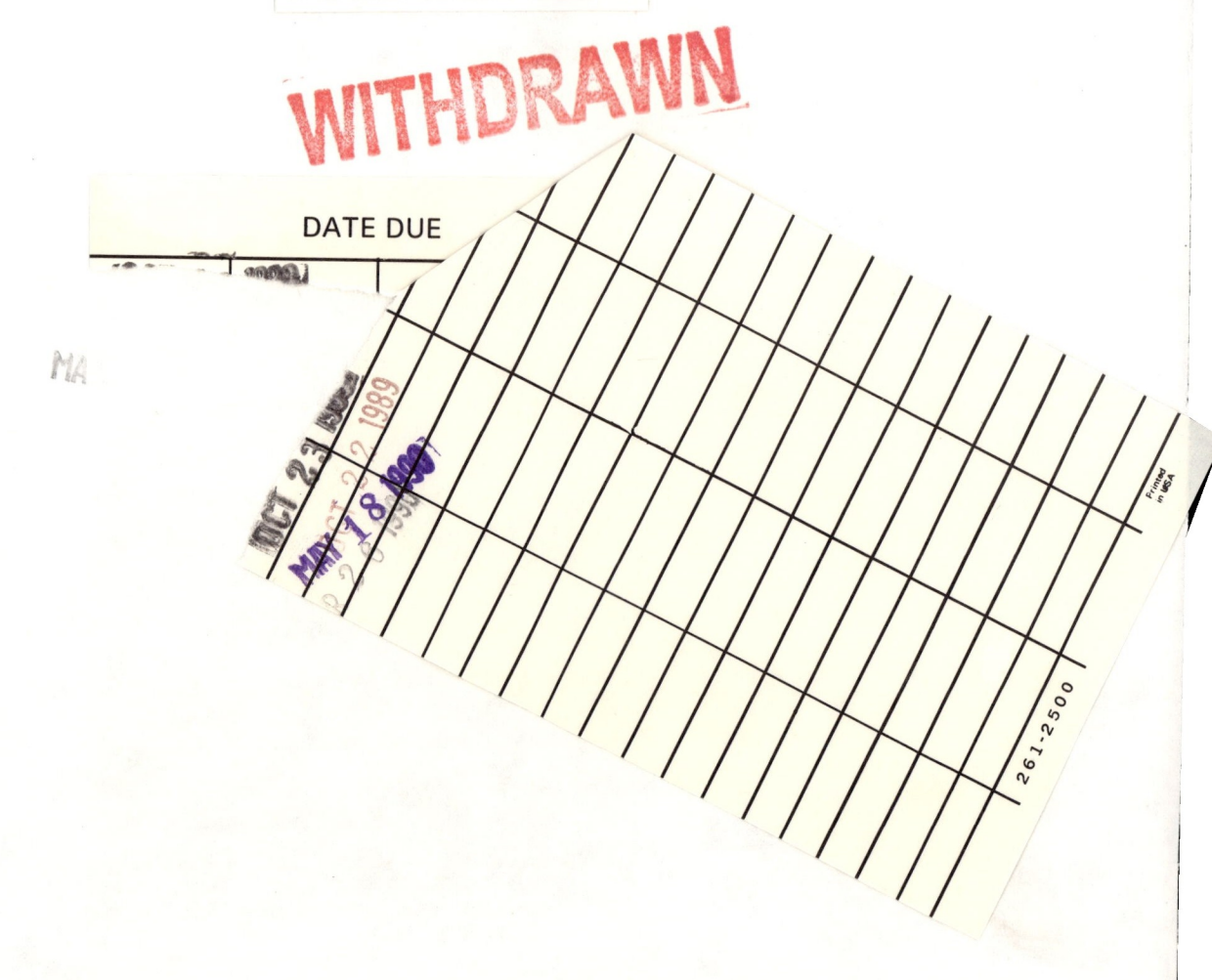

3 2922 00024 260 9

WITHDRAWN

DATE DUE